YIDDISH IN ISRAEL

PERSPECTIVES ON ISRAEL STUDIES

S. Ilan Troen, Natan Aridan, Donna Divine, David Ellenson,
Arieh Saposnik, and Jonathan Sarna, *editors*

Sponsored by the Ben-Gurion Research Institute for the Study of Israel and
Zionism of the Ben-Gurion University of the Negev and the Schusterman
Center for Israel Studies of Brandeis University

YIDDISH IN ISRAEL

A History

Rachel Rojanski

INDIANA UNIVERSITY PRESS

This book is a publication of

Indiana University Press
Office of Scholarly Publishing
Herman B Wells Library 350
1320 East 10th Street
Bloomington, Indiana 47405 USA

iupress.indiana.edu

© 2020 by Rachel Rojanski

All rights reserved

No part of this book may be reproduced or utilized in any form or by any means, electronic or mechanical, including photocopying and recording, or by any information storage and retrieval system, without permission in writing from the publisher. The paper used in this publication meets the minimum requirements of the American National Standard for Information Sciences—Permanence of Paper for Printed Library Materials, ANSI Z39.48-1992.

Manufactured in the United States of America

Cataloging information is available from the Library of Congress.

ISBN 978-0-253-04514-0 (hdbk.)
ISBN 978-0-253-04515-7 (pbk.)
ISBN 978-0-253-04518-8 (web PDF)

1 2 3 4 5   25 24 23 22 21 20

For Adam,
mayn basherter

CONTENTS

Acknowledgments ix

A Note on Transliteration, Translation, and Archival Signatures xiii

Introduction: "They Are Ashamed of Us Yiddish Writers" 1

1 "Even the Stones Speak Hebrew": The Melting Pot and Israel's Cultural Policy 26

2 The Heart of Yiddish Culture: The Yiddish Press 1948–1968 48

3 "We Are Jewish Actors from the Diaspora": Yiddish Actors, Yiddish Theater, and the Jewish State, 1948–1965 101

4 "To Assemble the Scattered Spirit of Israel": High Yiddish Culture—*Di goldene keyt* and the Yiddish Chair at the Hebrew University 154

5 "We Are Writing a New Chapter in Yiddish Literature": The Literary Group Yung Yisroel and the Zionist Master Narrative 188

6 "You No Longer Need to Be Afraid to Love Yiddish": 1965, the Production of *Di megile*, and the Return of Eastern Europe to Israel's Collective Memory 225

7 The End of the Twentieth Century: Private Memory, Collective Image, and the Retreat from the Melting Pot 250

Epilogue 281

Bibliography 295

Index 313

ACKNOWLEDGMENTS

WRITING THIS BOOK HAS BEEN PART OF MY life for a long time. It started in Israel with a review I published in the daily *Ha'aretz* of a TV show about Yiddish. The review generated a heated debate about the history of Yiddish in Israel and its place there, and this aroused my interest in the subject. Sometime later, I thought that maybe I should write a book about it. I had no idea then that I was embarking on a journey that would take me back to my childhood years in Tel Aviv.

I owe this book (as well as many other things) first and foremost to my parents, Ida (née Sapir) and Dov-Ya'akov (Yasha) Rojanski z"l, who came to Israel from the Jewish communities of Kovna and Bialystok respectively, at different times and under very different circumstances. They loved Yiddish but chose Hebrew as the language of our family. In our small apartment in the old north of Tel Aviv, the walls were covered with Hebrew books only, and a Hebrew daily was waiting at the door every morning. Nonetheless, Yiddish had a huge presence in our life—not in written form but as a day-to-day language. My parents spoke Yiddish with each other and with other Yiddish speakers. They never spoke it in public and certainly never to me. They strongly believed that the generation that was born in the state of Israel should speak Hebrew, not Yiddish.

Writing this book has made me understand that this childhood experience not only aroused my scholarly interest in Yiddish and pushed me to study it seriously in a later stage of my life but actually enabled me to understand how subtle was the negotiation of Yiddish speakers with both languages and how complicated and nuanced was the tension between the two for those who loved Yiddish and wanted a Hebrew future for the next generation. I thank my parents for this, as well as for instilling in me the love of learning, for teaching me the values of hard work and honesty, and especially for their unconditional love that made me who I am.

I would like to thank the institutions and foundations that supported this research with grants over the years. I am especially grateful to the Israel Science Foundation, which gave me a generous three-year grant that enabled me to do intensive research in archives and libraries in Israel and the United States, the Yad Ben Zvi Institute in Jerusalem, the Research Authority at the University of Haifa, the Katz D. Center for Advanced Judaic Studies at the University of Pennsylvania, the Humanities Research Funds, and the Program in Judaic Studies at Brown University.

I benefited a lot from the help of many librarians and archivists who shared with me their knowledge and demonstrated much goodwill. The veteran librarians of the Jewish studies reading room at the National Library of Israel in Jerusalem, Elona Avinezer, Ruth Flint, Tzipora Ben-Abu, and Aliza Alon; the devoted archivists of the YIVO institute in New York, Fruma Mohrer and especially Leo Greenberg, who has been a source of knowledge and good advice to me ever since I started visiting the YIVO archives as a graduate student; and Judith Leifer, the unique reference librarian of the Herbert D. Katz Center for Advanced Judaic Studies Library, who knew how to unearth long-forgotten Yiddish newspapers, after I had lost hope of ever finding them. I thank them all.

I was privileged to be helped by some veterans of the world of Yiddish in Israel. The writer Yossel Birstein z"l, who opened his heart to me and shared his knowledge of the archives at the National Library of Israel, as well as his wonderful and unforgettable stories; the legendary editor and leader of Yiddish in Israel, Mordechai Tsanin z"l, who told me his life story, gave me some documents from his personal archives, and, more importantly, provided me the opportunity to meet in person the greatest fighter for Yiddish in Israel, and the veteran writer and journalist Yitzhak Luden z"l, who edited the last Yiddish newspaper in Israel and was a great source of knowledge about Yiddish in Israel. I benefited greatly from meeting with the poet and remarkable woman Rivka Basman-Ben Haim, who told me her life story and discussed with me Yiddish literature in Israel in the 1950s and 1960s. Shmuel Atzmon-Vircer, the founder and longtime director of the Yiddish theater in Israel, Yiddishpiel, shared with me documents and information on the history of his theater, told me its story, and answered difficult questions, and Lidya Ophir, Israel Shumacher's daughter, generously helped clarify some matters.

Over the years I have benefited from the help of several research assistants: Amy Simon, Boris Tarnopolsky, and especially Ilya Vovshin, who is now a scholar in his own right.

I am grateful to the many friends and colleagues who, over the years, provided help and advice, put at my disposal their knowledge, read parts of the manuscript, and gave me helpful comments. Avrahan Novershtern shared with me his broad knowledge of Yiddish literature and Yiddish sources; David Engel read the entire manuscript and offered helpful and important suggestions and comments; Benny Mer and Ella Bauer read parts of the manuscript; Joel Berkowitz graciously read the chapters on Yiddish theater and provided invaluable comments; Mordechai (Motke) Naor, a scholar, writer, and one of the veterans of the Israeli journalistic scene, answered patiently and generously numerous specific questions and proved again that Google can't compete with an extraordinary human mind and memory. Pnina Lahav helped clarify some of the legal questions raised in the book and offered friendly support along the way.

My Yiddish teacher, who became a good friend, Esther Rollansky, was always there for me to answer questions, to support, and to listen in a most helpful way.

Shlomo Berger z"l, who was a partner for stimulating intellectual conversations and ideas, passed away suddenly and untimely, leaving his many friends all over the world shocked and devastated.

Other colleagues answered questions, referred to sources, clarified matters, or provided ideas, comments, and insights: Dalit Assouline, Yaakov Barnai, Justin Cammy, Kimmy Caplan, Shimon Cohen, Jonathan Decter, Hasia Diner, Ofer Dynes, Gennady Estraikh, Tuvia Friling, Aviva Halamish, Dov-Ber Kerler, Rafi Mann, Kenneth Moss, Leonid Roitman, and Jonathan Sarna.

Special thanks go to Elissa Bemporad, who gave me much-needed advice at a critical moment.

Since English is not my first language, I used the help of some editors. Most important was the contribution of my father-in-law, Neville Teller, MBE. A professional English writer and experienced editor, he generously read the entire manuscript, edited it, and made very useful comments. I thank him for this very much.

I would like to extend my deepest thanks to S. Ilan Troen, the chair of the Publications Committee of the list Perspectives on Israel Studies at Indiana University Press. Ilan supported my project enthusiastically and generously, always giving his wise and friendly advice and offering encouragement at times when it was very much needed.

Many thanks to Dee Mortensen at Indiana University Press who believed in my manuscript from the first time we were in contact and navigated the publication process in a professional and friendly way, to the anonymous readers for their helpful comments, and to the entire team at Indiana University Press.

Special thanks also go to Rebecca Wolpe, who proofread the manuscript and especially the multiple transliterations of Hebrew and Yiddish.

And finally, the most important people in my life.

My daughter, Inbal, who grew up with this book, taught me important lessons of life, commitment, joy, and love. Although her interests are far from the topic of this book, she found a very creative way to connect with it. She drew the picture that decorates the cover of this book, making her a part of this project, and me grateful and proud.

Adam Teller, my life partner, intellectual companion, and best friend, stood by my side throughout this project and much more. Without his patience, wisdom, and love, this book would never have come to completion. I dedicate it to him with all my love.

A NOTE ON TRANSLITERATION, TRANSLATION, AND ARCHIVAL SIGNATURES

ALMOST ALL THE PRIMARY SOURCES, INCLUDING THE NEWSPAPER articles, as well as much of the scholarly literature that I used for the research on this book, were written in either Yiddish or Hebrew. For the Yiddish transliterations, I have used the YIVO romanization system. For Hebrew transliterations, I have used the guidelines of the Academy of the Hebrew Language (2011 edition). According to these updated guidelines, Hebrew prepositions that are part of the following noun form part of the noun and so are not be separated by a hyphen (e.g., *ha-*, *ve-*) although in some cases the academy suggests using an apostrophe (e.g., *ha'*, *ve'*). Since the guidelines permit the transliterator a little liberty, I decided that using an apostrophe after all Hebrew prepositions would be clearer (*ha'*, *ve'*, etc.). In addition, though the Hebrew letter כ is now to be transliterated *kh*, I have continued to use *ch* since it is more familiar for readers. I have used *h* for the letter ה, as suggested by the guidelines.

Names of Yiddish writers are spelled as they appear in English in their books and not in Yiddish transliteration and pronunciation, for example, Abraham Sutzkever. The same is true for titles of newspapers and names of places. Hebrew words used in Israeli Yiddish have been transliterated in the Hebrew-Sephardi pronunciation (e.g., *agudut*, not *agudes*, as might be expected), because this is how they are pronounced in Israeli Yiddish.

Some of the Hebrew-language scholarly books and articles quoted here have been published in English translation. However, in many cases I have had to quote from the Hebrew original because the English translation is abridged and omits the parts referred to. All translations from Hebrew and Yiddish within the text are mine, except where indicated.

Since I started the research for this book, the Israel State Archive, where many of the sources are to be found, has set up an online catalog and, in doing so, has changed the signatures of all the files. I used both the old signatures, as they still appear on the files themselves, and added in brackets the new signatures to reflect the online catalog.

YIDDISH IN ISRAEL

INTRODUCTION

"They Are Ashamed of Us Yiddish Writers"

> But A. M. Fuechs remained unimpressed and glum. He considered that the Jewish National Fund hadn't treated him with enough respect. A Hebrew writer, he said to me, they would have taken to a luxury hotel in Tel Aviv. Over a lavish dinner they'd have delivered a speech of greeting. Maybe even two speeches. But Yiddish writers? Us they took off for a whole day of wandering. I won't deny that the bus was nice—it had comfortable seats—but where did they take us? To Sodom! An empty sandy desert. Not a soul to be seen. Not a bird. They say there's not even one live fish in the Dead Sea.
>
> They're ashamed of us Yiddish writers.
>
> —Yossel Birstein, *"Ha'sofer A. M. Fuechs kevar haya zaken,"* 1986

IN MAY 1976, THE READERS OF *SIMAN KERI'A*, one of Israel's leading Hebrew literary journals at the time, came across a name most had never seen before: Yossel Birstein.[1] The sixth issue of the quarterly ran a Hebrew translation of a story that Birstein had written in Yiddish, alongside a lengthy interview with him. This came at a time when Yiddish was at one of its lowest points in Israel and Yiddish writers were largely unknown to the Israeli public.

Yossel Birstein was born in Poland in 1920 and immigrated to Australia in 1937. He came to live in Israel in 1950, after having published a book of Yiddish poetry.[2] In Israel, he published four books of Yiddish prose. Yet despite excellent Hebrew translations of Birstein's writing—the editor of *Siman keri'a* called his works "gems of new Israeli prose"—their status as translations from Yiddish put them squarely on the margins of Israeli culture.[3]

Birstein's breakthrough came in 1976. The publication of his story in the prestigious Hebrew quarterly won him his entry ticket into Israeli culture.[4] In 1986 he published a volume of short stories, *Ketem shel sheket* (A Drop of Silence), the first collection he wrote originally in Hebrew. It was well received. Birstein became recognized as a Hebrew writer and eventually came to be considered an important Israeli author.[5]

Still, many of Birstein's Hebrew stories are peopled with Yiddish speakers, and some hint at the status of Yiddish in Israel as a forgotten culture that belongs in the archives or the cemetery.[6] The short story "Ha'sofer A. M. Feuchs kevar haya zaken" (The Writer A. M. Feuchs Was Already an Old Man), quoted in the epigraph above, may be the most nuanced and complex statement of this issue made by a writer whose biography had been indelibly marked by the dramatic changes in Jewish culture after the Holocaust.

"They're ashamed of us Yiddish writers," complains the protagonist, an aging and not very successful Yiddish writer, railing against the attitude of the Jewish National Fund (JNF) toward them. "A Hebrew writer," he objects, "they would have taken to a nice hotel in Tel Aviv."[7] Yiddish writers, however, were brought to the arid wasteland of Sodom.

In Birstein's story, the trip was organized by the JNF—still a powerful national institution even in the 1980s—and it was done as a tribute to the Yiddish writers. Of course, the destination of the trip was not Tel Aviv, "the first Hebrew city," but Sodom, the biblical town that had been destroyed in fire and brimstone while those escaping were forbidden to look back at it.[8]

So what was the message? The words Birstein put in A. M. Feuchs's mouth expressed a view that was widely held (and still is) that the state of Israel indeed was ashamed of its Yiddish writers and rejected them. On the other hand, it is possible to see the text as Yossel Birstein—the embodiment of the post-Holocaust transformation of Jewish culture, especially in Israel—giving the Hebrew reader a nuanced view of the complicated relationship between the state of Israel and the Yiddish language and culture. After all, Birstein's story included a mixture of acceptance, distancing, rejection, and affection, hardly a portrayal of inordinate hostility.

It is the relationship between Yiddish and the state of Israel, in all its complexity and nuance—as well as the ways both the leaders of the state, on the one hand, and Yiddish speakers, writers, actors, and artists, on the other, understood it—that forms the topic of this book. Its goal is to explore the transformation of Jewish culture after the Holocaust and in the wake of the emergence of the state of Israel. At its heart is the story of Yiddish, the major language, literature, and culture of the vast majority of Jews worldwide before the Holocaust, and its struggle to survive following the destruction of most of its speakers and readers. It focuses on the encounter of Yiddish, the traditional transnational Jewish languge and culture, with the burgeoning new Hebrew culture in Israel—the newly born Jewish nation-state.

This study challenges the long-held view that Yiddish was suppressed and even rejected by the state of Israel for ideological reasons—that is, as a direct result of the Zionist ideology of the "negation of the Diaspora." Instead, it not only gives a picture of the vibrant development of Yiddish popular and high culture in Israel's first decades but actually presents Yiddish in Israel as an integral part of the country's culture. It does so by examining and analyzing the development of Yiddish-language culture in Israel and charting the dialectical tensions and reciprocal influences of its interaction with Israeli Hebrew culture (not to mention, the Yiddish-language culture of the Jewish Diaspora).

In short, this book is a comprehensive history of Yiddish in Israel, viewing it as an integral part of the new, complex, and multifaceted culture that developed in the Jewish state.

Yiddish and Hebrew before the Holocaust: Ideology, Images, and Linguistic Reality

Hebrew and Yiddish are usually understood as being in tension with each other for ideological reasons. Since the days of the Haskalah movement, and especially since the emergence of Jewish nationalism in the late nineteenth century, there were ideological conflicts between proponents of Yiddish and those who supported Hebrew, with both sides claiming to be the bearers of the Jewish national language. This has led to the attitude toward Yiddish in Israel being explained as a manifestation of an ideological conflict—between the Diaspora and its negation in the land of Israel, between the new Jew and the old Jew, between the past and the future. Yet, in the actual cultural and lingual reality of Jews in the Diaspora from the end of the nineteenth century to the Holocaust, the relationship between the two languages was more dialectical than binary, and the linguistic and cultural situation in which the Jews found themselves influenced this relationship no less than ideological world views. In order, then, to understand the background of the complex attitude toward Yiddish in Israel, we need to examine the place of Yiddish in the Jewish society of the time and the relations between its supporters and opponents in the years before the establishment of the state of Israel.

On the eve of World War II, Yiddish was the language of the majority of Jews worldwide. Of some 16.6 million Jews throughout the world, approximately 11 million (about 66 percent) were Yiddish speakers or at least knew the language.[9] They were to be found first and foremost in eastern Europe and then in the United States, Latin America, and some smaller centers.

Yiddish was the vernacular of Ashkenazi and eastern European Jews at least until the end of the eighteenth century.[10] In the nineteenth century, too, it remained the main language of eastern European Jews and for many of them the only language they knew. Yet until the middle of that century, Yiddish literature was sparse and consisted mostly of books related to the Jews' religious tradition.[11] The rise of the Haskalah movement in Germany engendered the first fundamental opposition to the language, which it viewed as a corrupt form of German, an idea that made its way to Russia in the early nineteenth century.[12] Yet, paradoxically, it was the emergence of the Haskalah movement in Russia that encouraged Jewish writers to start writing in Yiddish. It turned out that their aspiration to reach a broad audience that could read their writings was stronger than their opposition to Yiddish. The publication of *Kol mevaser* (The Herald Voice, Odessa 1862–1873)[13] and the subsequent decision of Mendele Moykher Sforim—the pen name of Sholem Yankev Abramovitsh, the first of the three great Yiddish masters (known in Yiddish as "the classics")—to publish his first Yiddish story in that paper opened a new era in the history of Yiddish and Yiddish literature.[14]

Perhaps the most dramatic turning point in the history of Yiddish, which resulted in Yiddish becoming not only a language of culture and politics but also an ideological element in its own right, took place with the emergence of Jewish nationalism at the turn of the twentieth century.

In 1897 two major Jewish national movements were founded: the Zionist movement and the Bund (the General Jewish Labor Bund in Lithuania, Poland, and Russia). Together they became the symbol of the ideological tension between Hebrew and Yiddish. The fundamental goal of the Zionist movement was the rebirth of the Jewish people in the land of Israel. The revival of the Hebrew language was an integral part of this goal, and one could not exist without the other. The Bund was founded as a socialist-Marxist organization representing the Yiddish-speaking working class in the Pale of Settlement and Congress Poland. Its ideological program developed gradually over the first few years of the twentieth century. It came to define itself as a Jewish national movement, opposing Zionism and any territorial solution for the Jewish people. Instead, it adhered to the concept of *doikayt* ("here," i.e., the current places where Jews were living as opposed to going to Israel) and adopted the idea of "national cultural autonomy" in the Diaspora based on the Yiddish language. In 1905, the Bund declared itself an anti-Zionist movement.[15] These two opposing ideas created the binary equivalence that became prominent in Zionist discourse: Hebrew and its supporters were identified with Zionism while Yiddish and its supporters were equated with anti-Zionism. This binary even appeared in books published in Israel during the 1950s.[16]

The reality, however was different. During 1904–1906, other Jewish political parties emerged in the Pale of Settlement. Most were proletarian but still maintained strong ties to Zionism. (The most important of these was Poalei-Zion.)[17] Nonetheless, they all used Yiddish as the language of both their activities and their ideological publications. This use of Yiddish was not ideological but reflected the linguistic reality of the time. According to the census held in the Russian empire in 1897, almost 98 percent of the Jews declared Yiddish as their mother tongue.[18]

In 1908, the famous Shprakh konferents (Language conference) was held in Czernowitz, the capital of Bukovina, then part of the Austro-Hungarian Empire. The goal of the conference was to discuss the state and status of Yiddish. The main issue on its agenda was a proposal to declare Yiddish the national language of the Jewish people. Yet alongside militant Yiddishists, such as Chaim Zhitlowsky (1865–1945), who opposed Zionism, there was also a significant number of Zionists and members of Poalei-Zion among the organizers and participants. The question of Hebrew was not even on the original agenda; only after Y. L. Peretz, the oldest and most distinguished participant in the conference, put serious pressure on the organizers did they add it. In the end, after heated debate, the conference adopted a resolution declaring Yiddish "a national language of the Jewish people." The status of Hebrew was left a matter of individual choice.[19] Zionist activists at the conference supported the decision.[20] The Czernowitz resolution did not, therefore, position Yiddish in opposition to Hebrew and did not encapsulate any conflict between Yiddish and Hebrew—and certainly not between Zionism and anti-Zionism. The supporters of the resolution understood language as an organizing element for Jewish nationalism, and the realistic choice at the time was Yiddish.

That same year, 1908, also saw the founding of the Yiddish daily *Haynt*, in Warsaw. It explicitly identified with the Zionist cause and quickly became the most widely read Yiddish paper in eastern Europe. In 1910, the daily *Der moment* was established and soon became the second major Yiddish newspaper in Poland. Pro-Zionist at first, after 1916 it became the unofficial organ of the Folkist Party, whose values it promoted. These were similar, in part, to those of the Bund, including supporting the idea of Jewish cultural autonomy based on the Yiddish language and culture. At the same time, *Der moment* also came out in favor of Zionism, settling in Israel, and the use of Hebrew. In 1935, *Der moment* became the mouthpiece of the Alliance of Revisionist Zionists and regularly published essays by its leader, Ze'ev Jabotinsky. Notably, other Yiddish newspapers appeared in eastern Europe over the years, voicing orthodox, socialist, and various forms of Zionist-socialist views.[21]

The Yiddish scene at the turn of the twentieth century, combining culture and politics, was not limited to eastern Europe. Mass emigration from eastern Europe as of 1882 created a large, vibrant Yiddish center in the United States, which maintained ongoing ties with the centers in eastern Europe. Almost every national-socialist Yiddish-speaking party and political movement that developed within the Pale of Settlement had an equivalent in the United States.

One of the most active among them was Poalei-Zion of North America—a socialist Zionist political party with a clear orientation toward the land of Israel and its settlement. Over time, this organization issued various newspapers in Yiddish, set up Yiddish secular schools, and until the 1940s conducted all of its activities in Yiddish.[22] And it was not alone.

From the turn of the twentieth century, a whole range of Yiddish newspapers started to come out in the United States. In 1905 four dailies were already being published, one expressing a religious-Zionist world view (*Yidishes tageblat*);[23] another, conservative and orthodox values (*Morgn zhurnal*); the third, a liberal world view (*Di varhayt*); and of course the *Jewish Daily Forward* (*Forverts*), founded in 1897 and, with its socialist orientation, soon became the most important Yiddish daily in the world.[24] Over the following years, additional dailies were founded, as well as dozens of weeklies, monthlies, and quarterlies—all in Yiddish and representing a spectrum of different views. Yiddish literary centers also sprang up in eastern Europe, especially Poland, as well as in the United States.[25] On either side of the Atlantic, Yiddish schools, theaters—popular as well as artistic—sprang up and flourished. And since Yiddish publications made their way across the water—as occasionally did the writers and artists themselves—the result was a creative, vibrant, transregional Yiddish world.

Yiddish and Hebrew in Prestate Palestine

Things were different in the land of Israel. Here the struggle was to create a new linguistic reality—the opposite of that in the Diaspora—in which the majority of the Jewish population would be Hebrew speaking. In that situation, there was indeed a clear tension between Hebrew and Yiddish, and those who emphasized the conflict between them had a significant practical goal: creating the conditions that would give Hebrew supremacy.

The Jewish Yishuv in prestate Palestine was known for its vehement, sometimes violent opposition to Yiddish, news of which spread throughout the Jewish world. Beginning during the Second Aliya (1904–1914), the leaders of the Poalei-Zion movement in Eretz Israel, who later became the heads of the Yishuv and of the state of Israel, promoted the strong opposition toward Yiddish. Zealous supporters of the Zionist ideology, who considered the revival of Eretz Israel their most sublime ideal, and the revival of the Hebrew language an integral part of that, they made the struggle for Hebrew a top priority, targeting not only Yiddish but also other languages.[26] Yet the opposition to Yiddish took center stage, as they played on the anti-Zionist image that Yiddish had in the Yishuv.

In fact, the opposition to Yiddish in prestate Palestine also stemmed from a practical consideration: the language's growing power in the Diaspora in those years led to a fear that a large wave of immigration of Yiddish speakers would prevent the revival of Hebrew. This resulted in strong public opposition to the use of Yiddish, with Yiddish speakers branded as holding an anti-Zionist ideology. Things could even get physical. During Chaim Zhitlowsky's visit to Israel in 1914, high school students, led by their principal, physically prevented him from leaving the house where he was staying to give a lecture in Yiddish. The talk was canceled.[27]

In the 1920s, however, the situation changed: Hebrew took firmer root and became the major language spoken in the Yishuv. Moreover, the 1922 British Mandate for Palestine defined Hebrew as one of the three official languages in Mandatory Palestine, giving the language an official status for the first time in its history. As of 1924, the land of Israel also became a growing center of Hebrew literature.[28] The number of Yiddish newspapers that circulated in prestate Israel was very small, and with the exception of Left Poalei-Zion's *Nayvelt*, which was founded in 1934 and continued to appear until 1955, they were very short-lived. While original Yiddish literature was written in the Yishuv and even described various facets of life there, it was scant and certainly posed no threat to the burgeoning Hebrew literature.

Nonetheless, in 1923, an organization called Gedud meginei ha'safa (Defenders of the [Hebrew] Language Battalion) was founded. Mainly high school students, some high school graduates, and even a few from the Lewinsky teachers' seminary, they engaged in teaching Hebrew, putting out pro-Hebrew propaganda, and participating in public activism against the use of other languages, especially Yiddish. This small group had a very loud voice, which allowed it to influence public opinion way beyond its actual power.[29]

The struggle against Yiddish intensified during the period of the Fourth Aliya (1924–1929). This wave of immigration that started after the United States implemented immigration restrictions in 1924 was very different from previous ones. Unlike the Second and Third Aliyot, the Fourth Aliya was not ideological in nature. Most of the immigrants were Jews fleeing antisemitism and economic hardships, particularly in eastern Europe, who chose the land of Israel for lack of an alternative. Most spoke Yiddish, settled in urban centers, and started small businesses. Veteran immigrants who had come for ideological reasons and were part of the Labor movement treated them with disdain.[30] They sneered at their petit bourgeois occupations, accused them of ideological inferiority, and cast the fact that they spoke Yiddish as the major expression of this decadence.[31]

In reality, the immigrants' choice to start small businesses and use Yiddish as their everyday language was practical in nature and did not represent any ideological preference, but this did not prevent the attacks on them, especially by people with a strong ideological connection to the Labor movement. The unjustified nature of the hostility becomes even clearer when we take into account the fact that there was a significant number of *halutzim* (highly ideological "pioneers," especially farmers) among the immigrants.[32] The use of other languages in the Yishuv at that time was widespread and did not arouse any opposition.[33]

This practice of presenting Yiddish as inferior and worthy of rejection evolved over the years and became a kind of general truth in its own right. It was seen clearly in 1927, when a significant public debate broke out over the proposal to establish a chair in Yiddish at the Hebrew University. The idea had first been proposed by the owner of the New York Yiddish daily *Der tog*, who even expressed his willingness to endow the chair himself. The plan was that whoever held it would primarily engage in research, with a limited amount of teaching in Hebrew. Nonetheless, the idea became enormously controversial not just within the university but among the public at large as well. Zionist leaders wrote to the president of the university, warning him that the Yiddish chair would destroy the Hebrew University. The Gedud meginei ha'safa was even harsher. Drawing on the idea that the Hebrew University was a flagship of the Zionist enterprise in Palestine, the organization's flyers described the Yiddish chair as a "crucifix in the sanctuary," elevating Hebrew to divine status and presenting Yiddish as its, presumably demonic, opponent.[34] In the wake of this storm, the project came to nothing. The chair in Yiddish had to wait to be founded until 1951, a few years after the establishment of the state.

In the late 1930s and especially in the 1940s, the general public in prestate Palestine lost interest in the question of Yiddish. Small pockets of resistance continued to exist, and even cases of extreme violence, such as torching newspaper stands that sold copies of *Nayvelt*, erupted, yet the Hebrew press did not discuss the Yiddish question, and neither did *Nayvelt* itself.

Despite that reticence, the image of the Israeli leadership as zealous opponents of Yiddish became fixed in the public memory. An incident that took place in February 1945, at the sixth convention of the Histadrut, had an enormous impact. Following a speech given in Yiddish by Rozka Korczack, a heroine of the Vilna ghetto and later a partisan, David Ben-Gurion referred to her as speaking a "foreign and grating language." Though he withdrew this statement a few years later, it was too late. His supposed implacable hostility toward, not to say hatred of, Yiddish became a permanent part of his political persona—and remained so for a very long time.[35]

"Immigrating Home": Yiddish Speakers and the State of Israel

The proclamation of the state of Israel on May 14, 1948, opened a new period in the history of Yiddish. The background to this was painful. World War II and the Holocaust had fundamentally changed the shape of Jewish culture and shifted the balance of power within it. Yiddish, once the spoken tongue of most Jewish people and the main language of secular Jewish culture, had lost its status forever. In eastern Europe, the Holocaust had all but eliminated it, and in the United States, it was in decline. The children of Yiddish-speaking immigrants from eastern Europe had turned their backs on the language while immigration restrictions to the United States stopped the influx of new Yiddish speakers to the country. In Israel, Hebrew—the ideological language of Zionism and the actual language of the Yishuv—had become the main language of the Jewish nation-state. Yiddish was left at its lowest ebb, the language of the lost Jewish past.

This was the linguistic reality that immigrants from eastern Europe faced when they arrived in the newly founded state of Israel. On the day the state was declared, about 650,000 Jews lived there: some 55 percent were immigrants from Europe and the United States, and another 35 percent were the descendants of immigrants. In other words, on the eve of the declaration of Israel's independence, about 90 percent of Jews in Palestine were of Ashkenazi origin.[36] Most of them had a good command of both Hebrew and Yiddish, though many preferred not to use the former.[37]

By September 1948, most of the displaced persons from the camps in Germany, Austria, and Italy had reached Israel; in the winter of 1948–1949, the Jews from British detention camps in Cyprus joined them. All of these were Holocaust survivors, known in Hebrew as *she'erit ha'pleita* (the surviving remnant).[38] In terms of the geographical background of the Ashkenazi immigrants, 106,000 were from Poland, 118,000 from Romania, and another 10,000 or so from other places. This made more than 225,000 immigrants from the Yiddish-speaking heartlands.[39]

It is hard to tell precisely how many of the immigrants spoke Yiddish on a daily basis. According to Roberto Bachi, among Israelis whose first language was other than Hebrew in late 1948, 46.8 percent spoke Yiddish; this dropped to 33.3 percent with the immigration of Jews from Arab countries.[40] On the other hand, Bachi also noted that 60 percent of Israel's Jewish population in 1954 used more than one language on a daily basis, which suggests that the number of Yiddish speakers was higher than his first figures suggested.[41] Other sources, particularly journalistic reports and stories, describe the extensive daily use of Yiddish by these immigrants.[42] The existence of an extensive Yiddish press with a substantial circulation in the early years of the state also strongly indicates that a significant body of people used the language every day.[43]

The fairly homogenous nature of the immigrant population would change dramatically in terms of both their cultural and linguistic backgrounds in the course of the early 1950s. From May 14, 1948, until the end of 1953, more than 700,000 immigrants arrived in Israel. Of these, immigrants from Europe constituted only 48.6 percent of the total, with immigrants from Asia and Africa making up 50.7 percent. (The rest came from the Americas.)[44]

These figures have many implications for our discussion. First, in terms of raw statistics, this is a rare case in the history of immigration in which the immigrant population outnumbers the host society. This situation created massive difficulties in the resettlement process, particularly providing work and housing. Second, the heterogeneous demographic structure of the immigrants strengthened the sense of urgency among the Israeli leadership to develop a single and comprehensive cultural policy for all immigrants, to ensure greater cohesiveness in the society that would emerge once they were resettled. Such was the policy of the melting pot, which, together with the Zionist ideology of "the negation of the Diaspora," worked by demanding that the new immigrants abandon their old cultures, especially the Diaspora cultures in which they grew up, and adopt instead the new Israeli Hebrew culture. The jewel in the crown of that culture was of course the Hebrew language, so the immigrants were to accept the rejection of past Jewish languages (such as Yiddish, Judeo-Spanish, and various Jewish dialects of Arabic), which were henceforth to be defined in Israel as "foreign languages."

However, the migration of Jews to Israel, their own nation-state, involved the unique notion of *aliya* (literally, "ascent"), which carried with it the connotations of both returning to one's homeland and reaching a more exalted level of Jewish existence. The Israeli sociologists Edna Lomsky-Feder and Tamar Rapoport have termed migrating to one's nation-state, as was the case in Israel, an "ethno-national home-coming migration." They explain that, in such situations, the ethnic-national collective welcomes the immigrants on the basis of an assumption of historical belonging determined by blood ties.[45] The author Itamar Yaoz-Kest's more literary term, "immigrating home," beautifully evokes the feelings of the immigrant who expects to be treated as a prodigal son in his new home.[46] For the immigrants in Israel and especially for the Yiddish speakers among them, the feeling of immigrating home and the country's linguistic policy seemed to be in conflict with each other.

As Hanna Yablonka has noted, many of the Yiddish speakers who came to Israel after 1948, mostly Holocaust survivors, soon reverted to their old ways of making a living and falling into the patterns of everyday life.[47] That, of course, included their use of language, which reflected their life experience rather than any ideology. In fact, the majority had not actively espoused Zionist ideology before the war, and their decision to settle in Israel had been the outcome of their traumatic experiences rather than any ideological choice.[48] Nonetheless, they fully identified with the state, wanted to integrate into their new home, and were quite willing to take part in building it. In fact, many of the Yiddish speakers—and even writers—who survived the Holocaust and came to Israel not only accepted Hebrew as the language of the Jewish nation state but also chose not to pass on their own language, Yiddish, to the next generation.[49]

And yet, as people who were "immigrating home," they expected their nation-state to treat the Jewish cultures of the past with respect. This was all the more true as far as Yiddish speakers were concerned. Unlike other groups of new immigrants, especially those from the Arab countries, they considered themselves to belong to the very same social group as the leaders of the state, almost all of whom were Jews from eastern Europe who knew Yiddish well. Many of those who rejected Yiddish on ideological grounds actually liked the language and culture. Many Yiddish speakers, especially writers and activists, could not accept this and expected the leaders of the state to support Yiddish and allow it to exist alongside Hebrew. The fact that some policy makers in the state of Israel saw Yiddish, their common *mame loshn* (mother tongue), as a "foreign language" and an impediment to establishing Hebrew as the national language caused some tension between Yiddish loyalists and the state. The attempts to limit the Yiddish press and theater that were made in the early 1950s ramped up the tension still further. Those who actively promoted Yiddish through journalism, literature, theater, and the like experienced these attempts as active persecution on the part of the state of Israel.

Yiddish in Israel: Major Questions

This, then, raises the question of whether there was, in fact, a clearly defined official policy toward Yiddish in Israel. What was the nature of the attempts to restrict it in the early 1950s, and did they really play a central role in the development of Yiddish in Israel? What were the most important influences that shaped the development of Yiddish in Israel? Were these the actions of the state, or did other factors come into play? Can the development of Yiddish be isolated from the broader processes that took place in Israel and in Jewish culture in general over the years? And finally, what were the connections between Yiddish in Israel and Yiddish in the post-Holocaust Jewish world?

To provide answers to these questions, this book analyzes the history of Yiddish in Israel within the broader context of the state's cultural and political history and examines the development of Yiddish-language culture within the context of its reciprocal relations with the state. As should be clear by now, its point of departure is that Yiddish speakers in Israel constituted an immigrant society. The development of their language and culture should, therefore, be examined with the theoretical tools used for examining such societies.[50] At the same time, one should not forget the unique features of this history. The ideologically Zionist character of the state of Israel, on the one hand, and the concept of these immigrants "immigrating home," on the other, mean that this history should also be examined as a phenomenon sui generis.

The main questions that the book asks are clustered around three major issues, which form the threads connecting the various chapters: (1) the development and nature of cultural hegemony in the state of Israel; (2) attitudes toward the past like nostalgia, the creation of a "usable past," and the tension between individual and collective memory; and (3) problems arising from the tension between the transregional nature of the Yiddish language and the local nature of Hebrew-Israeli culture.

Hegemony

The concept of hegemony, as defined by Antonio Gramsci, holds that the control over society is currently wielded by a dominant group, the bourgeoisie, which by propagating its own cultural values makes the other groups in society subordinate to it and its desires. For the proletariat to assume control, it—or the state acting on its behalf—has to deploy a range of its own cultural and spiritual measures in the same way. It is this "cultural hegemony" that will assure its ascendancy as much as, if not more than, legislation on social and economic issues.[51] The question of hegemony is thus central to understanding the relationship between the state of Israel and Yiddish, especially during the years in which the socialist-Zionist Mapai regime worked to buttress its control over Israeli society.

Israel's primary goal was, of course, to create a society that would be able to absorb the mass immigration as part of the Zionist ideology of "ingathering the exiles." The challenge was to do this for such a large and disparate group while preserving the existing political, economic, and cultural order.[52] The creation of the new Hebrew-Israeli culture was undoubtedly part of Zionist ideology, but it also had another role to play. It was to become part of the state's hegemonic system of control over its citizens by creating a kind of "intellectual and moral unity," of the type that Antonio Gramsci theorized.[53] For this to work, it was crucially important to create a unified Hebrew culture and to ensure that the citizens of the country adopted it. Israel's policy makers believed that the use of foreign languages would obstruct this project and prevent new immigrants from learning Hebrew. They considered all non-Hebrew languages foreign, including Jewish ones. Yiddish was, for historical reasons, deemed the greatest threat in this regard. Just a few years previously, it had been the language of the majority of the Jewish people, had wielded considerable ideological power, and had been Hebrew's greatest rival. Not unnaturally, the leaders of the state assumed that a robust cultural scene in Yiddish in Israel would put their program at serious risk. The image of Yiddish as the language of Zionism's opponents played into this.

The perception of foreign languages in general and Yiddish in particular as a threat involved government ministers and senior officials in extensive debate over the best ways to make sure that Hebrew and the new Hebrew culture would be accepted by the whole of Israeli society. A central question was whether the effort to ensure the success of the Hebrew project should include limiting the use of foreign languages, especially Yiddish, by the use of existing law or even new legislation. In the end, the preferred alternative was to promote Hebrew through hegemonic mechanisms, such as the use of propaganda and the enlistment of volunteers.

This activity was not aimed against foreign languages in general or Yiddish in particular but for promoting Hebrew. However, the discourse that surrounded these efforts, the ways in which action was taken, and the overt and covert messages that it conveyed all had far-reaching effects on the status of Yiddish in Israel.

There was another side to the issue, however. In order to retain its hegemonic power in the Israeli democracy, the ruling Mapai party needed the support of the Israeli public, including the groups that used foreign languages. To win it, Mapai had to reach out to these people in their own languages and cultures. While this had to be done on a day-to-day basis, it became extremely important during election campaigns. The leaders of Mapai, who were also the leaders of the state, saw Yiddish speakers as the most important of all the groups. They viewed Yiddish speakers as the most literate and educated of the groups, as well as the most sophisticated and critical. As a result, they invested a great deal of thought and effort in opening channels of communication with the Yiddish-speaking public, primarily by means of the press. They thus found themselves acting in the Yiddish-speaking space and supporting cultural activity in Yiddish to bolster their political standing—a move that seemed to contradict their objections to Yiddish as a threat to the spread of Hebrew. An inherent conflict thus developed between Mapai's goal of creating cultural hegemony (by rejecting, among other things, Yiddish) and its need to maintain political hegemony (for which it needed to use Yiddish). The tension between these contradictory aspirations had a significant effect on the development and achievements of Yiddish in Israel.

Nostalgia, Usable Past, and Individual and Collective Memory

Nostalgia, says Svetlana Boym, is "the longing for a home that no longer exists—a sentiment of loss and displacement, but is also a romance with one's own fantasy."[54] So while hegemony played a pivotal role in shaping the attitude of the leadership to Yiddish, nostalgia and the creation of a usable past were important vehicles in shaping the attitude of the Israeli public toward Yiddish, playing a role both in bringing Yiddish back to Israeli culture and in marginalizing it. Nostalgia also was very instrumental in shaping the image of Yiddish as a "popular" and "warm" language, not to say "funny" or even "ridiculous."

Although life in the first decade of the state of Israel did not leave much room in the public sphere for nostalgia, an underground current of nostalgia for the eastern European past continued to exist in Israeli society. In the first half of the 1960s, thanks to the passage of time but also in the wake of the Eichmann trial, this current began to bubble to the surface. A new and more acceptable form of memory was therefore needed—a "usable past" that could legitimize this nostalgia for the lost world of eastern Europe. This gave rise to theatrical performances that presented the east European Jewish past in a romantic and imaginary way. One of these performances actually came from Broadway: *Fiddler on the Roof*, a musical based on Yiddish stories by Sholem Aleichem. However, it was far from the Yiddish original. Embroidered with songs and dances, it presented an invented image of a happy life in the Jewish shtetl of the past—a fantasy in which people could channel their yearnings for a better past. The production opened the way for Yiddish literature and culture to penetrate the public cultural arena. Adaptations of Yiddish literature offered an even more highly developed imaginary past, embedded not in a Broadway-style musical but in the real Yiddish words of the poems and stories that many people knew and cherished. And the theater that staged these plays suddenly became a "realm of memory," to use Pierre Nora's term.[55]

However, after the 1967 war, Israeli culture changed again. The nostalgia for the east European Jewish past was replaced with yearnings that were connected to a new vision of the land of Israel. The nostalgic window for Yiddish closed.

It took some two and a half decades for it to reopen. This time, Yiddish appeared not as part of a kind of collective memory but in the private memories of immigrants and their children. With the passage of time, Israelis who had come to Israel from eastern Europe began to see in Yiddish itself the embodiment of their past. This feeling was even stronger for the second generation, who had been born after the Holocaust and knew little Yiddish or none at all. For them, Yiddish theater, where they could hear the sound of the language, became once again a "realm of memory," but this time in a very personal and private way.

However, this nostalgia for the past through Yiddish—loving the language without understanding it and valuing the literature without reading it—also shaped the image of Yiddish in the public imagination as a popular, even low culture, known only for its jokes. This has, over the years, taken a heavy toll on the language and its culture.

Transnationality

Yiddish literature was transregional in nature and had been so for centuries.[56] As early as the beginning of the seventeenth century, in the introduction to the *Mayse-bukh*, the writer urged readers in Ashkenaz (i.e., the German lands) to buy a copy without delay before all the rest were sent to be sold in other countries, such as Bohemia, White Russia, and Poland.[57] The transnational nature of Yiddish reached its peak in the interwar years of the twentieth century, when centers of Yiddish flourished on both sides of the Atlantic—in the United States and in Europe—and maintained reciprocal ties. The Yiddish press became international in nature and was read across the Yiddish-speaking world, in Europe, North America, and Latin America. In addition, Yiddish theater and cinema became transnational: Yiddish theater and movie stars also began to travel the world, transferring the forms of Yiddish art and culture from one part of the world to another.[58]

In stark contrast to this, Israeli culture was not only local but did its best, as a matter of principle, to cut itself off from the Jewish cultures of the diasporic past. On the other hand, the Israeli leadership saw Israel's relations with the Jewish world—particularly with American Jewry—as extremely important. The transnational nature of Yiddish did not escape these leaders. They were also aware of the fact that, although Yiddish was in decline when the state of Israel was founded, many Diaspora Jews continued to embrace Yiddish, value Yiddish literature, and admire Yiddish writers and even actors.

One of their central goals was to make world Jewry see the state of Israel as the nation-state of the entire Jewish people, not only of its citizens, and to give it the status of the spiritual or cultural center for Jews everywhere. Against this background, it is important to distinguish between the Israeli leadership's attitude toward Yiddish popular culture and Yiddish high culture. The Israeli leadership was willing to give public, financial, and moral support to small pockets of high culture in Yiddish as a means of bolstering the image of the Jewish nation-state as a home to the Jews' most important spiritual and cultural assets. Yiddish was clearly perceived by the Israeli leadership as one of these.

For that reason, famous Yiddish actors, big stars known across the Jewish world, were not only made very welcome in Israel but also were invited to settle there. Attempts were even made to establish a Yiddish repertory theater, funded with public money, to tempt them to move to Israel and turn it into the center of high-quality Jewish art theater. It never worked. However, the project of creating a Yiddish literary journal with public money that would take center stage in the international Yiddish literary community was a great success. In this way, Israel used Yiddish not only to become part of the transnational network of post-Holocaust Jewish culture but also—in an unstated and subtle way—to establish itself as a kind of cultural "nodal center," to which other centers of Jewish culture would be tied, to use the terminology of research on transnational mercantile networks.[59]

These are the main axes around which the discussion here turns. The book's various chapters are dedicated to topics that show how the history of Yiddish in Israel was closely intertwined with the social, political, and cultural developments of the state. The first chapter discusses the attitude of the state toward Yiddish in its earliest years. The chapters that follow deal with the way those issues at the heart of Yiddish-language culture—the press, the theater, literary production and publication, and the academy—developed in the Israeli environment. The final chapter shows how these issues played out over the decades by returning to the state and its changing attitude toward Yiddish at the turn of the twenty-first century.

As a final point here, I should like to mention important groups of Yiddish speakers that will not be discussed in the book and explain why: These groups are part of the ultraorthodox community, which is in fact made up of a number of different groupings. In Israel, the Hasidic groups, as well as those remnants of the ultraorthodox society in nineteenth-century Jerusalem who still speak Yiddish, saw (and still see) Yiddish as something quite different from the modern, secular culture discussed here. In fact, these specific ultraorthodox groups use Yiddish as a barrier to separate themselves from Israeli Zionist society and to define their identity as different from the general Israeli Hebrew-speaking population. As far as they are concerned, the modern, secular Yiddish literature, drama, and press are *tarbut anashim hata'im* (a culture of sinners), and they have no interest in it. So, though their Yiddish has many aspects of great interest and importance, it is not part of the story being told here. It awaits its own historian.[60]

Approaches to the Subject

The full history of the Yiddish language and culture in the state of Israel and especially the nexus of the development of Yiddish with that of Israel's Hebrew culture has yet to be told. The development and use of languages in general in the prestate Yishuv, however, has been studied in some detail, alongside broad studies on the emergence of Hebrew culture in Ottoman Palestine, the creation of Hebrew culture in the prestate Yishuv from the First Aliya to 1948, and the multilingual nature of society in Mandatory Palestine.[61] Two monographs specifically devoted to Yiddish before 1948 have been written. The first is Arye L. Pilowsky's *Tsvishn yo un neyn: Yidish un yidish-literatur in Erets-Yisroel, 1907–1948* (Yiddish: Between Yes and No, Yiddish and Yiddish Literature in Eretz Israel 1907–1948), published in 1986.[62] Drawing on a wide range of primary sources, including archival materials as well as Yiddish publications, the book provides a detailed account of the development of Yiddish language and culture in prestate Palestine and attitudes toward it. The second book, *What Must Be Forgotten*, by Yael Chaver, was published in 2004 and grounds its thesis on a close reading of Yiddish literature.[63] By focusing on three Yiddish authors, two prose writers and a poet, Chaver argues that because Yiddish did not bear the same ideological significance in prestate Palestine as Hebrew, its literature was freer to be less conservative in its choice of themes than Hebrew.

Only a limited number of shorter studies devoted to Yiddish in the state of Israel have been published. Some important sociolinguistic and historical aspects of the issue have been discussed by Joshua Fishman and David Fishman in their pioneering study of the Yiddish press, radio, theater, and book publishing in Israel.[64] In addition, various articles on, among other things, the teaching of Yiddish in Israeli universities have also been published.[65]

Most research, however, has focused on specific aspects of Yiddish literature in Israel. These include a number of papers on the poet Abraham Sutzkever, parts of which dealt with his writing in Israel.[66] Some studies were done on the group of young Yiddish poets Yung Yisroel, in particular a series of articles by David Roskies in the 1970s.[67] In recent years, Shachar Pinsker has published a number of papers arguing that the work of the group, especially its poetry, had a great deal in common with the work of the Hebrew poets of the day and so constitute an important component of early Israeli literature.[68]

Two doctoral dissertations written at The Hebrew University of Jerusalem in the last few years also discuss various aspects of Yiddish in Israel. The first is a study of the long career of the very famous comic duo Dzigan and Shumacher, which includes two chapters on their career in Israel.[69] The second deals with Yiddish prose written in Israel in the years 1948–1968.[70] Both dissertations, however, discuss their topics from an artistic point of view. The first focuses on satire as social critique; the second is a literary reading of various short stories and novels aimed at demonstrating their unique nature. Neither attempts to reexamine the relations between the state of Israel and Yiddish-language culture, with both studies—albeit in very different ways—continuing to reiterate the accepted view that the attitude to Yiddish in Israel was one of rejection and suppression.[71] This idea clearly remains current even in the most recent scholarship.

While a comprehensive study on Yiddish speakers and the development of the culture created in Yiddish in the state of Israel has not yet been written, Jeffrey Shandler has devoted a monograph to the development of Yiddish in post-Holocaust United States, *Adventures in Yiddishland: Postvernacular Language and Culture*. In it, he discusses the transformation of Yiddish during the second half of the twentieth century.[72] Tracing the encounters of American Jewry with the Yiddish language, he demonstrates how Yiddish was transformed from a language of daily life to the bearer of symbolic value for those who used it in any way. He coined the term "post-vernacular language" to describe this kind of usage. Shandler also found traces of the postvernacular use of Yiddish in Israel at the turn of the twenty-first century.

On the other hand, the mass immigration to Israel that forms the backdrop to this study has been examined in depth. Various studies have focused on Israel's absorption of the immigrants, dealing with, among other things, questions of education and changes in language culture.[73] Others have devoted special attention to the specific experience of Holocaust survivors as new immigrants in Israel.[74] In cultural terms, much has been written about images of the Israeli New Jew vis-à-vis those of the diasporic Jew, a topic essential for the discussion of Yiddish in Israel.[75]

The question of cultural hegemony in Israel's first decade, particularly in the context of immigrant absorption has also been studied. The focus of this research has been Jews who did not come from the same cultural background as the hegemonic leadership—that is, the Mizrahi Jews, who emigrated from Arab countries.[76] This issue is the focus of two fundamental books that approach the question from different points of view, through the use of two different disciplines.

The first one, the literary study *Al saf ha'ge'ula: sipur ha'ma'abara dor rishon ve'sheni* (On the Threshold of Redemption: The Story of the Ma'abara [transit camp] First and Second Generation), by Batya Shimony, examines the immigration and absorption experience of Jewish immigrants from Arab counties, as portrayed by authors who came from those countries.[77] By also examining how the absorption of the Mizrahi Jews in Israel was portrayed in the literary work of veteran Israelis, Shimony is able to point out the gap that existed between the Zionist vision of redemption and the liminal place occupied by the Mizrahi Jews as Israel's Jewish Others.

In his sociological study of the group he terms the "Arab Jews," Yehuda Shenhav also examines—though in an entirely different way from Shimony—the same encounter between "European Jews" and "Arab Jews" in Israel. Focusing on the decade of the 1940s rather than the years post-1948, Shenhav discusses the relationship between the Zionist leadership and the "Arab Jews" and explains why the leadership encouraged the image of the Mizrahi Jews as a religious group, emphasizing the leadership's orientalist attitude toward them.[78]

What unites these two disparate books is their examination of cultural hegemony through the examination of an "out-group"—that is, the Mizrahi Jews, whose cultural background was seen as not only different from that of the Zionist leadership but also inferior to it. My book, however, changes the focus by examining the relations between the Zionist leadership and other Ashkenazi Jews, who shared with them the same culture. This focus brings a new perspective to bear on the question of cultural hegemony and Israel's development in its first decades. In doing so, it also adds another layer to the study of the transformation of Jewish culture after the Holocaust. It examines both the development of post-Holocaust Yiddish and its encounter with the Jewish nation-state and the ways in which the burgeoning Israeli Hebrew culture encountered this new phase of Yiddish-language culture.

The Sources

This study is based on a broad range of primary sources: archival sources of various kinds; printed materials, such as official reports and other records; newspapers and periodicals in Hebrew and Yiddish; interviews with Yiddish journalists, writers, and actors (or their sons and daughters); and a number of literary sources.

The archival materials consist mainly of documents from the files of the Israeli Ministry of Education and Ministry of Internal Affairs, kept in the Israel State Archive in Jerusalem, which help clarify the complex and contradictory forces in the attitude toward Yiddish. The materials reveal a broad picture of the different—sometimes conflicting—considerations that were involved in the plans to create a new Hebrew culture, to develop Hebrew teaching, and to encourage the use of the language. The documents used here include minutes of the meetings of special committees, correspondence of government officials, reports of committees, and policy papers. Of special interest are reports of the police and the Council for the Control of Films and Plays concerning unauthorized Yiddish performances. Other important archival materials are the minutes of special committees of the Mapai on the foreign-language press, kept in the Archive of the Israeli Labor Party, and documents on Yiddish theater and Yiddish writers from other archives in Israel, as well as the YIVO archive in New York. The printed materials on which the discussion is based consist mainly of minutes of meetings of the Israeli government and the Knesset (the Israeli parliament), as well as official publications, such as pamphlets issued by various organizations, activity reports, policy papers, and public relations material.

Periodicals, especially the weekly and daily press in both Hebrew and Yiddish, form a very rich source for learning about approaches toward and opinions of Yiddish. The Hebrew publications reflect the ways in which the Yiddish language and culture was presented to the Israeli Hebrew reader, giving insights into the opinions and attitudes that were common and so had an enormous influence on attitudes to Yiddish in Israel. On the other hand, a close reading of the Israeli Yiddish press provides us with a fascinating picture of how Israel was portrayed to the Yiddish readers and especially how this press described to its readership attitudes toward Yiddish in Israel. It also sheds light on the expectations of various Yiddish journalists and writers for the future of Yiddish in the Jewish nation-state.

In addition, I conducted a number of interviews with people who had been active in Yiddish life in Israel. They included Yiddish writers and journalists, Yiddish actors, and, on occasion, members of their families. These interviews were interesting and engaging, though their usefulness for my research was quite limited. Conducted many years after the events in question, the interviews revealed the personal points of view of their subjects, sometimes limited by the weakness of human memory and sometimes colored by partisan positions taken in conflicts long past. Their often unbalanced nature meant that they had to be supported by additional sources that I felt to be more reliable. Nonetheless, this oral testimony was very valuable as it added a human dimension that the other sources often lacked.

The last group of sources are literary in nature, consisting mainly of Yiddish prose written in Israel, and form an important aspect of the book. These works are an excellent reflection of their authors' encounters with the experience of immigration and life in the new country, giving us important insights into their feelings, thoughts, and hopes as the bearers of Yiddish-language culture in the Jewish nation-state. I analyzed them not for their artistic or aesthetic value but as historical sources that provide a window into states of mind, thoughts, hopes, and ideas that the archival documents do not express. This material thus adds an extra layer to the study, deepening and enriching our understanding of the processes at work and helping create a nuanced and complex picture of the development of Yiddish in the state of Israel.

Notes

1. *Siman keri'a* (Exclamation Mark) was founded in 1972 as an Israeli Hebrew literary quarterly that published both literature and scholarship. The goals of the new quarterly were to challenge the poetics of the previous generation, to broaden the span of Israeli literature, and to introduce the Israeli reader to new voices. Birstein was one such voice.
2. For a detailed discussion of Birstein, see chapter 4.
3. Menachem Perry, "Kavim yehefim u'tzlil," in Yossel Birstein, *Sipurim me'ezor ha'shalva* (Tel Aviv: Hakibbutz Hameuchad, 2004), 325. Perry was the editor of *Siman keri'a* and became Birstein's literary patron. For the 1976 interview, with a biographical introduction by Perry, see pp. 323–346.
4. Yaakov Meir, "Al sheloshet ha'halomot ha'genuzim shel Birstein," *Ha'aretz*, December 28, 2005.
5. Shiri Lev-Ari, "Yossel Birstein—1920–2003," *Ha'aretz*, December 28, 2003.
6. Yossel Birstein, "Lif'amim ani tofes et atzmi," *Ketem shel sheket* (Tel Aviv: Hakibbutz Hameuchad, 1986), 143–144; "Keshe'bati le'veito shel ha'sofer A. M. Fuechs," *Ketem shel sheket*, 135–136.
7. Yossel Birstein, "Ha'sofer A. M. Feuchs kevar haya zaken," *Ketem shel sheket*, 133.
8. On Tel Aviv as the "first Hebrew city," see Maoz Azaryahu, *Tel Aviv, Mythography of a City* (Syracuse, NY: Syracuse University Press, 2007), 33–71.
9. Sergio DellaPergola, "Merkaz u'periferya ba'olam ha'yehudi: hamishim shana be'perespektiva sotzyo-demografit," *Yahadut zemaneinu* 8 (1993): 269–299; Max Weinreich, *History of the Yiddish Language* (Chicago: Chicago University Press, 1980), 723.
10. Chava Turniansky, *Sefer masa u'meriva le'R(eb) Aleksander be'R(eb) Yitshok Pafen Hofen (1627)* (Jerusalem: Magnes, 1985), 126–134.
11. Traditional Yiddish literature included *Tsene-rene, tkhines, mayse bikhlekh*, stories about Hasidic leaders, and so forth.
12. The main opponent to Yiddish in Russia was Yitzhak Ber Levinson, also known by the acronym Ribal, who explained it clearly in his book *Te'uda be'Israel* (Vilna and Grodno, M. Man and Sh, Zimel, 1828), 8.
13. On the history of modern Yiddish during the first half of the twentieth century, see David E. Fishman, *The Rise of Modern Yiddish Culture* (Pittsburgh: University of Pittsburgh Press, 2005).
14. The other two were Sholem Aleichem and Y. L. Peretz.
15. Jonathan Frankel, *Prophecy and Politics, Socialism, Nationalism and the Russian Jews, 1862–1917* (Cambridge: Cambridge University Press, 1981), 171–257.
16. Mendl Zinger, *Be'reishit ha' tzyonut ha'sotzyalistit* (Haifa: Yalkut, 1956), 32–33. Zinger describes Zionism and Bund as two opposites that were born together (32–33).
17. Frankel, *Prophecy and Politics*, 131–170.
18. On this census, see Shmu'el Ettinger, "Demuta ha'yishuvit ve'ha'kalkalit shel yahadut Rusya be'sof ha'mea ha'esrim," in Shmu'el Ettinger, *Bein Polin le'Rusya* (Jerusalem: Zalman Shazar Center and Bialik Institute, 1994), 257–279.

19. *Di ershte yidishe shprakh-konferents: barikhtn, dokumentn un opklangen fun der tshernovitser konferents, 1908*, Vilna, 1931; Joshua A. Fishman, "Attracting a Following to High-Culture Functions for a Language of Everyday Life: The Role of the Tshernovits Language Conference in the 'Rise of Yiddish,'" *International Journal of the Sociology of Language* 24 (1980): 43–73; Yechiel Szeintuch, "Ve'idat Tshernovitz ve'tarbut Yidish," *Khulyot* 6 (Spring 2000): 255–285; Matityahu Mintz, "Tziyonim ve'Poalei-Zion ba'shprakh konferentz be'Tshernovitz, 1908," *Shvut* 15 (1992): 135–147.

20. Leon Chazanowitz, a prominent member of the world leadership of Poalei-Zion, proposed a similar resolution. *Di ershte yidishe shprakh-konferents: barikhtn, dokumentn un opklangen fun der tshernovitser konferents, 1908*, Vilna, 1931, 106–107.

21. For a detailed survey on the Yiddish press in Poland, see Nathan Cohen, "Itonut yomit yehudit be'Polin," in *Kiyum va'shever: Yehudei Polin le'doroteihem*, ed. Israel Bartal and Israel Gutman (Jerusalem: Merkaz Zalman Shazar, 2001), 301–323.

22. On Poalei-Zion in North America, see Rachel Rojanski, *Zehuyot nifgashot: Poalei-Zion bi'tzefon Amerika 1905–1931* (Sede-Boker: Ben-Gurion University Press, 2004).

23. Joseph Chaikin, *Yidishe bleter in Amerike* (New York: self-published, 1946), 56–62.

24. For a survey of the Yiddish press in the United States, see Moshe Shtarkman, "Vikhtikste momentn in der geshikhte fun der yidishe prese in Amerike," in *Finf un zibetsik yor yidishe prese in Amerike, 1870–1945*, ed. Jacob Glatstein, Shmuel Niger, and Hillel Rogoff (New York: Y. L. Peretz Farayn, 1945), 5–54.

25. On Yiddish in the United States, see Irvin Howe, *The World of Our Fathers* (New York: New York University Press, 2005, reprint), 217–551. On the Yiddish center in Warsaw, see Nathan Cohen, *Sefer sofer ve'iton: merkaz ha'tarbut ha'yehudit be'Varsha, 1918–1942* (Jerusalem: Magnes, 2003).

26. For example, the struggle against setting German as the teaching language at the Technion in 1913–1914: Yuval Dror, "Reishit ha'technion ha'ivri be'Haifa, 1902–1950, me'ha'tochnit le'beit sefer gavoha yehudi ve'ad tom tekufat nihulo shel Shlomo Kaplanski," *Iyunim bi'tekumat Israel* 6 (1996): 333–334.

27. Aryeh Leyb Pilowsky, *Tsvishn yo un neyn: Yidish un yidish literatur in Erets Yisroel, 1907–1948* (Tel Aviv: World Council for Yiddish and Jewish Culture, 1986), 17.

28. Zohar Shavit, "Ha'shelabim be'hitpathuto shel ha'merkaz be'Eretz Israel ve'hafihato le'merkaz hegemoni," in *Toldot ha'yishuv be'Eretz Israel me'az ha'aliya ha'rishona—beniyata shel tarbut ivrit be'Eretz Israel*, ed. Zohar Shavit (Jerusalem: Israel Academy for Science and Humanities, 1998), 91.

29. See Shimon Shur, *Gedud meginei ha'safa be'Eretz Israel, 1923–1936* (Haifa: University of Haifa, Mosad Herzl, 2000).

30. Dan Giladi, *Ha'yishuv bi'tekufat ha'aliya ha'revi'it* (Tel Aviv: Am Oved, 1973), 40.

31. Yael Chaver, *What Must Be Forgotten: The Survival of Yiddish in Zionist Palestine* (Syracuse, NY: Syracuse University Press, 2004), 35–36.

32. Giladi, *Ha'yishuv*, 9.

33. Liora Halperin discusses the use and place of other languages in the Yishuv. Liora R. Halpein, *Babel in Zion: Jews Nationalism and Language Diversity in Palestine, 1920–1948* (New Haven, CT: Yale University Press, 2015).

34. Aryeh Pilowsky, "Lashon, tarbut u'leumiyut ba'yishuv ha'hadash—ha'diyun ha'tziburi ba'tochnit le'hakim katedra le'Yidish bi'Yrushalayim be'shilhei 1927," *Katedra* 21 (1981): 103–134; Chaver, *What Must Be Forgotten*, 113–120.

35. See below, Chapter 1, note 6.

36. Moshe Sikron, *Ha'aliya le'Israel 1848–1953* (Jerusalem: Falk Center for Statistical and Economic Research, 1957), 36–37.

37. Yael Enoch, "Aliya u'kelita: nitu'ah sotzyologi," *Israel ba'asor ha'rishon* (Tel Aviv: Open University, 2001), section 2, 88.

38. The definition of *she'erit ha'pleita* has been broadly discussed by historians, especially in Israel. In this book, I use the term to mean all Jews who survived the Holocaust. See Israel Gutman, "She'erit ha'pleita: be'ayot ve'havharot," in *She'erit ha'pleita 1944–1948, ha'shikum ve'ha'ma'avak ha'politi*, ed. Israel Gutman and Adina Drechsler (Jerusalem: Yad Vashem, 1990), 461–479; Zeev W. Mankowitz, *Life between Memory and Hope: The Survivors of the Holocaust in Occupied Germany* (Cambridge: Cambridge University Press, 2002), 4–5.

39. Moshe Sikron, *Ha'aliya ha'hamonit, memade'ha, me'afyene'ha ve'hashpa'ata al ha'uchlusya be'Israel* (Jerusalem: Ministry of Education and Culture, Center for Information, 1989), 5, 8. Table 1. Also see Hanna Yablonka, *Ahim zarim: nitzolei ha'sho'a bi'medinat Israel 1948–1952* (Jerusalem: Yad Ben Zvi, 1994), 9.

40. Roberto Bachi, "A Statistical Analysis of the Revival of Hebrew in Israel," in *Studies in Economic and Social Sciences* (Jerusalem: Magnes, 1956), 194, table 2. On the immigration from Arab countries in 1949–1950, see Sikron, *Ha'aliya le'Israel*, 24–25.

41. Bachi, "Statistical Analysis," 199

42. See Rachel Rojanski, "A Yiddish Shtetl in Tel Aviv," in *Yiddish Cities: Montreal, Melbourne, Tel Aviv*, ed. Shlomo Berger (Amsterdam: Menasseh Ben Israel Institute, 2013), 65–81.

43. See below, chapter 2.

44. Sikron, *Ha'aliya le'Israel*, 33.

45. For a theoretical discussion of immigration to a nation-state, see Edna Lomsky-Feder and Tamar Rapport, *Israelim be'darkam: sipurei hagira shel tzeirim mi'brit ha'mo'atzot le'she'avar* (Jerusalem: Magnes, 2013), 1–7. This assumption also underlies the Law of Return, which was passed in 1950, which assumes that the person returning home naturally belongs to the collective and also grants that person a number of rights, which are not given to anyone who is not part of the ethnic collective. On the various forms of ethnonational rhetoric in the Law of Return, see Yfaat Weiss, "Golem and Its Creator: How the Jewish Nation State Became Multiethnic," in *Challenging Ethnic Citizenship: German and Israeli Perspectives on Immigration*, ed. Daniel Levy and Yfaat Weiss, 82–106 (New York: Berghahn, 2002).

46. Itamar Yaoz-Kest, *Ha'mehager ha'baita: Stories 1970–2005* (Tel Aviv: Eked, 2005).

47. Yablonka, *Ahim zarim*, 13.

48. Israel Gutman describes the decision to come to Israel as "a result of a difficult and cruel experience" ("She'erit ha'pleita," 20).

49. The problematic attitude to Yiddish in the Yishuv was known throughout the Jewish world; some Yiddish intellectuals even expressed concern about the status of Yiddish in Israel after the proclamation of the state.

50. Judith R. Blau, Min Thomas, Beverly Newhouse, and Andrew Kavee, "Ethnic Buffer Institutions: The Immigrant Press; New York City, 1820–1984," *Historical Social Research* 23, no. 3 (1998): 20; Susan Olzak and Elizabeth West, "Ethnic Conflicts and the Rise and Fall of Ethnic Newspapers," *American Sociological Review* 56, no. 4 (August 1991): 458–459.

51. Antonio Gramsci, *A Selection from the Prison Notebooks*, ed. and trans. Quintin Hoare and Geoffrey Nowell Smith (New York: International Publishers, 1971, 2014 printing), 3–14.

52. Baruch Kimmerling, *Mehagrim, mityashvim, yelidim, ha'medina ve'ha'hevra be'Israel bein ribui tarbuyot le'milhamot tarbut* (Tel Aviv: Am Oved, 2004), 142–147.

53. Gramsci, *Selection*, 181–182.

54. Svetlana Boym, *The Future of Nostalgia* (New York: Basic, 2001), xiii.

55. Pierre Nora, *Realms of Memory: The Construction of the French Past*, trans. Arthur Goldhammer (New York: Columbia University Press, 1996), 1–20

56. I use the term "transregional" for the premodern area and "transnational" for the post–World War I world.

57. Introduction to *Eyn shoyn mayse bukh*, excerpt in original Old Yiddish in Jerold C. Frakes, *Early Yiddish Texts 1100–1750* (Oxford: Oxford University Press, 2004), 491.

58. On Yiddish-language culture as a transnational culture in the interwar period, see Rebecca Kobrin, *Jewish Bialystok and Its Diaspora* (Bloomington: Indiana University Press, 2010), 190–191.

59. Sebouh David Aslanian, *From the Indian Ocean to the Mediterranean: The Global Trade Networks of Armenian Merchants from New Julfa* (Berkeley: University of California Press, 2011), 13.

60. For sociolinguistic studies of Yiddish in Haredi society in Israel, see Lewis Glinert and Yosseph Shilhav, "Holy Land, Holy Language: A Study of an Ultraorthodox Jewish Ideology," *Language in Society* 20, no. 1 (March 1991): 59–86; Solomon Poll, "The Sacred-Secular Conflict in the Use of Yiddish among the Ultra-Orthodox Jews of Jerusalem," *International Journal of the Sociology of Language* 24 (1980): 109–125. On the use of Yiddish in Haredi communities in Jerusalem, see Dalit Berman-Assouline, *Shimur u'temura ba'yidish ha'haredit be'Israel* (PhD diss., The Hebrew University of Jerusalem, 2007).

61. Of most importance on Hebrew in Ottoman Palestine is Arieh Saposnik, *Becoming Hebrew: The Creation of a Jewish National Culture in Ottoman Palestine* (Oxford: Oxford University Press, 2008). An important study on Hebrew in the Yishuv is Zohar Shavit, *Toldot ha'yishuv be'Eretz Israel me'az ha'aliya ha'rishona—beniyata shel tarbut ivrit be'Eretz Israel* (Jerusalem: Israel Academy for Science and Humanities, 1998.) And on the multilingual society in Mandatory Palestine, see Halperin, *Babel in Zion*.

62. Pilowsky, *Tsvishn yo un neyn*.

63. Chaver, *What Must Be Forgotten*.

64. Joshua A. Fishman and David E. Fishman, "Yiddish in Israel: The Press, Radio, Theater and Book Publishing," *Yiddish* 1-2 (1973): 4–23.

65. Abraham Noverstern, "Between Town and Gown: The Institutionalization of Yiddish in Israeli Universities," in *Yiddish in the Contemporary World: Papers of the First Mendel Friedman International Conference on Yiddish*, ed. Gennady Estraikh and Mikhail Krutikov (Oxford: Legenda, 1999), 2–20.

66. Justin Cammy, "Vision and Redemption: Abraham Sutzkever's Poems of Zion(ism)," in *Yiddish after the Holocaust*, ed. Joseph Sherman (Oxford: Boulevard, 2004), 240–265; Dan Miron, *Sheleg al kenaf ha'yona: pegishot im Avraham Sutzkever* (Tel Aviv: Eked Le'shira, 1999).

67. David Roskies, "Di shrayber grupe Yung Yisroel," *Yugntruf*, 27–28 (1973), 7–12; 33 (1975), 7–8; 34 (1976), 4–7. This study emphasizes the synthesis between the tradition of Yiddish literature and the Zionist ideas in their work.

68. Shachar Pinsker, "Choosing Yiddish in Israel: Yung Yisroel between Home and Exile, the Center and the Margins," in *Choosing Yiddish: New Frontiers of Language and Cultures*, ed. Lara Rabinovitch, Shiri Goren, and Hanna S. Pressman (Detroit: Wayne State University Press, 2013), 277–294; Shachar Pinsker, "Ata marvad me'ofef, ein'cha yoter me'hazaya shel am te'atrali," *Haaretz*, December 11, 2009. In addition, some work has been done on Yossel

Birstein's Yiddish writing: Assaf Inbari, "Sipurei ha'kibutz shel Yossel Birstein," *Keshet ha'hadasha*, 21 (2007): 138–149.

69. Diego Rotman, *Performans ke'vikoret tarbut, mif'al ha'te'atron shel Dzigan ve'Shumacher 1927–1980* (PhD diss., The Hebrew University of Jerusalem, 2012).

70. Gali Drucker Bar-Am, *'Ikh bin dayn shtoyb'? yitzug ha'havaya ha'israelit be'siporet yidish be'Israel 1948–1968* (PhD diss., The Hebrew University of Jerusalem, 2013).

71. Drucker Bar-Am states explicitly that this is not her goal. Drucker Bar-Am, *Ikh bin dayn shtoyb*.

72. Jeffrey Shandler, *Adventures in Yiddishland: Postvernacular Languge and Culture* (Berkeley: University of California Press, 2006).

73. Of utmost importance is the pioneering work Dvora Hacohen, *Olim bi'seara: ha'aliya ha'gedola u'kelitata be'Israel 1948–1953* (Jerusalem: Yad Ben Zvi, 1994). Translated by Gila Brand as *Immigrants in Turmoil: Mass Immigration to Israel and Its Repercussions in the 1950s and After* (Syracuse, NY: Syracuse University Press, 2003). The English translation is shorter than the Hebrew original, and some sections are missing from it.

74. A pathbreaking work was Yablonka, *Ahim zarim*. Translated by Ora Cummings as *Survivors of the Holocaust: Israel after the War* (London: MacMillan, 1999).

75. Anita Shapira, *Yehudim hadashim yehudim yeshanim* (Tel Aviv: Am Oved, 1997). Oz Almog, *The Sabra: The Creation of the New Jew* (Berkeley: University of California Press, 2000).

76. See, for example, Moshe Lissak, "The Demographic Social Revolution in Israel in the 1950s: The Absorption of the Great Aliyah," *Journal of Israeli History* 22 (Autumn 2003): 5–8.

77. Batya Shimoni, *Al saf ha'ge'ula: sipur ha'ma'abra dor rishon ve'sheni* (Or Yehuda: Kineret, Zmora-Bitan, Dvir, 2008).

78. Yehuda Shenhav, *The Arab Jews: A Postcolonial Reading of Nationalism, Religion, and Ethnicity* (Stanford, CA: Stanford University Press, 2006).

1

"EVEN THE STONES SPEAK HEBREW"
The Melting Pot and Israel's Cultural Policy

AT 11:00 A.M. ON SUNDAY, JULY 18, 1948, Meir Vilner, the editor in chief of the Israeli Communist Party daily, *Kol Ha'am*, reported to the military recruitment office on Kalischer Street in Tel Aviv.[1] When the official on duty asked him what languages he spoke, he replied: "Hebrew, German, Yiddish, and Polish." "Yiddish is not a language," the man replied. Vilner, taken aback at this dismissal of a language spoken by millions of Jews, protested vigorously. Unmoved, the official said, "I have been given orders, approved by the Supreme Command, not to list Yiddish, because it is not a language."

Although seemingly inconsequential, this exchange was covered the following day in brief reports in a number of Hebrew dailies. They depicted the incident, however, as unsurprising.[2] In their accounts, the officer's response to Vilner was presented as consistent with the long-standing objection to Yiddish from prestate days that had now been transferred to the state of Israel. Yiddish was to be rejected and suppressed for ideological reasons.

Israel's negative attitude toward Yiddish was well known across the Jewish world. It was mentioned from time to time in American Yiddish periodicals, as well as in the Hebrew and the Yiddish Israeli press.[3] In fact, so pervasive was the idea that the rejection of Yiddish was the official policy of the Israeli government that the second, more optimistic part of Vilner's story was largely ignored by the press.

This is what happened. The day after the incident in the recruiting office, Shmuel Mikunis, the Israeli Communist Party delegate to the State Council (the institution that preceded the Knesset) submitted a parliamentary question to Prime Minister David Ben-Gurion asking whether such an order about the status of Yiddish actually existed. Ben-Gurion replied immediately: "No order to the effect that Yiddish is not a language has been issued, and no official is authorized to make such a statement. I will find out who he was and he will be reprimanded appropriately."[4] The next day, the recruitment office also issued a statement that the official who had refused to recognize Yiddish as a language had acted of his own accord and that he would be removed from his position. It was this dry statement, rather than a report of the prime minister's response, that appeared in small type in the Hebrew dailies *Davar* and *HaTzofe*.[5]

Little surprise, then, that in the coming years public opinion continued to perceive the official attitude toward Yiddish as both hostile and driven by the ideological views of the Israeli leadership, especially Ben-Gurion himself.[6] A clear example of this can be found in the Yiddish weekly *Ilustrirter vokhnblat* (Illustrated weekly), which in its early days also included large sections in Hebrew. In February 1949, it published in bold print a poem by the veteran Yiddish poet Yosef Papyernikov meant to sum up the situation of Yiddish in Israel. Entitled "Tsar fun Yidish" (The sorrow of Yiddish), the poem described the rejection of Yiddish in Israel as part of the state's ideological negation of the Diaspora and the Jewish culture created there. "Such is the fate of Yiddish," the poet lamented, in the "Holy Land of the Patriarchs," where "even the stones speak Hebrew."[7]

The history of the status of Yiddish in Israel and the attitude toward it there has not yet been systematically studied. Opinions on the question, even at the beginning of the twenty-first century, have tended to be impressionistic, sharing the assumption that opposition to Yiddish was part of the ideological opposition to the Diaspora and the Jewish culture created in it. Statements such as "the Zionists chose to change their own language by force," "the Zionists trampled on Yiddish," or "the Ashkenazi establishment spurns the language and culture of the Jews of eastern Europe for ideological reasons" still appear as the definitive explanation for the fate of Yiddish in the state of Israel.[8]

This chapter adds depth to the discussion by providing a systematic examination of the basic attitude of the Israeli authorities not just to Yiddish but to all the cultures and languages brought to the state in its early years. The backdrop to the discussion is the construction of the new Israeli culture at this time and the role played in it by the ideology of "negating the Diaspora." I present two arguments. The first is that though the ideological negation of the Diaspora did underpin formal efforts by political and intellectual elites to shape a new Israeli culture in the first decade of the state's existence, it did not lead to a defined or cohesive policy toward either the languages and cultures of the Diaspora in general or Yiddish in particular.

In fact, the background to the attitude toward Yiddish in Israel was far more complex and developed out of dialectical tensions between diverse and sometimes contradictory impulses. These included ideas of rejecting Yiddish and feelings of affection toward it, placing great importance on the principle of a "Hebrew state" while understanding the centrality and power of Yiddish in Jewish culture until just recently, and the desire to sever ties with the Diaspora alongside the sense of a permanent connection to the Jewish culture of eastern Europe, seen by many leaders of the day as the only Diaspora culture of any value.

My second argument here is that the attempt to come up with an official policy aimed at constructing a new Hebrew culture and ensuring its success through legislation and law enforcement proved largely unsuccessful. In the end, such actions as promoting the teaching of Hebrew, encouraging its use, issuing propaganda in favor of Hebrew and against other languages and cultures, and using the various tools of the hegemonic state proved much more successful than legislation.

The "Negation of the Diaspora," the New Jew, and the New Hebrew Culture

The concept of the negation of the Diaspora emerged in late nineteenth-century eastern Europe and evolved into one of the cornerstones of Zionist ideology. It held that Jewish life in the Diaspora—or the "diasporic situation" as some Zionist leaders called the political, economic, social, and cultural conditions in which Jews had lived in the Exile—endangered Jewish existence as it did not allow Jews to live a full Jewish life. For that reason, Zionist thinkers and leaders argued that the Jews needed to change the parameters of the relationship between Jews and non-Jews and to create a sovereign state of their own with a Jewish majority. This analysis of Jewish life in the Diaspora became part of the Zionist ideology whose main goal was to galvanize the Jewish masses into leaving the Diaspora en masse and creating the Jewish state.

However, the idea that Jewish life in the Diaspora was bad for the Jews had additional ideological implications and was not perceived by all Zionist leaders in one single way.[9] Classical Zionists like Theodor Herzl and Leon Pinsker viewed the Diaspora as a sociological anomaly that could bring Jewish life to a tragic end, using the concept as an analytic framework to support the argument that the Jews should leave the Diaspora for their own sovereign state. Ahad Ha'am, who actually coined the phrase "negation of the Diaspora" (in Hebrew, *shelilat ha'galut*) and developed the theory that the Jewish state should be the Jews' spiritual center, maintained that the Diaspora would continue to exist alongside the Jewish state.[10]

There was also a third, more radical approach that called for the total liquidation of the Diaspora. Thinkers like Micha Yosef Berdyczewski and Yosef Haim Brenner demanded its eradication, not only physically but also psychologically.

People of the Second Aliya (1904–1914) were fascinated with this radical idea and embraced the view that negating the Diaspora meant the rejection not only of the Diaspora of the present but also of its very essence as a historical phenomenon. The idea of erasing from the continuum of Jewish history whole historical periods—and especially that of the Diaspora and its values—suggested by Berdyczewski was the basis of the idea of the negation of the Diaspora as it evolved in the Eretz Israeli Zionism at the beginning of the twentieth century.[11]

The leaders of the Labor Zionist movement from this period, Yitzhak Ben Zvi and David Ben-Gurion, adopted the related concept of the jump from the time of classical Judaism to the emergence of modern Jewish nationalism. Often termed "the historical leap," this idea actually meant excising from the historical continuity of the Jewish people the whole period after the destruction of the Second Temple, thus stressing the historical and cultural contrast between the Hebrew living in his own land and the Jew living in the Diaspora.[12] As early as the days of the Second Aliya, Ben-Gurion wrote that the "New Jew, who is proud and willing to take up arms, will not submit to fear and go back [to the Diaspora]. He is not weak and not frightened."[13]

Ben-Gurion remained faithful to these ideas for the next five decades. However, by the 1930s and 1940s, there were some Labor Zionist leaders and intellectuals in Palestine who did not support the complete rejection of the Jews' Diaspora past and even expressed concerns about the negative ramifications of these ideas for the development of the younger generation.[14]

This tension was felt on the ground too in the prestate years. The main organizing element of the new Hebrew culture then being created remained the contrast between Jewish diasporic culture and the Hebrew culture of the Yishuv. However, as Zohar Shavit has shown, other cultures, especially those brought from Western Europe, continued to exist alongside the new Hebrew culture. True, it continued to be viewed as the most important, while the other cultures were either ignored or sometimes made the target of public attack. Still, they were never destroyed, and the Hebrew culture that developed in Eretz Israel even incorporated non-Hebrew components.[15]

Itamar Even-Zohar has emphasized strongly that the new Hebrew culture did not consist only of "new" elements. On the basis of the polysystem theory that he developed, he has shown that Hebrew had existed for centuries before the Zionist revolution as part of a polysystem of diasporic Jewish culture. It was simply not a spoken language. Based on that same pattern, he argued that Hebrew in Palestine, although it was preferred for ideological reasons, remained part of a linguistic-cultural polysystem.[16] Hence, alongside "the [ideological] introduction of new elements, quite a large body of the 'old culture' remained in place."[17]

The tension between the ideology of the new Hebrew culture and the reality of the Yishuv that contained elements from the old world of the Diaspora has been well described by Israel Bartal. He saw it as "a dialectical relationship, fraught with tension and contradictions, [that] existed between the presence of the Diaspora as a source and frame of reference for the Yishuv, and the rejection of the Diaspora as a phenomenon and symbol." He understood this as "a tension between a source and an outcome that is also antithetical."[18]

It should come as little surprise then that, in total opposition to the view entrenched in Israeli public opinion, Ben-Gurion's attitude toward Yiddish was not unequivocal and contained at least an element of acceptance and understanding. It is true that Ben-Gurion described the historical reality of his day by using the biblical image of the transition from the generation of the desert to the generation of the settlement in the land of Israel. In his eyes, the history of the "desert generation"—the period after the loss of independence and nationhood, which also included the Diaspora of eastern Europe—was of no value.[19] After the founding of the state of Israel, Ben-Gurion continued to hold to the idea of negation of the Diaspora, though his attitude to Yiddish became much more nuanced, and he tended to unlink it, as a practical issue at least, from the concept of the historical leap.

One of the main sources of the very widespread idea that Ben-Gurion always had a negative attitude toward Yiddish was an incident that took place in 1945. On February 1 of that year, at the sixth convention of the Histadrut, Ben-Gurion reacted to a speech in Yiddish delivered by Rozka Korczack, a hero of the Vilna ghetto and the partisans, who had arrived in the country only a few weeks earlier. He related to her words as having been spoken in "a foreign, grating language."[20] This was unquestionably a very harsh statement, a blatant and disdainful rejection of Yiddish.

However, after that one outburst, Ben-Gurion never returned to the idea that Yiddish is a "foreign" language and his views on Yiddish began to reveal much greater complexity. In April 1950, he met with the Yiddish author H. Leivick, who was visiting Israel at the time. Leivick, regarded as one of the greatest Yiddish writers of his generation, discussed with him the cultural path being taken by the state of Israel, as well as the language question.[21] After the meeting, Ben-Gurion wrote in his diary: "At four-thirty, Leivick came to see me. He has questions about how the character of the State will be shaped ... What is the cultural path of the Jewish people in the State—Hebrew and Yiddish? ... What is to be the fate of Yiddish? Is its role over? Should its demise be hastened?"[22] He added:

> And as for the danger of distancing ourselves from the diaspora and the near past—as far as I'm concerned, I am in favor of this "distancing." ... I feel closer

to the distant past when we lived in our land than to the near past, because our life in the diaspora was flawed, and with that "material" flaw, the spirit was flawed too. . . . What took place in the time of the Second Temple is closer to me than what happened a hundred or fifty years ago.

As for Yiddish, if he [Leivick] had spoken to me forty years ago, I would not have wanted to hear about Yiddish at all. We were forced to be fanatical about Hebrew because the revival of the language was almost unnatural; in Ireland they have not succeeded in doing it until today. Now I am able and ready to discuss Yiddish with greater openness—and I am glad that my children understand the language.[23]

Ben-Gurion expressed a similar view in a cabinet meeting in July 1951. The topic of that meeting was the Goldfaden Theater, a Yiddish repertory theater from Jaffa, which had appealed to the supreme court against the government for putting a ban on Israeli-run Yiddish theater. Ben-Gurion voiced his personal opinion on the subject: "I think we are wrong from a substantive point of view. When there were only a few of us [Hebrew speakers] in Israel, I was a zealot. Today, I am still zealous about the Hebrew language—but we can't deny a hundred thousand people a little pleasure."[24]

Thus, while the ideology of the negation of the Diaspora does seem to have remained a formative principle in the process of nation building, at least during the first decade of the state, some political leaders were willing to consider finding a place in Israeli culture for non-Hebrew cultures too. Ben-Gurion himself does seem to have understood at a very early stage—perhaps before anyone else—that the Holocaust had not only changed the demography of the Jewish people but had also created far-reaching ramifications for the development of Jewish culture. Following the destruction of east European Jewry, Yiddish no longer posed a significant threat to Hebrew. This understanding was one of the factors that shaped his complex attitude to Yiddish in the post-Holocaust years. For other leaders and policy makers, factors like affections, nostalgia, and memory were at play.[25]

To understand the complexity of the attitude toward Yiddish in the state of Israel, we need to see how, in the early fifties, the Israeli political leadership tried to consolidate, or perhaps even to create, the new Israeli culture and make sure that it was accepted in the country at large. Such a project involved lengthy discussions led by government representatives and public officials and with the participation of writers and intellectuals. They discussed what the character and structure of this new culture should be and particularly how Hebrew was to be made the major organizing element of life in Israel. Hovering over all of these discussions—explicitly or implicitly—was the issue of the cultures brought by Jews from the Diaspora and what their place was to be in the cultural and social life of the Hebrew-language state.

"A Hebrew Style That Does Not Yet Exist": The Formation (or Invention) of Israeli Hebrew Culture

The early years of the state were a period of mass immigration to Israel. Within three years (1948–1951) its Jewish population had more than doubled. The new immigrants came from all over the world and brought to the country a whole range of different languages and cultures.

While immigration to Israel, the so-called ingathering of the exiles, was one of the mainstays of Zionist ideology, in practical terms, the mass immigration was an enormous challenge—economically, socially, and culturally—to the newborn state.[26] Israel's main goal was, of course, to renew the political sovereignty of the Jewish people in its own state, but at the same time it was supposed to bring about the Jews' social and cultural renaissance and the revival of the Hebrew language. "In Israel, not only was a new polity established, a new people was created too," wrote Dvora Hacohen, in her pioneering study of the mass immigration in 1948–1953.[27]

The leaders of the state were undoubtedly aware of the demographic revolution that this mass immigration was causing. They also understood that, alongside the great challenges to Israel's security and economy it posed, there were severe cultural and linguistic problems that had to be faced.[28] So while the state was struggling with an acute housing shortage for new immigrants, setting up special transit camps (*ma'abarot*) for them, and trying to find employment for them, its leaders viewed the issue of language and culture—creating a single unified society and culture—as an equally important task, if not more so.

Crucial in this was the adaption of the Hebrew language and the creation of the new Hebrew culture that was to be hegemonic in the new state. As a newly created state with an immigrant population that outnumbered those already settled and that spoke many different languages, Israel faced a practical need to make Hebrew the actual common spoken language of all its Jewish citizens. In this way the practical and ideological aspects of the language question became two sides of the same coin, although the ideological issues were usually more heavily emphasized and attracted more attention.

The greatest visionary of the new Hebrew culture and the driving force behind its development and acceptance was the prime minister, David Ben-Gurion. At an early meeting in the home of the prominent actor Aharon Meskin of the Habima Theater in November 1948, he gave his vision clear and succinct expression: "We need to make a deliberate, though not artificial, effort to give our lives their own unique and unified shape." At the same meeting he also spoke of "the lack of a Hebrew character to our lives, our dress, our names, our lifestyle, and our holidays."[29] Here, then, was the practical aspect of Ben-Gurion's vision: Hebrew was to be not just the language of the new state but its very way of life.

Earlier, in the summer and early fall of 1948, Ben-Gurion held a series of meetings with writers and intellectuals in the hope of harnessing them to his political and social program.[30] In February 1949 he established a "scientific council" with the participation and leadership of scientists from the Weizmann Institute of Science, the Hebrew University, and the Technion.[31] Later in the year, he held two meetings with writers to "consult them on ways to encourage authors and intellectuals to play a role in shaping the character of the nation in the State of Israel."[32] On March 27, 1949, thirty-five writers participated in the first of two meetings held to discuss that issue. Ben-Gurion opened his speech by stressing that the government would not deal with shaping the spiritual and moral nature of the nation and would never interfere with scientific truth or literary style. However, the reality of the mass immigration meant that great efforts had to be made to create a "unified nation." To this end, said Ben-Gurion, "we need to create a Hebrew character and style that does not yet exist; [one] that could not have existed in the diaspora, in a [Jewish] people lacking a homeland, independence and national self-determination." He then added: "We need to revive and strengthen the link with the inspiring light of our past, without chaining ourselves to a fossilized and obsolete heritage. . . . We need to impart a culture to the masses of immigrants that is both Jewish and universal. And I believe that what the previous generations of the Jewish people—or the other peoples of the world— have left us will not be enough. We will want to make our own contribution to mankind's cultural treasures."[33] The "deliberate effort" to create a totally new Hebrew lifestyle thus became an issue of paramount importance in future discussions about Israeli culture.

Some of the participants in that meeting expressed similar views. Haim Gouri, a young poet and former member of the Palmach, even connected the new Israeli culture directly to the concrete reality of the day. "Today," said Gouri with poetic license, "culture is being created on 'twisting Burma roads,' with the blow of the pick-axe, and in the youth volunteer labor camps."[34] The children's writer Anda Pinkerfeld (later Amir) spoke directly against Yiddish. "There are many dangers now [facing the creation of Israeli culture]," Anda said at that meeting, "and we have to stand in the breech. I want to warn you, for example, about the danger of Yiddish. I have already heard rumors that the Bialik Prize is going to be awarded to a translation from Yiddish and not to an original work [in Hebrew]."[35] Several of the participants hastened to deny the rumor, but the very fact that the subject was raised at all shows that, in the minds of some people at least, east European Jewish culture in general and

Yiddish in particular was felt to be a danger to the creation of the new Israeli culture.[36]

An important participant in that meeting was Ben-Zion Dinaburg (later Dinur), a professor of Jewish history at the Hebrew University. Dinur agreed with Ben-Gurion's approach and worked in tandem with him. However, his view about the place of the Jewish past in Israeli culture was more nuanced than that of the prime minister. While Ben-Gurion talked about creating a new "character" and "lifestyle," Dinur focused on the issue of tradition. He spoke explicitly about both the invention of a new tradition and the existence of a link between any Israeli tradition and the Jewish historical past. While he stated clearly that not every aspect of Jewish history had a role to play in the life and thought of the current generation, he did not stress the historical leap as Ben-Gurion did. Instead, he suggested examining what parts of Jewish history were relevant for the current generation and how to shape the essential character of Jewish life in the state of Israel.[37] "In my view," Dinur said, "the way [to preserve the Jewish character of life] is to revitalize new [i.e., hitherto unused] layers of the Jewish tradition." He added: "As a matter of fact, with the Destruction of the Temple, Jewish tradition withered somewhat ... [so] now we need to find different tools, different options for reviving it." Having said that, he asserted that the newly created tradition was to have "an original, Israeli character."[38]

The idea of inventing a cultural tradition as part of the nation-building process is by now well known. Eric Hobsbawm, who, together with Terence Ranger, coined the term "the invention of tradition," claimed that the conscious invention of new traditions takes place in situations of rapid social change and is meant to meet the immediate needs of the nation-building process.[39] He also stated that Israeli nationalism had no connection to the Jewish historical past and therefore had to be invented.[40]

Dinur's vision, however, was more nuanced, expressing a dialectical attitude toward pre-Holocaust east European Jewish culture that comprised both rejection and some form of affinity. He was not the only one to do so. Other participants, particularly the Hebrew University professor of philosophy Samuel Hugo Bergmann and the writer Eliezer Steinman, expressed similar thoughts.[41]

Almost all the speakers at the meeting suggested setting up some kind of organization to deal with the "genuine absorption [of the mass immigration] and shaping their [cultural] character to fit the patterns of the nation," to use the words of Martin Buber, professor of philosophy at the Hebrew University.[42] Ben-Zion Dinur, who, like Ben-Gurion, wanted to put the discussion on practical lines, proposed establishing "a small council, an executive committee, [representing] all the intellectuals, and to let it plan the spiritual [i.e., cultural] work—acting fast and effectively."[43]

Making "the spiritual absorption of the immigration" a practical reality was the focus of Ben-Gurion's second meeting with the writers on October 11, 1949.[44] Ben-Gurion and Dinur had previously reached an understanding with the writer and literary activist Asher Barash, who drafted a practical proposal for setting up the council proposed by Dinur.[45] Barash suggested calling it the Council for Humanities and Culture (Mo'atza le'tarbut ha'ruah).[46]

Toward the end of the October meeting, Ben-Gurion read out Barash's proposal: The council was to consist of writers, philosophers, historians, artists, and educators, plus a representative of the government. It would be chaired by the minister of education. Altogether, it would comprise fifteen members. It would be authorized to hold regular discussions on the state of the culture and its needs and to recommend cultural projects that would serve national and social goals in their broadest sense. The council's budget would be allocated by the state, and its decisions would be binding morally and would be taken into account by the state authorities. "I have no doubt," read Ben-Gurion, "that if the proposed council receives the required authority from the government (including the proper standing and a budget) . . . it will be respected by the entire public and will be a boon to all those engaged in shaping the character of the nation."[47]

The proposal passed without a vote, and on the next day a small committee convened and drafted a detailed plan for the creation of a Council for Cultural Matters. However, the poor health of the minister of education and political developments in the coalition that created a political constellation unfavorable for Ben-Gurion convinced him that it would not be a good idea to raise the idea of the council at a cabinet meeting. The realization of the plan was delayed until after the next general election.[48]

"Nation and Language Are Almost Synonyms": B. Z. Dinur, the Hebrew Language, and the Issue of Jewish Historical Continuity

The third government of the state of Israel took office in October 1951, and Ben-Zion Dinur was appointed minister of education. Less than three months later, at its meeting on January 6, 1952, the government decided to set up a Supreme Council for Cultural Affairs. This was to be a public body working on behalf of the government and charged with the task of shaping Israeli culture.[49]

Dinur, by then the minister of education and culture, was named head of the council. Its secretary was Shmuel Yavnieli, a veteran of the Second Aliya and head of the cultural committee of the Histadrut (the General Federation of the Hebrew Workers in Israel).[50] The members of the council were prominent figures in all aspects of the country's cultural life, including Zalman Shazar, the previous minister of education; Professors Shmuel Hugo Bergmann and Dov Sadan from the Hebrew University; and Professor Yohanan Ratner from the Technion. Other members were representatives of the Jewish Agency and of the religious parties (Mizrachi, HaPoel HaMizrachi, Agudat Yisrael).[51]

The council's first meeting was held on March 13, 1952, and was largely devoted to a talk by Dinur on cultural problems in Israel. Dinur was a well-known historian, and one of the leading professors at the Hebrew University. However, on this occasion he was also speaking as Israel's minister of education and the head of a state committee established at the prime minister's initiative. So although Dinur's words clearly reflected his personal views, they were also an important official voice on the new Hebrew culture and its relationship with the Jewish cultures of the Diaspora. As such, they are worth examining in some detail.

As a historian, Dinur framed his discussion theoretically. He found in Jewish history, Jewish fate, and common Jewish spiritual values the organizing principles for the existence of the Jewish people.[52] However, more important even than those for him was the Hebrew language, in which he saw the heart and soul of the Jewish nation. "The common language is a precondition for the very existence of our people," he stressed in his opening statement. "In the Hebrew language, we say '*uma ve'lashon*' [nation and language] and use them almost as synonyms."[53]

He went on to say that Jews in the Diaspora had spoken many languages but had only had one in common. This was "because the inner life of the individual Jew and the public life of the Jewish people were structured by the Hebrew language, by the elements of Hebrew that became part of every language spoken by Jews, and that is what set them apart." Dinur was referring to the element of *loshn koydesh* (literally, "the holy tongue")—that is, the Hebrew of the Bible and the prayer book and the Aramaic of the Talmud, which formed an inseparable part of all Jewish languages and was particularly important in Yiddish. "Hebrew," Dinur continued, "was the language not only of Jewish Law *halacha*, but also of the Jews' special way of life; it was the language of our historical fate. . . . [The Jews] divided the year according to the weekly Torah readings. The biblical and traditional terms 'Ashkenaz' (Germany), 'Tzarfat' (France), 'Sepharad' (Spain), and 'Togarma' (Turkey) have become part of modern [Jewish] geography [as the names of countries or peoples], and each period has had its own 'Haman' and its own 'Pharoah.'"

At this point, Dinur turned to the nature of diasporic Jewish culture. And while describing it, he drew a very subtle—and at the same time quite clear—dividing line between the culture of the Jews from eastern Europe and that of those who had come from Muslim countries, pointing to the superiority of the former, he said,

> We find ourselves in a situation in which those parts of our people who most faithfully preserved our cultural heritage, through their language and recognition of our shared fate and through their expression of the nation's spiritual values and unique lifestyle, have been destroyed. That huge and terrible Holocaust that killed a third of our people caused even greater destruction to the essence of our nation. Those diasporas that are now being ingathered here, are not very rich in spiritual heritage. It was their historical fate to be more-or-less cut off from the high road of Jewish history. . . . They did not share in the historical development of recent generations. They knew nothing of Hasidism and the extensive religious revival it brought in its wake with the Gaon of Vilna and his disciples, [and were unaware] of the establishment of the great yeshivas in Lithuania, Poland, and Hungary. They were untouched by the spirit of the Haskalah that gave life a new meaning through the Hebrew language. . . . They were not galvanized by the Hibbat Zion and Zionist movements in their rejection of exile . . . and were not caught up in the awakening of the Jewish working masses to a life of equality [i.e., Jewish socialism].[54]

Dinur's words certainly expressed a paternalistic and orientalist attitude toward the Mizrahi Jews and even perhaps an attempt to exclude them from the history of Jewish culture. There was nothing new in that. Similar and even more explicit statements that depicted the Oriental Jews as people of an inferior culture had appeared in the Hebrew press as far back as 1949 and had also been expressed by senior officials of Israel's immigrant absorption authority.[55] It is not, however, what I want to focus on here. What is interesting for this discussion is the first half of Dinur's statement—his description of the eastern European Jews. To understand the status of Yiddish (and east European Yiddish-language culture generally) in Israel, it is not the rejection of the Oriental that is important but the embrace of the east European. It was that Jewish culture that Dinur presented as the true—perhaps the only—culture of the Jewish people, and which he saw as the bridge to the new Israeli culture that was to be created, or in Dinur's terms, as "our spiritual heritage."

One can understand Dinur's words as suggesting that the negation of the Diaspora was aimed mainly at the cultures of Jews from the Arab countries; however, what is interesting for the discussion here is the other side of the coin.[56] It seems that Dinur's view that east European Jewish culture was the only genuine Jewish culture was not meant to denigrate other Jewish cultures but to impart to east European Jewish culture itself a special importance.

While Ben-Gurion remained faithful to the idea of the historical leap, Dinur favored a view of Jewish history as one long, unbroken line.[57] He, like the other participants in the discussion, regarded Hebrew as the Jewish language that had been common to all the diasporas and as the bedrock on which Israeli culture would be built. However, he saw in the culture of east European Jewry a vital transitional phase in the creation of modern Jewish culture and the development of the modern Hebrew language.

Hence, the opening speech of the first meeting of the Supreme Council for Cultural affairs did not present an unequivocal negation of diasporic Jewish culture but rather a dialectical attitude to it. On the one hand, these cultures and languages were, in principal, rejected to make way for Hebrew, while on the other, east European Jewish culture and especially its components that were connected to Yiddish—Hasidism and particularly the Jewish Labor movement, which supported Yiddish ideologically—were embraced and appreciated.

Legislation and Enforcement: The Proposed "Language Inculcation" Law

The last part of Dinur's speech and the discussion that followed focused not just on the Hebrew language as the very heart of Israeli culture and identity but also on the need to find ways to make it, in practice, the main language of speech in the state of Israel and its language of culture.

"The situation [today] is that one person does not understand the language of the other," Dinur said. "So some people have proposed ... that the ... [government] pass a State Language Law to ensure that the language is [fully] adopted."[58] Following this line, he went on to list a number of possible sanctions that the state could take against people who did not learn Hebrew, such as making eligibility to receive public services contingent on knowing the language. He then rejected them, arguing that unless the citizens agreed with the law, it would be almost impossible to enforce it. It would be much better, Dinur said, to inculcate Hebrew culture and language by other means available to the state.[59]

Dinur then presented his own program for ensuring that the culture and the language would be fully accepted by the Israeli people and proposed doing so by means that can be called hegemonic rule. The strategies he wanted to adopt were of the type identified and critiqued by Antonio Gramsci, in particular, that one part of the collective in the state can assume ideological control over its other parts by taking over the foci of cultural power. Dinur proposed establishing a statewide public mechanism to instill the correct cultural values "into every house, into every corner," and to establish "special authorized bodies" that would deal with the various practical aspects of diffusing Israeli-Hebrew culture. He envisioned the establishment of a special authority for this purpose, which would be situated within the Ministry of Education and Culture and work in cooperation with the local municipalities. This authority would supervise not only Hebrew teaching but also supplying the new immigrants with reading material and theatrical performances in the language. Dinur concluded by saying, "The state cannot and should not take on this whole project but it should serve as a source of planning and encouragement."[60]

The discussion that ensued was summed up by the secretary of the council, Yavnieli, as follows: "The government, by appointing the Council for Culture, has shown its desire to take responsibility for directing the people's cultural life. . . . To do this, the Government can act through legislation, supervision, organization, and the allocation of appropriate funding."[61] In other words, two clear-cut options seemed to be on the table: the Hebrew language and Israeli culture could be imposed either by means of legislation and enforcement or by wielding hegemonic control (to be achieved through budgetary allocation).

At first, legislation seemed the more reasonable choice. A meeting of a small forum of the Supreme Council for Culture, held on March 30, decided to demand that a regulation be passed to the effect that all applications to a public authority had to be written in Hebrew. Alongside that, however, it also decided to call for the appointment of what they called "language trustees" (*hever ne'emanei ha'lashon*), who would promote the study of Hebrew in immigrant towns.[62]

The second plenary meeting of the Supreme Council for Culture, held two months later, focused largely on Dinur's proposal to formulate a bill on Hebrew teaching. He made it absolutely clear that the law would apply not to "those learning the language but to those imparting it"; that is, it would oblige the state to make the teaching of Hebrew to adults part of the compulsory education system.[63] Nonetheless, he also suggested that the law include a sanction against those who did not learn the language, by linking knowledge of Hebrew with opportunities for employment in the public sector. In the discussion that followed, there was complete agreement on the need to impart Hebrew through both legislation and enforcement, such as prohibiting the employment in any public institution of any person who had been living in the country for a certain period and had not yet proven sufficiently fluent in Hebrew.[64]

Further meetings were held, but in the end the discussions on the "Law for the Inculcation of Hebrew" reached a dead end in the summer of 1953. The major reason for this was funding problems, though personal issues also played a part.[65] By the end of the year, the bill had ended up in the archives.[66] This fact does not minimize in any way the ideological importance of Hebrew for the leaders of the state; nor does it signify that instilling the language had ceased to be a major policy goal in shaping Israeli society. It just meant that a different strategy would be needed.

In 1954, the government started a huge campaign to spread the use of Hebrew. More than three thousand volunteers from among veteran Israelis joined hundreds of female soldiers doing their military service to act as Hebrew teachers. In this program, the language was to be instilled not through legislation and enforcement but through the expansion of hegemonic control, partly by using female soldiers as teachers but more by using one part of the population—the volunteers—to coerce another, the new immigrants. "Soldiers of hegemony" was the epithet that the Israeli sociologist Baruch Kimerling used for these volunteers.[67]

Instilling Hebrew through the exploitation of cultural hegemony proved quite effective, even more so than through legal means. Legislation and enforcement were likely to have aroused opposition, whereas spreading Hebrew with the tools of hegemonic control was not only effective in terms of numbers but also provoked no objection. Quite the reverse: it gave those teaching the language and those learning it, and more importantly the public at large, a largely positive feeling about the program, underlining for all concerned its great importance for Israeli society as a whole. The process of disseminating Hebrew was thus seen by the public as a national cultural project of paramount importance.

However, there was another side to this coin. Anything perceived as not supportive of this process—and especially anything viewed as detrimental to it—became the object of opposition. Disseminating Hebrew entailed not only the encouragement of reading, writing, performing, and broadcasting in the language but also opposition—even outright hostility—to the use of any other language, especially the Jewish ones. Little surprise then that one of the questions raised during the discussions of the Supreme Council for Culture on promoting Hebrew concerned the obstacles to this process and how they should be dealt with.

Hegemony: Creating a "Suitable Public Atmosphere" for Disseminating Hebrew

A key obstacle as far as the members of the Supreme Council for Culture were concerned was the non-Hebrew press. It was discussed as early as the council's second meeting. Dinur, as minister of education and culture, suggested harnessing this press to the Hebrew-language effort by compelling each non-Hebrew paper to include a Hebrew section so that the readers of "foreign language" newspapers would get a "Hebrew lesson."[68] Other speakers went further, suggesting that the supply of paper to any such publication would depend on its including a daily section teaching Hebrew.[69] Still others rejected the idea entirely, preferring to use the non-Hebrew press as a means of reaching a broader readership and so extending their political power.[70] In the end, the final version of the bill for the inculcation of Hebrew did include a provision making it mandatory "to include a Hebrew section in every publication appearing in the state that is intended for Jews and is not in Hebrew."[71]

On August 18, 1952, a subcommittee of the Supreme Council for Culture held its own discussion on the "problems of the foreign press in Israel," making explicit mention of Yiddish. There was general opposition to the large number of non-Hebrew periodicals being published, which those present viewed as a "destructive element in the very fact that they were not addressing the reader in the language of the state."[72] At the end of the discussion, the committee decided that "a demand should be submitted to the government that it stop giving licenses to the foreign-language press (published for the Jewish population).... A principle of priority should be introduced for the paper supply: first and foremost for the Hebrew press."[73]

A few months later—in November 1952—at a plenary meeting of the Supreme Council for Culture, Dinur announced, "We are not going to wait for the law to be published. We are going to do our utmost to convince the foreign-language press [to print Hebrew sections], in order that they will do so willingly and not out of coercion."[74] Dinur was speaking following an opinion given by the acting attorney general that it would not be possible to apply the "Law for Enforcement of the Language" to the non-Hebrew press.[75] But beyond that, Dinur does seem to have understood that creating an atmosphere hostile to the use of non-Hebrew languages, and particularly the foreign-language press, was a more effective strategy for inculcating Hebrew than legislation.

The whipping up of opposition to the non-Hebrew newspapers can be clearly seen in the 1953 annual of the Journalists Association, *Sefer ha'shana shel ha'itonaim* (The journalists' yearbook), in which a large section was devoted to the question of the "foreign" press in Israel. It opened with an article by Yosef Ulitzky, which gave a detailed survey of the newspapers, publishing houses, and radio broadcasts in languages other than Hebrew. "We are being flooded by foreign languages in a deluge of foreign newspapers, most of which are low quality," Ulitzky opened his article, and he went on trenchantly to oppose the very existence of these non-Hebrew media. He ended with a call to "uproot foreign languages" and a demand that the Ministry of Education wage a "war" against them.[76] This article was followed by a long series of brief responses, written by well-known public figures, all of whom unreservedly supported efforts to instill the Hebrew language and opposed the non-Hebrew press. However, the issue they discussed in their responses was whether Hebrew should be imposed through legislation or unofficial means (i.e., hegemonic control).[77]

With the exception of Dr. Herzl Rosenblum, the editor of *Yedioth Aharonoth*, who resolutely favored the prohibition of non-Hebrew newspapers by law, most people who wrote responses felt that cultural control was more effective than legislation.[78] For many, it was the creation of an atmosphere supportive of Hebrew and hostile to other languages that promised the greatest success in the struggle to make Hebrew the language of all.[79] Dinur, who also contributed to the same volume, wrote at great length about the "public volunteer movement" and the use of state-run radio as an effective way of spreading the use of Hebrew.[80] Even the mayor of Tel Aviv, Haim Levanon, who argued that "the immigrant should be forced to speak Hebrew by law," noted that in order to disseminate Hebrew, "we have to create a suitable public atmosphere."[81]

It seems then that during the early 1950s, the creation of a new Hebrew culture was one of the main concerns of the state's leadership, which made serious efforts to develop policy on the issue and perhaps even to find ways to enforce it. However, examining the debates on the question seems to show that alongside the aspiration to accelerate the process of nation building by negating the old diasporic cultures and creating a new unified Israeli Hebrew one, other thoughts, ideas, and feelings were also at play. Alongside the very determined ambition to create a new culture, there was also an understanding that this could not happen without taking the old ones into consideration. Some leaders even gave east European Jewish culture (which, of course, includes Yiddish) a special role in acting as a kind of bridge to the new Israeli one.

In the absence of a clear policy of legally enforcing the Hebrew culture in Israel, two forces were at play: one pushed for some continuation (or at least for the inclusion of some parts) of east European Jewish culture within it and one that wanted to make it an entirely new culture, cut off from the diasporic past. This tension became crucial in determining the status of Yiddish in Israel since it created a complex dialectic between its total rejection and some sense of affinity and even respect for it.

At the same time, the extensive use of hegemonic tools to spread the use of Hebrew in Israel, which included the rejection of other languages, both openly and by implication, helped create a negative public image in Israel particularly of the Yiddish language and culture, which was still identified as the major threat to Hebrew. However, since the policy against non-Hebrew Jewish cultures was not legally enforced, Yiddish did find space to develop and even thrive in Israel and to become part of Israeli culture. It is this process that will be the subject of the chapters to come.

Notes

1. *Kol Ha'am* was the Hebrew daily of the Communist Party of Palestine (PKP—Palestinishe Komunistishe Partey) that was transformed into the Israeli Communist Party (Maki). It was in existence from 1937 to 1975. The verdict in an appeal the daily submitted against its closure in 1953 is one of the most important manifestations of freedom of speech in Israel.
2. "Rosh ha'memshala meshiv li'she'elat Sh. Mikunis," *Kol Ha'am*, July 23, 1948; "Yidish eina safa," *Maariv*, "Sihot," July 19, 1948.
3. See, for example, "Inyen Yidish in Yisroel," *Di tsukunft* (September 1951): 291–299.
4. "Rosh ha'memshala meshiv li'she'elat Sh. Mikunis," *Kol Ha'am*, July 23, 1948.
5. "Merkaz giyus mak'hish," *Davar*, July 23, 1948, 2; "Ha'pakid she'pasal Yidish ke'safa huhlaf," *HaTzofe*, July 23, 1948, 6.
6. His image as a bitter enemy of Yiddish had been shaped years previously and has proved remarkably long-lasting. See Rachel Rojanski, "Ha'omnam safa zara ve'tzoremet? li'she'elat yahaso shel Ben-Gurion le'Yidish aharei ha'shoa," *Iyunim bi'tekumat Israel* 15 (2005): 463–482.
7. Yosef Papyernikov, "Tsar fun Yidish," *Ilustrirter vokhnblat*, February 11, 1949, 12.
8. Yosef Grodzinsky, "Lo ha'yidish tavi aleinu et ha'ketz mi'bayit," *Ha'aretz*, November 20, 1998; Avner Shapira, "Safa tze'ira la'netzah," *Ha'aretz*, July 14, 2009; Yitzhak Luden, "Ha'Yidish mekupahat," *Ha'aretz*, May 8, 1997.
9. Shmuel Almog, *Le'umiyut, tziyonut, antishemiyut: masot u'mehkarim* (Jerusalem: Ha'sifriya ha'tziyonit, 1992), 243–261.
10. A'had Ha'am, "Shelilat ha'galut," *Al parashat derachim* (Berlin: Judische Verlag, 1921), 4: 106–109.
11. Ehud Luz, *Makbilim nifgashim: dat u'le'umiyut ba'tenua ha'tzyonit be'mizrah eiropa be'reshita 1882–1904* (Tel Aviv: Am Oved, 1986), 224–230.
12. Yitzhak Conforti, *Zeman avar, ha'historyographya ha'tzyonit ve'itzuv ha'zikaron ha'le'umi* (Jerusalem: Yad Yitzhak Ben Zvi, 2006), 124–134.
13. David Ben-Gurion in a letter in Bracha Habas and Eliezer Shohat, *Sefer ha'aliya ha'sheniya* (Tel Aviv: Am Oved, 1957), 348. On the attitude to the *Galut* in the land of Israel during the first *aliyot*, see Israel Kolat, "Ha'im ha'yishuv haya hagshamat ha'leumiyut ha'yehudit?," in *Le'umiyut ve'politika yehudit: perspektivot hadashot*, ed. Yehuda Reinharz, Joseph Salmon, and Gideon Shimoni (Jerusalem: Merkasz shazar, 1996), 225–252.
14. See Conforti, *Zeman avar*, 131; Anita Shapira asserts that Berl Katzenelsson saw Jewish history as including some diasporic components, Yitzhak Tabenkin was against cutting off the continuity of Jewish history, and Shlomo Lavi and David Maltz thought that this view was damaging the education of the next generation in the land of Israel. Anita Shapira, "Whatever Became of 'Negating Exile'?," in *Israeli Identity in Transition*, ed. Anita Shapira (Westport, CT: Praeger, 2004), 69–108.
15. Shavit, *Toldot ha'yishuv*, 2–3, 5.
16. On the polysystem theory, see Itamar Even-Zohar, "Polysystem Theory," in "Polysystem Studies," ed. Itamar Even Zohar, special issue, *Poetics Today* 11, no.1 (1990): 9–26.
17. Itamar Even-Zohar, "The Emergence of a Native Hebrew Culture in Palestine, 1882–1948," in *Essential Papers on Zionism*, ed. Jehuda Reinharz and Anita Shapira (New York: New York University Press, 1996), 727–744. See also Itamar Even-Zohar, "Tahalichei maga ve'hitarvut be'hivatzrut ha'tarbut ha'ivrit ha'hadasha," in *Nekudat tatzpit: tarbut ve'hevra*

be'Eretz Israel, ed. Nurit Gertz, Dan Miron, and Shalom Reichman (Tel Aviv: Open University, 1988), 129–140.

18. Israel Bartal, "Yishuv and Diaspora in Changing Perspectives," in *Major Changes within the Jewish People*, ed. Israel Gutman (Jerusalem: Yad Vashem, 1996), 387–397.

19. Anita Shapira, "Ben-Gurion and the Bible: The Forging of an Historical Narrative?," *Middle Eastern Studies* 33, no. 4 (October 1997): 645–674.

20. On this affair, see Rojanski, "Ha'omnam safa."

21. On the status of Leivick in Yiddish literature of his day, see Abraham Noverstern, *Kesem ha'dimdumim. apokalipsa u'meshihiyut be'sifrut Yidish* (Jerusalem: Magnes, 2003), 214.

22. Ben-Gurion's diary, April 29, 1950, the Ben-Gurion archives, Sede-Boker.

23. Ibid.

24. Minutes of cabinet meeting no. 55, July 7, 1951, "Theater performances in Yiddish," Israel State Archives. For a detailed discussion on this topic, see chapter 3.

25. Amnon Raz-Krakotzkin asserts that "the declared policy was to achieve cultural uniformity, based on the acceptance of a system of values and images of the hegemonic elite," in fact, "in the complex reality, phenomena that were not consistent with this guiding principle obviously continued to exist, and sometimes even expressed (consciously or not) opposing concepts." Amnon Raz Krakotzkin, "Galut be'toch ribonut, le'bikoret shelilat ha'galut ba'tarbut ha'israelit," *Teoria u'bikeret* 4 (1993): 24.

26. The Israeli sociologist Moshe Lissak described it as a cloudburst. Lissak, "Demographic-Social Revolution."

27. Hacohen, *Olim bi'se'ara*, 1. An abridged version of this book was published in English: *Immigrant in Turmoil: Mass Immigration to Israel and Its Repercussions in the 1950s and After* (Syracuse, NY: Syracuse University Press, 2003). The parts that deal with the creation of an Israeli culture were not included in the English version. All references to this book refer to the Hebrew original.

28. Hacohen, *Olim bi'se'ara*, 145–146.

29. Ben-Gurion's diary, November 26, 1948, the Ben-Gurion archives, Sede-Boker.

30. Hacohen, *Olim bi'se'ara*, 146–153.

31. Hacohen, *Olim bi'se'ara*, 146.

32. Minutes of the first meeting, March 27, 1949, Divrei sofrim ba'pgisha ha'rishona she'zimen rosh ha'memshala (Tel Aviv, Ha'madpis ha'memshalti, June 1949), 1:3–4.

33. Ibid., 4.

34. Divrei sofrim, 1:20. The Burma Road was a road paved during the war of 1948 as a bypass to get to Jerusalem, which was under siege.

35. Divrei sofrim, 1:20.

36. Ibid.

37. David Myers asserts that Dinaburg (Dinur) was forever negotiating the balance between the forces of continuity and change in the Jewish past. "The motif of continuity in Jewish history, even in the diaspora, prominently figured in Dinaburg's historical work." David N. Myers, *Re-inventing the Jewish Past* (New York: Oxford University Press, 1995), 142.

38. Divrei sofrim, 1:7.

39. Eric Hobsbawm, "Introduction: Invention of Tradition," in *The Invention of Tradition*, ed. Eric Hobsbawm and Terence Ranger (Cambridge: Cambridge University Press, 1983), 1–13.

40. He made the same point about Palestinian nationalism. Hobsbawm, "Introduction," 13–14.

41. Divrei sofrim, 1:14, 15.
42. Divrei sofrim, 1:5.
43. Divrei sofrim, 1:8.
44. See also Ben-Zion Dinaburg to Ben-Gurion, July 18, 1949, State archives, 29/335 (ISA-PMO-PMO-000wd15).
45. Hacohen, *Olim bi'se'ara*, 148. On August 24, Ben-Gurion wrote to Shmuel Yavnieli that the role of the council would be "to outline principles that will serve [our] social and national goals." Ben-Gurion to Yavnieli, August 24, 1949, State archives, 29/335 (ISA-PMO-PMO-000wd15).
46. Asher Barash to Ben-Gurion, August 30, 1949, State archives, 29/335 (ISA-PMO-PMO-000wd15).
47. *Divrei Sofrim ba'pgisha ha'shniya she'zimen rosh ha'memshala*, October 11, 1949, (Tel Aviv, Ha'madpis ha'memshalti 2: April 1950), 27.
48. Hacohen, *Olim bi'seara*, 151.
49. Minutes of the first meeting of the Supreme Council for Cultural Affairs, March 13, 1952, State archives, 858/6-G (ISA-education-education-000ylbg). On the circumstances leading to Dinur's appointment as minister of education and the appointment process, see Zvi Zameret, *Alei gesher tzar: ha'hinuch be'Israel bi'shnot ha'medina ha'rishonot* (Sede-Boker: Ben-Gurion University of the Negev Press, 1997), 221–231. On Dinur's accomplishments as minister of education and the impact he made on Israeli education, see Zvi Zameret, "Ben Zion Dinur: intelektu'al bone medina," *Ha'tzyonut* 21 (1998): 321–332.
50. Hacohen, *Olim bi'se'ara*, 151.
51. Minutes of the first meeting of the Supreme Council for Cultural Affairs, March 13, 1952, State archives, 1086/16-GL (ISA-education-education-000hq4p). For the full list of the council's members, see State archives, 1086/18-GL (ISA-education-education-000hq4p).
52. Minutes of the first meeting of the Supreme Council for Cultural Affairs, State archives, 858/6-G (ISA-education-education-000ylbg).
53. Minutes of the first meeting of the Supreme Council for Cultural Affairs, State archives, 858/6-G (ISA-education-education-000ylbg), 2.
54. Minutes of the first meeting of the Supreme Council for Cultural Affairs, State archives, 858/6-G (ISA-education-education-000ylbg).
55. See Lissak, "Demographic-Social Revolution," 168–171; Sami Shalom Shitrit, *Ha'ma'avak ha'mizrahi be'Israel, bein dikui le'shihrur, bein hizdahut le'alternativa 1948–2003* (Tel Aviv: Am Oved, 2006), 61–66. On the reflection of this attitude in Israeli Hebrew literature, see Shimoni, *Al saf h'geula*, 38–40.
56. Raz-Krakotzkin, "Galut be'toch ribonut."
57. On Dinur's view on Jewish history, see David N. Myers, "History and Ideology: The Case of Ben Zion Dinur, Zionist Historian Par Exellence," *Modern Judaism* 8, no. 2 (1988): 167–193.
58. Minutes of the first meeting of the Supreme Council for Cultural Affairs, State archives, 858/6-G (ISA-education-education-000ylbg). As a matter of fact, attempts to compel the public through legislation or legal enforcement to use Hebrew had already been made in the past, with little success. In the 1930s, the Tel Aviv municipality had tried to pass a bylaw obliging businesses within its boundaries to have signs in Hebrew. However, because Hebrew was only one of three official languages (along with English and Arabic) in Mandatory Palestine, the municipality lacked the legal jurisdiction to enact the law.

Instead, attempts were made to impose Hebrew through hegemonic control, both by means of a committee of writers and teachers affiliated with the Tel Aviv municipality, which suggested proper Hebrew names for businesses, and later through the Public Council for the Enforcement of the Hebrew Language, which worked under the auspices of the Culture Department of the National Executive. See Azaryahu, *Tel Aviv*, 79–92. It should be noted that although starting in 1935 the struggle for Hebrew was waged mainly against German, opposition to Yiddish was not abandoned, and an article printed in *Ha'aretz* at the end of that year expressed dissatisfaction with the work performed by the Hebrew names committee established by the Tel Aviv municipality, labeling some of the names they had suggested *ivri taytsh*, a term used to describe translations of the Pentateuch into Yiddish. A. Safra, "Fifiyot: ir be'ivri taytsh," *Ha'aretz*, December 5, 1935, 6. See also Yoav Gelber, *Moledet hadasha: aliyat yehudei merkaz eiropa u'klitatam, 1933–1948* (Jerusalem: Yad Yitzhak Ben Zvi, 1990), 306.

59. Minutes of the first meeting of the Supreme Council for Cultural Affairs, State archives, 858/6-G (ISA-education-education-000ylbg).

60. Minutes of the first meeting of the Supreme Council for Cultural Affairs, March 13, 1952, State archives, 858/6-G (ISA-education-education-000ylbg).

61. Ibid.

62. Minutes of the committee for working with the public, as part of the activity of the Supreme Council for Cultural Affairs, March 30, 1952, State archives, 1086/16-GL (ISA-education-education-000hq4p).

63. Minutes of the second meeting of the Supreme Council for Cultural Affairs, May 28, 1952, State archives, 1086/16-GL (ISA-education-education-000hq4p).

64. Ibid.

65. The Ministry of Interior, which was supposed to provide part of the funding, alongside the local municipalities, blocked the legislation. Meeting of the ministry's committee dealing with the Supreme Council for Culture, July 24, 1953, State archives, GL-16/1086 (ISA-education-education-000hq4p); the minutes of the meeting also mention the termination of Yavnieli's term as secretary of the Supreme Council for Culture. At the beginning of March 1953, the Hebrew press reported that the budget allocated to the Ministry of Education for instilling Hebrew was reduced. "Zutot ha'taktziv," *Al HaMishmar*, March 6, 1953.

66. Hacohen argues that the minister of interior, Moshe Shapira of Ha'poel Ha'Mizrahi (National Religious Labor Party) was concerned that the real aim of this law was to distance new immigrants from religious values and therefore opposed it. Hacohen, *Olim bi'se'ara*, 156. On February 3, 1954, a member of Knesset, Israel Bar-Yehuda, submitted the bill of this law to the Knesset, but the law was not passed. "Hugsha hatza'at hok hanhalat ha'lashon," *Al HaMishmar*, February 4, 1954.

67. Kimmerling, *Mehagrim mityashvim yelidim*, 153.

68. Ministry of Education, Meeting of Supreme Council for Culture, May 28, 1952, State archives, GL-16/1086 (ISA-education-education-000hq4p).

69. Ibid.

70. Dr. M. Perry, representative of the city of Tel Aviv. Ibid., The list of the members of the Supreme Council for Culture, State archives, GL-16/1086 (ISA-education-education 000hq4p).

71. Shmuel Yavnieli to the minister of education, August 21, 1952, State archives, GL-16/1086 (ISA-education-education 000hq4p).

72. The Supreme Council for Culture, the meeting of the committee for literature, August 17, 1952, State archives, GL -16/1086 (ISA-education-education-000hq4p).

73. Supreme Council for Culture, the meeting of the committee for literature, August 18, 1952, State archives, Gl-1086/16 16 (ISA-education-education ooohq4p).

74. The meeting of the Supreme Council for Culture, November 6, 1952, State archives, GL-16/1086 (ISA-education-education ooohq4p).

75. Interim Attorney General to Yavnieli, June 9, 1952, State archives, GL -16/1086 (ISA-education-education ooohq4p).

76. Yosef Ulitzky, "Ha'la'az be'rosh hutzot," *Sefer ha'shana shel ha'itonaim,* 1954, 39, 50.

77. Ulitzky, "Ishey ha'am al hanhalat ha'lashon," *Sefer ha'shana shel ha'itonaim,* 1954, 53–55.

78. Dr. Herzel Rosenblum, "Be'hatzi emtza'im lo sagi," *Sefer ha'shana shel ha'itonaim,* 1954, 62–63. It should be noted that there were those who took a softer line. The editor of *Maariv,* Ezriel Carlebach; the chief education officer of the Israel Defense Forces (IDF), Ze'ev Aharon; and the editor of *HaBoker,* Joseph Heftman, argued that the non-Hebrew press and theater could serve as a bridge between the cultures of the Diaspora and the new Hebrew culture. It was their view that these institutions should be allowed to exist even while every effort was being expended on teaching Hebrew. See Ezriel Carlebach, "Machshir le'hitbadlut o le'hishtarshut," *Sefer ha'shana shel ha'itonaim,* 1954, 61–62; Ze'ev Aharon, "Hatafat musar lo to'il," ibid., 56; Joseph Heftman, "Al yahafoch ma'avar le'keva," ibid., 55.

79. See Yitzhak Kariv, "Ma osa Yerushalayim," *Sefer ha'shana shel ha'itonaim,* 1954, 61, Abba Hushi, "Het'a shel ha'medina," ibid., 56–57.

80. Ben-Zion Dinur, "Hitnadvut ke'hok," *Sefer ha'shana shel ha'itonaim,* 1954, 53.

81. Haim Levanon, "Ha'yishuv hiniah nishko," *Sefer ha'shana shel ha'itonaim,* 1954, 57–58.

2

THE HEART OF YIDDISH CULTURE
The Yiddish Press 1948–1968

As another hot summer's day in 2006 drew to a close, a number of people could be seen climbing the stairs to the apartment of Mordechai Tsanin, on one of the pleasant streets in the old north of Tel Aviv. They were journalists and writers, the old guard of Yiddish-language culture in Israel, coming to inform the founding editor of the most important Yiddish newspaper ever published in the country, *Letste nayes*, that it was to close: the project to which he had devoted his life was coming to its end. Only a few months earlier they had celebrated his hundredth birthday with him. In speeches given at the party, they had feted him as "the founding father" of Yiddish in Israel and as "the head of the family of Yiddish writers in Israel and abroad." An article published in Yiddish around the same time was entitled, simply, "Tsanin—meynt: Yidish" (Tsanin means Yiddish).[1]

Although a prolific writer, Tsanin did not achieve his fame through his literary accomplishments. He was certainly involved in many aspects of Yiddish cultural life and had fought for Yiddish in Israel with great determination. But above all, he had been the founder and editor in chief of more than one major Yiddish newspaper in Israel. In response to his initiatives, other Yiddish newspapers had begun to appear in Israel, some even set by people who opposed the use of Yiddish in principle. So, while Tsanin's place of honor in the world of Yiddish and beyond can be attributed, to some degree, to his personality and achievements, it was primarily the result of his status as the leading editor of the Yiddish press. There is perhaps no better sign of the centrality of the press in Yiddish cultural life in Israel.

During the prestate years, there had barely been a Yiddish press in Palestine. From the turn of the century to 1948, only a handful of Yiddish newspapers had appeared, most of them short-lived. The only one that appeared for a long time was *Nayvelt*, issued by the Left Poalei-Zion, which was founded in 1934 and appeared regularly for over twenty years.²

In July 1948, about a month and a half after Israel's declaration of independence, Mordechai Tsanin founded his first paper, *Ilustrirter vokhnblat*, which made him the owner and editor of the first Yiddish newspaper to be established in the state of Israel. Others followed within weeks, and within less than a year, there were several dozen Yiddish periodicals in circulation in Israel, including newspapers, political periodicals, and literary journals. A decade later, the Yiddish press in Israel boasted sixty-one regular publications, some of them put out by public bodies or political parties.

These numbers reflect the vibrant world of the Israeli Yiddish press in the 1950s and, to some extent, in the 1960s too. This is extremely surprising given the state of Israel's linguistic policy in its early years. So the question needs to be asked how the Yiddish press managed to emerge and flourish despite an official policy that not only stressed the cultivation of Hebrew as the national language but also tried actively to limit the non-Hebrew press and officials and bureaucrats tried to apply this policy, especially to Yiddish.

One issue that needs to be considered is that Yiddish had always been the language of a minority group in the countries where Jews lived; its newspapers were those of an ethnic religious minority group and were considered a foreign-language press. In Israel, the readership of the Yiddish press—Jews who came from eastern Europe—might have been immigrants, but they were not an ethnic or national minority. Quite the opposite: they were part of the Jewish majority; they saw themselves as an integral part of Israeli society, and they understood the Yiddish press to be a central component in the history of Jewish culture. However, even in Israel, the Jewish nation-state, Yiddish and its press continued to be seen as foreign, due to the national cultural and linguistic policy that defined the general acceptance of Hebrew as one of its main goals and viewed Yiddish as a foreign, even a pariah, language. As a result, the Yiddish readership of these papers was driven into the position of being a *cultural* minority in their own nation-state. The tension between the sense of coming home felt by eastern European new immigrants in Israel and the state's Hebrew policy that did not recognize either their language or its culture played a central role in shaping the status of Yiddish in Israel. It was particularly significant in the development of the Israeli Yiddish press.

This chapter deals with the history of the Yiddish press in Israel, its struggles against the state's linguistic policy, and its efforts to become an influential power in Israeli society and political life. I posit as a main argument that it was the conflict between the desire of newspapers' editors and founders to play an active role in Israeli journalism, as well as in Israeli politics, that caused Israel's leaders to prefer political interests over cultural ones. This conflict actually contributed to the development of the Yiddish press.

The Yiddish press in the Diaspora had been deeply engaged with Jewish politics. Many newspapers in eastern Europe and the United States had had a clear political agenda and were an influential force in Jewish politics. The first Yiddish newspapers in Israel, on the other hand, were founded by individuals who defined themselves as apolitical. It did not take long, however, before they were publishing political commentary and perhaps even showing signs of wielding political influence. This led the political parties, including Mapai itself, to start their own Yiddish papers and compete with each other for readers. The result was a very lively and diverse Yiddish press that existed for more than a decade, sometimes with the support of forces ideologically opposed to Yiddish.

"A Yiddish Newspaper Is an Entirely Different Category": Background

The press has always been at the heart of modern Yiddish culture and provided fertile soil for its growth. It not only played a major role in the development of modern Jewish politics in eastern Europe and the United States but also acted as a crucial platform for the development of modern Yiddish literature.[3] More than anything else, however, it was a minority press. Written in a language that was not the language of the country where it appeared, it focused on the specific social and political interests of the Jewish minority and sometimes on their needs within majority society.

Since the Jews were, before 1948, a stateless people, their press—and prominent within that, the Yiddish press—provided its readers with what Benedict Anderson has termed an "imagined community," serving as an organizing element of Jewish national identity. "A Yiddish newspaper is an entirely different category from a non-Jewish newspaper," wrote Jacob Glatstein, Shmuel Niger, and Hillel Rogoff—three leading writers and intellectuals in the world of Yiddish in the United States. "The Yiddish newspaper has taken the Jewish immigrants, organized them into a group and shaped them."[4]

Scholars of the ethnic-minority press use, sometimes interchangeably, the terms "ethnic press," "minority press," "foreign-language press," and "immigrant press" to describe their subject.[5] Throughout its history, the Yiddish press had always belonged to the first three categories and sometimes to the fourth too. In the state of Israel, however, it started out as simply an immigrant press.

A universal characteristic of immigrant societies is the establishment of institutions to act as a kind of bridge between the new country and the country of origin. The purpose of these bodies is to help the immigrants undergo the complex processes of migrating from country to country and culture to culture. Some scholars call them "buffer institutions."[6] The immigrant press is generally perceived as the most important of these institutions, whose most basic role is to help the immigrants orient themselves to the fundamental realities of life in their new home.[7]

However, as early as the first quarter of the twentieth century, scholars began to identify other important roles played by the immigrant press. In his pioneering 1922 study of the foreign-language press in the United States, Robert E. Park argued that the major function of these papers was not only to help immigrants to navigate the realities of life in a strange environment but also to expedite their adaptation to and acculturation in their new society. This press, claimed Park, made it possible to introduce newcomers to the dominant values of the new society not only in their own language but also using concepts familiar to them, making it much easier to assimilate them.[8] Therefore, according to Park, the immigrant press helped readers both take their first steps in a new society and become an integral part of it.

Carl Wittke, who studied German-speaking immigrants in the United States, expanded the definition. He suggested that the immigrant press plays a double role by preserving the cultural ties of the immigrants with their lands of origin and by helping them adapt to the new country.[9] Hannah Arendt understood this process a little differently, arguing that these newspapers allowed immigrants to retain their group identity by helping them stay in touch with their former home. She, too, viewed the east European Jews in the United States as a special case, as they did not identify with their country of origin but still developed a group identity with the help of the press.[10]

Nonetheless, many scholars agree that an immigrant press must, by its very nature, be living on borrowed time.[11] As the sociologist Morris Janowitz put it: the success of an immigrant press is measured by its ability to render itself unnecessary. If an immigrant press survives over time, that means that the immigrant ghetto continues to exist.[12]

Yet the Yiddish press in general outlived the immigrant generation and filled a variety of functions that went beyond the needs of the immigrants themselves. In the United States, it served as an organizing element of secular Jewish identity, while both there and in Israel remaining loyal to Yiddish came to symbolize an attachment to the Jewish culture of the Old World and a desire to preserve it.

In many ways, however, the Yiddish-language press that developed in Israel following the immigration from eastern Europe was a unique phenomenon in the history of the immigrant press. This was, in large part, due to the nature of the immigration to Israel itself as an "immigration home."[13] Though the state of

Israel did make absorbing immigrants a top priority and invested great efforts in their integration, this welcoming attitude was coupled with a demand that they leave their old cultures behind and adopt the state's new Hebrew culture.

Tsanin meynt Yiddish (Tsanin Means Yiddish): Mordechai Tsanin and the Beginnings of the Yiddish Press in Israel

In the years leading up to the creation of the state of Israel, some ten Yiddish periodicals were published. Most were little more than propaganda pamphlets issued by public institutions—the Histadrut (General Federation of Hebrew Workers), the Jewish Agency, and the World Zionist Organization—and all appeared irregularly.[14] After the founding of the state, several new Yiddish publications appeared, mostly the same kind of pamphlets issued by the military or by different political parties.[15] These did not even meet the most basic needs of the mass of Yiddish readers who had recently immigrated to Israel—a group that formed some 50 percent of non-Hebrew speakers in Israel in 1948 and still as much as a third in 1950.[16]

Into this void stepped Mordechai Tsanin (1906–2009), an aspiring journalist and man of many talents and a forceful disposition, who combined great vision with great courage. Mordechai Yeshayahu Tsanin (Tsukerman) was born in 1906 in Sokolow Podlaski, a district town in the Lublin Province of Poland. After being educated at a *heder* and a *yeshiva*, he moved with his family to Warsaw at age fifteen and attended a Polish gymnasium.

He was drawn to Yiddish literature at a young age and published his first story in 1928 in *Oyfgang*, a Warsaw monthly that showcased young Yiddish writers.[17] While working as an administrator at Di tsentrale yidishe shul-organizatsye (the Central Yiddish School Organization, TSYSHO), he published in various Yiddish literary journals, such as *Literarishe bleter* (The literary pages), *Faroys* (Forward), and *Vokhnshrift far literatur, kunst un kultur* (Weekly journal of literature, arts, and culture). In 1933, his collection of short stories *Vivat lebn* (To life) was published, and 1935 saw the appearance of his debut novel, *Oyf zumpiker erd* (On swampy ground), which dealt with the poverty of village life.[18] From 1937 to 1939 he was employed regularly at the periodical *Bikher nayes* (Books news).[19]

When Germany invaded Poland in 1939, Tsanin fled to Vilnius yet returned shortly afterward to bring news of what was happening there to the Jews who remained in Warsaw. After a short stay in the city, he again traveled east, leaving Poland, and after a journey that spanned Lithuania, Japan, India, and Egypt, he reached Palestine in 1941.[20] He settled in Tel Aviv and opened a bag store, from which he made his living while devoting most of his energy to furthering

Figure 2.1. *From right to left*: Dora Tsanin, Mordechai Tsanin, Golda Meir, Shimon Dzigan. Courtesy of Ze'ev Tsanin.

his literary aspirations in Yiddish. Almost immediately on his arrival in Palestine, he began publishing in *Nayvelt*, and a year later, he published his first book there: *Vuhin geyt Yapan, reportazhn fun vaytn mizrekh* (Where is Japan headed? Reports from the Far East, 1942), a compilation of impressions from his travels through East Asia on his way to Palestine.[21]

Starting from late 1945, Tsanin spent a year in postwar Poland under the guise of a British journalist from Mandatory Palestine. The outcome was a series of articles published in the New York–based Yiddish daily *Forverts* (*Forward*) describing the decimation of one hundred Jewish communities in Poland. The articles were later collected and published in a book entitled *Iber shteyn un shtok: A rayze iber hundert khorev gevorene kehiles in Poyln* (Of stones and ruins: A journey through one hundred destroyed communities in Poland).[22] His return to Poland that year was a profound turning point for Tsanin: when he came back to Israel, he decided to dedicate his life to Yiddish as a journalist, an author, and eventually a newspaper editor.

Perhaps his two greatest achievements apart from his contribution to the Yiddish press were his 1982 Yiddish-Hebrew and 1994 Hebrew-Yiddish dictionaries—a groundbreaking endeavor that was, for many years, the only dictionary that bridged the gap between Yiddish and modern Israeli Hebrew. His most significant literary accomplishment was his six-volume *Artapanus kumt tsurik aheym* (Artapanus comes back home), an epic novel telling the entire history of the Jewish people from the days before the great Hasmonean revolt in Judea to the war of 1973, through the life story of a single Jewish family.[23]

He also wrote and edited more than twenty books in Yiddish, some literary but most collections of his writings on the fate of the eastern European Jews and Jewish, especially Yiddish, culture. However, without a doubt, Tsanin's greatest achievement was the Yiddish press. This was what made his name and turned him into a very influential figure in the world of Yiddish, both in Israel and abroad, as well as in Israeli politics and journalism. His reward came in the form of membership in two of Israel's most prestigious bodies: the Israeli Editors Committee and the Israel Press Council.[24]

Ilustrirter vokhnblat: An Illustrated Yiddish Weekly

Even before mass immigration to Israel began in September 1948, Tsanin decided to start a Yiddish weekly, clearly understanding the cultural importance of such a publication for the Yiddish-speaking immigrants who would come from eastern Europe.[25] He chose the format of a photo magazine with little accompanying text and gave it a bilingual name: *Ilustrirter vokhnblat* in Yiddish and *Shavu'on metzuyar* in Hebrew, both of which mean "Illustrated Weekly."

The new magazine ran for sixty-three weeks, from July 1, 1948, to October 14, 1949. The first issue contained no declaration of a program or a credo of any kind. Its editorial column was, just that once, in both Hebrew and Yiddish and discussed the question of Israel's defense. The other articles also dealt with matters of pressing importance to the new state, especially in the realm of the military. On the face of things, then, the new periodical had nothing to do with Yiddish culture but was just a weekly magazine on Israeli affairs written in Yiddish. In practice, however, it was not quite that simple.

Weekly photo magazines were a popular format around the world in the 1940s and the 1950s; Israel alone had three such periodicals in 1948. In fact, there were many similarities between *Ilustrirter vokhnblat* and its two Hebrew-language contemporaries: *HaOlam Haze* (This world)[26] and especially *Devar Ha'shavua* (The weekly news). All three offered a combination of current affairs, culture, and a smattering of entertainment, and they all frequently published photographs of soldiers, especially on the front and back covers. Nonetheless, *Ilustrirter vokhnblat* had important differences from the other two, and not just because it was in Yiddish.

Two major, intertwined themes featured in every issue of the magazine. One was the Holocaust, and the other was the development of the state of Israel in the face of the war for independence. Although war reportage was common at the time and appeared in all Israeli periodicals as a matter of course, *Ilustrirter vokhnblat* devoted special attention to it in terms of both content and graphics. Its stories always focused on the Jewish individual, while in the background, whether implicitly or explicitly, was the Holocaust. Stories about soldiers on guard duty always noted, openly or by implication, that they had come from "there" (i.e., from the Holocaust). This also found expression in the cover illustrations: one prominent example was a drawing of a soldier holding a rifle and wearing a helmet with the Star of David on it, while elderly Jews leaned on him for support, their hands shackled and the yellow star on their arms. The caption, in both Yiddish and Hebrew, read: "Soldiers of the Israel Defense Forces breaking the chains of their enslaved brothers, ensuring the independence of their country and the freedom of their people."[27]

All this was very much in line with the Zionist ethos and the image of the New Jew, who was physically strong and bravely faced his enemies, unlike the weak and very timid Diaspora Jew.[28] Nonetheless, *Ilustrirter vokhnblat* took a more nuanced approach. The Israeli Jew it featured was not born in Israel but was an immigrant Holocaust survivor. In contrast to the Zionist ethos and its negation of the Diaspora, this Jew did not cut himself off from his past. Instead, he was described as moving seamlessly from the Diaspora past into the Israeli present, with living in Israel always described as a kind of closure. In other words, in the *Ilustrirter vokhnblat*, the Israeli experience could not exist without its diasporic roots.[29]

Ilustrirter vokhnblat also fulfilled the traditional roles of an immigrant press. It regularly ran articles providing immigrants with useful information about life in their new country, such as the structure of the political system and the workings of the government. Beyond that, however, when mass immigration to Israel began on October 29, 1948, readers who needed it were also invited to seek help or advice at the magazine office. "The editor has office hours every Tuesday between ten and twelve," read the back cover.[30]

This was not an entirely new idea in the world of the Yiddish press; after all, the editor of *Forverts*, Abraham Cahan, had also invited readers to come to his office for similar reasons. Yet the two cases were not alike. While *Forverts* as a classic minority newspaper worked to help Jewish immigrants find their way in a foreign country, *Ilustrirter vokhnblat* was offering assistance to people "immigrating home."

Scholars of the immigrant press note that immigrant newspapers can also reflect their readers' reservations about their new country or government policies.³¹ Indeed, initially *Ilustrirter vokhnblat* not only was reticent of expressing any reservation about the policy of the Israeli government; it sang the praises of the new state and basked in its glory. Life in Israel was portrayed as better than in the Diaspora and Israelis as better than Diaspora Jews. Even the humor section sometimes ran jokes depicting those born in Israel as cleverer and more resourceful than their new immigrant counterparts.

However, this lasted for only the first few months of circulation. Offering the editor's help to newcomers was the first sign of the critical line Tsanin would soon take against the leadership of the country. Gradually, the weekly began looking less at the state itself and more at Yiddish and Yiddish-language culture and to the life of the Eastern European Jewish immigrants in Israel.³² Not surprisingly, its attitude toward the state and its policies began to change too.

On October 14, 1949, some three months after the end of the war for independence, *Ilustrirter vokhnblat* announced that it would be making a number of changes, including adopting a new name: *Letste nayes* (The latest news). It implied that the changes would be merely cosmetic and that the paper would stay the same. In practice, however, *Letste nayes* would prove to be an entirely different project that would transform the Yiddish press in Israel and also leave its mark on the Hebrew press there too.

An Informative, Democratic Newspaper Suited to the Times: *Letste Nayes*

As with *Ilustrirter vokhnblat*, Tsanin was the founder, editor, and living spirit of *Letste nayes*. This time, however, he had two partners: Israel Hadash and Matzliah Zeitouni. The first, Hadash, was born in Vilna in 1912, received a traditional Jewish education, and was active in Left Poalei-Zion circles. He immigrated to Israel in 1936 and made a living from various jobs at *Nayvelt*.³³ In 1946 he established his own publishing house, *Naye lebn* (A new life), which published books in Yiddish for forty years.

Records of the establishment of the Tsanin-Hadash partnership are missing, but we can assume that it had at least been discussed before *Letste nayes* began to appear.³⁴ It was definitely in place by October 5, 1950, when Matzliah Zeitouni, the owner of Carmel Printers on Lewinsky Street in Tel Aviv, joined Tsanin and Hadash—who already owned *Letste nayes*—as third partner. It was this new partnership, dubbed ZeTsaKh (an acronym of the three surnames), that published *Letste nayes*.³⁵

Unlike Tsanin and Hadash, Zeitouni was a descendant of a Sephardic family that had lived for many generations in Palestine. He did not know Yiddish and never felt a connection with the language or the culture of east European Jews, so his reasons for joining the partnership are not clear. The available sources are not helpful. Tsanin presumably wanted a business partner or partners to offset the considerable financial burden of producing the newspaper,[36] while Hadash had a long-standing interest in the Yiddish press and Yiddish publishing in general. Zeitouni's motivation appears to have been purely financial. He seems to have grasped the business potential of a Yiddish newspaper in Israel in the early 1950s, particularly bearing in mind that Yiddish speakers were perceived at the time as a highly literate group with a strong tradition of reading. To his eyes, then, investing in a Yiddish newspaper might have seemed a financially worthwhile step.[37]

The name *Letste nayes* was probably chosen for its unambiguous meaning: it was to be a newspaper devoted to current affairs, which would hopefully turn into a major Israeli daily. It was also an accurate translation of *Yedioth Aharonoth*, the name of one of the first privately owned Hebrew dailies in Israel. However, it is not likely that Tsanin named his paper after that Hebrew daily, particularly because *Yedioth Aharonoth* was going through difficult times. It is more reasonable to assume that the name was chosen to forge a connection with the Yiddish press of the past: *Letste nayes* had been the name of a sensational Yiddish evening paper, combining politics and current affairs with sensational news from the Jewish street, that had appeared in Warsaw for several months after August 1929.[38] While the publishers of *Letste nayes* in Tel Aviv probably did not intend to create a specific tie to one of the Yiddish newspapers in interwar Poland, they might well have been interested in a title that would express a sense of continuity with the old world of Yiddish.

From the outset, *Letste nayes* was presented as a development of *Ilustrirter vokhnblat*, which even published the new paper's declaration of its editorial principles. *Letste nayes* was going to be "an informative, purely democratic paper to answer the needs of our time; it will offer diverse, nonpartisan discussion of all important issues relating to our country and its development, and especially to the painful questions concerning new immigrants. *Letste nayes* will help Yiddish-speaking immigrants strike root in Israel by keeping them up to date with economics, politics and cultural news." The new paper would report about international affairs, publish two serialized novels, have regular sections on medicine and practical advice, and feature op-eds. "*Letste nayes* will appear every Thursday in an eight-page format, and will cost 50 Prutot [0.05 Israeli Pound]."[39]

The new paper was clearly trying to follow the well-known pattern of the Yiddish press. It was shaped as an immigrant newspaper that would engage with domestic politics while helping immigrants put down roots in their new country and continue the traditions of the prewar Yiddish press in eastern Europe while forming part of the transregional Yiddish culture in the postwar world. However, Israeli life was very different from the reality in which the Yiddish press had developed in other countries, so *Letste nayes* quickly became a new type of newspaper: a Yiddish paper that was part of the country's political life and influenced it in ways that no previous Yiddish newspaper had succeeded in doing.

The first issue of *Letste nayes* appeared on November 3, 1949, and under its title printed the subheading "Umparteyish blat far gezelshaft, politik un kultur" (A nonpartisan newspaper for social, political, and cultural affairs). The issue was numbered 1, though it added the number 64 in brackets to indicate its continuity with *Ilustrirter vokhnblat*.[40]

Yet the great enthusiasm with which *Letste nayes* started out soon faded as the paper's energies had to be directed to the struggle against the state of Israel's policy on Hebrew. For the rest of their lives, Tsanin and many other Yiddish journalists would claim that this policy reflected a conscious governmental discrimination against Yiddish in general and the Yiddish press in particular. The reality, however, was more complex. I will argue that Tsanin's leadership of *Letste nayes* and his combative editorial policy won him and his paper a position of such strength in Israeli politics that the country's leadership felt it necessary to prefer their own political interest over their linguistic policy. This ended up making a significant contribution to the development of the Yiddish press in Israel.

"The Danger of Yiddish": Newspaper Licensing, Paper Supply, and the Yiddish Press

The basic legal document that regulated the press in the state of Israel and defined its relations with the authorities until well into the twenty-first century was the Press Ordinance of 1933, formulated by the British authorities. In 1945, as their relationship with the Jewish Yishuv deteriorated, mandate authorities added stringent regulations on newspaper licensing to the ordinance.[41] Like other laws made by the British in Palestine, this ordinance too was adopted by the state of Israel (and it remained in force until May 2017).[42] The Press Ordinance stated that "no newspaper may be printed or published in Palestine, unless its owners first obtain a license signed by the responsible district official."[43] The Press Ordinance was defined as a criminal law, so anyone violating it was liable to conviction in a court of law and to criminal punishment.

The Press Ordinance established basic criteria for those able to receive a license to publish a newspaper (having to be above a certain age, having no criminal record, etc.) but also left considerable discretion in the hands of the responsible officials, who in the state of Israel served in the Ministry of the Interior, to decide on questions of issuing and revoking such licenses.[44]

In May 1949, Yeshayahu Klinov, the head of the Press, Information, and Film Administration in the Ministry of the Interior, met with a special committee of the National Organization of Hebrew Journalists to discuss the policy of licensing non-Hebrew newspapers.[45] In a nuanced presentation, Klinov noted that the foreign-language press might hold new immigrants back from learning Hebrew and even create competition for the Hebrew daily press. At the same time, however, he acknowledged the need for a foreign-language press as a way of helping new immigrants navigate their daily lives in Israel. This led him to propose considering new legislation to deal with newspaper licensing.

All the participants in the meeting, including the editors of the large Hebrew evening papers (Herzl Rosenblum of *Yedioth Aharonoth* and Ezriel Carlebach of *Maariv*), vehemently opposed the publication of non-Hebrew dailies and demanded it be restricted. Two other participants—Joseph Gravitzky of the Government Press Office and Sh. Shevalov of *Ha'aretz*—voiced explicit concerns about Yiddish. Both expressed strident opposition to the publication of Yiddish newspapers and even referred to "the danger of Yiddish."[46] Another participant proposed "blocking the development of non-Hebrew press on the grounds of the paper shortage."[47] It was not an empty threat.

The mass immigration that had started soon after the establishment of the state and the consequent need to absorb hundreds of thousands of indigent immigrants while the country was waging the war of 1948 had put Israel in a difficult economic situation. In addition, the young state lacked means of production and, even more so, the foreign exchange reserves it needed to pay for food and basic raw materials. From 1949 to 1959, therefore, the state of Israel declared an austerity regime (called in Hebrew *tzena*) in which, among other things, the rationing of food and clothes was enforced.[48]

It was another form of rationing that affected the position of the Yiddish press. Israel faced a severe shortage of paper that lasted well into the 1950s. This hit newspapers especially hard since there was a shortage of newsprint in the world market and Israel did not have the foreign currency it needed to pay for imports.[49] A special government committee was set up to allot paper according to whatever criteria it determined. Paper rationing thus became a second way of controlling the Israeli press, and particularly non-Hebrew newspapers, giving the authorities a way to do so without having to pass laws or introduce concrete regulations against a specific language or publication.[50]

The most important general discussion on the issue of the foreign language press was held by the Supreme Council for Cultural Affairs, though in the council's first two sessions the question was addressed only indirectly. During the first session, Shmuel Yavnieli reiterated the idea that monitoring and controlling the paper supply for the printing industry might be one way to help shape Israeli culture,[51] while in the second, Ben-Zion Dinur proposed requiring "every foreign-language newspaper to devote a page or a section to Hebrew, so that readers will get a Hebrew lesson in every issue."[52]

Dinur's suggestion did not express opposition to the non-Hebrew press as such but certainly indicated his recognition of its power. It generated vigorous debate. All the participants stressed the important role of newspapers in instilling language and culture. A few objected to non-Hebrew press very vociferously and again recommended using paper rationing to restrict its publication. One speaker, a representative of the National-Religious Mizrachi movement, Rabbi Katriel F. Tchursh, referred directly to Yiddish and expressed his very strong objection to the appearance of what he called "jargonistic" newspapers.[53]

In August 1952, the subcommittee on literature formed by the Supreme Council held a special meeting to discuss the non-Hebrew press in Israel. It learned that there were ninety-one non-Hebrew periodicals in circulation at the time. Yiddish, with sixteen titles, was second only to English in terms of the number of publications.[54] No other language could boast more than a few titles.

Here, too, the participants were unanimous in their opposition to the non-Hebrew press and stressed that any move toward giving up on the use of Hebrew to communicate with Jewish Israelis would be harmful.[55] Eventually, the committee made two recommendations: first, that the government control the licensing of non-Hebrew papers for Jewish readers by limiting their publication to no more than three times a week and by revoking the licenses of inactive papers and, second, that low priority be given to the allocation of newsprint to non-Hebrew newspapers.[56] The decision was reiterated in meetings of other committees, which took place in fall 1952.[57]

While this policy certainly made it harder to publish Yiddish newspapers, especially dailies, it did not put a stop to the Yiddish press in Israel. The actual damage it caused Yiddish was probably much more a question of image since Yiddish was categorized as a rejected language. This did not mean that there was no discrimination at all, just that it played out in a much more minor key.

This can be seen quite clearly in the case of M. Stein's 1952 petition to the High Court of Justice against the Minister of the Interior.[58] Stein was the publisher of the *Demokratishe ovnt tsaytung* (Democratic evening paper), which had for a number of years appeared in five languages—Hebrew, German, French, Russian, and Yiddish. During the time of the British mandate, it had been properly licensed, but after the establishment of the state, it needed a new license. In 1951 Stein applied for one and was given permission to publish a daily in seven languages, including Hebrew and Yiddish. However, he ran into difficulties and in the first half of 1952 managed to publish only eight issues of his paper, all in Yiddish. His license was then revoked, following a stipulation of the press ordinance that the Ministry of the Interior was empowered to revoke the license of any daily that failed to publish twelve daily issues in a row (except for Saturdays) in a single month.[59]

Stein petitioned the high court on the grounds that the Ministry of the Interior had revoked his license to prevent the publication of a Yiddish newspaper, arguing that Hebrew newspapers that failed to come out regularly were not treated in the same way. The high-court justices, Yitzhak Olshan, Simha Assaf, and Shimon Agranat, denied Stein's petition, pointing out that his paper had clearly failed to meet the standard set out in the press ordinance. Still, Justice Yitzhak Olshan did address the claim of discrimination in his ruling: "We have no doubt that the justification for revoking the license was that the newspaper was not published as often as required. However, [the minister of the interior] was not willing to assist a non-Hebrew paper by overlooking the 'offense' and not using the power given him by law."[60]

So, while this ruling followed the letter of the law, it was discriminatory against Yiddish, in its justification of selective enforcement. Clearly the ideological stance of the judges had influenced their decision. On the other hand, it should not be forgotten that Stein did initially receive a license to bring out a multilanguage daily, including a Yiddish version.[61]

In fact, despite the preferential treatment of Hebrew, many Yiddish newspapers were licensed between 1948 and 1952—though on the condition that they appear no more than three times a week.[62] A whole range of publications received licenses: *Ilustrirter vokhnblat* was granted a license in September 1948.[63] In December of that year, the Herut movement received a license to publish three non-Hebrew newspapers: in Romanian, German, and Yiddish;[64] *Nayvelt*, the long-standing Yiddish paper of the Left Poalei-Zion was granted a license in February 1949 to appear three times a week.[65] Two months later, *Ihud olami* was licensed to appear as a Yiddish weekly;[66] in December that year, Shlomo Frank of Jerusalem was granted a license to publish a newspaper on cultural and national affairs, entitled *Yidishe bilder*, which he would edit.[67] On December 13, 1949, *Frayheyt*, a newspaper issued by the Herut movement (both words mean "freedom," the first in Yiddish and the second in Hebrew), was licensed to change its name to *Unzer moment* and appear as a weekly.[68] On April 28, 1950, the General Zionist Party received a license to publish the weekly *Unzer haynt*,[69] and in June, Yeshayahu Vinograd was given a license to put out the weekly *Unzer fraynt*, also on behalf of the General Zionist Party.[70]

So, while the licensing policy did limit the Yiddish press, it certainly did not prevent its growth.

Matters became more difficult when paper rationing for the press came into the picture. It was managed by the Book Publishers Association of Israel, based on quotas set in April 1949, and was a source of considerable tension. Israel's dailies cautioned that reducing their circulation due to a lack of paper endangered not only their own existence but also democracy itself.[71] Delegations from the large daily newspapers—*Davar, Maariv,* and *Ha'aretz*—met with the minister of trade and industry to discuss the issue.[72]

In late December 1950, printers, publishers, and journalists organized A Conference on the Printed Letter, held in Tel Aviv to discuss the implications of the paper shortage on the printing industry. In the presence of government officials, the speakers called on the government to recognize the printing industry as a fully-fledged branch of the economy and claimed that the paper shortage was preventing the dissemination of information and hampering literary creativity, not to mention scientific and other development. Some even demanded that the government establish a paper factory in Israel.[73]

The supply of paper, particularly newsprint, was the topic of frequent—and heated—discussions in the Knesset.[74] In early 1951, the tension reached a peak. In a debate on January 3, all the speakers accused the government of ignoring the importance of setting a paper policy in a country that was absorbing so many immigrants and warned that this was harming Israel's cultural development. The role of the non-Hebrew press was discussed in detail. Most speakers did agree that the non-Hebrew press played an important role in an immigrant-absorbing state and that it did not constitute a serious threat to the spread of Hebrew. At the same time, however, they noted the growing number of foreign-language newspapers, including the six Yiddish papers that were in circulation at the time, and recommended reducing this number. In the end, the plenum recommended referring the issue of paper supply to a special Knesset subcommittee to be composed of members of the economy, education and culture, and internal affairs committees.[75]

The special subcommittee convened two weeks later, and one of its first recommendations was to cut down paper consumption by reducing the number of licenses given to foreign-language newspapers.[76] It also recommended that licenses for foreign language newspapers be limited to six months, to enable frequent reconsideration and ensure that there was enough paper to print Hebrew books and periodicals.[77]

Back in the Knesset, MK Yitzhak Raphael, from the Mizrachi Party, submitted a motion on May 7, 1952, for a debate on the spread of foreign languages in Israel in general and of the foreign language press in particular, presumably with an eye to encouraging restrictive legislation. With the influence of Minister Dinur, the issue was referred to the Knesset's Committee on Culture, thus postponing the debate.[78] This was the legal and political reality into which *Letste nayes* was born.

Letste nayes, *Yidishe tsaytung*, and *Yidishe prese*: One Paper, Three Names

Letste nayes ran as a weekly for seventeen weeks and then, following its receipt of a new license,[79] as a twice weekly, which it did as of issue number 18 on February 27, 1950.[80] Within a couple of months, Tsanin filed a request to publish *Letste nayes* three times a week. He was refused, with no explanation.[81] In November, he applied to make *Letste nayes* a daily. In an internal memo sent to the Press, Information, and Film Administration in the Ministry of the Interior, its deputy head explained that "the foreign-language press, including Yiddish," could not be allowed to expand and that due to lack of paper it would not be possible "to fulfil Mr. Tsanin's request."[82]

Some eight months later, Tsanin made another application to the Ministry of the Interior for a license to publish his paper three times a week. This time, his request was approved, though the paper continued to appear twice a week for a number of months, apparently due to the paper shortage.[83] Still, on September 30, 1951, Rosh Hashanah eve, *Letste nayes* announced that it would soon begin appearing three times a week, with more pages and broader coverage. Readers were even invited to write in with ideas for new sections to add to the newspaper and interesting topics that could be covered. On November 4, 1951, *Letste nayes* began appearing three times a week—on Sundays, Tuesdays, and Fridays.

In late 1952, there was a massive increase in Israel's paper stocks.[84] This may have persuaded the publishers of *Letste nayes* to try and turn it into a daily. Though their request for a license was turned down, they did not give up on the plan. Instead, they decided to publish another newspaper that would also appear three times a week, on the days *Letste nayes* did not (i.e., on Mondays, Wednesdays, and Thursdays). The two together would form a daily paper.

So, in early August 1953, a big advertisement appeared in *Letste nayes* announcing the founding of a new Yiddish newspaper, *Yidishe tsaytung*, which would appear three times a week starting in September. The editor of the new paper would be M. Tsanin, and it would express the exact same values as *Letste nayes*. Tsanin's editorship was the guarantee that readers would find in *Letste nayes* and *Yidishe tsaytung* together a stable daily paper. The ad was signed by the publisher: the Da'at Association.[85]

The Da'at Association was the name of an organization run by Israel Hadash, one of Tsanin's partners in *Letste nayes*, and it was Hadash who held the license to publish the new newspaper. The title it was given, *Yidishe tsaytung* (which could mean either "Yiddish newspaper" or "Jewish newspaper"), was a popular one in the world of the Yiddish press. Newspapers of this name had appeared in Vilna and Buenos Aires, and, following the Holocaust, the titles of several Yiddish papers published in the displaced-persons camps included the words "Yidishe tsaytung."

The two papers made no secret of the fact that they were working around the licensing regulations. In fact, the front pages of both declared proudly that *Letste nayes* and *Yidishe tsaytung* were one and the same. When the first issue of *Yidishe tsaytung* appeared on Tuesday, September 1, 1953, it urged its readers, in large letters next to the logo, to "read tomorrow in *Letste nayes*." Equivalent wording appeared in the next day's *Letste nayes*. Just three weeks later, both papers began to appear with a single logo: "*Letste nayes* conjointly with *Yidishe tsaytung*" (Letste nayes *fareynikt mit* Yidishe tsaytung).

The two publications differed in terms of quality and importance. *Letste nayes* was clearly the flagship and *Yidishe tsaytung* a supporting player. So, while *Letste nayes* kept the weekend edition—the most important issue of the week—and looked like a daily paper in the full sense of the term, the first issues of *Yidishe tsaytung* were just two pages long and included mostly news, a section called Questions of the Day, and readers' letters.

It did not stay that size for long. On May 2, 1954, the paper doubled in size from two to four pages. There was now room to include a semi-regular section of reports from the Hebrew press, which appeared in almost every issue, as well as sections on current affairs in the Jewish world and in daily life in Israel. Six months later, almost every issue included coverage of economic issues and sports, too. *Yidishe tsaytung* was growing into a newspaper in its own right—a development that turned out to be a mixed blessing.

From One Joint Paper to Two Separate Projects: The Split in *Letste nayes*

On December 4, 1955, a new Yiddish newspaper began to appear under the title, *Yidishe prese* (The Jewish press). On the right-hand corner of its front page was a small, inconspicuous notice stating that, for technical reasons, it would be the companion paper to *Letste nayes* from that time on.[86] In fact, the change was far from technical: it was the result of a serious falling out between the two main partners of *Letste nayes*, Mordechai Tsanin and Israel Hadash. This story shows that the fate of the Yiddish press (and Yiddish in general) was determined not only by government policy or popular attitudes toward the language but by a range of factors—economic, personal, and others. It is therefore worth examining in some detail.

It is difficult to work out the precise motivations of those involved. Until his death, Tsanin never even alluded to Israel Hadash, whose name had also never appeared in *Letste nayes*, and conspicuously failed to mention that, in its early years, the paper had been under joint ownership. For his part, Hadash was by no means as reticent and published an account of the affair in an article that appeared in *Yidishe tsaytung* several weeks later.[87]

Any attempt to reduce this imbalance in the sources with the oral testimonies of other contemporaries is highly problematic since it is almost impossible to verify their accuracy.[88] What can be assumed with some confidence is that the relationship between the two men was tense, especially given Tsanin's forceful personality and his higher status in the world of Yiddish, both in Israel and abroad.[89] The formal grounds for the dissolution of the partnership seems to have been a disagreement over the political opinion expressed by the newspaper.

In the 1950s much of the Israeli press, in Hebrew as well as in other languages, was published by political parties. That was not the case with *Ilustrirter vokhnblat* and later *Letste nayes–Yidishe tsaytung*, which were privately owned and apolitical, as they made sure to proclaim on the front page of every issue. Still, defining a newspaper as apolitical did not, of course, prevent its editors from holding political opinions, which could sometimes differ from those they had held in the past or had previously expressed. This became an issue particularly during election campaigns.

The general elections for the second Knesset were held on July 30, 1951. They had been brought forward following a harsh public debate over child education in the *ma'abarot*, which had eventually led to the dissolution of the coalition and the resignation of the government.[90] *Letste nayes*, at the time still appearing only twice a week, did not take any position on the upcoming elections. On July 2, a small headline on the front page announced the beginning of the election campaign, and no more was said about it until just before the elections.[91] On the weekend before they were held (July 27), the paper devoted a great deal of space to explaining Israel's political parties to its readers. It presented the platforms of a number of the parties—Agudat Israel, Mapai, Mapam, and Herut—and explained how the election process worked but took no political stand.[92] Tsanin waited until election day itself to make his views known. On July 30, *Letste nayes* ran a lengthy article signed by Tsanin in person that criticized the very decision to hold elections.[93] In it, he sat in judgment on each of the parties, arguing that none of them were acting for the common good but out of narrow party interests. He went on to thunder that holding elections at that time did not benefit anyone and only caused the unnecessary expenditure of funds that could better have been diverted to genuinely vital concerns.

It is perhaps not surprising then that the split with Hadash was precipitated by the next general election, to the third Knesset, which was held as scheduled on July 26, 1955. In the coalition, the two major parties looking to return to power were the Mapai and the General Zionists. Both parties, each for its own reasons, were afraid of a drop in support.[94] Tensions around the elections ran high, and Tsanin ran articles in *Letste nayes* that could vaguely be interpreted as support for the General Zionist Party. His partner Israel Hadash was very upset and told Tsanin of a rumor circulating to the effect that he was being paid by party operatives.[95] Tsanin's response was a curt notification to Hadash in writing that their partnership would be terminated as of October 1, 1955.[96]

Stories that Tsanin supported the General Zionist party were nothing new. In late 1954, he had filed a libel suit against the Mapai-owned newspaper *Ha'dor*; its editor, Yona Yagol; and its former editor Haim Shurer, for running a story that he (i.e., Tsanin) was acting as part of the General Zionists' election campaign. The reports in *Ha'dor* also tied Uri Avnery and his paper, *HaOlam Haze*, to the party.[97] The suit ended in a settlement in which *Ha'dor* was required to publish a retraction and an apology and to pay Tsanin 1,450 Israeli pounds in compensation, which he agreed to donate to children in the *ma'abarot*.[98]

As well as reflecting the high tensions that preceded the elections, this affair also shows that the Yiddish press and Tsanin himself had become significant players in Israeli politics. Linking him with Uri Avnery, whose paper was very influential and was a thorn in the government's side, however preposterous it seemed given Avnery's ideological stance,[99] further reinforces the assumption that *Letste nayes* was powerful and had to be reckoned with.[100]

The *Letste nayes* partnership did not end immediately. On December 6, the Tel Aviv District Court, following a request by Israel Hadash, ordered the ZeTsaKh (Zeitouni, Tsanin, Hadash) partnership dissolved and forbad the use of the printing presses that belonged to it.[101] However, even that was not the end of the conflict. At the request of Israel Hadash, Tel Aviv District Court judge Dr. Joseph Lamm issued a court order preventing Tsanin from making any changes in the license of *Letste nayes*. In fact, Hadash had gone so far as to make a personal appeal to the minister of the interior on this matter.[102] On December 22, the parties finally reached a settlement in court that *Letste nayes* would continue circulating as usual, any joint property would be sold, and the partnership would be dissolved.[103]

On February 7, 1956, *Yidishe tsaytung* appeared independently for the first time, taking the opportunity to announce the separation between Tsanin and

Hadash and to reprint the receiver's ruling.[104] Hadash published a full account of the split from his point of view in the paper's weekend issue.[105]

As an independent periodical, *Yidishe tsaytung* consisted of only two pages of news and appeared three times a week. Nonetheless, its editor aspired to make it a daily and so started another newspaper, *Folksblat*, which appeared three times a week following the pattern of *Letste nayes*.[106] The paper closed after only three months, and *Yidishe tsaytung* returned to appearing thrice weekly, until in 1958 it was forced to cut back and become a weekly.

Although the partnership with Hadash had been dismantled, Zeitouni and Tsanin remained partners in *Letste nayes* until 1960.[107] Tsanin's new paper *Yidishe tsaytung*, which had replaced the *Yidishe prese*, came out under that title for some three months. Issue number 33, which came out April 28, 1956, appeared with a new title, *Hayntike nayes* (Today's news), the name of another Yiddish newspaper that came out in Warsaw in the interwar years.[108] Its publisher and license holder was—as had been the case with *Yidishe prese*—Dora (Deborah) Tsanin, Mordechai Tsanin's wife.[109] That situation lasted until the end of August 1959, when *Letste nayes* was finally permitted to become a daily and *Hayntike nayes* stopped appearing.

As we have seen, the titles of Tsanin's newspapers, including *Letste nayes* and *Hayntike nayes*, were drawn from the world of the Yiddish press. In this way, Tsanin situated his journalistic endeavors in Israel as a continuation of the world of Yiddish that had perished in the Holocaust. However, his newspapers were also a quintessential part of the new Israeli reality. This was achieved not by the papers' titles but by their content.

Israeli Politics, Yiddish, and Eastern European Jewish Memory: The Contents of *Letste nayes*

In terms of its structure and contents, *Letste nayes* looked like any other Israeli newspaper. Although it initially came out only once a week, it was still designed like a daily and retained that format for many years. The first issues had six or eight pages, depending on how much paper the publisher had managed to get his hands on. The first pages contained the news, political and financial, as well as op-eds. As in the Hebrew-language press, the news pages dealt mainly with matters related to the state of Israel and the Middle East,[110] focusing on the austerity regime then in effect in Israel, and the liquidation of the Diaspora through immigration to Israel.[111] Some of the columns were more similar to those found in the prewar Yiddish press: one section for women and household issues and one for medicine and popular science, as well as a chess column, and the crowning glory—a section on literature, theater and art.[112] There was also a selection of readers' letters and humor pieces.¹¹³ Nonetheless, *Letste nayes* had some qualities all its own that set it apart from both the Hebrew newspapers and the run-of-the-mill immigrant press.

As a paper whose readership consisted of people "immigrating home," it was not enough for *Letste nayes* just to help them integrate into Israel. Neither was its goal simply to help them consolidate as a distinct group within Israeli society. In fact, *Letste nayes* quickly became the voice of Yiddish-speaking Holocaust survivors within Israeli society and acted, among other things, to preserve the memory of eastern European Jewry and make it part of Israeli culture and Jewish historical memory.¹¹⁴ To achieve these goals, it had to become an interesting and relevant newspaper with its own unique voice.

First and foremost, it had to establish itself as an integral part of Israeli life. Tsanin's editorials were essential to this effort, which soon won a name for themselves outside the world of Yiddish. Always sharp and well written, these articles criticized government decisions and actions across a whole range of fields. These included immigrant housing,¹¹⁵ the segregated nature of Israeli education (which was split into a number of different "streams"),¹¹⁶ and even economic policy.¹¹⁷ While it was immigrant housing that mostly aroused Tsanin's ire,¹¹⁸ a great deal of his criticism was aimed directly at the prime minister, Ben-Gurion. This started as early as the second issue of *Letste nayes*, whose editorial attacked Ben-Gurion for his attitude toward Diaspora Jewry, and reached its peak during the Sinai Campaign of 1956¹¹⁹ and the Wadi Salib riots in 1959, during which Tsanin also sharply criticized the police.¹²⁰

Tsanin did not limit himself to expressing his opinions only in the editorials. He also printed a weekly column of political satire, entitled *Fun vokh tsu vokh, shabesdike shmuesn* (From one week to another, Shabbat conversations), which dealt with the same issues raised in the editorials but in a humorous way.¹²¹ He mocked the government and its ministers,¹²² the transit camps,¹²³ and relations between immigrants and old-timers in Israel.¹²⁴ He did not even spare the 1956 Sinai Campaign, which he called a "frivolous undertaking."¹²⁵

Tsanin's tone unquestionably reflected his forceful personality. But there was another factor at play. The criticism in *Letste nayes* was not ideological in nature. Tsanin wrote like a family member, clued in to everything happening at home but critical of the way it was being handled. Among the country's leaders, as well as in journalistic circles, Tsanin's tone earned him the reputation of an opposition figure, but it positioned *Letste nayes* as an institution that was part and parcel of Israeli society and as such had a right to criticize it.

Naturally, *Letste nayes* also had other elements aimed at its specific readership. Most important of these was the section on literature and culture. From its very first issue, *Letste nayes* had devoted a large section—relative to its size—to literature, theater, and art. Initially, its emphasis was on connecting readers to Hebrew culture. The paper printed translations of Hebrew literature, starting with the writing of Aharon Ashman, who was known as a radical "Hebraist,"[126] as well as articles on literature[127] and theater reviews from the Hebrew stage.[128] However, it was not long before *Letste nayes* began to turn to Yiddish literature, publishing an original serial novel and replacing Yiddish translations of Hebrew literature with original Yiddish writing. It tended to showcase the work of Yiddish writers who lived in Israel, some of whom had already published in the prestigious *Di goldene keyt*.[129]

Still, the paper's literary section was not aimed only at intellectuals with an interest in literature; it also reached out to the broader audience interested in Yiddish-language culture. For them, it provided general book reviews,[130] information about events connected to Yiddish-language culture (such as the visits in Israel of important figures from the world of Yiddish),[131] and news of Yiddish plays being performed in Hebrew translation.[132] In addition a section, "Fun altn oyster" (From the old treasure house), reprinted popular Yiddish literature, drawn mainly from eastern European Jewish folklore.

Keeping alive the memory of east European Jewry and particularly the Holocaust was one of *Letste nayes*'s major aims. Before the Eichmann trial in 1961, the Holocaust filled a very small space in the public memory in Israel.[133] For example, though the Knesset designated the twenty-seventh of the Hebrew month Nissan as Holocaust Remembrance Day in 1951, it did not become law until 1959.[134] The Hebrew press, too, devoted very little space to Holocaust issues.

Letste nayes was different. It published articles about the Holocaust and reviews of the scant literature about the Holocaust that appeared in those years.[135] However, it went even further and devoted space to printing detailed testimonies. On March 31, 1950, on the eighth anniversary of the Warsaw ghetto uprising, *Letste nayes* devoted two pages to the rebellion and to life in Warsaw before the war. One whole page was given over to an article on the uprising by Rachel Auerbach a writer, essayist, and historian who had survived the Holocaust in Warsaw.[136] In the middle of the page, a full-length column showed a memorial candle followed by text in memory of the victims of the ghetto, especially the fighters. "We will never forget," it read. "We will remember them all and will tell our children and our grandchildren about the heroism of the Jewish uprising in the Warsaw ghetto."[137]

Letste nayes, then, was not just another Yiddish paper. It was a complex combination of many things. It was a quality newspaper in the best traditions of the Yiddish press; it was also an Israeli paper deeply engaged in issues of the day, often with a strong oppositional slant, and it served too as a "realm of memory" for Holocaust survivors. It was this unique mix that made *Letste nayes* a significant, even powerful presence in the Israeli journalistic arena.

"The Difference between Foreign Language and Yiddish": The Knesset and the Government on the Foreign-Language Press and the Yiddish Press

The Ministry of the Interior was quite aware of the fact that *Letste nayes* was circumventing its refusal to license it as a daily by appearing as two papers that each came out three times a week. In fact, *Letste nayes* was not the only foreign-language newspaper to employ that tactic. Two Polish-language newspapers did so, and later other papers in Yiddish followed suit. For its part, the ministry looked for ways to stop all the newspapers, particularly *Letste nayes*, from appearing as they did.[138] However, Tsanin was not so easily deterred and, in the course of a long and detailed correspondence, managed to persuade the ministry's officials to see his newspapers as two separate projects.[139]

The Ministry of the Interior and its officials were not the only ones who knew about this stratagem. Government ministers, Knesset members, and even journalists in the Hebrew-language press were well aware of it, too. The ministry's policy was not to cancel the licenses of existing newspapers but to take steps to restrict them; new papers, on the other hand, were often denied a license.[140] Tsanin managed to get around these problems, too. Following the breakup of the partnership with *Yidishe tsaytung*, he requested—and received—a license for his new paper, *Hayntike nayes*, and no steps were taken to impede the publication of the two newspapers that actually made up one daily.

Nonetheless, the issue of the foreign-language press still remained a major concern, not just for the government and its officials but for various public figures and journalists, all of whom sought ways to restrict it. Since the press ordinance laid down clear-cut conditions for the granting of a license to publish a newspaper, no one who met them could be denied.[141] The opponents of the foreign-language press had to come up with a different strategy if they wanted to curb these papers and restrict their activity.

There were two major groups opposed to the spread of the non-Hebrew press. First, Hebrew journalists and editors viewed it as a serious competitor, and second, government ministers and Knesset members, but they were much less enthusiastic about the campaign. In other words, members of the press who had the power to influence public opinion were very much in favor of restrictive legislation, while members of the Knesset and government ministers were not as keen about the idea of creating such laws.[142]

The rhetoric both groups used focused on the importance of encouraging the use of Hebrew and the negative influence the non-Hebrew press had on it. At the end of 1952, however, the director of the department for the inculcation of Hebrew in the Ministry of Education proposed the idea of involving the foreign-language newspapers in this endeavor. The plan was to have the foreign-language papers include a twice-weekly column with a short lesson in Hebrew. The complete proposal in all its detail was brought before the editors of the foreign-language press at a meeting held at the end of September of that year, and they all reacted favorably.[143] It was not the first time that the idea of including a Hebrew section in those newspapers had been broached, either as a means of recruiting them in the effort to encourage the spread of Hebrew or as a form of restriction. Though nothing came of those proposals, they refused to disappear. Over the next two years, as public opposition to the foreign-language press grew greater, the idea of a law requiring those papers to include Hebrew translations became increasingly popular, a move that would have greatly increased their production costs and so created serious hardships for their owners.

As noted earlier, since the end of 1953, the minister of education, Ben-Zion Dinur, and the Supreme Council for Culture had tended to prefer using administrative measures to encourage the spread of Hebrew rather than passing laws to restrict the use of foreign languages. In this spirit, Dinur declared the seventh year after the establishment of the state, beginning from May 1954, as the year of "Imparting Hebrew."[144] The project began in August of that year.[145] What it involved in practice was a broad program of Hebrew teaching, largely by volunteers, under the slogan "The whole people will teach, the whole people will learn."[146] The government approved a detailed plan of action for the year, including an appeal to the foreign-language press to print Hebrew lessons and even to give major news items in Hebrew.[147]

It was only natural for the Hebrew press to give wide coverage to such an important national initiative. As part of it, a number of journalists, some of them very senior, took the opportunity to criticize the foreign-language newspapers as an obstacle to the spread of Hebrew and to call for a law that would force them to include Hebrew sections. The number of articles on the issue soon began to grow, and their authors hammered home the point that the foreign-language press was slowing down the integration of the new immigrants into Israeli society. Some went as far as to claim that the content of these newspapers was inconsistent with the national narrative and was sometimes even encouraging people to leave the country.[148] David Giladi, a leading journalist, bluntly called the foreign-language press an "anti-nationalist" element.[149] Interestingly, the discussion dealt with the foreign-language papers as a whole, barely even mentioning the Yiddish press in general or *Letste nayes* in particular.[150]

Although many of the writers admitted that in a country of immigration a foreign-language press was a genuine necessity, they still called on authorities to restrict it, by denying licenses to new papers and forcing every such paper to print a full Hebrew translation of its contents.[151] These were not new demands, as noted earlier, and had even been proposed in an editorial in *Maariv* written by its highly esteemed editor, Dr. Ezriel Carlebach.[152]

One thing that was new in the 1954 offensive against the foreign-language press was the use of economic arguments.[153] The writers of these articles noted that non-Hebrew papers were much more profitable than their Hebrew counterparts since their production costs were lower: they employed fewer writers, and much of their content consisted of translations from the Hebrew press. That made them—according to those articles—simply Hebrew newspapers in translation, so reading them saved the immigrant the need to buy a Hebrew paper. In other words, the foreign-language press was being cast as competition for the Hebrew-language press.[154]

Government officials had been preoccupied with the question of the foreign-language press from the time it had begun to develop. Throughout the 1950s, surveys and statistical studies were conducted to discover the number of foreign-language newspapers in Israel, the size of their readership, and their circulation. These were largely made by the Ministries of the Interior and Education, at the request sometimes of the ministers and sometimes of civil servants.[155] Still the strongest pressure on Knesset members to pass laws restricting the foreign-language press came not from within the government and its officials but from the journalists and editors of Hebrew newspapers.

Early in 1954, the Association of Hebrew Journalists established the Press Committee for Imparting Hebrew, chaired by Dr. Ezriel Carlebach. Its main goal was to limit the foreign-language press, and to that end it put together a detailed memorandum that surveyed the situation of that press, its circulation, and its readership. The conclusion it reached, not surprisingly, was that the non-Hebrew press was a significant impediment to the acquisition of Hebrew by the Israeli public and also hindered the integration of new immigrants into Israeli culture. To solve the problem, it suggested making several changes in the press ordinance, primarily to force every foreign-language newspaper to print a complete Hebrew translation of its contents and to rescind the license of any that failed to do so.[156]

In addition to this, a large part of the memorandum dealt with the competition that the foreign-language press presented to the Hebrew press. It included a detailed calculation of the lower production costs of the foreign-language papers compared to their Hebrew counterparts and the higher prices they were sold at. The memorandum also noted that the overall circulation of all non-Hebrew papers taken together was identical to that of all Hebrew papers and that at least some of their readers were not newcomers to Israel.[157]

A second memorandum by the committee dealt with the question of how to make the foreign-language press "a vehicle for citizenship in the state." It suggested three possible solutions, one of which was to make all foreign-language newspapers completely bilingual. This memorandum also reflected, albeit less blatantly than its predecessor, the Hebrew press's economic interest in the abolition of the foreign-language press.[158] Both memoranda were circulated among all the government ministers and Knesset members, but it seems that they aroused little enthusiasm for restricting the foreign-language press through legislation.

On January 6, 1954, Shalom Zysman, a Knesset member from the General Zionist Party, submitted a motion for the agenda to discuss the "spread of foreign-language periodicals in the country." Although he stated that the foreign-language press did not pose a real danger to the Hebrew language, he claimed that it slowed the pace of the "cultural absorption" of new immigrants and did not allow them to develop culturally, adding that its primary function was easy profit for its publishers.[159] The minister of the interior, Israel Rokach, agreed that it made some sense to restrict the foreign-language newspapers but showed no real desire to take any practical action.[160] In fact, in a conversation with a journalist from *Maariv* a few days before that debate, Rokach had said that he preferred improving the dissemination of Hebrew to restricting the foreign-language press.[161]

Attempts to pass a law restricting the foreign-language press caused great consternation among Yiddish writers in Israel. They viewed it as an attack on Yiddish and did their best to exclude Yiddish from the general category of foreign-language newspapers. In addition to the furious reactions in the Yiddish press, which called these proposals *gzeyres*,[162] the representatives of the Association of Yiddish Writers and Journalists applied to the minister of the interior, asking him to remove Yiddish from the list of foreign languages:[163] "The Association of Yiddish Writers in Israel is gravely concerned about the news that the government is planning to include Yiddish, the language of the people massacred in the Holocaust, in a law against foreign languages," the letter stated.[164] In reality, Knesset members and government ministers were in no hurry to pass a law against the foreign-language press, and they also noted explicitly that any restrictions on the foreign-language press would not apply to Yiddish.

Another motion for the agenda concerning the foreign-language press was submitted to the Knesset in May of that year. This time it was Knesset member Israel Bar-Yehuda of the Mapam party who proposed it. His motion was entitled "A Law for the Inculcation of the Hebrew Language (Publications)" and had two parts. Its main proposal was that every foreign-language newspaper be required by law to print part of its content in Hebrew translation.[165]

This time Minister Rokach reacted at greater length, focusing on two things in particular. First, he emphasized that the Israeli education system and the passage of time would do far more to encourage the spread of Hebrew than any law restricting foreign languages. Second, he made it clear that Yiddish and Judeo-Spanish were not to be put in the same category as other languages.[166]

The question of the foreign-language press was raised in a special cabinet meeting devoted to the topic in December 1954. The reason for the meeting was an upcoming Knesset discussion over the motions for the agenda on this issue that had been put off time after time.[167] In the final vote, the majority supported introducing legislation that would make it mandatory for the foreign-language press to include a Hebrew translation of 10 percent of its content, but things were not as clear-cut as they might seem.[168] First, the amount of Hebrew translation had been cut to just 10 percent, minimizing the damage to the newspapers. Second, even that small restriction passed only by a whisker, seven in favor and six against—barely 50-percent support. Third, and most importantly here, several of the ministers made it absolutely clear that a distinction had to be made between Yiddish and foreign languages.

There were two major voices who supported the new legislation. Pinhas Lavon, the minister of defense, and Golda Meir, the minister of labor, both of Mapai, used the term "foreign-language press" to refer just to the Yiddish press. Both compared the Yiddish newspapers in Israel to those in New York and noted that several of those in New York also printed a column in English, with no adverse effects. As a result, they felt no reason to oppose the addition of a column or a full page in Hebrew to the Yiddish newspapers.[169] On the other side, Joseph Burg, the minister of postal services and a senior member of the national religious HaPoel HaMizrachi Party, emphasized that Yiddish was a special language and still played a role in connecting Israel and the Diaspora. Even the prime minister, Moshe Sharett, went on the record as saying that "there is extreme sensitivity as regards Yiddish" and suggested that the Yiddish press merited special treatment.[170]

Still, the figure who spoke in favor of Yiddish most loudly and clearly was the minister of the interior, Israel Rokach. He expressed opposition to any legislation that would force non-Hebrew newspapers to include texts in Hebrew, pointing out that the number of foreign-language newspapers was not on the rise and that not only did they not impede the spread of Hebrew, but they were absolutely essential to older immigrants who, due to their age, found it difficult to learn the language. He also twice expressed his opinion that "a distinction should be made between foreign languages and Yiddish" and that "the attitude to Yiddish should be different . . . more liberal."[171] He did not provide a clear explanation for his stance, merely saying that Yiddish was closer to the hearts of its speakers than other languages.

In the end, despite the vote, the press ordinance was not amended. Officials at the Ministry of the Interior continued trying to discuss with the editors of the foreign-language newspapers some kind of agreement about including a Hebrew section in their papers but made no further attempts to introduce new legislation on the issue.[172]

It seems quite clear that one reason why the Knesset members never took seriously the attempts to pass laws restricting the foreign-language press was the fact that it never presented a real obstacle to the spread of Hebrew. More than that, during the years of the mass immigration, it had actually proved helpful in the absorption of the new immigrants. But there was also another reason, one that was explicitly mentioned both in some of the debates and in the press.[173] It turned out that many politicians had no opposition to the existence of the foreign-language press in general and the Yiddish press in particular. In fact, they had good reason to promote it as a way of reaching out to the new immigrants. Closer examination reveals that many of the Yiddish newspapers were actually published by political parties, including Mapai itself.

Israel's Political Parties and the Yiddish Press

During the 1950s, about one hundred newspapers and periodicals in Yiddish were created in Israel. Some were very short-lived, while others came out for several years, even several decades. In all, from 1948 to 1970, an average of between twenty and thirty Yiddish newspapers and periodicals were published in Israel every year.

Only a small number of these—most important among them, *Letste nayes*—were privately owned. In most of those cases, the owners were new immigrants, sometimes Holocaust survivors, who had been journalists or newspaper editors in the past and wanted to renew in Israel the publication of an older paper. One example of this was the biweekly *Yidishe bilder*, which was first published in Israel in 1958 as a continuation of the monthly with the same name that had come out in the displaced-persons camp in Munich after the Holocaust. In other cases, the papers were published by such organizations as Brit Avoda—the Bund in Israel, which published the monthly *Lebns-fragn*, which eventually became the last Yiddish newspaper to continue appearing in Israel, well into the twenty-first century. There were also editors of private Hebrew papers who published them in separate Yiddish editions. A good example of this was Uri Avnery who, in 1954, published *Veltshpigl*, a Yiddish version of his sensational, antiestablishment magazine, *HaOlam Haze,* in an attempt to reach out to the new immigrants from Eastern Europe.[174]

However, these privately owned newspapers were in the minority. The overwhelming majority of publications in Yiddish were published by public organizations and institutions, such as the Histadrut, or by the political parties, who were interested in reaching out to the new immigrants, as well as to those old-timers who read Yiddish.[175] This helps emphasize the fact that throughout the 1950s the Yiddish-speaking public was regarded as highly literate, which made it attractive to publishers looking for political or financial gain. Of course, to attract that audience and hold its attention, these papers had to be of a high quality, providing a range of content, including literary and cultural material. In paradoxical fashion, then, many of the same people and organizations that were opposed to Yiddish for ideological reasons actually contributed to the development of a vibrant Yiddish press in Israel.

Many of the earliest Yiddish newspapers in Israel were published by organizations with a radical left orientation that had traditionally promoted the Yiddish press. The first of these was *Fray Yisroel: Demokratisher vokhnshrift far politik, virtshaft un kultur* (Free Israel: a democratic weekly for politics, economics and culture), which came out from 1948 to 1964; though not officially connected to the Communist Party, its stance was communist in nature. The second was *Yisroel—Bleter fun ikhud olami (TS"S) hitakhdut,* published by the socialist-Zionist political movement whose name it carried (i.e., TS"S hitakhdut). It began to appear in 1949 and featured articles on current affairs, a few on Jewish issues and Jewish history, and one article—the last in every issue—that dealt with theater, literature, or art. It was published at irregular intervals until 1954, first as a monthly and later more infrequently.

However, political movements with a tradition of using or supporting the Yiddish press were not the only ones to publish Yiddish newspapers in Israel. The country's hegemonic political parties also soon became aware of the importance of the Yiddish-reading public as a target for their propaganda. The first of these was the ruling party, Mapai.

On January 7, 1949, even before the publication of the first issue of *Letste nayes,* Mapai began to bring out its own newspaper in Yiddish, *Dos vort.* The title was a precise translation of *Davar,* the name of the Histadrut's flagship daily that was identified by the public as the paper of Mapai. *Dos vort* actually started as a piece of party propaganda produced for the elections to the Constituent Assembly that were held on January 25 of that year. Each issue carried the heading "Onetime Edition," and alongside its logo, the letter aleph appeared, reminding readers that was Mapai's sign on the ballot sheet. As part of the party's campaign in the country's first election, *Dos vort* reflected the tension between it and its main competitor—Mapam, the Marxist socialist-Zionist party. "Once the State of Israel was created, Mapam ought to have disbanded," was a subheading on the second page of the second issue.[176]

After the elections, *Dos vort* did not close but continued to come out twice a week for almost two years, gradually becoming a regular Yiddish newspaper rather than just a party propaganda platform. In mid-February 1951, *Dos vort*, now expanded in size to six pages and featuring photographs, began to appear three times a week on Wednesdays, Thursdays, and Fridays.[177] Another sign of its character as a regular Yiddish paper came in January 1952, when it began to print a serial novel about life in Paris under the Nazis. Thus it came about that Mapai, whose leaders held the reins of power in Israel and spearheaded the country's militant Hebraistic policy, was actually the first public body in Israel to publish a Yiddish newspaper.

About eighteen months later, Mapai decided to set up a second Yiddish paper, *Di tsayt*, which would also come out three times a week.[178] In fact, it was not meant to be a new paper at all. *Di tsayt* was going to come out on Sundays, Mondays, and Tuesdays and so complement *Dos vort*. Together, they would form a full-scale daily. Its front page carried a notice informing readers that *Di tsayt* and *Dos vort* were together a single daily paper, edited by the same editorial committee and with the participation of the same writers.[179] So even before Tsanin adopted the idea of making a daily out of two papers appearing three times a week, Mapai, Israel's ruling party, had done so openly and unashamedly.

The combined newspaper *Dos vort–Di tsayt* lasted only a few months. However, in February 1957, Mapai began to publish a new Yiddish periodical. It was the weekly *Yisroel tog ayn tog oys—vokhnblat far gezelshaftlekhe, politishe, ekonomishe un kultur problemen* (Israel day by day—a weekly on social, political, economic, and cultural problems). Although it was meant to serve the interests of Mapai, it did so in a subtle and sophisticated way and was published in magazine format with a whole range of articles and many photographs. While it printed articles on Hebrew culture in Israel[180] and gave a lot of space to Yiddish literature and culture,[181] most of its content was of contemporary interest and put a positive spin on the achievements of the state, and so, without actually saying as much, it cast a favorable light on Mapai's leadership of the country. Editorials on current political issues and supporting Mapai explicitly appeared only rarely.[182]

Yisroel tog ayn tog oys never managed to become a weekly. It came out irregularly—usually once a month—for its first six months and then more regularly, twice a month. It closed after two years. However, the front page of the last issue in February 1959 announced that a new weekly, *Di vokh* (The week), would soon appear, boasting that it would be an "illustrated weekly in Yiddish like the most modern European newspapers . . . something new in the Yiddish press, a surprise for the Yiddish reader in the State of Israel and the Jewish world."[183] The first issue of *Di vokh* came out in March 1959; the last, a year later.

Though none of the other parties matched Mapai's level of activity in Yiddish publishing, two tried their hand. The General Zionist Party began publishing a Yiddish newspaper in early July 1950. It was called *Unzer haynt* (Our today) and was edited by Haim Levanon—a party leader, one of the founders of the party's Hebrew newspaper *HaBoker*, and a member of the Tel Aviv municipality council. The newspaper started its life in July 1950 as a small-scale weekly—with current news, political pieces, and a few ads. About nine months later, it began to come out three times a week, on Mondays and Wednesdays in a one-sheet format (two pages) and on Fridays at twice that size.

On September 1, 1953, on the day when *Yidishe tsaytung*, the paper that supplemented *Letste nayes*, appeared and two weeks after *Di tsayt* appeared alongside *Dos vort*, a supplementary paper for *Unzer haynt* also began to published under the title *Unzer fraynt* (Our friend). As with *Di tsayt*, *Unzer fraynt* was presented as an expansion of *Unzer haynt* into a daily paper. *Unzer haynt–unzer fraynt a teglekhe yidishe tsaytung* (Our today–our friend: a Yiddish daily) was how it was put on the front page of the first issue on September 1, 1953. The joint paper would continue under the existing editorial board, which had taken a series of steps to ensure that it would be a "fine, modern, vibrant, and popular" newspaper. It would also appear in an extended format with sections on literature and the arts, legal advice, and medical issues; there would also be a chess column and the like. Levanon, who had in the meantime been elected mayor of Tel Aviv, was replaced as chief editor of the two papers by B. Zilberberg. Among its contributors, the new joint daily could boast many leading journalists from the Hebrew press, and it also serialized Yitzhak Perlov's important novel *Jabalia*.[184] All this was squeezed into a publication that consisted of only four pages during the week and ten on the weekend.[185]

Unzer haynt–unzer fraynt existed as a daily for only five months. In January 1954, it returned to the weekly format under its original title, *Unzer haynt*, remaining in that format for another year and a half. In all, it appeared for about five years, during which time it played a major role in enriching Yiddish-language culture in Israel and contributing to its vitality and growth. In mid-1954 Mapam also jumped on the bandwagon and began to bring out a publication called *Oyf der vakh*, an exact Yiddish translation of *Al HaMishmar*, the Hebrew paper of the Ha'shomer Ha'tza'ir movement that was connected to Mapam. During its first year, *Oyf der vakh* appeared as a series of onetime issues that dealt with, among other things, Yiddish literature and culture and Israeli culture, too. This was not a lowbrow, popular publication.[186]

In early 1955 *Oyf der vakh* got a license to appear as a weekly, and it appeared in that format until May 1956, when it closed.[187] A year later, Mapam started a new weekly, entitled *Yisroel shtime—vokhnblat far gezelshaftlekhe, politishe un kultur problemen* (The voice of Israel—a weekly on social, political, and cultural problems).[188] Like the other Yiddish weeklies put out by the political parties, its goal was to bring high-quality Yiddish culture and essays on current affairs to the Yiddish readership.[189] And indeed, *Yisroel shtime* was in many ways similar to *Yisroel tog ayn tog oys* in both design and content.[190] *Yisroel shtime* appeared in that format until the end of 1967, when it began coming out once every two weeks. It eventually closed down in 1997, having been a monthly for its last decade.

Thus, by the end of the second Knesset (July 1955), all three large parties had begun publishing Yiddish newspapers. They were not the only public bodies to do so. During the first decade of the state, in addition to the Jewish Agency, two women's organizations started to issue their own newspapers in Yiddish—*Heym* (Home), published by Mo'etzet Ha'po'alot (connected to Mapai) and *Froyen buletin*, put out by the Organization of Democratic Women in Israel, which was a Communist organization.[191]

However, while Tsanin's motivation in opening *Letste nayes* stemmed from his interest in Yiddish literature and Yiddish-language culture in general, the political parties had totally different goals. They wanted to reach out to Yiddish readers to make them supporters of their parties. More importantly, they wanted their votes on election day. To this end, basic propaganda materials were not enough; the Yiddish readership needed quality newspapers to be swayed. This, however, led to some tension with *Letste nayes*, which also adopted a political stance but one that was often in opposition to the ruling government, sometimes in extremely harsh tones. Little wonder, then, that the ruling party, Mapai, invested much time and energy, not to mention resources, in finding ways to deal with the Yiddish newspapers in general and with *Letste nayes* in particular.

From Opposition to Establishment: Mapai Purchases *Letste nayes*

As the hegemonic party that led the state from its establishment until 1977, Mapai was deeply committed to its official linguistic policy and to strengthening the Hebrew language. However, at the same time, it needed to consolidate, if not strengthen, its position of power in Israeli society, particularly at election time. The most important and effective way to control public opinion during those years was undoubtedly the written press.

In the state's first decades, the newspapers owned and run by the political parties formed the backbone of the Hebrew press.[192] Their main aims were not only to expand the circle of the parties' supporters but also to reach out to the unaffiliated readership.[193] Mapai ascribed enormous importance to the written press and, of all Israel's political parties, controlled the highest number of papers. Alongside the daily *Davar*, published by the Histadrut but identified with Mapai and supportive of its positions, Mapai itself published the daily *Ha'dor*, as well as the weeklies *Ashmoret*, *Ha'po'el Ha'tza'ir*, and *Ha'molad*.[194] With the exception of *Ha'molad*, none of these publications were profitable, but Mapai saw them as essential and so went on bringing them out regardless.[195]

When mass immigration began in the late 1940s, Mapai sought ways to reach out to the new immigrants. It started publishing party bulletins in ten different languages, including Yiddish and Judeo-Spanish (Ladino). Some of these publications—especially those in Bulgarian and Serbo-Croatian—were successful; others failed. Prominent among the latter was the one in Yiddish—*Dos vort*.

In April 1950, a discussion was held at the Mapai headquarters on the party's foreign-language newspapers, during which the attitude of the party to Yiddish and its readers, as well as its interest in the Yiddish press, was made clear. Based on the estimate of the secretary-general of the party, Zalman Aharonowitz-Aran, the Yiddish readership in Israel at the time numbered about a hundred thousand.[196] The most popular Yiddish papers were *Letste nayes* and *Nayvelt*, both of which were hostile toward Mapai. Consequently, the party decided to bring out its own Yiddish newspaper to impart its views to Yiddish readers, but the newspaper they founded, *Dos vort*, had a hard time competing with those two papers and attracting readers.

The participants in the discussion at Mapai headquarters understood well that their paper was unsuccessful not due to its political message but because of its journalistic quality. The fact that the Yiddish readership could distinguish between a quality newspaper and a propaganda pamphlet was very clear to the leaders of Mapai. They were therefore quite anxious to find a way of getting the party's message to those readers via the press despite the problems involved. The leaders of Mapai, then, did not even consider the possibility of trying to halt the publication of the existing Yiddish papers; they were inclined to instead start their own newspapers of a high enough standard to compete with them.

This was not a simple matter at all. In addition to the financial investment involved, a professional team that could bring out a quality paper of the required standard to break into the market had to be put together. Finding good writers was not too difficult. The tough job was to find an editor. The first name raised was that of Dr. Meir (Marc) Dvorjetski, the well-known physician from the Vilna ghetto, but it did not work out.[197] Mapai continued to publish *Dos vort* and even added a weekly, *Bleter far oylim—Alim la'olim*, which ran for about ten months from July 1949 to April 1950.

In 1952, Mapai founded the United Printing Company in Israel as a party printing house.[198] After five years it changed its name to Pirsumim (Publications) and became an independent affiliated publisher that printed mainly foreign-language newspapers, including all of Mapai's foreign-language publications.[199] In the meantime, *Dos vort* seems to have closed in 1953, and for a while it might have seemed as if the press landscape was going to change.[200]

In the first half of the 1950s, huge waves of new immigrants arrived in Israel. These people were not guaranteed to support Mapai, and the party was constantly looking for ways to win their votes.[201] However, many of the immigrants were from North Africa and were described by the Mapai leadership as a public that "does not read, and certainly does not buy newspapers."[202] So, in the run-up to the elections to the third Knesset, which took place in July 1955 after the Lavon affair and Ben-Gurion's return to the party leadership following a brief period of retirement at Sede-Boker, Mapai did not even discuss the issue of the foreign-language press.[203] It was not until 1957 that it returned to the party agenda with a vengeance.

In January 1957, Tsanin founded a new Yiddish periodical, an illustrated weekly entitled *Tsanins yidishe ilustrirte velt* (Tsanin's illustrated Jewish world), a sign of his very strong position in the world of Yiddish. Mapai had serious concerns about the paper because even though it focused mainly on entertainment, it at times expressed views that were, like those of *Letste nayes*, "not wanted" by the party.[204]

Within a month, in February 1957, Mapai, via Pirsumim, began to bring out *Yisroel tog ayn tog oys*, edited by Pesach Pyekatsh, a Yiddish journalist with experience from both prewar Poland and the state of Israel.[205] In fact, in early 1957, Mapai was publishing, with the help of the Pirsumim press, nine non-Hebrew weeklies (in Rumanian, French, Polish, Judeo-Spanish, Bulgarian, Hungarian, Arabic, Persian, and Yiddish).[206] In May of that year, a document summing up the situation of the foreign-language press in Israel was submitted to Giora Yoseftal, the secretary of Mapai. The document discussed two issues relevant to the Yiddish press: one was the efforts to improve the weekly *Yisroel tog ayn tog oys*, and the second was the status of *Letste nayes* and possible ways to reduce its hostility to Mapai.[207]

This attitude of Mapai to the Yiddish press, especially its efforts to publish Yiddish newspapers of its own, clearly exemplified the tension it felt between the struggle to maintain cultural hegemony by encouraging the development and spread of the Hebrew language and culture, on the one hand, and the ambition to maintain and even strengthen Mapai's political hegemony, on the other. It was to help achieve this second goal that the party needed to reach out to the new immigrants who read the non-Hebrew press. The Mapai leadership was well aware of the tension between its support for the state's cultural policy and its need to maximize its political standing. The chair of the party's foreign-press committee, set up in 1957, even mentioned it in a comprehensive report he submitted a year later: "The party should take into consideration . . . the political necessity of maintaining a foreign-language press to provide correct information," he wrote. "Publication of these papers in no way interferes with the efforts to encourage the use of Hebrew. On the contrary, . . . it seems . . . that by means of the foreign-language press . . . we will bring people closer to Hebrew than [we would if we] abandoned the immigrants to the rival newspapers."[208]

In the fall of 1957, Mapai decided to form the Committee for the Foreign-Language Press, to be headed by Moshe Kitron, a Poalei-Zion member and founder of the Dror movement in Argentina.[209] The committee's main task was to monitor the coverage of Mapai in the foreign-language press in Israel, gather information on the reading habits of the non-Hebrew readers, take steps to improve the party's existing non-Hebrew papers, and create more such periodicals if they were deemed necessary to meet the party's needs.

The members of the committee, especially its chairman, Kitron, were aware of the difficulties of establishing new papers—setting up editorial boards and developing readerships. They preferred acquiring existing papers, retaining, as far as possible, their editorial staff, and continuing to publish them in their original format. The only major change they wanted to make was to ensure that any content hostile to Mapai was removed and that content supportive of the party was published as much as possible.[210]

Although, in principle, the committee related equally to papers in all languages, as Kitron stated explicitly in a summary report he wrote before resigning from his position as chairman in March 1958,[211] the committee minutes show a clear preference for Yiddish papers. The Yiddish readership was described approvingly as an educated and literate group, well worthy of being provided with high-quality reading materials.[212] Unquestionably, one of the reasons for this was the fact that most of the Mapai leadership, including the members of the Committee for the Foreign-Language Press and their chairman, Kitron, were originally from Eastern Europe and so had warm feelings toward the Yiddish language, its culture, and its papers. However, the party's real motive for creating its own Yiddish newspaper was far more specific—to counter the influence of Tsanin and his papers, and this too was noted by

Kitron in his final report, which described *Letste nayes* as the leading foreign-language newspaper in Israel.

The significance for Mapai of competing with Tsanin can be seen in the history of the party weekly, *Yisroel tog ayn tog oys*. About a year after it began to appear, its editor, Pyekatsh, informed Mapai that his paper had made a name for itself as the best Yiddish paper in Israel and that it was serving the party in the best possible way by acting as a counterweight to Tsanin's papers and to those of Mapam.[213] A survey conducted by the editorial board in early 1958 found that the paper had about twenty-six thousand readers.[214] In actual fact, it was floundering. Although meant to be a weekly, it had for its first six months appeared only irregularly—between once and twice a month. So bad did the situation become that its publisher asked that its name, which meant "Israel day by day" be changed to *Yisroel bleter* (Israel pages).[215] On February 18, 1959, two years after it began to appear, the paper closed down, and Mapai decided to replace it with another Yiddish weekly, *Di vokh* (The week), also to be published by Pirsumim.

The elections of November 1959 brought the issue of the foreign-language press to the fore in party discussion once again. Mapai was at the peak of its influence and achieved its best elections results ever. Still, during the campaign, the Committee for the Foreign-Language Press kept a very close eye on the non-Hebrew papers, particularly on the writers who specialized in party matters.[216] It also brought out bulletins that were distributed as special supplements with some of the foreign-language newspapers.[217] It made a concerted effort to disseminate these bulletins through the Yiddish press—it had thousands distributed with its weekly, *Di vokh*, but more importantly reached an agreement with *Letste nayes* that it would distribute twenty thousand such bulletins to its readers.[218] *Letste nayes* also promised not to distribute the bulletins of any other party.[219] On the very eve of the elections, Mapai printed an additional pamphlet in Yiddish, entitled *Faktn* (Facts).[220]

The emphasis that Mapai put on *Letste nayes* during the election campaign is a clear sign of just how much importance it attributed to the paper. After the elections, in early 1960, Mapai held a discussion on "restraining *Letste nayes*." A memorandum sent by the Committee for the Foreign-Language Press to the party secretary signaled the new direction, noting that "there is a possibility for some type of partnership with Mr. Tsanin, and contacts have already been made in that regard."[221] And indeed, later that year (probably in June), Mapai arrived at an agreement with Mordechai Tsanin regarding the party's acquisition of *Letste nayes*.

The details of the transaction are rather obscure. The archives of Mapai, as well as those of Tsanin's personal papers available to scholars, do not mention it at all, and it seems that both parties had no interest in making the deal public knowledge.²²² The only written source that mentioned it was the Hebrew press, which reported in early May 1960 that Mapai had purchased *Letste nayes* from Tsanin for the sum of a quarter of a million Israeli pounds.²²³ The party itself probably did not want to have the paper labeled as a party publication for fear it might lose its influence. For his part, Tsanin denied the reports of the sale. In reply to a journalist's question, he said that he had sold a share in the newspaper to private investors who may in turn have sold it to Mapai. He also said that his partners in the paper had sold their shares too but did not specify to whom.²²⁴

It seems very likely that Tsanin wanted to conceal just how much he had received for the newspaper (the equivalent at the time of $139,000, an enormous sum in Israel). However, his main reason for wanting to keep the transaction out of the public eye can probably be found in an article printed in the Yiddish monthly *Lebns-fragn*, which never spared its criticism of anyone, not even Tsanin: "The last stronghold has fallen," declared the article dramatically. "Mapai has purchased *Letste nayes* from Tsanin. Tsanin denied it . . . so we kept quiet and waited. We did not want to believe it." It concluded, "What is left of the struggle Tsanin has kept up for years to preserve the importance of Yiddish [in Israel] and its rights? He is certainly not naïve enough to think that Mapai will continue it. Is everything permissible for the sake of doing 'business'?"²²⁵

Tsanin apparently did not feel comfortable with the sale to Mapai either; he certainly never acknowledged it until the day he died.²²⁶ However, the fears expressed by the *Lebns-fragn* turned out to be baseless. Under the auspices of Mapai and Pirsumim, *Letste nayes* continued to appear for another four decades. In 1995, Mapai sold the paper to a private businessman, and it continued coming out into the twenty-first century.²²⁷

Letste nayes was not the only Tsanin publication that the party wanted to control. On July 6, 1960, *Tsanins yidishe ilustrirte velt* merged with Mapai's *Di vokh*. The readers learned about the merger in an announcement printed in the newspaper. "To our readers," it read, "from this issue on, *Ilustrirte velt* will appear together with *Di vokh*, under the title *Ilustrirte velt vokh*. With a combined editorial board, it will become a top-notch family newspaper."²²⁸ Tsanin, who had previously been both publisher and editor, became "editor in chief," while the paper itself was edited by Yosef Magen, a writer and veteran member of Mapai. Though this seems to have been a genuine merger rather than a sale, it was still hushed up. I could not find any document about the merger in either the Mapai archives or Tsanin's personal papers.²²⁹ The weekly continued to appear unchanged until 1975, when Tsanin announced its closure due to a dramatic decline in readership.²³⁰

Tsanin did not leave *Letste nayes* after its sale, continuing as its editor until 1977, when he was replaced by Yitzhak Brat.²³¹ The change of ownership was never mentioned in the paper, which actually remained precisely the same as it had been before, with no changes of any sort. Only once, before the elections to the fifth Knesset in August 1961, did Mapai use it for the election campaign. These were the last elections during which Ben-Gurion headed the party, and things went badly. Still, a few weeks prior to the elections, *Letste nayes* came out with a kind of supplement entitled *Faroys: Far zikherheyt, demokratye, un oyfboy, dos vort fun mifleges poaley Erets Yisroel* (Forward: For security, democracy, and building, the word of the workers party in Israel). It resembled the paper *Dos vort*, from the 1950s, and like it, was simply election propaganda for Mapai.²³²

During the 1960s, the overall circulation of *Letste nayes* decreased compared to the previous decade, though it still remained high and could even match that of some Hebrew newspapers.²³³ On the other hand, the total number of Yiddish papers declined sharply. Most of the private newspapers founded in the 1950s had very short lives. The papers of the various political parties held out a little, but they too did not last long. *Unzer haynt–unzer fraynt*, of the General Zionist Party, folded in the mid-1950s; *Oyf der vakh*, of Mapam, also shut its doors and was replaced in 1958 by *Yisroel shtime*, which came out once every two weeks and sometimes even less frequently. Mapai also closed most of its newspapers and replaced them with *Letste nayes* but, as already noted, did not turn it to a party organ.

It seems that after the purchase of *Letste nayes* Mapai actually began to lose interest in the Yiddish press. Its leaders probably realized that the Yiddish readership was shrinking and so the influence of its press was declining. In addition, Tsanin moderated his critique. Ben-Gurion's resignation as prime minister and Tsanin's sense that he was now part of the Israeli establishment probably led him to see things in a less critical way.

At the end of the 1950s and during the 1960s, a number of new periodicals were published in Yiddish. Several were in the format of magazines that combined politics, society, and culture. The most prominent of these was *Tsanins ilustrirte velt* (and later *Ilustrirte velt vokh*), mentioned above, which was an illustrated weekly dedicated to Israeli society, politics, and art, as well as the Jewish world in general. It published many stories on culture, entertainment, and fashion but at the same time discussed current events, often quite critically, especially in the editorials.²³⁴ *Ilustrirte velt vokh* came out in this spirit until 1975.²³⁵

The other stable—and longest-lived—Yiddish publication in Israel was the monthly (sometimes bimonthly) *Lebns-fragn*, published by the Arbeter

Ring (Brit-Avoda) in Israel. Founded in 1951 it continued appearing regularly until 2014.

Letste nayes was, then, the only daily newspaper in Yiddish that came out in Israel for decades. Ironically, for most of its life it was published by Mapai, which meant that Israel's hegemonic political party enabled the existence of this long-lived Yiddish daily.

"The Carlebach of the Yiddish World" and the Secret of *Letste nayes*

To conclude the discussion here, three questions need to be answered: What enabled the number of Yiddish newspapers to grow in the 1950s? Why were most of these publications short-lived? And how did *Letste nayes* manage to survive for such a long time?

The Yiddish press in Israel began its life as an immigrant press, and the early Yiddish newspapers were classical immigrant institutions, encouraging integration into the new country. At the same time, however, they were also classical Yiddish newspapers, providing their readers with news from the world of Yiddish and Yiddish literature.

For all his importance, Tsanin was not alone in the world of the Yiddish press in Israel. Even before he started his journalistic endeavors, many Yiddish papers were being published in Israel, and during the 1950s this number grew further. The vibrant arena of Yiddish newspapers that developed encouraged others to start Yiddish newspapers. Some did so as a continuation of their careers in the Yiddish press from before they came to Israel; others, as a way of expanding the readership of Hebrew periodicals. The best example of the latter was Uri Avnery, who, as already mentioned, published in 1954 a Yiddish edition of his sensational weekly *HaOlam Haze*, under the title *Veltshpigl*.

In fact, Avnery's excursion into Yiddish publishing failed, and *Veltshpigl* folded after only ten weeks. Though this was presumably because the Yiddish audience did not want to read a typical Hebrew newspaper in Yiddish translation, it does raise the question why the other, more traditionally orientated Yiddish papers failed too.[236]

One possible cause often given to explain this is government policy aimed at putting an end to the use of Yiddish in Israel. However, on closer examination, this is not as clear-cut as was once thought. Certainly, the government's policy on licensing newspapers seems to have had only a minimal influence on the Yiddish press. The struggle to obtain a license, which could sometimes involve submitting multiple requests, was definitely a hurdle for the Yiddish newspapers, but not one they could not jump. In practice, all the Yiddish papers were granted licenses, and some even found ways to overcome the restriction of appearing as a daily.

The shortage of paper, on the other hand, was apparently a real obstacle. The Yiddish papers do seem to have been discriminated against in the allocation of newsprint, though some publishers managed to solve the problem by buying it on the black market.[237] Unfortunately, however, no reliable data regarding paper allocation from these years are available, so it is difficult to determine precisely how it affected the development of the Yiddish press.

Probably the most important factor that influenced the development of the Yiddish press in Israel was not connected with government policy but with the special character of immigrant society in Israel and its relations with the hegemonic authorities. The immediate target audience of the Yiddish press in Israel was the approximately two hundred thousand new immigrants that came to Israel from Eastern Europe during the state's first two years. Even when taken together with other Yiddish readers who had arrived in the country previously, this was too small a group to support the large number of publications that were initially set up.

In addition, most of the Yiddish-speaking immigrants were Holocaust survivors, more than half of them aged fifteen to twenty-nine. According to Hanna Yablonka, this population integrated into Israeli society rapidly and effectively and had a strong commitment to Zionist ideals.[238] The immigrants' drive toward integration, combined with the fact that no further great waves of Yiddish speakers reached the country, accelerated the integration processes that are typical of immigrant societies. These naturally meant that the Yiddish press, as an immigrant press, would have only a short life. If they were to survive in this overcrowded arena and acquire a loyal readership over time, it was not enough for the Yiddish papers simply to serve immigrants or satisfy a nostalgic yearning for the papers of the past. This task proved well beyond the capabilities of most Yiddish publications of the 1950s, 1960s, and beyond.

How then was *Letste nayes* different and what enabled it, even in the 1960s, to maintain a circulation that was higher than that of several Hebrew papers? First and foremost, it was a quality newspaper that knew how to strike the right balance between its various sections, and, just as important, it came out regularly, something most Yiddish papers did not manage to do. Beyond that, Tsanin seemed intuitively to understand how to adapt his newspaper to its target audience. While his previous publication, *Ilustrirter vokhnblat*, had devoted a lot of space to providing practical help for new immigrants in their daily lives, *Letste nayes* treated its readers as people who had "immigrated home," doing everything it could to make them an integral part of Israeli political and social discourse. It expressed clear-cut positions on current issues, not only those of relevance to new immigrants but also—in fact mainly—on those of central importance to the state of Israel. The editorials in *Letste nayes* were sharply critical of the government, giving the paper a unique voice of its own in the Israeli public arena. *Letste nayes* never stopped being a Yiddish newspaper, with a large section on Yiddish literature, reviews of the Yiddish theater or of Yiddish plays staged in the Hebrew theater, and articles about the Jewish world. However, above all, it made itself an Israeli institution—the voice of Yiddish-speaking Israelis.

The power of *Letste nayes* found expression in Tsanin's growing influence in the world of the Israeli press, while the strengthening of his status there in turn boosted *Letste nayes*. Among Hebrew-language journalists, he became known as "the Carlebach of the Yiddish world," a very complimentary comparison with Ezriel Carlebach, one of the leading editors of the Hebrew press and a very prominent journalist.[239] Tsanin was an active and respected member of the Israeli Journalists Association.[240] He was regularly invited on journalists' tours,[241] joined leading Hebrew newspapermen for interviews and press conferences, and, toward the end of the 1950s and the beginning of the 1960s, was also a member of the Editors Committee of the Hebrew Press.[242] All this, in addition to his preeminent status among Yiddish journalists, made him a figure of importance in the world of Israeli journalism and was ultimately a major factor in Mapai's decision to acquire his paper—a move that enabled *Letste nayes* to survive for more than five decades.

Nonetheless, a natural dynamic, typical of every immigrant society, came into play. Most Yiddish readers gradually went over to the Hebrew press and lost interest in the perspectives provided by a Yiddish paper. Though Mapai and its successor, the Labor Party, continued to publish *Letste nayes* as part of its regular activity, the paper's readership dwindled to just a very small group of those who remained, despite everything, loyal to Yiddish.

Notes

1. Yitzhak Luden, "Tsanin—meynt: Yidish, tsu Mordkhe Tsanins 100st geboyrntog," *Lebns-fragn* 641–642 (March–April 2006): 17.

2. *Nayvelt* was founded in 1934 as a biweekly and was issued at varying intervals until 1955 (two or three times a week and eventually once a week). On the Yiddish press in Palestine from its inception until 1934, see Arye L. Pilowsky, "Itonut Yidish be'Eretz Israel mi'tehilata ve'ad hofa'at *Nayvelt* 1934," *Katedra* 10 (1979): 72–101.

3. On this, see Cohen, *Sefer, sofer ve'iton*, 187–193. On the beginning of the Yiddish press in Eastern Europe, see Avraham Noverstern, *Ha'sifrut ve'ha'hayim, tzemihat sifrut Yidish ha'hadasha* (Tel Aviv: Open University, 2000), 27–28. On the restrictions placed by czarist Russia on Yiddish newspapers at the end of the nineteenth century, see Fishman, *Rise of Modern Yiddish Culture*, 21–25.

4. Jacob Glatstein, Shmuel Niger, and Hillel Rogoff, eds., *Finf un zibetsik yor yidishe prese in Amerike 1870–1945* (New York: Y. L. Peretz Farayn, 1945).

5. Stephan Harold Riggins, "The Media Imperative: Ethnic Minority Survival in the Age of Mass Communication," in *Ethnic Minority Media: An International Perspective*, ed. Stephan Harold Riggins (New York: Sage, 1992), 2–3.

6. Blau et al., "Ethnic Buffer Institutions," 20.

7. Olzak and West, "Ethnic Conflicts," 458–459; Leonard Dinnerstein and David Reimers, *Ethnic Americans: A History of Immigration* (New York: Columbia University Press, 2009).

8. Robert Ezra Park, *The Immigrant Press and Its Control* (New York: Harper and Brothers, 1922).

9. Carl Wittke, *The German Language Press in America* (Lexington: University of Kentucky Press, 1957), 2–3.

10. Hanna Arendt, *Essays in Understanding 1930–1945: Formation, Exile, and Totalitarianism*, ed. Jerome Kohn (New York: Harcourt Brace, 1994), 81–105.

11. Dan Caspi and Yehiel Limor, *Ha'metavchim: emtze'ei ha'tikshoret be'Israel 1948–1990* (Tel Aviv and Jerusalem: Am Oved and Machon Levi Eshkol, 1992), 49. See also Wittke, *German Language Press*, 3.

12. Morris Janowitz, *The Community Press in an Urban Setting: The Social Elements of Urbanism* (Chicago: University of Chicago Press, 1967), 19. See also Caspi and Limor, *Ha'metavchim*, 49.

13. For a theoretical discussion of this concept, see the introduction to this book.

14. Such as *Buletin fun prese byuro*, published by the Zionist Federation; *Di histadrut un di medine*, published by the Histadrut; *Di vokh in Erets-Yisroel*, published by the Jewish Agency; *Karneinu*, published by the Jewish National Fund; and others.

15. Such as *In der heym*, published by the Israel Defense Forces, and *La'olim*, published by Mapai.

16. According to Roberto Bachi, in 1948, Yiddish speakers were 11.7 percent of the Israeli population and almost half (46.7%) of the non-Hebrew speakers. In 1950, Yiddish speakers constituted 13.4 percent of the Israeli population and 33.3 percent of the non-Hebrew speakers. See Roberto Bachi, "Tehyat ha'lashon ha'Ivrit be'aspaklarya statistit," *Leshoneinu* 20 (1956): 75–76. Bachi also notes that while immigrants to Israel quickly abandoned such languages as Polish or Romanian, they did not give up Yiddish. According to Hanna Yablonka's calculations, Jewish displaced persons constituted 86 percent of immigrants to Israel in 1948. See Yablonka, *Ahim zarim*, 4.

17. On *Oyfgang, khoydesh shrift farn yungn yidishn vort*, see Cohen, *Sefer, sofer ve'iton*, 218.

18. Mordechai Tsanin, *Vivat lebn: novelen* (Warsaw: Shprayzn, 1933); Mordechai Tsanin, *Oyf zumpike erd* (Warsaw: Shprayzn, 1935).

19. Auerbach, Birnboin, Shulman Shtarkman, eds., *Leksikon fun der nayer yidisher literatur* (New York: Congress for Jewish Culture, 1968), vol. 7, 533.

20. Interview with Mordechai Tsanin, Tel Aviv, May 2000.

21. See, for example, *Nayvelt*, August 31, 1941, January 19, 1943; Mordechai Tsanin, *Vuhin geyt Yapan: reportazhn fun vaytn mizrekh* (Tel Aviv: Eeygns, 1942).

22. Mordechai Tsanin, *Iber shteyn un shtok: a rayze iber hundert khorev gevorene kehiles in Poyln* (Tel Aviv: Letste nayes, 1952).

23. For further information on Tsanin, see Abraham Liss, "Mordechai Tsanin—shtraykhn tsu zayn shafn," *Yerushalaymer almanakh* 25 (1995): 280–287; David Sephard, "Mordechai Tsanin," *Yidishe kultur* (September–October 1980): 33–37; Rachel Rojanski, "Tsanin," in *Leksikon heksherim le'sofrim isra'elim*, ed. Zissi Stavi and Yigal Schwartz (Or Yehudah: Kineret Zmora, Bitan-Dvir, 2014), 752–753.

24. "Ba'asefa ha'kelalit shel va'adat ha'orchim," *Maariv*, May 17, 1965; "Ba'tzibur," *Davar*, December 22, 1968.

25. On the stages of mass immigration in the first two years of Israel's existence, see Moshe Sikron, *Ha'aliya le'Israel 1948–1953* (Jerusalem: Falk Center for Statistical and Economic Research, 1957), 24–30.

26. HaOlam Haze was founded in 1937, by the journalist Uri Kesari, and focused on entertainment and cultural matters. In 1950 Uri Avnery and Shalom Cohen bought the weekly and changed its nature entirely.

27. *Ilustrirter vokhnblat* no. 4, August 6, 1948.

28. Almog, *Sabra*, 77.

29. This will be discussed broadly in chapter 5.

30. See, for example, "The editor has open office hours for the public every Tuesday between 10AM to 12PM in Shlomi Press, 29 Zvulun street, Tel Aviv," *Ilustrirter vokhnblat*, December 10 , 1948, back cover; *ibid.*, December 31, 1948, back cover.

31. Blau et al., "Ethnic Buffer Institutions," 21.

32. See for example (unsigned) "Yidish un Terkish," *Ilustrirter vokhnblat*, March 18, 1949, 11.

33. Mikhele Rosnboym, *Ondenk bukh fun Yisroel Khadash z"l* (Tel Aviv: Naye Lebn, 1973), 17–23.

34. Israel Hadash, "Vos iz geshen in *Letste nayes*?" *Yidishe tsaytung*, February 10, 1956. Yitzhak Luden also believed this was the case (correspondence with Yitzhak Luden, 2007).

35. "Tzav peruk le'hotza'at *Letste nayes*," *HaTzofe*, December 7, 1955; "Sichsuch bein ba'alei *Letste nayes*," *Davar*, December 18, 1955.

36. When he was almost one hundred years old, Tsanin recalled that the success of *Ilustrirter vokhnblat* had motivated him to turn it into a real newspaper that would gradually become a daily. Interview with Mordechai Tsanin, April 2005. Also, although Tsanin was fully lucid, time may have blurred his recollections or caused forgetfulness; his account must therefore be treated with great caution. Furthermore, as of 2000 I held several conversations with Tsanin, in which he never mentioned having had partners at *Letste nayes*.

37. Matzliah Zeitouni's son, Shlomo Zeitouni, believes that this was the case: he recalls that for his father, the Yiddish newspaper was a business venture that did not bear fruit (conversation with Shlomo Zeitouni, 2010). Attitudes toward the power of the Yiddish press can also be discerned from the large number of political newspapers in Yiddish—as will be detailed further on.

38. Cohen, *Sefer, sofer ve'iton*, 97, 100–101.

39. *Ilustrirter vokhnblat*, October 14, 1949.

40. The last issue of which was numbered 63.

41. The ordinance was handed down after the Royal Commission of Inquiry on the Palestine Disturbances of August 1929 found that Arab newspapers had played a role in inciting the Arab population and recommended introducing regulations to enable supervision of the press. Caspi and Limor, *Ha'metavchim*, 146–147.

42. "Hahlata historit," *Ha'ayin ha'shevi'it*, May 29, 2017, http://www.the7eye.org.il/250493.

43. Press Ordinance of 1933, Section 4, https://www.nevo.co.il/law_html/Law19/p185_001.htm#Seif11.

44. Ibid. See also Moshe Ha'negbi, *Hofesh ha'itonai ve'hofesh ha'itonut be'Israel, dinei tikshoret ve'etika itona'it* (Ra'anana: Open University, 2011), 66–70. On the history of press regulation in Mandatory Palestine and Israel, see Pnina Lahav, "Governmental Regulation of the Press: A Study of Israel's Press Ordinance," *Israel Law Review* 13 (1978): 230–250, 489–524.

45. The National Organization of Hebrew Journalists, or, as it later became, the National Association of Israeli Journalists, was founded in 1946 and represents the interests of the journalist community in Israel, including salary concerns. Caspi and Limor, *Ha'metavchim*, 20.

46. Minutes of a meeting between the head of the Press Administration and the Committee on Foreign Languages of the National Organization of Hebrew Journalists, May 16, 1949, State archives, G-718-10 (ISA–MOIN-MOIN-000102a).

47. Ibid., the words of Mr. Rubinowitz from the daily *HaBoker*.

48. Some of the limitations were canceled following the reparations agreement with Germany in 1953, and though it was further relaxed in the years that followed, the austerity regime remained in force until 1959. On the austerity regime and social processes in Israeli society during the 1950s, see Orit Rozin, *The Rise of the Individual in 1950s Israel: A Challenge to Collectivism* (Waltham, MA: Brandeis University Press, 2011), 3–64.

49. "Ha'mahsor be'neyar metzamtzem pe'ulat hotz'aot ha'sefarim," *Al HaMishmar*, July 3, 1949; "Devar ha'yom – ha'matzav be'aspakat ha'neyar la'itonim," *Davar*, August 3, 1950.

50. On the press ordinance and other legislation concerning press supervision, see Michael Harpazi, "Hofesh ha'itonut le'or hukei Israel," *Sefer ha'shana shel ha'itona'i'm*, 1957, 22–30

51. Minutes of the first session of the Supreme Council for Cultural Affairs, March 13, 1952, State archives, 1086/16-GL (ISA-education-education-000hq4p).

52. Minutes of the second session of the Supreme Council for Cultural Affairs, May 28, 1952, State archives, 1086/16-GL (ISA-education-education-000hq4p).

53. Ibid.

54. English came in the first place with twenty-two publications; many of these were issued by public institutions for readers abroad.

55. The Supreme Council for Cultural Affairs, meeting of the Subcommittee for Literature, August 17, 1952, State archives, GL-1086/16 (ISA-education-education-000hq4p).

56. Sh. Yavnieli to the Minister of Education, August 21, 1952, State archives, GL-1086/16 (ISA-education-education-000hq4p); Minutes of the Subcommittee for Arts and Theater, August 18, 1952, State archives, GL-1086/16 (ISA-education-education-000hq4p).

57. Meeting of Hever pe'ilei ha'lashon, November 6, 1952, State archives, GL-1086/16 (ISA-education-education-000hq4p).

58. High Court of Justice file number 213/52 *M. Stein v. Minister of interior*. (The court files and the newspaper don't provide Stein's first name.) On this subject, see also Pnina Lahav, "Ha'oz ve'ha'misra: beit ha'mishpat ha'elyon ba'asor ha'rishon le'kiyumo," *Iyunei mishpat* 14, no. 3 (August 1989): 492–495.

59. High Court of Justice file number 213/52 *M. Stein v. Minister of interior*, 868–869.

60. Ibid., 872.

61. Stein was the only writer for this paper and thus had not been able to create an interesting product.

62. Requests to increase circulation to three times a week or more were sometimes rejected. See, for example, the request by Dr. Rubin, the editor of *Unzer moment*, to expand circulation and publish the newspaper three times a week instead of once a week, based on the existing license, which was refused. Letter from M. Goldstein to *Unzer moment*, April 28, 1950, State archives, G-716/71 (ISA-MOIN-Moin-000qlvr).

63. Klinov and J. Gravitzky, head of the Press, Information and Film Department at the Ministry of the Interior, to Y. Gubernik, Tel Aviv District Supervisor at the Ministry of the Interior, September 21, 1948, State archives, G-716/71 (ISA-MOIN-Moin-000qlvr).

64. J. Gravitzky, head of the Press, Information and Film Department at the Ministry of the Interior, to Y. Gubernik, Tel Aviv District Supervisor, December 7, 1948, State archives, G- 716/71 (ISA-MOIN-Moin-000qlvr).

65. Klinov and J. Gravitzky, head of the Press, Information and Film administration at the Ministry of Interior, to Y. Kuperman Tel Aviv District Supervisor at the Ministry of the Interior, February 3, 1949, State archives, G-716/71 (ISA-MOIN-Moin-000qlvr).

66. Y. Klinov and J. Gravitzky, head of the Press, Information and Film Administration at the Ministry of the Interior, to Y. Kuperman, Tel Aviv District Supervisor at the Ministry of the Interior, April 22, 1949, State archives, G- 716/71 (ISA-MOIN-Moin-000qlvr).

67. Notice of License Given to Publish *Yidishe bilder*, December 2, 1949, State archives, G-716/71 (ISA-MOIN-Moin-000qlvr).

68. Letter written by Tel Aviv District head of the Press, Information and Film Administration, August 8, 1950, State archives, G-716/71 (ISA-MOIN-Moin-000qlvr). (The letter details the entire development of licensing for these newspapers.)

69. Y. Kisilov, head of the Press, Information and Film Administration at the Ministry of the Interior, State archives, G-716/71 (ISA-MOIN-MOIN-000qlvr).

70. Notice of License Given to Publish *Unzer haynt*, June 29, 1950, State archives, G-716/71 (ISA-MOIN-MOIN-000qlvr).

71. "Devar ha'yom," *Davar*, May 28, 1950.

72. "Hoser neyar me'ayem shuv al ha'itonut," *Maariv*, November 21, 1950.

73. "Be'kinus ha'ot ha'mudpeset: ha'memshala nidreshet le'havtiah melai tziyud ve'helkei hiluf le'batei defus," *Al HaMishmar*, December 25, 1950; "Ne'erach kenes ha'ot ha'mudpeset,'" *Herut*, December 25, 1950; "Kinus ha'ot ha'mudpeset," *Davar*, December 24, 1950; M. D., "Ha'ot ha'mudpest mevakeshet al nafsha," *Davar*, December 27, 1950.

74. Meeting no. 176 of the first Knesset, August 8, 1950, *Divrei ha'knesset*, 2512–2518.

75. Meeting no. 209 of the first Knesset, January 3, 1951, *Divrei ha'knesset:* 673–681.

76. Report of Subcommittee for Paper, meeting of January 16, 1951, State archives, G-54/716 (ISA-MOIN-MOIN-00083z5).

77. Report of the Subcommittee on Paper [undated in document text], State archives G-716/54 (ISA-MOIN-MOIN 00083z5).

78. Meeting no. 78 of the second Knesset, May 7, 1952, *Divrei ha'knesset* 1055–1056; Report of the Subcommittee on Paper, from a meeting held on January 15, 1951, State archives, G-54/716 (ISA-MOIN-MOIN 00083z5).

79. Letter to the Tel Aviv District Supervisor at the Ministry of the Interior by Y. Klinov, head of the Press, Information and Film Administration, December 30, 1949, State archives, G-71/716 (ISA-MOIN-MOIN-000q1vr).

80. "Fun montik den 27 h. kh. dershint *Letste nayes* 2 mol a vokh," *Letste nayes*, February 24, 1950.

81. Correspondence between the Tel Aviv District Supervisor at the Ministry of the Interior with the head of the Press, Information and Film Administration, April 19, 1950; April 28, 1950, State archives, G-71/716 (ISA-MOIN-MOIN-000q1vr).

82. Letter from the deputy head of the Press, Information, and Film Administration, December 10, 1950, State archives, G-71/716 (ISA-MOIN-MOIN-000qlvr). The letter details Tsanin's request.

83. The Press, Information and Film Administration in the Ministry of the Interior to *Letste nayes* editorial board, July 22, 1951, private papers of Mordechai Tsanin. The letter includes the details of the letter of request by the editorial board of *Letste nayes*.

84. "Rishyonot yevu le-882 ton neyar sefarim," *Davar*, July 22, 1952; "Huvtah melai neyar itonim ad sof shana ha'ba'a," *HaTzofe*, December 26, 1952.

85. *Letste nayes*, August 7, 1953.

86. *Yidishe prese*, no. 1, December 4, 1955.

87. Israel Hadash, "Vos iz geshen in *Letste nayes*," *Yidishe tsaytung*, February 10, 1952.

88. I conducted interviews with Yitzhak Luden, who had been a senior journalist in *Letste nayes*, and with Judge Haim Hadash, the son of Israel Hadash. As so much time had gone by, Luden remembered things in only very general terms, while Haim Hadash, who had been a boy at the time, simply reiterated his father's version.

89. This tension is strikingly evident in the way in which Hadash described the rift with Tsanin. Hadash, "Vos iz geshen." Luden also alluded to this complicated relationship, though very delicately.

90. Hacohen, *Olim bi'se'ara*, 151.

91. "David Ben-Gurion, ongehoybn di val kampanye in land," *Letste nayes*, July 2, 1950.

92. "Agudas Yisroel—der fon treger fun toyre yidntum"; "Di birger un di valn"; "Tenu'at ha'Herut"; "Dos vort fun Mapai"; "Dos vort fun Mapam," *Letste nayes*, July 27, 1951.

93. "Di hayntike valn," *Letste nayes*, July 20, 1951.

94. Yechiam Weitz, *Israel ba'asor ha'rishon*, Unit no. 9, Ha'behirot la'knesset u'mashberim memshaltiyim (Tel Aviv: Open University 2001), 61–62.

95. The affair was described in Hadash, "Vos iz geshen," here, note 34.

96. Letter from Tsanin to Israel Hadash, July 29, 1955, quoted in Hadash, "Vos iz geshen." According to the letter, the partnership was supposed to end on October 1, 1955.

97. "Tevi'at nezikin neged *Ha'dor*," *Herut*, December 31, 1954. In fact, Uri Avnery did not know about these reports and, predictably, denied any connection with the General Zionists—in keeping with his political views.

98. "Al *Ha'dor* le'hitnatzel, le'hakhish u'la'shalem pitzuyim," *Herut*, January 1, 1955.

99. Conversation with Uri Avnery, May 2011. Avnery totally denied the story and said that he had never heard about it.

100. On the attitude of newspaper editors to Uri Avnery and *HaOlam Haze*, see Nitza Erel, "Beli mora, beli maso panim," *Uri Avnery ve'HaOlam Haze* (Jerusalem: Magnes, 2006), 313–326.

101. "Tzav peruk le'shutfut hotza'at *Letste nayes*," *HaTzofe*, December 7, 1955.

102. "Sichsuch bein ba'alei *Letste nayes*," *Davar*, December 18, 1955; "Tzav neged ha'iton *Letste nayes*," *HaTzofe*, December 22, 1955.

103. "Hotza'at *Letste nayes*," *HaTzofe*, December 23, 1955.

104. Announcement by the Receiver, Dr. Procaccia, regarding the dissolution of the *Letste nayes* partnership, *Yidishe tsaytung*, January 30, 1956.

105. Hadash, "Vos iz geshen."

106. In the first few months, the editor of both papers was David Lutzky, a relative of Israel Hadash.

107. Conversation with Shlomo Zeitouni, Matzliah Zeitouni's son.

108. On *Hayntike nayes* in Warsaw, see Nathan Cohen, *Sefer, sofer ve'iton*, 96–97.

109. *Hayntike nayes*: editor, M. Tsanin; publisher, Dora Tsanin; no. 33, April 28, 1956. In March 1958 the license was transferred to Mordechai Tsanin.

110. "Groys gever transport ongekumen keyn Mitsraim un Sirye," *Letste nayes*, November 3, 1949; "Derklert milkhome dem shvartsen mark," *Letste nayes*, October 6, 1950.

111. "Masn bager fun poylishe yidn tsu kumen keyn Yisroel," *Letste nayes*, November 10, 1949; "Fuftsik toyzent yidn befrayte fun Irak kumen keyn Yisroel," *Letste nayes*, May 15, 1950.

112. "Far der froy," and later "Froy un heym." On sections for women and the household in the Yiddish press in the United States, see Rachel Rojanski, "Yiddish Journals for Women in Israel: Immigrant Press and Gender Construction (1948–1952)," in *Yiddish Studies Today (Leket)*, ed. Marion Aptroot, Efrat Gal-Ed, Roland Gruschka, and Simon Neuberg (Dusseldorf: Dusseldorf University Press, 2012), 585–602.

113. *Unzer fraye tribune*, sometimes with a subheading "Red zikh arop fun harts" (Get it off your chest).

114. On this, see Rachel Rojanski, "Shomer ha'zikaron," *Ha'aretz*, February 13, 2009.

115. "Der ershter milyon," *Letste nayes*, November 24, 1949; "Di shuldike tsum mishpet" [On the situation in the transit camps], *Letste nayes*, December 30, 1949.

116. "Ven men zeyt vint," *Letste nayes*, February 27, 1950.

117. "Unzere virtshaft," *Letste nayes*, March 27, 1950; [untitled], *Letste nayes*, February 12, 1951. The article without a heading deals with the shopping craze in clothing stores, following a rumor that the ration stamps would lose their value; no merchandise was left in the stores.

118. See also articles in later years, for example, "Di arbetsloze viln broyt" [On unemployment], *Hayntike nayes*, February 15, 1957.

119. Editorial, March 8, 1957.

120. "Vider oysgebrokhen umru in Vadi Salib," *Hayntike nayes*, July 28, 1959.

121. In the introduction to a collection of these columns, Tsanin wrote that their purpose was to describe wrong things in a funny way and thus cause the government to correct them. M. Tsanin, *Shabesdike shmuesn* (Tel Aviv: Farlag Letste nayes, 1957), 7.

122. "Meshiekh volt gekumen, ven ale manhigim vern ministorn," *Letste nayes*, January 17, 1950.

123. "Sof fun lagern onheyb fun ma'abarot," *Letste nayes*, November 4, 1950.

124. "Oylim kritikirn un vatikim shtrekhelirn," *Letste nayes*, June 22, 1951.

125. "Vegn der Sinai aktsye," *Letste nayes*, March 22, 1957.

126. Aharon Ashman, "Toyves," *Letste nayes*, November 3, 1949.

127. Y. Blum, "Der konflikt tsvishn yunge un alte," *Letste nayes*, December 30, 1949.

128. Z. Marin, "Fir teater premyeres," *Letste nayes*, December 30, 1949.

129. Abraham Liss, "Yung yisroel," *Hayntike nayes*, November 15, 1957.

130. Mordechai Yafet, "Zekhtsig yor yidishe poezye in Amerike," *Letste nayes*, December 11, 1956.

131. "Brukhhim haboim, Mark Turkow, der shefer fun a monument farn poylishn yidntum," *Letste nayes*, February 10, 1950

132. "Mirele Efros in Habima," *Hayntike nayes*, November 20, 1957.

133. Anita Shapira, "The Holocaust: Private Memories, Public Memory," *Jewish Social Studies* 4, no. 2 (1998): 40–58.

134. See "Martyrs' and Heroes' Remembrance Day Law, 5719–1959," https://knesset.gov.il/shoah/eng/shoah_memorialday_eng.pdf.
135. Volf Yasni, "Der kidesh hashem fun Yerakhmiel Briks," *Letste nayes*, December 11, 1950
136. Rachel Auerbach, "Der yidisher oyfshtand—Varshe 1943," *Letste nayes*, March 31, 1950.
137. Ibid.; the next page had a long article by Tsanin about prewar Warsaw and a story by the partisan writer Shmerke Katsherginsky. M. Tsanin, "Dos yidishe Varshe vos iz avek in flamen," *Letste nayes*, March 31, 1950; Shmerke Katsherginsky, "Di ershte diversye," *Letste nayes*, March 31, 1950.
138. Letter from A. Avior of the Ministry of the Interior to the ministry's legal advisor, regarding *Letste nayes*, *Yidishe tsaytung*, and two Polish newspapers, *Express Izraelski* and *Kurier Izraelski*, January 17, 1954, State archives, G-2221/12 (ISA-MOIN-MOIN-0003p1s).
139. Letter from the attorney Yaakov Zalivansky, Tsanin's representative, to the Ministry of the Interior, April 26, 1954, State archives, G-2221/12 (ISA-MOIN-MOIN-0003p1s); Dr. Kremer, the official responsible for special duties in the Ministry of the Interior to the official in charge of the Tel Aviv District in the ministry, March 12, 1954, State archives, G-2221/12 (ISA-MOIN-MOIN-0003p1s); the official in charge of the Tel Aviv District in the ministry wrote to the official in charge of special affairs in the ministry that it was impossible to legally prove that *Yidishe tsaytung* and *Letste nayes* were one newspaper, and hence it was impossible to annul their license. State archives, G-2221/12 (ISA-MOIN-MOIN-0003p1s).
140. Dr. Kremer, the official responsible for special duties in the Ministry of the Interior, to the director general of the ministry, February 16, 1954, State archives, G-2221/12 (ISA-MOIN-MOIN-0003p1s).
141. The conditions for obtaining a license to publish a newspaper were as follows: the responsible editor had to have a high school education, and the publisher had to pay a very small sum as a guarantee. See Reply by M. Shohetman, deputy director of the press section in the Ministry of the Interior, to questions referred to him on the radio program, *Questions from the Balcony*, October 29, 1952, State archives, G-2221/12 (ISA-MOIN-MOIN-0003p1s).
142. This group also tended to distinguish between the Yiddish press and the rest, seeing the former as a greater danger.
143. Letter from press and information officer in the Ministry of Education and Culture, to M. Shohetman, deputy director of the press section in the Ministry of the Interior, September 25, 1952, State archives, G-2221/12 (ISA-MOIN-MOIN-0003p1s).
144. "Shenat mivtza hanhalat ha'lashon," *Herut*, February 18, 1954; "Tuchraz shenat hanhalat ha'lashon," *Davar*, February 17, 1954.
145. "Mivtza hanhalat ha'lashon la'am" (Operation of Imparting the Hebrew Language) was a proposed program approved in its entirety by the government in its session on July 11, 1954. State archives G-5551/7 (ISA-PMO-PMO-000v8gn).
146. Ibid., and handbill distributed by the Committee for Inculcation of Hebrew calling on citizens to volunteer to teach Hebrew. State Archives, ISA-Privatecollections-BenZviRelations-000fm3z.
147. "Mivtza hanhalat ha'lashon la'am" (note 145).
148. See, for example, Asher Nahor, "Yerushat ha'hefker ha'nimkeret bi'rehovot Tel Aviv—keitzad gadal mispar ha'itonim ha'lo'aziyim ad she'higi'a le'mala mi'me'a," *Yedioth Aharonoth*, December 28, 1953; "Seyag la'itonut ha'lo'azit" (editorial), *HaBoker*, January 8, 1954.

149. David Giladi, "Me'a ve'arba'a itonim mefitzim la'az be'Israel," *Maariv*, January 1, 1954. On David Giladi, see Rafi Man, "Ha'hashuv im ha'me'anyen, hesped le'David Giladi," *Ha'ayin ha'shevi'it*, http://www.the7eye.org.il/25210.

150. Only one article did this: "Misrad ha'penim ma'alim ayin mi'ribui ha'itonut ha'lo'azit," *Al HaMishmar*, September 7, 1953.

151. "Sofreinu ba'knesset, esrim ve'arba'a kitvei-et lo'aziyim pog'im be'kosher ha'kelita shel ha'olim," *Herut*, January 7, 1954; "Itonut ha'la'az ve'hafatzat ha'sefer ha'ivri be'diyunei ha'knesset," *Davar*, January 7, 1954; "Arba'im itonim be'shteim esrei leshonot lo'ez be'Israel," *Davar*, September 30, 1953.

152. Ezriel Carlebach, "Safa la'kol," *Maariv*, April 12, 1951.

153. Yizhar Arnon, "Ha'itonut ha'lo'azit doheket et ha'Ivrit," *Herut*, February 6, 1953; Regina Elazari, "Inflatzya shel itonut la'az," *Hador*, December 25, 1953.

154. This idea had been brought to the attention of the minister of the interior in an internal memorandum even before the 1953–1954 wave of articles in the press: "The Hebrew press has recently been very vociferous on this subject. In part, this is due to sincere concerns about the Hebrew culture and the Hebrew language. But it seems to me that the newspapers were clamoring a great deal because they were anxious about economic competition." S. B. Yeshayahu to the Minister of the Interior, February 18, 1952, State archives, G-2221/12 (ISA-MOIN-MOIN-003pls).

155. Memorandum on the foreign-language press in Israel by Maximilian Apolinari Hartglass, advisor to the Ministry of the Interior, sent to the minister, April 5, 1950, State archives, G-2221/12 (ISA-MOIN-MOIN-003pls); Survey of the foreign-language press in Israel, Ministry of the Interior, May 1952, State archives, G-2221/12 (ISA-MOIN-MOIN-003pls); Deputy Minister of Trade and Commerce to the Minister of Interior, on the foreign-language press, December 5, 1953, State archives, G-12/2221 (ISA-MOIN-MOIN-003pls); A section from the memorandum on the weekly meeting between the director general and deputy director in the Ministry of the Interior, January 8, 1954, State archive, G12/2221 (ISA-MOIN-MOIN-0003pls); Review on the foreign-language press, submitted to the director general of the Ministry of the Interior, February 16, 1954, State archives, G-12/2221 (ISA-MOIN-MOIN-0003pls).

156. Memorandum from the Press Committee for Imparting Hebrew, probably February 16, 1954 (date was added in handwriting), State archives, GL-14/1787 (ISA-education-education-000fzw8).

157. Ibid., 11. The text of the memorandum speaks about the foreign-language newspapers providing a Hebrew translation. But the writers argue that since a large part of the material in these papers is translated from Hebrew, the readers would prefer to read the original in a Hebrew paper and not in a foreign-language paper.

158. The Press Committee for Imparting Hebrew, second memorandum, June 9, 1954, State archives, Gl-14/1787 (ISA-education-education-000fzw8).

159. 350th session of the second Knesset, January 6, 1954, *Divrei ha'knesset*, 584–585.

160. Ibid., 585.

161. "Sar ha'penim al sakanat ha'la'az" (conversation between the minister of the interior and the *Maariv* journalist), *Maariv*, January 1, 1954.

162. *Gzeyres* (*gezeirot* in Hebrew) are extremely harmful laws or regulations. Traditionally, Ashkenazi Jews used the word *gzeyres* to describe attacks on Jews by non-Jewish authorities.

163. Y. Satmer, "Erev naye gzeyres kegn Yidish," *Lebns-fragn*, February 1, 1954.

164. Letter from the Association of Yiddish Writers to the Minister of the Interior Israel Rokach, signed by Sutzkever, Gross-Zimmerman, and D. Rubinstein, February 28, 1954, State archives, G-2221/12 (ISA-MOIN- MOIN -003pls).

165. The second part of the proposal dealt with the language of street signs.
166. Session no. 428 of the second Knesset, May 26, 1954, *Divrei ha'knesset*, 1777–1778.
167. Minutes of meeting 14/1954 of the cabinet, December 12, 1954, 27.
168. Ibid., 40.
169. Ibid., 36.
170. Ibid., 38.
171. Ibid., 28.
172. Memorandum of understanding following a meeting between the deputy director for special matters in the Ministry of the Interior and the editors of non-Hebrew newspapers, October 25, 1957, State archives, Gl-14/1787 (ISA-education-education-000fzw8).
173. See, for example, David Giladi, "Me'a ve'arba'a itonim mefitzim la'az be'Israel," *Maariv*, January 1, 1954.
174. Nitza Erel claims that Avnery's aim was to use that paper to reach Jews in the United States who were opposed to Zionism, such as the reform rabbi Elmer Berger. Nitza Erel, *Uri Avnery ve'HaOlam Haze*, 154. In a telephone conversation in 2009, Avnery told me that he published *Veltshpigl* to reach a readership among the new immigrants.
175. The Jewish agency also published a Yiddish periodical, but its prospective readership was the Jews outside Israel.
176. *Dos vort*, no. 2, onetime publication, January 11, 1949.
177. *Dos vort*, no. 1, February 16, 1951.
178. It began publication in mid-August 1953.
179. "Tsu unzere leyener," *Di tsayt*, September 1, 1953.
180. For example, "Ohel—dos arbeter teater in Yisroel," *Yisroel tog ayn tog oys*, no. 7, June 1957.
181. S. Kantz, "Yidishkeyt un yidishe kultur," *Yisroel tog ayn tog oys*, no. 20, December 30, 1957, 6.
182. For example, no. 20, December 30, 1957, 2.
183. *Yisroel tog ayn tog oys*, February 18, 1959.
184. *Unzer haynt*, September 1, 1953.
185. Including Y. M. Neiman, a member of the *Davar* editorial board; Meir Grossman, member of the Jewish Agency board and previously one of the editors of *HaBoker*; Dr. Herzl Rosenblum, the editor of *Yedioth Aharonoth*, who was in the past active in the Yiddish press in Kovno.
186. For examples of its literary and theater sections, see "Literatur un kunst," Y. Ts. Shragel, "In der velt fun kultur," *Oyf der vakh*, September 9, 1954; Volf Yasni, "Shekiye un morgnshayn in gezang fun Yisroel-dikhter Arye Shimri," *Oyf der vakh*, October 5, 1954; Yosef Opatoshu, "A zingerin," *Oyf der vakh*, November 4, 1954; "Dos vort hot Sholem Asch," *Oyf der vakh*, October 21, 1954; "Zikh ongehoybn teater-sezon in Yisroel" and "Filharmonisher orkester," *Oyf der vakh*, October 5, 1954; and A. Shlonskis, "Gezamelte lider"; H. Bartov un A. Megged, "Premirt mitn Usishkin priz far literatur"; Dov Bar-Nir, "H. Bartov, der humanist-vegn zayn bukh *Shesh kenafayim la'ehad*"; M. Z. Tal, "'Shlomik und mir': tsu der oyffirung fun *Hedva va'ani*," *Oyf der vakh*, October 28, 1954.
187. Announcement of the editorial board, *Oyf der vakh*, January 27, 1955.
188. The editorial board, the management, and the printing house were the same as those of *Oyf der vakh*. The editor was A. Efrat, and the offices were located in the Al HaMishmar building in Tel Aviv.
189. "Tsu di leyener," *Yisroel shtime*, no. 1, June 13, 1957.
190. For example, the section Fun vokh tsu vokh (From week to week) dealt with day-to-day matters, such as "Yisroel far naye politishe problemen," *Yisroel shtime*, June 30, 1957. The

literary section brought articles like "Oyf a shpatsir mit Peretz Markish" and "Vegn bukh dertseylungen *Di ban* fun Tzvi Eisnman," *Yisroel shtime*, June 20, 1957.

191. Various weekly magazines and biweekly newspapers also appeared but proved ephemeral.

192. Caspi and Limor, *Ha'metavchim*, 40–43.

193. Yitzhak Galnoor, *Reishita shel ha'demokratya be'Israel* (Tel Aviv: Am Oved, 1985), 215.

194. Ibid., 44.

195. Words of the secretary-general of Mapai, Zalman Aharonwitz-Aran, at meeting of Mapai headquarters. Minutes of party headquarters, April 26, 1950, Archives of the Labor Party, Beit Berl, folder of the minutes of the party headquarter meeting.

196. Ibid. This number was also mentioned by Itzhak Luden and Mordechai Tsanin, who talked about a circulation of thirty thousand copies for *Letste nayes*, with each copy being read by four readers.

197. Meir (Marc) Dvorjetski, who immigrated to Israel a few months earlier, was active in many Yiddish newspapers in France, the United States, and Argentina. Conversation with his daughter, Zvia Balshan, March 23, 2009.

198. It was funded by the International Ladies Garment Workers Union in the United States (ILGWU), with additional party financing, and began to function in 1953. Report of United Printing Company, March 1, 1957, Archives of the Labor Party, no. 9/48/56.

199. United Printing Company Ltd., report March 1, 1957, Archives of the Labor Party, file no. 9/48/56. See also Report of Kidum Co. regarding "Pirsumim," April 8, 1957, Archives of the Labor Party; "Ha'avarat ha'shevu'onim le'hevrat Pirsumim," report signed by Moshe Kitron, 1957, Archives of the Labor Party, no. 9/49/57; Letter from Moshe Kitron to Giyora Yoseftal, March 17, 1958, Archives of the Labor Party, no. 9/49/58.

200. In the National Library of Israel there are volumes until that year. I found no other volumes in any other library in Israel or the United States.

201. Weitz, *Israel ba'asor ha'rishon*, 73–74.

202. Kitron's report, March 17, 1958, Archives of the Labor Party, no. 9/49/58. For remarks about the scant importance of the newspaper in Bulgarian and Romanian, see also "Ha'avarat ha'shevu'onim le'hevrat Pirsumim," report signed by Moshe Kitron, 1957, Archives of the Labor Party, no. 9/49/57.

203. On the attitude toward that immigration, see Avi Pikar, *Olim bi'mesura, medinyut Israel kelapei aliyatam shel yehudei tzefon Afrika 1951–1956* (Sede-Boker Ben-Gurion University Press, 2013), 1–26.

204. On the appointment of members to follow up the foreign-language press, see To Gotthelf from A. Ufner, October 5, 1959, Archives of the Labor Party, no. 3707; Ufner to L. Kuperstein, October 2, 1959, Archives of the Labor Party, no. 3707; Memorandum on the foreign-language press in Israel, January 21, 1960, Archives of the Labor Party, no. 9/48/60.

205. Niger and Shatzky, *Leksikon*, 7: 157–58.

206. Kitron report, March 17, 1958.

207. "The situation of the foreign-language press," Memorandum for Giora Yoseftal, August 29, 1958, no name of writer, Archives of the Labor Party, no. 9/49/57. The document mentioned the names of four Mapai members who regularly wrote for *Letste nayes*, including Knesset member Herzl Berger, with the recommendation that they go on writing for that paper to counter its spirit, which was hostile to Mapai.

208. Report by Moshe Kitron submitted to Giora Yoseftal, March 17, 1958, Archives of the Labor Party, no. 9/49/58.

209. Letter from Moshe Kitron to Y. Avidov in the party's absorption department, November 11, 1957, Archives of the Labor Party, no. 9/49/57; Invitation to the first meeting of the Committee on the Foreign-Language Press, Moshe Kitron to members of the committee, November 21, 1957, Archives of the Labor Party, 9/36/57. On Moshe Kitron, see Naomi Kitron, *Bein shalosh yabashot: hayei Moshe Kitron* (Jerusalem: Carmel, 2005).

210. Kitron report, March 17.

211. Moshe Kitron to the party secretary-general, Giora Yoseftal, March 17, 1958, Archives of the Labor Party, no. 9/49/58.

212. Report on meeting regarding information dissemination in Yiddish, February 10, 1958, Archives of the Labor Party, no. 9/49/57.

213. Pyekatsh to Moshe Kitron, February 4, 1958, Archives of the Labor Party, no. 9/49/57.

214. Pyekatsh to Moshe Kitron, February 2, 1958, Archives of the Labor Party, no. 9/49/57.

215. Letter from the official in charge of the Tel Aviv District in the Ministry of the Interior, to the Pirsumim Company, September 18, 1957, Archives of the Labor Party, no. 9/48/57.

216. Notes by the Committee on the Foreign-Language Press, 1959, Archives of the Labor Party, no. 9/49/59.

217. Israel Shapira to Y. Paldi, August 27, 1959, Archives of the Labor Party, no. 9/49/59.

218. Letter to P. Pyekatsh from Israel Shapira, August 28, 1959, Archives of the Labor Party, no. 9/49/59.

219. Israel Shapira to Himelfarb, August 26, 1959, Archives of the Labor Party, no. 9/49/59.

220. I. Shapira to Ruth Rali, September 7, 1959, Archives of the Labor Party, no. 9/49/59.

221. Memorandum on the foreign-language press in Israel, January 21,1960, Archives of the Labor Party, no. 9/49/59.

222. Tsanin's archives are kept in the Gnazim Institute in Tel Aviv. They contain some correspondence, but the main bulk is manuscripts of his books and articles.

223. M. Meisles, "Mapai rocheshet itonim," *Maariv*, June 24, 1960.

224. Sofrenu be'Tel Aviv, "Mapai rachsha et *Letste nayes* be'reva milyon lirot," *Herut*, June 2, 1960.

225. Ben Yaakov, "Oykh di *Letste nayes*," *Lebns-fragn*, July 1, 1960, 9.

226. In his article "Konformizm," published in 1992, Tsanin told about the struggles of *Letste nayes* but did not mention at all the selling of the paper. Mordechai Tsanin, *Zumershney* (Tel Aviv: H. Leivick farlag, 1992), 176–178.

227. In 1995, Mapai sold the paper to a private businessman, who kept it alive into the twenty-first century. Conversation with George Edry, April 2008, who purchased all the foreign-language newspapers of the Pirsumim Company in 1995.

228. *Ilustrirte velt vokh*, no. 57, July 6, 1960.

229. Neither in the Gnazim Archive of Hebrew Writers, in Israel, where his papers are archived, nor in the papers he gave me.

230. On this, see Chapter 7.

231. *Yidish literatur in medines Yisroel* (Tel Aviv: H. Leivick farlag, 1991), 191.

232. For example, *Letste nayes*, July, 12, 1961.

233. Ruth Shaul, the person in charge of public inquiries in the office of the president of Israel, to Mordechai Tsanin, editor of *Letste nayes*, January 20, 1966, Gnazim Institute, Archives of Mordechai Tsanin, 504 2551/15.

234. It carried many stories dealing with the Yiddish-culture world and especially the stars of the Yiddish stage. See, for example, "Di tokhter fun yidishn teater, Ida Kaminska," *Tsanins ilustrirte velt*, no. 27, July 24, 1957; "H. Leivick der treger fun derleyzung un der yidisher

literatur," *Tsanins ilustrirte velt*, no. 28, July 31, 1957; "Di tsvey shtern vos bavegn zikh" [On Dzigan and Shumacher], *Tsanins ilustrirte velt*, September 29, 1960; "Max Perlman un Gita Galina," *Tsanins ilustrirte velt*, December 14, 1960. In December 1960, the cover showed a photograph of Ben-Gurion with a nuclear cloud in the background. The headline read: "The world says that Israel owns a nuclear bomb." The headline of the next issue was, "A look at the Nuclear Reactor Center run for peaceful purposes," *Tsanins ilustrirte velt*, no. 51, December 21, 1960; no. 52, December 28, 1960.

235. See chapter 7.

236. In a conversation in 2012, Uri Avnery told me that he decided to publish a paper in Yiddish to reach out to the thousands of new, Yiddish-speaking immigrants in Israel then, but the paper did not sell.

237. Tsanin said on many different occasions that this is what he used to do to get printing paper.

238. Yablonka, *Ahim zarim*, 10. See also Hanna Yablonka, "Kelitat nitzolei ha'sho'a bi'medinat Israel—hebetim hadashim," *Iyunim bi'tekumat Israel* 7 (1997): 285–298.

239. Ezriel Carlebach was an astute, highly esteemed journalist. See the words of the journalist Levi Yitzhak Ha'yerushalmi, https://www.youtube.com/watch?v=vQsN-aXiH2Q.

240. See, for example, the request by the secretary of the association asking to print the association's regulations of professional ethics in *Letste nayes*, February 26, 1958, Gnazim Archive of Hebrew Writers, Israel, Tsanin's archives, 504 2504/15.

241. M. Ron, secretary of the national union of Israeli journalists, to Tsanin, December 11, 1960, Gnazim Archive of Hebrew Writers, Israel, Tsanin's archives, 504 2610/15.

242. On Tsanin's membership in the editors committee, see "Nesi'ut hadasha be'va'adat ha'orchim," *Davar*, May 1, 1961; "Ba'asefa ha'kelalit shel va'adat ha'orchim," *Maariv*, May 18, 1965.

3

"WE ARE JEWISH ACTORS FROM THE DIASPORA"

Yiddish Actors, Yiddish Theater, and the Jewish State, 1948–1965

In the summer of 1951 Nathan Wulfowitz, a Yiddish actor and new immigrant from Poland, appeared before a magistrate in Haifa. He had been summoned for staging two plays in Yiddish without a permit and was fined twenty Israeli pounds. One of the plays was *Hershele Ostropolyer*. Wulfowitz described his experience in a satirical article published in *Letste nayes* under the title "*Hershele Ostropolyer* in Court." Wulfowitz wrote, "Today the judge's sentence will make our dear Hershele illegal. . . . Among the goyim, Hershele could speak freely, but here in Israel they want to padlock his mouth."[1]

Ostensibly it was a humorous piece describing the frustrations of a Yiddish actor in the Israel of the early 1950s, facing the restrictions the state was imposing on Yiddish theater. Actually, though, the article in *Letste nayes* reflected a much broader reality. It was not only about the new immigrant, Nathan Wulfowitz. It was about Hershele, the well-known Hassidic jester, the hero of popular jokes and tales and one of the cornerstones of Yiddish popular culture. As much as Wulfowitz, it was Hershele, the east European Yiddish-speaking Jew, who was being put on trial by the state of Israel.

"How dare you drag the Diaspora here, lock, stock and barrel?" thundered the magistrate in Wulfowitz's humorous article.[2]

Despite the verdict, and undeterred by his experience in court, Wulfowitz went back to Tel Aviv and continued performing in Yiddish. He was by no means the only actor to ignore rulings of this kind.

The main argument in this chapter is that the steps taken against Yiddish theater during the state's first years had almost no direct influence on its development. They lasted for only a very short time and were not effectively enforced. They did, however, have a psychological impact. They shaped the image of Yiddish theater as an art form rejected by the new Israeli culture, in effect perpetuating its existing status as inferior, even vulgar. The state was intent on creating an Israeli Hebrew cultural hegemony; for Yiddish theater this was a problem.

The officially inspired effort to suppress Yiddish theater was, however, only part of the story. There were Yiddish performers who enjoyed a stunning and lengthy success in early Israel and were even enthusiastically supported by members of Israel's political, social, and cultural elite. Some were visitors—internationally renowned artists, stars of the Yiddish and sometimes even the American stage. Artists such as these were supported by the Israeli establishment either in the interests of advancing the state's cultural hegemony in the Jewish world or because they brought to Israel outstanding and high-quality Jewish theater.

I will open with a discussion of the official policy toward Yiddish theater, the ways Yiddish actors tried to fight it, and the effect their struggle had on the development of Yiddish theater in Israel. I will then examine the visits to Israel of three great Yiddish actors—Maurice Schwartz, Joseph Buloff, and Ida Kaminska—and discuss how intellectuals, journalists, and sometimes even politicians reacted to them. The last part of the chapter will focus on the famous comic duo Dzigan and Shumacher, whose unique story demonstrates the power of quality theater when it was faced with the state's cultural policy.

Yiddish Theater in Israel: The Background

From its earliest days, Yiddish theater was characterized by the polarization between high and low. The unique character of modern Yiddish theater coalesced to a great extent in the days of its founder, Abraham Goldfaden, who staged his first Yiddish play in the fall of 1876 in Iași, Romania. For his troupe Goldfaden recruited singers, who based their art on the tradition of the Jewish *batkhn* (jester), as well as young comic actors.[3] He started with plays in vaudeville style, comedies, melodramas, and operettas, later adding dramatic plays.[4] Goldfaden's plays were staged all over eastern Europe, and his company laid the foundations for the subsequent popular Yiddish theater. The model of presenting light entertainment alongside dramatic plays remained widespread for many decades.[5]

In 1883, the Russian Empire declared a comprehensive ban against Yiddish theater, which remained in effect until the twentieth century, and caused many Yiddish actors to leave eastern Europe and migrate to England and the United States.[6]

The mass immigration of Jews from eastern Europe during the last quarter of the nineteenth century to the United States, and especially to New York City, created there a significant audience that was interested in this theater. Here too Yiddish theater soon adopted the pattern of combining a large number of popular light entertainment performances with attempts to establish high-quality drama. Of the companies specializing in the latter, arguably the most important was Maurice Schwartz's Yiddish Art Theater (Yidisher kunst teater), founded in 1918 and active for some thirty years.[7]

The renaissance of Yiddish theater in eastern Europe began in 1905 when the Russian authorities loosened their reins. Yiddish theater troupes flocked to Warsaw, Poland, and performed mainly simple comedies for an uneducated audience that was interested in light entertainment.[8] Here it was Y. L. Peretz and his disciples who expressed great opposition to Yiddish popular theater which they called *shund*.[9] And again, alongside the popular companies, high-quality art theaters were also established, culminating with that of the legendary actress Ester-Rokhl Kaminska, who brought Yiddish theater to previously unknown artistic heights.[10] The fact that Yiddish theater was only rarely supported by public money increased the tension that was felt between the aspiration to create quality theater and the need to have a popular repertoire that would draw well at the box office by appealing to a broader audience.

Yiddish theater was at its zenith during the interwar years. By now transnational in nature, it played an important role in all the large Jewish cultural centers in the world: New York, Warsaw, Paris, Buenos Aires, and a number of cities in the USSR.

However, this golden age did not last long. By the 1940s the Yiddish theatrical arena in the United States had shrunk. The processes of acculturation had moved Yiddish speakers to the general English-speaking theater, and the immigration restrictions of 1921 and later had stopped the flow to the United States of new Yiddish-speaking immigrants, the audience of the Yiddish theater. In addition, newer forms of entertainment, especially films, were now competing successfully with Yiddish theater. In Eastern Europe—the ancestral home of Yiddish—the Holocaust had, at once, put an end to Yiddish theater, almost entirely.[11]

Among the Holocaust survivors who came to Israel during the first years of the state were, of course, also Yiddish actors, for whom it was only natural to want to return to their theatrical careers. The realities of Israeli life during the first years of the state made this very difficult for them.

Since there was no Yiddish theater in Israel at that time, the new immigrant actors had to create their own opportunities to perform. Faced with the urgent need to make a living and with very restricted financial resources at their disposal, they were forced either to settle for very modest artistic productions or to focus on the kind of popular Yiddish theater—melodramas, operettas, and revue—that was already looked down upon in the Jewish world.

On top of that, these Yiddish actors also had to deal with Israel's cultural policy, which not only made the development and inculcation of Hebrew its top priority but also supported limiting non-Hebrew Jewish cultures, especially Yiddish. How this was done in the theater world will shed a great deal of light on the status and development of Yiddish in the early years of the state.

The Official Policy: "Yiddish Theater Is Dangerous Not Just Because of the Language"

In fact, the struggles of the Yiddish theater in the first three years of the state are very revealing when we try to weigh the relative importance of legislation and enforcement as opposed to the power of the Zionist ethos and the state's cultural hegemony in determining cultural policy and shaping Israeli culture.

The newly founded state enacted no official rules or laws regarding non-Hebrew Jewish theater in general and Yiddish theater in particular. Nonetheless, in a way similar to what happened with the Yiddish press, a legal means was found to limit its development. This was through theater censorship done by the Council for the Control of Films and Plays. Based in the Ministry of the Interior, the council drew on the Public Theater Ordinance of 1927 and its amendment in 1937, both from the time of the British Mandate for Palestine. According to these laws, anyone wishing to stage a play needed a permit from the council, which was made up of public figures in the fields of education and culture and was chaired by an official of the Ministry of the Interior. However, the council had no official guidelines governing its activity since the ordinance itself did not determine any explicit criteria for approving or rejecting plays. In 1949, a senior official in the Ministry of the Interior wrote a letter to the editor of the daily *Maariv* explaining that the council "sees its role as an educational public activity of great responsibility."[12] Such a definition left the council with a lot of leeway to decide what was appropriate for approval and so allowed it to play a kind of voluntary role in the service of the regnant Zionist ideology and its cultural world view.[13]

Although there was no law or rule related directly to Yiddish, in August 1949, the council announced the following limitations on Yiddish theater as part of a more general declaration of principles: (1) in general, performances in Yiddish were to banned; (2) troupes who came to Israel for short visits would be permitted to hold performances; (3) Yiddish theater shows would be permitted for a limited time inside new immigrants' transit camps.[14] A short time later the council added a clarification determining that non-Hebrew artists visiting from abroad would be permitted to perform in a non-Hebrew language for a period of six weeks. Performances in Yiddish were included in this category.[15]

On March 3, 1950, the council held a special meeting to revisit these principles. Those opposed to them argued that Yiddish was not exactly sweeping the country and that no language should be disqualified on principle. However, those that supported them —first and foremost the representative of the Ministry of Education—insisted that everything should be done to protect the Hebrew language. They also claimed that other countries, too, did not open their gates to a language that was not the official language of the state, although this argument was not based on reliable information. "A theater is a sort of school," claimed the opponents of foreign languages, "and if we give a theatrical company permission to perform in a language other than Hebrew, we are starting to provide the nation with education in foreign languages."[16]

In the end, the council did not only accept the restrictions (which were aimed at anyone who put on a theatrical performance without a permit) but also considered ways of collaborating with the police in enforcing them. In practice, Yiddish actors—who found it difficult to get the necessary permit—often had to appear without one. The law did not allow a play to be stopped once it had begun, even if it was performed without a permit, but the Yiddish actors who appeared in it were later brought to court and fined—usually a small sum.[17]

Its inability to close down performances that had already begun irritated the council, which continually sought legal means to stop unlicensed performances while in progress. It even tried to bring about an amendment to the Public Theater Ordinance that would allow the police to stop unlicensed performances after they had started and arrest the actors on the spot.[18] The amendment was not passed, but the original law made it possible to act against persons regarded as aiding an unlicensed performance: any owner of a movie theater who rented it out for an unlicensed performance would be regarded as having committed a criminal offence, with the same true of those selling tickets for such performances.[19] As a result, theater owners would sometimes refuse to rent out their venue to Yiddish theaters or to sell their tickets.

The laws against those who performed without a permit remained in force for years, but the guidelines specifically banning Yiddish theater were canceled in the summer of 1951. In June of that year, responding to a petition to the High Court of Justice submitted by the Goldfaden company, the Israeli government instructed the council to cancel all restrictions on Yiddish theater and no further attempts were made to impose any.[20] Shows in Yiddish were still sometimes required to pay an "entertainment stamp tax," which was not required for theatrical performances in Hebrew; however, this tax was not directed explicitly against Yiddish theater and was subject to negotiation.[21] Nevertheless, the bureaucratic hostility toward Yiddish theater continued for at least another decade.

The next major challenge the Yiddish theater faced came from the Supreme Council for Cultural Affairs, which was founded in March 1952.[22] On April 24 of that year, the council's Art and Theater Committee met for the first time. Although only six months had passed since the government had decided to abolish all restrictions on Yiddish theater, the committee included among its goals "reducing the influence of Yiddish theater." In the discussion, various committee members went on the record as saying that "Yiddish theater is dangerous not just because of the language," and that "in order to wean the audience from Yiddish theater, other appropriate entertainment options should be created for them and popular Hebrew artistic troupes should be established."[23] However, though there were those on the committee who opposed Yiddish theater and tried in various ways to push it to the margins of Israeli culture, no further legal limitations were imposed.

From 1951 until the 1960s hundreds of applications for permits for Yiddish plays were submitted to the council. All of them—without exception—were approved. However, more than once council members added disparaging comments to the permit, such as "lacking content and foolish" or "lowbrow comedy." These notes had no practical significance but served to express their writers' feelings toward Yiddish in general and Yiddish theater in particular.[24]

Yiddish Theater until 1950: Theater Shows without a Permit

The most prominent characteristic of the Yiddish theatrical scene in the newly founded state was its temporary nature. The first artists to perform in Yiddish in Israel were visiting actors touring from abroad and new immigrants who had just arrived. Evenings of poetry reading were most common at this time, though some of the new immigrants did try to stage plays from the traditional repertoire of the Yiddish theater. These productions often ran into difficulties due both to the limited number of Yiddish actors available in Israel and also, perhaps mainly, to the lack of the financial means needed for a proper staging.

Perhaps the most important long-term consequence of the official policy on Yiddish theater was the constant psychological pressure it put on Yiddish actors. They certainly felt rejected and maybe even came to see themselves as part of a counterculture. Above all, however, it forced many Yiddish actors to understand that the only way to have a viable theatrical career in Israel was to move to the Hebrew theater.

The actual restrictions on Yiddish theater had few significant consequences. Only a small number of owners refused to allow Yiddish performances in their theaters, and on the whole the performances that were advertised did in fact take place. A common trick was to give the wrong starting time in the ads. The audience knew that it had to come early, but when the police showed up at the given time, the show was already in progress and so could not be stopped.[25] As we have seen, some Yiddish actors were brought to court after the fact, where they were sentenced to a fine of one Israeli pound, which they could exchange for a one-day imprisonment.[26] This was double the license fee for a performance.

Some of the early Yiddish performers immediately after the founding of the state were female singers: Jenny Lubitz, who also performed very successfully in Hebrew to great acclaim, and Lola Folman, wife of the author Yitzhak Perlov.[27] Folman was also one of the first Yiddish artists to have to contend with the censor's restrictions.[28] Similar performances were held by Rachel Holzer and Yaakov Weislitz, two Yiddish actors with a distinguished reputation from the prewar Yiddish theater in Poland, who separately visited Israel from Australia in 1950–1951. Both performed "reading soirees" in which they read from the works of Y. L. Peretz, Sholem Aleichem, Peretz Hirschbein, Der Tunkeler, Aaron Zeitlin, Eliezer Steinberg, and Yosef Papyernikov, among others.[29]

At the same time immigrant actors began to set up companies to stage plays in Yiddish. Many of them were in Jaffa, which had a significant Yiddish-speaking population. Their budget was usually limited, which is probably why they did not advertise their performances in the Yiddish or Hebrew press. Paradoxically enough, the best way to learn about the Yiddish theatrical arena in these years is from the records of the Council for the Control of Films and Plays. The documents reflect extensive theatrical activity in Yiddish. Bearing in mind that plays staged without a permit were not known to the council and so did not appear in its records, we can assume that the actual number of plays in Yiddish was even greater.

Among the more prominent companies at this time was the Yafo profesyonaler Yidish teater (Jaffa Professional Yiddish Theater), which was set up by Joseph Lichtenberg in the summer of 1950 and staged several plays in Yiddish. Some received police visits, following which the actors and the manager of the troupe were summoned.[30] Despite this the theater continued to perform, putting on the plays *Dos Volge meydl*, *Der vilner mentsh*, and *Kol nidre*,[31] all of which were staged in a cafe in Jaffa.[32] In addition, Eliezer Getler produced the plays *Yidishe mame* and *Tsipke fayer* in Jaffa and was duly brought to court for both of them. At the same time *Khasye di yesoyme* was produced at the Ohali club in Jaffa.[33] Some of these plays belonged to the traditional repertoire of

Yiddish theater;[34] others were low comedies. In nearby Tel Aviv, the Aviv Theater was founded with a repertoire consisting mostly of light entertainment and operettas, such as *Der rebe hot geheysn freylekh zayn*.[35] There were ten actors in the company, and, quite unusually for the time, they managed to earn a living from it.[36] And, of course, these productions formed only a part of what was a very active Yiddish theatrical scene in Israel in these years.

At the beginning of 1950, the renowned Yiddish actor Zygmunt Turkow, who was living in Brazil at the time, visited Israel to direct a play for the Cameri Theater in Tel Aviv.[37] That production was a failure, but while in the country, Turkow organized and participated in a number of Yiddish shows together with his wife, the actress Rosa Turkow. Since they did not obtain permits for these shows, the celebrity couple from abroad were fined one and a half Israeli pounds and given an additional suspended fine of twenty Israeli pounds to be paid if they performed without a permit again.[38]

In the same year the famous comic duo Dzigan and Shumacher visited Israel for the first time. Though they were extremely successful, they ran into serious trouble with the Council for the Control of Films and Plays (more on that below).

The year 1950 also saw the founding of the Abraham Goldfaden Yiddish Theater. This was the first attempt to establish a permanent Yiddish repertory theater in Israel. There would not be another one until the 1970s.[39] The company's actors also conducted a determined struggle against the policy that forbade performances by Israeli actors in Yiddish. As we have seen, their success led to the abolition of the ban on Yiddish theater in Israel. Following that, the troupe continued for a while without having to fight restrictions, but it did not flourish and was soon forced to disband. The reasons for its initial successes and its eventual failure have a great deal to teach us about the place of Yiddish in Israeli culture in the 1950s.

The Abraham Goldfaden Theater, 1950–1952: "We Will Not Permit a Yiddish Play"

In December 1950 a group of actors, new immigrants from Poland, came together in Tel Aviv to form a Yiddish repertory theater.[40] The leading members of the group were Nathan Wulfowitz, David Hart, and Israel Segal. Wulfowitz, an acclaimed Yiddish actor, had been a member of the Yung teater in Warsaw until 1939, had spent the war years in the USSR, and immediately after that found a place in the Jewish theater in Łódź under the leadership of Ida Kaminska. He had also appeared with some success in a number of Dzigan and Shumacher's shows. David Hart came from a family of Yiddish actors in Galicia and had been active in various companies in Poland before the war. He played in the State Yiddish Theater in Lwów in its early days and after the war performed in the displaced-persons camps. Israel Segal had been one of the founders of the Yiddish theater in the Vilna ghetto and was later involved in theatrical initiatives among Holocaust survivors in postwar Germany.[41]

Although some of them knew Hebrew, the group decided to establish a Yiddish theater company to provide employment opportunities for new immigrants who—like themselves—had previously had a stage career but had been unable to break into the Hebrew theater.[42] Their target audience was new immigrants who had not yet learned Hebrew and wanted to experience Yiddish theater as they had known it before the Holocaust.[43] In this spirit they chose the theater's repertoire, which mainly consisted of plays that were mainstays of the Yiddish theater in eastern Europe and so familiar to the theater's prospective audience. The first play to be presented was Goldfaden's classic comedy, *Di tsvey Kuni Lemel*.

From its earliest days, the Goldfaden Theater had many obstacles to overcome. First and foremost was the challenge to find a permanent home. This it finally found in the Migdal Or Garden, the garden of a deserted Arab house in the Givat Aliya (Jabalia) neighborhood in Jaffa.[44] The company also struggled with a limited budget, which meant the scenery, the stage, and even the curtain were made on the cheap.[45] In addition to all this, the theater had also to contend with the official policy that prohibited Yiddish theater.

As the law demanded, a representative of the theater contacted the Council for the Control of Films and Plays on December 27, 1950, and asked for a license to stage *Di tsvey Kuni Lemel* in Yiddish. The request was rejected.[46] Undaunted, the company began to perform anyway, and on February 16, 1951, the premiere of *Di tsvey Kuni Lemel* was held in the Armon movie theater in Holon.[47]

The actors' decision to appear without a permit led to a series of sanctions against them. A few days after the play opened in Tel Aviv, the troupe traveled to Migdal-Gad (later the city of Ashkelon). This may have been the first time that theater was to come to this township, where transit camps for new immigrants were beginning to be built; certainly none of the Hebrew-language companies had yet performed there. Nonetheless, when the actors arrived, they found the local movie theater where they were supposed to put on the play locked as the result of a police order forbidding the owner to permit a performance in Yiddish.[48]

Following this, the troupe sent a long letter to the Council for the Control of Films and Plays, explaining that the performances in Yiddish were only a temporary measure and that the company had a detailed plan for a gradual transition to performing in Hebrew. "We are Jewish actors from the Diaspora," their letter ran. "It has been our fate to suffer much trouble and persecution abroad. [So] how great is the pain and the shame [we feel] that we are suffering in much the same way in the independent Jewish state."[49] This request for a performance permit was also rejected.[50]

In light of this response, David Hart, acting as the representative of the Goldfaden company, met with the minister of the interior, Moshe Shapira, and asked him to intervene. The minister promised to do so, but nothing happened.[51] Following this, Nathan Wulfowitz met with Yeshaya Kisilov, the chair of the Council for the Control of Films and Plays, and asked to appear before the council to explain the company's motives. The council refused his request, reiterating that staging Yiddish plays in Israel would not be permitted.[52]

Meanwhile, the troupe continued to perform. It staged *Di tsvey Kuni Lemel* and Jacob Gordin's *Mirele Efros*, also without a permit from the Council for Control of Films and Plays,[53] and preparations began to stage *Hershele Ostropolyer* by Moyshe Gershonson.

On June 3 David Hart asked the Council for the Control of Films and Plays for a permit to stage the play, but, as in the past, the council answered: "We will not permit the play to be staged in Yiddish."[54]

Israeli audiences knew *Hershele Ostropolyer*; it had been performed in Hebrew at the Ohel Theater as recently as June 1948.[55] In fact plays translated from Yiddish were an integral part of the Hebrew theater's repertoire: the Habima Theater staged during the 1930s Hebrew-language productions of *Meshiyekh's keytn* (The chains of messiah) and *Ver iz ver?* (Who is the man), both by Leivick, as well as Jacob Gordin's *Mirele Efros*. In the years to come, a number of dramas by Sholem Aleichem, including *Di gold greber* (The gold diggers), *Oyfn fidele* (On the fiddle), *Der farkishefter shnayder* (The enchanted tailor), *Shver tsu zayn a yid* (It's hard to be a Jew), *Kleyne mentshelekh mit kleyne hasoges* (Little men with small horizons), and *Tevye der milkhiker* (Tevye the dairyman), were also staged in Habima.[56]

With the founding of the state, the number of plays translated from Yiddish included in its repertoire fell dramatically—part of the policy of encouraging original drama, characteristic of Israeli theater at that time—though Habima did produce a Hebrew version of Goldfaden's play *Kaptsnzon et Hungerman* (A tale of a prince) in 1953.[57] The Ohel Theater also staged a translation of *A farvorfn vinkl* (A forsaken corner) by Peretz Hirschbein.[58] The objection to the Goldfaden Theater's repertoire was therefore not to the plays themselves but to the language in which they were performed—Yiddish.

Although they had not received approval, the actors continued with rehearsals for *Hershele Ostropolyer*, and the premiere was scheduled for June 1, 1951. Further performances were scheduled for June 2, June 5, and June 29.[59]

As most of the company's performances took place without a permit, a policeman turned up at the theater almost every evening and issued the troupe with a report on which it had to pay a fine.[60] And, as we have seen, Nathan Wulfowitz was tried in the Haifa Magistrates Court and fined twenty Israeli pounds.[61]

At the end of June 1951, the police commander of the Tel Aviv region summoned David Hart and notified him that it was absolutely prohibited to hold theatrical performances in Yiddish. In addition, a police sergeant and two policemen appeared in the theater itself on June 28, notifying Hart and Israel Segal that they were strictly forbidden to stage plays in Yiddish and warning them not to perform the next day.[62]

Frustrated beyond measure, the actors of the Goldfaden troupe decided that they would not take this lying down. They would go to court to safeguard their right to perform in Yiddish.

Yiddish Theater in the High Court of Justice and in the Israeli Government: "To Condemn a Hundred Thousand People to Losing Their *Nakhes*"

The next day, June 29, 1951, the morning of the festive premiere of *Hershele Ostropolyer*, three actors representing the Goldfaden company petitioned the supreme court in its capacity as the High Court of Justice. The petitioners were Nathan Wulfowitz, David Hart, and Israel Segal. The respondents were the minister of the interior, the Council for the Control of Films and Plays, the National Headquarters of the Israel Police, the Central Investigation Department, and the police commander of the Tel Aviv District.[63]

The petitioners argued that the decision of the Council for the Control of Films and Plays to prohibit staging plays in Yiddish overstepped its authority and that the prohibitions it imposed on staging *Di tsvey Kuni Lemel* and *Hershele Ostropolyer* were illegal and contradicted "Israel's Declaration of Independence that promises freedom of language, education, and culture in the State of Israel."[64] The petitioners then argued that the council's decisions and prohibitions, as well as its instructions to the Police National Headquarters and the Tel Aviv police, were "in complete contradiction to the Public Plays Ordinance . . . which forbids discrimination between residents of the country on the basis of nationality, religion or language," and that the council had exercised its authority illegally and arbitrarily in banning plays in Yiddish, adding that it had perpetrated "malicious discrimination against the Yiddish language, which was created by the people in its Diaspora, and which is used by millions of Jews throughout the world and tens of thousands of Jews in Israel, and is a great cultural asset of the Jewish people."65 The petitioners also argued that the council's decision had no legal force because it had refused to allow the petitioners' representatives to appear before it and voice their claims. In the meantime, its actions had caused the appellants severe damage. They therefore appealed to the High Court of Justice to issue an order nisi ordering the Council for the Control of Films and Plays to explain to the court why it banned Yiddish plays in general and the two plays under discussion in particular. They also requested that the police be prohibited from interfering with the troupe's performances.66

On July 1, 1951, the High Court of Justice considered the appeal and issued an order nisi ordering the Council for Control of Films and Plays to explain its refusal to abolish the ban on performing in Yiddish in general and on the two specific plays in particular. The signatories to the order were the judges Menachem Dunkelblum, Moshe Zilberg, and Shimon Agranat.67

The court held another session on July 17, 1951, in which the state prosecutor notified the court that the Council for the Control of Films and Plays had decided not to oppose staging plays in Yiddish by local troupes. In response, the court canceled the order nisi it had previously issued.68 On the same day, the supreme court judges Shneur Zalman Heshin, Simha Assaf, and Yoel Zusman issued a court order determining that in accordance with the settlement reached between the petitioners and the respondents—that is, in view of the agreement by the Council for the Control of Films and Plays not to continue opposing the performance of plays in Yiddish—no further limitations would be imposed on Yiddish theater. The court also ordered the Council for the Control of Films and Plays to pay the Goldfaden company's legal costs.69

The case also generated a discussion on Yiddish theater at the cabinet meeting of July 18, 1951. While some ministers seemed unhappy with the very existence of a Yiddish theater, they did not say so explicitly, and there was unanimous agreement that legal and bureaucratic restrictions were no longer a practical possibility. Prime Minister Ben-Gurion was absolutely forthright in saying that Yiddish theater should be permitted in the state of Israel:

> I fear that we will lose [in court]. I also think that this matter in itself is not right. When there was just a small number of us in this country, I was a zealot. Today too I am still zealous about the Hebrew language, but when there were only a few of us we could afford to be cruel [to Yiddish]. Today we simply cannot condemn a hundred thousand people to losing a little *nakhes*.... This is the only enjoyment that these people have. It is indeed a great responsibility,... but it seems to me that we have to permit plays in Yiddish.70

The foreign minister, Moshe Sharett, added, "We cannot let the word spread that it is forbidden to act in Yiddish in Israel. However difficult it may be, we must concede."⁷¹ In the end the government decided that the minister of the interior would annul the Council for the Control of Films and Plays' decision on banning theatrical performances in Yiddish.⁷²

It was a stunning victory. The Goldfaden company was not only the pioneer in creating a Yiddish repertory theater in Israel, but also it had managed single-handedly to create an official policy that forbade interfering with Yiddish theater and made sure it would be allowed to perform without any interference.

The End of the Goldfaden Theater: "In Memory of 13 Tłomackie Street"

After its success in lifting the ban on Yiddish theater, the Goldfaden company went into a period of expansion. By the end of 1951 it had staged eight plays: *Mirele Efros* and *Kroytser sonate*, by Jacob Gordin, *Hershele Ostropolyer*, by Moshe Gershenzon; *Dos groyse gevins* (The great windfall) and *Shver tsu zayn a yid*, by Sholem Aleichem, and *Grine felder*, by Peretz Hirschbein; and also *Er kumt haynt bay nakht*, a translation of a French play, *Un ami viendra ce soir*, by Jacques Companéez and Yvan Noé, about the French resistance in World War II, directed by Nathan Wulfowitz.⁷³

In a radio interview in February 1952, on the occasion of the theater's first anniversary, the actor Israel Segal said that during the first year of its existence the theater had been a great success and played to ever greater audiences. He stated that the company had given 180 performances and estimated the number of people who had watched it to be about a hundred thousand.⁷⁴ However, the theater's report of December 1951 gave different figures, showing that only half of the tickets had been sold.⁷⁵ Reports of ticket sales made by various ticket offices and theatrical venues pointed in the same direction. The Goldfaden management blamed the problem on not having a permanent location and invested much effort in acquiring one. The hope was that a permanent location would not only become a familiar venue for theatergoers but might also turn into a Yiddish cultural center like those in prewar Warsaw on "13 Tłomackie and 2 Leszno" streets, as the author Yitzhak Perlov put it.⁷⁶

However, the Goldfaden Theater did not manage to translate its victory in court into stability and success. Its attempts to rent the Ohel Shem Theater in Tel Aviv came to nothing, and its efforts to rent places outside Tel Aviv failed too.⁷⁷ Undaunted, it staged a festive celebration of the Y. L. Peretz centennial on May 15, 1952,⁷⁸ and expanded its repertoire to include *Got, mentsh un tayvl* (God, man, and the devil), by Jacob Gordin, and Ansky's famous drama *Der dibek*.⁷⁹

Things must have seemed to be looking up during the winter season of 1951/1952 when the Goldfaden Theater staged its plays in Tel Aviv at the Hapoel

Sports Club on Nahmani Street. At the beginning of the summer, however, the lease ran out and the company had to return to Jaffa. In its letter to the management of Hapoel asking to extend the lease, the theater management admitted—in contrast to what Segal had said on the radio—that the audience in the Migdal Or Garden in Jaffa was very small. This it attributed to the venue's distance from the center of Tel Aviv. In the end, though, the Hapoel Sports Club did not accede to their request, and the Goldfaden Theater had to go back to performing in Givat Aliya in Jaffa.[80]

From there, things went downhill quite rapidly. The troupe amassed debts it could not repay and was forced to close. On July 29, 1952, an actors' meeting in the Migdal Or Garden in Jaffa decided to sell the theater to Meir Tennenbaum of Tel Aviv, who had already been dealing with the company's affairs for the past few months. Tennenbaum undertook to purchase the name of the Goldfaden Theater and to pay the company's debts to the sum of 1,205 Israeli pounds. On July 30, 1952, the company ceased to exist.[81]

It might be argued that the Goldfaden Theater failed because of all the limitations and restrictions imposed on it in its early years. There is no doubt that these weighed on it heavily, depleted its funds (which were in any case meager), and forced it to spend time and energy in legal battles. However, its success in having the ban on Yiddish theater lifted did not improve its fortunes. To the contrary, it brought its end nearer. Once the ban on Yiddish theater had been lifted, rather than enjoying success, it would seem that the Goldfaden company was forced to come to terms with the other difficulties it had faced all along, most especially the lack of an audience for a repertory theater in Yiddish. How that issue played out would eventually determine its fate.

The Audience for the Goldfaden Theater: "Sholem Asch or Sholem Aleichem"

From its financial statements it appears that although the theater performed in many places in Israel, most of its performances took place in the Migdal Or Garden in Givat Aliya, Jaffa, which actually became its home venue.[82] While the troupe ended up there because it had no other option, at the end of the day that meant that it was performing in the heart of a neighborhood full of new immigrants from Eastern Europe.

When mass immigration to Israel began in 1948, newcomers were settled in those urban neighborhoods in the center of Israel that had been vacated by their Arab residents during the war.[83] No less than 40 percent of the immigrants who arrived in 1948–1949 from Eastern Europe and the Balkans (Poland, Bulgaria, Yugoslavia, and Greece) were concentrated in and around Tel Aviv or, more precisely, Jaffa.⁸⁴ There are no statistical data to shed light on these residential neighborhoods, but semiliterary sources make it possible to construct a picture of how things must have been. These sources also refer to the cultural aspects of life in the neighborhoods and particularly to the place of Yiddish and its culture.⁸⁵

In February 1951 a long article was published in *Der yidisher kemfer*, the weekly of the Labor Zionist movement in the United States, which portrayed Givat Aliya as almost identical to an Eastern European shtetl.⁸⁶ The author, Moshe Grossman, a Yiddish writer and editor who had come to Israel from Poland, described the place as "a Yiddish-speaking territory," home to the culture and atmosphere of Eastern European Jewry: the billboards were full of Yiddish advertisements, typical Eastern Europe food was sold on the street, and the sounds of Yiddish radio broadcasts blared out from the houses. "Hebrew is hardly heard on the street," he wrote. "It is Eastern European languages, particularly Yiddish, that dominate."

Grossman also noted that Givat Aliya was not the only place of its kind and that in Yazour, an abandoned Arab village, there were also eight thousand people of Eastern European origin, and Yiddish theater performed there.⁸⁷ The author Y. D. Mittelpunkt published a similar description of Givat Aliya in *Letste nayes*, which also mentioned the Goldfaden Theater.⁸⁸

At least two articles published in these years dealt just with the Goldfaden Theater. One was written in Yiddish by Bronya Lev and appeared in *Letste nayes*,⁸⁹ the other was by Shabtai Tevet and was published in the highbrow Hebrew daily *Ha'aretz*.⁹⁰ Both articles focused specifically on the audience that came to the theater. Both described entire families carrying baskets packed with food and making a great deal of noise, and both made much of the fact that during the performance the audience would sing along with the actors and chat with the people sitting next to them. Tevet added a further detail to his article, which he called "Kasrilevke in Jaffa," after Sholem Aleichem's imaginary shtetl: from discussions he had with the audience who had watched Sholem Aleichem's *Dos groyse gevins*, it emerged that most did not know who had written the play. Some thought the author was Sholem Asch, while others did not even know who Sholem Aleichem was. They all, however, knew the songs.⁹¹

These descriptions suggest that it might have been the nature of the audience, as much as if not more than official policy, that effectively put an end to the development of Yiddish repertory theater in Israel. The character and level of an audience are determined by its "cultural capital"—that is, the knowledge with which it goes into the performance, or cultural norms. An audience needs this cultural capital to understand the play presented by the theater, and it is a function not only of its education but also its social and cultural background.⁹²

In 1950s Israel, country of origin and time of immigration were also determining factors. What this means is that the repertoire of any theater can determine the nature of the audience that will attend the shows.

The Goldfaden Theater aspired to improve its status by attracting audiences with greater cultural capital. In May 1951 it tried unsuccessfully to stage a play translated from Hebrew called *Eilat koret* (Eilat calls).[93] A year later the theater planned to put on a new comedy by David Pinsky entitled *Zi hot a dire* (She has an apartment) but changed its mind, explaining in a letter to the playwright that the company had no comic actors. The letter added that the management usually chose plays in which the actors had already appeared in prewar eastern Europe. That made life easy because the actors knew their parts and even remembered the direction, allowing the theater to manage without a director.[94] Financial necessity dictated this kind of choice, but the choice also influenced the theater's artistic level and marked it as old-fashioned and irrelevant to the new cultural realities in Israel.[95]

The Goldfaden Theater was therefore an almost direct transplant of Yiddish theater from Eastern Europe, not only in its repertoire but also in its acting style, direction, and the atmosphere created. "The entire performance," asserted an article in *Letste nayes* about a performance of *Mirele Efros* in the Goldfaden Theater, "is reminiscent of Yiddish theater fifty years ago . . . the same enthusiasm . . . and the same participation of the audience in the play."[96]

So while the Goldfaden Theater was struggling against the authorities that wanted to ban it, just carrying on performing was the best it could manage. To a certain extent the struggle itself might have given the company a degree of cohesion and strength and perhaps even raised the hope that when the restrictions on appearing in Yiddish were abolished, its financial situation would also improve. It did not happen. Once the troupe had overcome its legal problems, it then had to develop a repertoire that would attract an audience that would go on buying tickets. This it proved unable to do.

The audience that wanted Yiddish theater just for the atmosphere usually preferred light entertainment, like operettas and revue shows. Those who were interested in Yiddish repertory theater looked for performances on a high level. The Goldfaden Theater could not come up with either of the two.

Yiddish Theater after the Ruling of the High Court of Justice: "Yiddish Is Everywhere

Success in court did not save the Goldfaden Theater, but it did pave the way for an explosion in the number of Yiddish shows after the summer of 1951. Some of the performers had come to Israel as immigrants; others were only on tour. The

Yiddish theater season was relatively short, lasting for just the winter months, and the repertoire was mostly limited to reading, singing, and a few comic turns. Only a few artists tried to stage plays.[97] Nevertheless, there was a feeling that Israel was becoming the world capital of Yiddish theater. "Yiddish Is Everywhere" was the headline of a news story in the *Maariv* daily that reported on two troupes that performed in Yiddish in 1954.[98] "The Audience Continues to Flock to the Yiddish Theaters," shouted the headline to another story in the same daily a few months later.[99]

At the beginning of 1952, Zygmunt Turkow came to Israel for a second time. Among the leading Yiddish actors in prewar Poland, he had lived out the war years in Brazil before deciding finally to settle in the Jewish state.[100] In April of that year Zygmunt Turkow opened the Yidish folks teater (Popular Yiddish Theater) on Reines Street in central Tel Aviv, hoping to make it a high-class artistic theater.[101] His plan was to continue in the footsteps of the by-then-closed Goldfaden Theater and establish the company as a quality Yiddish repertory theater. Nonetheless, he had enough experience to understand that in order to succeed where the Goldfaden Theater had failed, he had to find his own way.[102]

Born in Warsaw in 1896, Zygmunt Turkow had been an actor from a very young age. One of the senior members of the well-known Der vilner trupe (The Vilna Troupe), he had also founded, together with his first wife, the famous actor Ida Kaminska, the Varshever yidisher kunst teater (VYKT, Warsaw Yiddish Art Theater).[103] Before the war, he performed in eastern and western Europe and Latin America, and once he had settled in Brazil in 1940, he opened a Yiddish theater, as well as a local theater that staged plays in Portuguese. At the beginning of 1949 he went on an extended tour of Europe, which ended with his first visit to Israel.[104] It was only in 1952, however, that he finally moved there.

From his broad theatrical experience in different Jewish communities, Turkow decided to make his theater in Tel Aviv a kind of bridge between Yiddish and Hebrew that might eventually lead to a transition to performances in Hebrew.[105] The starting point of the Yidish folks teater was far better than that of the Goldfaden Theater that preceded it. Turkow had financial resources, and although the Goldfaden Theater had had experienced actors, Turkow had an international reputation that his predecessor did not.[106] The fate of his initiative then can help us better understand the possibilities and difficulties in creating Yiddish repertory theater in 1950s Israel.

The repertoire Turkow chose for his theater was more modern and more diverse than that of the Goldfaden. His first presentation was a monodrama by the Brazilian Jewish playwright Pedro Bloch, *Back to a New Life*, which Turkow himself translated into Yiddish.[107] Though the reviews of the production were very positive, there were only a few of them, and more importantly, the audience did not come.[108] He went on to stage *Onkl Mozes*, by Sholem Asch; *Tevye der milkhiker* (Tevye the dairyman), by Sholem Aleichem; a number of Yiddish translations of Hebrew plays; and plays that combined Hebrew and Yiddish.[109] They were all failures. The audience voted with its feet, and those who did attend the theater were, as Turkow put it years later, "white-haired and bald."[110] The few reviews of Turkow's theater that appeared in the Hebrew press described it as "over sentimental" and "overly theatrical" and as a "typical Yiddish theater."[111]

Although Turkow's theater was in some respects different from the Goldfaden Theater, there were also many similarities between the two: their high-quality repertoire did not appeal to those seeking light entertainment, while their old-fashioned acting style was not attractive to the small audience that was interested in art theater in Yiddish. And while the Goldfaden Theater went on performing in Yiddish until it closed down, Turkow gave up on Yiddish.

In 1953, after only a single year, he decided to give up on Yiddish theater and move to Hebrew.[112] In 1956, about four years after settling in Israel, Turkow—together with Meir Yannai, one of the outstanding figures of the Israeli stage during the 1950s and 1960s—founded the Zuta Theater, a traveling Hebrew company of three actors, which performed throughout Israel with some success for over a decade.[113]

While Turkow succeeded in making the transition to Hebrew, limiting his Yiddish performing to just one or two evenings of readings, other artists continued to perform only in Yiddish. Almost all these shows were comedies or melodramas with a lot of singing, and they were all very similar. They gave the audience laughter, songs to sing along with, and the familiar atmosphere of the Yiddish stage, but in doing so, they also reinforced the image of Yiddish theater as light, even vulgar, entertainment of a low artistic level.

This kind of light entertainment remained popular throughout the 1950s. In 1953 Max Perlman and his wife, Gita Galina, visited Israel for the first time. Perlman, who had already performed in Eastern Europe, the United States, and Latin America, was famous for the stage character he created, which combined aspects of Maurice Chevalier and Fred Astaire, and was known in the Yiddish theater as a *kupletist*.[114]

Immediately on their arrival Perlman and Galina participated in a play by the Hebrew Matate Theater, *Zehirut ha'derech be'tikun* (Caution: Roadworks), which was defined as "a political satirical revue," the kind of performance in which they excelled.[115] In 1954, they founded their own Yiddish theater with the Hebrew name Te'atron komedya (Comedy Theater), where they staged melodramas and musical comedies based on simple songs and jokes.[116] Perlman staged

Yiddish entertainment of this kind in Israel for three decades but only for short periods.¹¹⁷ This was because he and his wife spent many long months during these years touring the Jewish world, particularly South Africa and Argentina, where there were still active Yiddish-speaking communities.¹¹⁸

In 1954 the Burstein family came to Israel to settle—the father, Pesach Burstein, and the mother, Lillian Lux, and the twins Mike and Susan (Motele and Zisele), who were just beginning to perform with their parents. On their arrival in Israel, the Burstein family found their way straight into the Yiddish scene. They moved into the Bristol Hotel on Ben Yehuda Street in Tel Aviv, the home of many visiting Yiddish actors, and took to the stage immediately.¹¹⁹ Their first shows were concerts, employing a large orchestra, which were immense successes. Their audiences included the leading lights of the Yiddish world, Israeli public figures, and even the mayor of Tel Aviv, Haim Levanon.

The Bursteins, however, wanted to expand. They had their own repertoire, which they had performed for decades throughout the entire Jewish world, and they wanted to present it in Israel too. In 1954, with a troupe of new-immigrant Yiddish actors, they produced the musical melodrama *A khasene in shtetl* (A wedding in the shtetl). It had been written by William Siegel especially for Pesach Burstein and had become the signature of the Burstein family. The Bursteins performed throughout Israel and were well received by both the Yiddish and the Hebrew press. They did not stay long, however; personal issues led them to return to the United States in 1955.¹²⁰

In that same year another pair of actors, survivors of the Warsaw ghetto, Jonas Turkow and Diana Blumenfeld, came to Israel from the United States.¹²¹ They were received with great honor as the only two artists who had survived the ghetto, giving evenings of Yiddish readings and participating in a play by H. Leivick.¹²²

In 1956 Ben-Zion Witler and Shifra Lerer visited Israel. The couple, well-known in both the United States and Argentina, appeared in several melodramas, such as *Yankel der shmid* (Yankel the blacksmith), but left Israel on the eve of the Sinai Campaign (October 1956), for which they were strongly criticized in the Hebrew press.¹²³ They returned in 1958 and staged a few more plays, all of them comedies and musical operettas.¹²⁴ At the same time, the Te'atron komedya be'Yidish, run by the famous actress Dina Halperin, produced several plays of the same kind.¹²⁵ The company also tried to expand its repertoire beyond the traditional comedies and operettas by staging a play on the struggle against the British mandate in prestate Israel.¹²⁶ In 1958, another famous Yiddish actor from the United States, Herman Yablokoff, visited Israel and performed with Joseph Lichtenberg's popular Yiddish theater in a number of musicals, particularly *Papirosn* (Cigarettes), which included the very well-known song in tango rhythm "Koyft zhe papirosn" (Please buy cigarettes), written by Yablokoff himself.[127]

This trend continued at the beginning of the 1960s. In 1962 the Burstein family returned to Israel and remained until 1964, staging their traditional repertoire, including *A khasene in shtetl* and other plays.[128] The Perlman-Galena couple also returned to Israel at that time to perform several musical melodramas.[129]

Throughout the early 1960s many Yiddish plays were staged, most of them musical comedies. The three most active companies were the Te'atron opereta ve'komedya of Joseph Lichtenberg; the Misgav Theater, which staged various plays, including *Nokhem der khokhem* (Wise Nahum), *A khasene in tfise* (A wedding in jail), and *Heym zise heym* (Home, sweet home);[130] and the Te'atron olim of H. Evron, which staged the play *Sha, sha der rebe geyt* (Hush, the rabbi's coming) and many other plays, most for only a few performances.[131]

In 1962, Eni Liton made another attempt to establish an artistic Yiddish repertory theater in Israel, alongside the Yiddish entertainment theater. Liton, a well-known actor originally from a family of Yiddish actors in Poland, came from Chile to Israel and started a Yiddish art theater.[132] Like Zygmunt Turkow's Folks teater before it, Liton's theater centered around one experienced and well-known Yiddish actor. However, unlike previous Yiddish theaters, especially the Goldfaden Theater, Liton ignored the traditional repertoire of Yiddish theater, choosing instead to stage the best of world drama translated into Yiddish. This was a new and daring attempt, aimed at a different audience from the one that normally attended Yiddish theater.

She began with *Mir froyen* (We women), a play for three actresses by the Polish author, Maria Mironowicz. The production, which had already been a success in Europe and Argentina, dealt with the love of three women for one man and focused on their intimate psychological experience.[133] *Mir froyen* was successfully performed 124 times.[134]

The next play was *Der shotn* (The shadow) by the Italian-born playwright Dario Niccodemi. This had a larger cast, which included a number of Yiddish actors who had been settled in Israel for some time, such as David Hart, one of the founders of the Goldfaden Theater.[135] In the fall of that year, Liton staged *Froy minister* (Madam minister), a political satire by the Yugoslav playwright Branislav Nušić, who was well thought of at that time; Abraham Karpinovitsh had translated the play into Yiddish.[136] At the beginning of 1963, she produced *Lucy Crown*, a family drama based on a novel by the American Jewish author Irving Shaw.[137] Over the next two years, she went on staging plays translated from Italian and Russian.[138] While the reviews in the Hebrew press were enthusiastic, the audiences did not come, and she left Israel for an extended foreign tour in 1965.[139]

There can be no doubt, then, that there was an active and vibrant Yiddish theatrical scene in Israel throughout the 1950s and 1960s. As in the pre-Holocaust Diaspora, it was characterized by a tension between a great deal of low-level popular entertainment and a small number of high-quality theatrical productions. However, in Israel, not only did Yiddish art theater never take off but also even the popular sector failed to establish itself, always remaining unstable. Since the formal restrictions on Yiddish theater had been lifted in 1951, they cannot have been the cause of this situation. To find that, we need to look elsewhere. It is by examining the perceptions of Yiddish theater in Israel and how it and its audience were viewed by Hebrew-speaking society that we will better understand the possibilities of development open to Yiddish theater in those decades.

Attitudes toward Yiddish Theater and Its Audience: "Yiddish Theaters . . . Whose Artistic Value Is Nil"

On the eve of Rosh Hashanah 1952, the daily *Davar* printed an article that summarized the past year in Israeli theater. Interestingly and very unusually the article included a section on Yiddish theater. However, it did not deal with the theater itself but with its status and attitudes toward it. Some anonymously quoted Israeli theater people were derisive. "One could justify the existence of top-class Yiddish theater," wrote Zvi Berachia, quoting an anonymous Israeli actor, "but Yiddish theaters . . . whose artistic value is nil?"[140]

When they wrote on the issue, all Israeli theater critics drew a clear connection between the cultural capital of the Yiddish theater's audiences and the level of the theater. Inherent in this was the idea that the audience's cultural capital determined the level of the theater and not the reverse. In other words, they argued that Yiddish theater in Israel positioned itself at a low level in order to adapt itself to the cultural capital of the audience that was interested in it.

This approach was to be found in both the Hebrew and the Yiddish press, though with one difference. While the Hebrew writers would present this phenomenon in a contemptuous or patronizing way and sometimes even with pity, the Yiddish writers reacted first angrily and then with sarcasm. An article in *Letste nayes* in 1952, signed with only the initials of the writer, made an impassioned call to fight *shund* on the Yiddish stage. It argued that Yiddish theater that was nothing but *shund* was exploiting the abolition of the ban on it and canceling out the Goldfaden Theater's great achievement. The article called on all those to whom Yiddish was dear to walk away from the *shund* theaters in order to put an end to them, recommending that the *shund* theaters close their doors on their own initiative, "before a struggle against them" was undertaken by people who were really concerned about the future of Yiddish.[141] This was a clear expression not only of the view of the more educated among Yiddish speakers but also of the gaping chasm between them and the audience that continued to attend the Yiddish theater. The latter were people without much cultural capital, who wanted low-level entertainment.

The Hebrew press made this very clear, reporting that the audience flocked "to the Yiddish theater despite its total provinciality" and emphasizing the uncultured nature of the audience and its behavior that would normally be unacceptable in theaters, as well as the fact that the Yiddish shows were "cabaret-like" and "with no pretense of being art."[142] In *Al HaMishmar* Stephan Gelbert made much of "the low artistic level and inferior repertoire" of some Yiddish theaters; while in the *Herut* daily newspaper, Moshe Ben-Shahar emphasized that Yiddish theater could no longer "stuff the audience with stories of the shtetl and needed more plays on current topics."[143]

It is worth emphasizing that none of the articles on the Yiddish theater in the press opposed it on principle or argued that it was an obstacle to the spread of Hebrew. On the contrary, most of the writers who wrote on the subject had great respect for Yiddish literature and drama and believed they had the power to advance Hebrew culture in Israel. "If there was a genuine Jewish theater in Yiddish that would bring to us, [here] to Israel, Sholem Aleichem or Y. L. Peretz in the original," wrote Dr. David Lazar, the editor of *Maariv*'s literary section,

> it is doubtful that it could be opposed from the point of view of the interests of Hebrew culture. We were not against Rachel Holzer's performance in Yiddish—she was performing ... art. The foreign language [i.e., Yiddish] "theater" [quotation marks in the original] that has sprung up in Israel ... is not, however, a cultural factor.... It represents theatrical *shund* in its worst form, in the style of *Khinke pinke*, and it addresses the coarsest and basest instincts. It spreads bad taste.... Anyone who enjoys its shows will no longer go to performances of any quality, cultural and clean, whether in Hebrew or a foreign language, [instead] he will demand *shund*.[144]

The attitude considering the Yiddish stage as low-level theater and its audience as having correspondingly low levels of cultural capital was surprisingly also reflected in the enthusiastic reactions to Eni Liton's productions.

"The production, in which Liton is currently performing," said the theater critic Dov Ber Malkin in a 1962 radio broadcast following the first few performances of *Mir froyen*, "lets us see that it is possible to stage Yiddish theater without embarrassment, and in a way that adds dignity to, and increases [our] faith in [Yiddish theater]. You sit in the theater and see ... a great Yiddish play."[145]

Malkin expressed himself similarly, a little later, after the opening of *Der shotn*. "The general impression [the production gave me] is of a miracle. A breath of fresh air is blowing in the Yiddish theater in Israel, and once again there is hope of a renaissance.... The audience itself"—he added, unlike the usual Yiddish theater audience—"sits tensely and fascinated, participating in the experience, it smiles and sheds a tear."[146]

Malkin was not alone in his views. Other theater critics wrote in the same spirit.[147] Uri Kesari of *Maariv* was quite outspoken: "Usually, I avoid the Yiddish shows that have flooded our stage.... [But recently] I have had the chance to be amazed at the level and finesse of the actress, Eni Liton."[148]

At the end of 1963 the weekend edition of *Maariv* devoted a double-page spread to Yiddish theater. In a long, illustrated article, the theater critic Shraga Har-Gil discussed the state of Yiddish theater in Israel. Although it was written with sympathy and compassion concerning the difficulties faced by Yiddish actors, it is hard to ignore in his words a touch of arrogance, perhaps even contempt, not for the actors but for the audience who came to see them. "Shmaltz" was what Har-Gil called the material that the Yiddish theater presented. For him, its audience were "simple people," and he noted that the theater troupes had to travel to distant and out-of-the-way places to find them. "A simple audience," he wrote, quoting one of the producers of the Yiddish troupes, "has special requirements. It is not interested in classical plays or modern plays. If I want to succeed, I have to stage bad plays, the names of whose authors I don't even remember. If, despite everything, I want to present good art and stage a serious play, as I am occasionally tempted to do, I lose a lot of money.... I earn good money from bad plays and lose it on an artistic production."[149]

This image of Yiddish theater became so widespread, even among lovers of the language, that in later years the phrase "Yiddish theater" was used to describe melodramatic and pathetic behavior.[150] In fact it was also extended to Yiddish in general—a point I will return to later.

This view of Yiddish theater was not limited just to the Hebrew press. In 1964, a satirical article in the Yiddish monthly *Lebens-fragn* described Yiddish theater as a kind of street market where all the traders were selling poor-quality merchandise and all the clients wanted to buy it. "Only a small minority is interested in good theater," claimed the writer sarcastically, "people who might read a book when they have some free time." He added: "These are the people who are interested in seeing Eni Liton and [Joseph] Buloff."[151]

However, reality was much more complex. Liton and Buloff were by no means the same thing. Liton, as we have seen, was an excellent Yiddish actress who offered modern international drama in Yiddish translation to the Israeli audience. She received rave reviews from the Israeli press but attracted only small audiences. Buloff was an internationally renowned star of stage and screen as well as a huge celebrity in the Jewish world. Though his repertoire was classical (and included both *Othello* and *Death of a Salesman*), his name alone was enough to attract the mass audience.

The power of this kind of celebrity was not lost on the Israeli authorities, and it welcomed international stars like Buloff, Maurice Schwartz, and Ida Kaminska with open arms and even invited them to stay and join the Hebrew stage. This formed part of an unofficial but very practical policy using Yiddish to help constitute Israel's cultural hegemony over the entire Jewish world.

"Let Him Settle Down with Us and Become a Hebrew Actor": Foreign Stars in Israel

Throughout the 1950s and 1960s, performances by the great actors of the international Yiddish stage played an important role in the Israeli Yiddish theatrical world. For the guest artists, visiting the new nation-state of the Jewish people was unquestionably an emotional experience. However, it was also an important professional move. The significant decline of Yiddish theater in both post-Holocaust Europe and the United States was forcing Yiddish actors to seek out new audiences. Many traveled to Latin America to perform,[152] but after the establishment of the state and the large-scale immigration of survivors from Europe, Israel became the preferred destination. In fact, Israel became the largest and most diverse arena for Yiddish theater worldwide.

This situation undoubtedly gave a boost to the "top end" of Israeli Yiddish theater but at the same time also increased the traditional tension between the popular and artistic tendencies in the Yiddish theater. The audience that the foreign stars attracted included not only new immigrants but also, perhaps especially, Yiddish-speaking old-timers in Israel—intellectuals, public figures, journalists, and writers, whose primary interest was to see a great actor or one of the classic Jewish plays, not necessarily Yiddish theater as such. These people generated a new, enlightening public discourse on Yiddish theater in Israel. These visits were viewed with favor by public figures, journalists, and high officials as they helped strengthen the status of Israel as a highly desirable venue for successful Jews with strong reputations and thus helped strengthen the position of Israel as the nation-state and cultural center of the entire Jewish people. This also demonstrated how Yiddish art theater was respected and welcomed, as opposed to the popular theater, and thus reflected strongly the traditional dichotomy between the two kinds of Yiddish theater. And while Yiddish popular theater was considered a negative influence in the process of creating a Hebrew culture, Yiddish art theater was perceived as among the Jewish historical cultural assets.

It is perhaps no surprise that some of these visiting actors—in particular Maurice Schwartz, Joseph Buloff, and Ida Kaminska—were invited, each in a different way, to settle in Israel and start their own companies. Their stories, therefore, are important if we want to understand the Israeli leadership's complex and multifaceted approach to Yiddish theater and Yiddish in general.

Maurice Schwartz: "To Redeem the Yiddish Theater from *Shund* and '*Kitsch*'"

During the 1950s, Maurice Schwartz (1890–1960) was probably the best-known representative of Yiddish theater worldwide. An actor, director, adapter, and producer, he had been the major personality in American Yiddish theater between the two world wars. In 1918, he had founded the Yiddish Art Theater (Yidisher kunst teater), a first-rate institution, and managed it until it closed in 1950. Schwartz was its director, producer, and leading actor and so created the model of a Yiddish theater based on one man—a "star"—which dominated the Yiddish theater world in the United States.[153]

Schwartz started visiting Israel, then Mandatory Palestine, in the late 1930s with the decline of Yiddish theater in the United States.[154] On his first two visits, he staged Hebrew versions of two plays that he had adapted from novels by I. J. Singer, *Yoshe kalb* (Yoshe the calf) and *Di brider Ashkenazi* (*The Brothers Ashkenazi*)—the two greatest box-office successes in his career. He also acted in them. The fact that he had appeared on the Hebrew stage could not but shape the way he was viewed and treated by public figures and in the Hebrew press both before and after the establishment of the state.[155]

It is not surprising, then, that when he came on his first visit to the newly established state in 1951, he was welcomed with great enthusiasm by leading political figures, including the minister of education and the mayor of Haifa, as well as by writers and journalists. This time, however, Schwartz did not come to Israel to contribute to the Hebrew theater. His aim was to create a local version of his own theater, the Yiddish Art Theater in New York, which had closed down a year earlier. On his arrival, he declared that he would be willing to move to Israel and settle there permanently on the condition that it would be possible for him to establish a Yiddish art theater that would perform locally and go on tours throughout the Jewish world.[156]

Not surprisingly, Schwartz's knowledge of the Hebrew language, as well as his expressed desire to settle in Israel, dominated all three of his visits there, in 1951, 1956, and then finally in 1960, during which he fell ill and died. Nonetheless, the theater he hoped to found in Israel was intended to be a Yiddish theater, and the way in which the idea was received is highly relevant here.

During his 1951 visit, Schwartz directed a Hebrew-language version of the classic Yiddish play *A farvorfn vinkl* (A forsaken corner—*Pina nidahat* in Hebrew) by Peretz Hirschbein, at the Ohel Theater. Also, in keeping with the tradition of Yiddish actors, he gave some evening performances that included the reading of mainly Yiddish literature and some Hebrew.[157] The reviews in the Hebrew press in Israel naturally focused on the artistic aspects of Schwartz's production: the excellence of the play, the direction, and the acting. Most also reflected a quite complex view of Yiddish theater as enriching Israeli Hebrew culture and particularly as representing the transition from the Jewish culture of the Diaspora—mainly in Yiddish—to a culture centered in Israel and integrated into Israeli society. They particularly noted how that kind of production would help make Israel the center of Jewish culture worldwide. In addition, newspaper articles also appeared discussing the integration of the Yiddish stars into Israeli culture not as something important in and of itself but as a significant contribution to Israeli culture and society.

Y. M. Neiman, a member of the editorial board of the daily *Davar* and a former journalist for the Warsaw Yiddish newspaper *Haynt*, who at that time was rather hostile toward Yiddish,[158] praised Schwartz for his intention to invest his talent and his reputation in Israel and to establish a Yiddish theater there that would maintain the link with the Diaspora. "It is nice to welcome an artist who is not just 'stopping by for the night' but is totally prepared to be a citizen," he wrote. He concluded by saying that by receiving Schwartz with lavish applause, the audience was expressing its intention to accept him as "a faithful son of the homeland." Neiman went even further by describing a one-man show during which Schwartz read from the works of major Yiddish writers as an "abbreviated *Shulhan aruch* [A set table—the book of Jewish law] of the Jewish theater," contrasting that with the "Hebrew theater" and singing the praises of the former.[159]

Other theater and literary critics presented Schwartz's performance similarly as a positive contribution to the Israeli stage, not however as Yiddish theater in itself but as a way to include the east European Jewish past in Israeli culture as what Pierre Nora has termed "a realm of memory."[160]

Maurice Schwartz visited Israel twice more. His 1956 declaration that he would settle there if he could found a Yiddish theater did not stir many waves,[161] but his last visit in 1960 was entirely devoted to this cause.[162] That year he produced *Yoshe Kalb* in Yiddish, but the reviews were meager and unenthusiastic.[163] They did, however, praise Schwartz himself and supported his initiative to revive his Yiddish theater in Israel,[164] emphasizing the fact that it would be aimed at Jewish audiences worldwide and tour extensively.[165]

Clearly, by 1960 nobody believed that Yiddish theater could still be an obstacle for Hebrew. The praises heaped on Schwartz as an exceptional artist only strengthened the image of most Yiddish theater as lowbrow.[166]

Schwartz's plan came to nothing, for during his last visit to Israel in May 1960, he fell ill and died.[167] *Davar*, the daily of the dominant Mapai party, described the expectations from his theater in an unsigned piece published a day after his death: "Schwartz came to Israel with many plans. He wanted to set up an artistic Yiddish theater whose center would be in Israel, from where it would tour the Diaspora. His dream was to redeem the Yiddish theater from the *shund* and the kitsch that has characterized most of the Yiddish plays put on in Israel, and to revive the glorious tradition of Yiddish theater from the prewar years."[168]

A high-quality Yiddish theater to be founded in Israel and bring high Jewish culture to Jewish communities in the Diaspora was how opinion formers in Israel wanted to see Yiddish theater at the beginning of the second decade of the state's existence. As we shall see, that attitude was not restricted to Maurice Schwartz and his plans.

Joseph Buloff: "He Did Not Get the Special Attitude towards Yiddish Prevalent Here"

If Maurice Schwartz was the best-known representative of Yiddish theater, Joseph Buloff was the embodiment of the Jewish actor who made it from the Yiddish stage to Broadway and Hollywood. Born in Vilna in 1899, Buloff was a member of the mythological Vilner Troupe and appeared alongside its greatest actors until, in 1927, he migrated to the United States to act in Maurice Schwartz's Yiddish Artistic Theater. There he became a star and was invited to appear on Broadway in some of the most popular musicals (*Oklahoma*, 1943–1948). Following that, he appeared in Hollywood movies and TV programs, which were enormously successful. He did not forget his roots, however, and in 1951 translated Arthur Miller's *Death of a Salesman* into Yiddish and played the title role, which was considered a huge artistic achievement.[169] Buloff visited Israel many times, where he was given celebrity treatment as a virtuoso artiste and an international star who had begun his career in the Jewish theater. Nonetheless, the context of Yiddish and of Yiddish theater in Israel eventually came to the fore.

Buloff's first visit to Israel lasted from March to September 1953.[170] It was regarded as a top-notch artistic event, and he was warmly received by the world of the theater and the Israeli Hebrew media.[171] The program for his visit, during which he gave no fewer than fifty-two performances, included evenings of readings in Yiddish, at which he was joined by the Yiddish actors David Hart and Fela Feld.[172] Still, though Buloff's performances were in Yiddish, the reactions to them during his first visit did not focus on Yiddish. The reaction in the Hebrew press included the following: "A visit by an artist like Buloff is an event in artistic life,"[173] "a unique, once-in-a-lifetime talent as an actor," "an experience of pure art,"[174] and "true art."[175]

His next visit was in 1956.[176] This time, he himself linked it to the world of Yiddish, when he announced on arrival that he wanted to appear in Israel with a Yiddish company and present good theater, not *shund*.[177] And indeed, not only did he put on marvelous Yiddish theater while he was there, he also provoked a media discussion about Yiddish theater, its future in general, and its place in Israel in particular.

All the articles that dealt with Buloff noted—favorably—that since the establishment of the state it had become a magnet, drawing Yiddish actors in search of an audience. They all lavished praise on Buloff's acting, and expressed the opinion, in one way or another, that a Yiddish theater on a high artistic level would have a serious contribution to make to Israeli culture and society.[178] "The Yiddish audiences are also thirsty for true art and will know how to appreciate it if it is made available to them," wrote the theater critic Dr. Emil Feuerstein.[179] There were also other opinions. Another critic, Asher Nahor, of the daily *Herut*, raved about Buloff but concluded his article with the words: "Let him settle down with us and become a Hebrew actor, and we will receive him with open arms as a Jew returning to his homeland."[180]

Buloff returned to Israel early in 1958[181] to stage top-quality plays in Yiddish, foremost among them his own Yiddish translation of Arthur Miller's *Death of a Salesman*. As in the past, he was highly praised for his acting.[182] Following that success, about three months into his visit, he announced at a press conference that he intended to remain in Israel and found a quality Yiddish theater that would also represent Israel abroad. He went on to say that in recent months he had noticed in Israel "profound and positive changes in the attitude to Jewish culture in general and to the Yiddish language in particular."[183] In response, the writer Shlomo Shva noted, "Because of his great talent—people did not relate to Buloff or to his plays with the special attitude towards Yiddish prevalent here—love, nostalgia, or ridicule."[184] There was some truth in that.

A few months after Buloff's announcement, the Ministry of Finance issued an order exempting a number of theaters from the "stamp tax." Buloff's was one of them.[185] In practical terms, the exemption was not very significant because the tax was completely rescinded two years later.[186] However, this tax, which was not imposed uniformly and was not collected from the large Hebrew theaters, was perceived as just one more instance of the state's harassment of Yiddish theater.[187] By exempting Buloff, and shortly thereafter Maurice Schwartz,[188] the finance ministry was giving expression to the government's wish to woo the Yiddish stars and encourage them to go on appearing in Israel, even in Yiddish.

During his next visit to Israel in 1961, Buloff put on the play *Tevye and His Seven Daughters* together with a company.[189] This time, too, the Israeli media was enthusiastic. Still, the idea of establishing a Yiddish theater in Israel was not mentioned anymore, while several writers did express the hope that Buloff would settle in Israel and join the Hebrew theater.[190] What changed during this visit was the holding of the Eichmann trial, which set in motion a dramatic shift in the attitude of Israeli society toward the eastern European Jewish past.[191] For the first time the Hebrew press described Yiddish theater in positive and nostalgic terms as "a pleasant, precious reminder of Jewish life in the Diaspora, in a world that once existed but is no more."[192]

Starting in the mid-1950s, then, Yiddish stars from abroad who appeared in Israel were thought to be making a significant contribution to Israeli culture by enriching it with works from classical Jewish culture and bringing to Israel the aura of international celebrity. Above all, however, they were thought to help make Israel the center of Jewish culture worldwide. In an article he wrote following another of Buloff's visits in 1966, Nahman Ben-Ami stated explicitly that Israel was becoming the one place in the world that actually nurtured Jewish culture and was helping it continue to survive.[193] He was not the first to say this. The point had already been made during the visit to Israel of another Yiddish star, Ida Kaminska.

Ida Kaminska: "A Valuable Asset for the State of Israel"

If Schwartz and Buloff represented to Israelis the Yiddish theater in the United States and the New World in all its aspects, Kaminska symbolized the Yiddish artistic theater of eastern Europe and the Old World in general.

As the daughter of Ester-Rokhl Kaminska, the legendary Yiddish actress known by the sobriquet "the mother of Yiddish theater," Ida Kaminska began her acting career at the age of five. Together with her first husband, Zygmunt Turkow, she founded the Varshever yidisher kunst teater (VYKT—The Warsaw Yiddish Art Theater), 1922–1928, managed Yiddish theaters in various parts of the Soviet Union (where she had fled on the outbreak of World War II), and reestablished Yiddish theaters in Łódź and Wrocław when she returned to

Poland after the war. In 1950, those theaters were nationalized and named the Ester-Rokhl State Yiddish Theater after her mother; Ida Kaminska was director. In 1955 the State Yiddish Theater moved to Warsaw. Despite the fact that the Polish government maintained the theater as a propaganda tool meant to show the world its positive attitude to minority cultures, and though its audience was small, Ida Kaminska continued to be greatly admired by Holocaust survivors and promoters of Yiddish theater and drama throughout the world.[194]

She visited Israel twice in the late 1950s, and her performances were given glowing reviews by the critics.[195] Her first visit to Israel in the summer of 1957 was described as a private visit, but she also met with public figures, government ministers, and leading actors and participated in special press conferences.[196] In addition, before leaving, Kaminska told the press of her plan to tour Israel with her company a few months later. Like Schwartz and Buloff, she also raised the possibility of moving to Israel and founding her own Yiddish theater.[197] However, what differentiated her visits from those of the other two was the fact that official Israeli agencies were involved in organizing them.[198]

The Israeli tour that Kaminska promised was delayed for almost two years, as a result of various bureaucratic problems, but this in no way diminished the enthusiasm and great excitement with which she and her company were received. The tour opened with *Di beymer shtarbn shteyendik* (The trees die standing tall), a Yiddish translation of the play *Los arboles mueren de pie*, by the Spanish playwright Alejandro Casona. The play had been staged in Hebrew by Habima during the months before Kaminska's visit and so was familiar to theatergoers in Israel.

On Saturday night, November 28, 1959, a gala performance of the play was held in the Ohel Shem in Tel Aviv. The large audience that filled the hall and welcomed the actress and her company with loud cheers included government ministers, members of the Knesset, and officials of the Foreign Ministry, as well as public figures and famous actors.[199] Rave reviews in the Hebrew press described the production as a great emotional and artistic experience.[200]

Kaminska and her company staged four more plays in Israel—all from the classical repertoire of the Yiddish theater. These were *Sender Blank*, based on a story by Sholem Aleichem; *Mirele Efros* by Jacob Gordin, one of the mainstays of the Yiddish theater; *Professor Mamlock* by Friedrich Wolf; and *Meylekh freylekh* (Happy king) by Jacob Preger. All the productions were described in the reviews as moving because of who the actors were, though Kaminska herself was praised rather more than the company.[201] One element common to all the reviews was the view, expressed implicitly or explicitly, that Kaminska's visit should not be judged by the same criteria as those of other Yiddish actors.

Perhaps because she came from the old world of eastern Europe, the issue of her settling in Israel seemed to take on a greater importance than it did during the visits of other Yiddish stars.²⁰²

This was certainly the case with the government, which was far more interested in Kaminska and even had the Foreign Service act behind the scenes to promote her visits. A short time before she came to Israel for the first time (in 1957), Kaminska and her company toured London, where the secretary in the Israeli embassy set up a meeting with her and members of her company to discuss, among other things, the possibility of their moving to Israel. Following the conversation, the first secretary of the Israeli embassy in London cabled the foreign minister, Golda Meir, raising the issue of Kaminska and her company perhaps moving to Israel. "From an artistic viewpoint," he wrote, "the theater is a valuable asset in which Israel has an interest too." He suggested that immediate steps be taken to move the theater to Israel in its entirety. Such a theater, he wrote, could go on tours throughout the Jewish world and "bring culture and art in Yiddish from the State of Israel to those Jewish centers for which Yiddish is still a precious language. I regard such tours," he went on, "as great opportunities to create a solid, living bridge between Israel and the Jewish communities of the Diaspora. There is no need to explain just how important that can be."²⁰³

The Israeli consul in Warsaw, Katriel Katz, wrote in a similar vein in a secret report that he submitted to the Foreign Ministry several weeks later: "It would be a good idea to move the base of the [Kaminska's] theater to Israel and, with the help of Jewish institutions abroad, give it the support [it needs to maintain] a high [artistic] level and an Israeli repertoire; we can then have it carry the message of Israel and Zionism to those Jewish communities whose language is Yiddish."²⁰⁴

The plan to move Kaminska's theater to Israel never materialized,²⁰⁵ though it was raised again in the next few years. However, the internal correspondence between members of the Foreign Ministry clearly reveals the idea, referred to only between the lines in the press, that such a move could enhance Israel's status in the Jewish world and put it at the head of the transnational network of Yiddish theater.

Two years later, at a party held by the daily *Davar* for Kaminska and her actor husband, Meir Melman, toward the end of another visit to Israel, the newspaper's editor, Haim Shurer, expressed the same idea but in reverse. Israel, he said, had now become the largest center in the world of Yiddish. Hence, he suggested, Kaminska and her husband should not rush to settle there. It would be better if they went on appearing before the Jews in Eastern Europe, who were cut off from Jewish culture.²⁰⁶

Di royte fatsheyle (The Red Kerchief): The Comic Duo Dzigan and Shumacher

While Yiddish actors who were new immigrants to Israel represented the theater's struggle for survival and the lowbrow entertainment that gave Yiddish theater its bad name and while the stars from abroad represented prestige and fine acting in which the state of Israel gladly took pride, Dzigan and Shumacher—the satirical, comic duo from Poland—were a phenomenon without parallel. For the Holocaust survivors living in Israel (and, of course, not only there) they symbolized the survival of the Jewish people, their will to overcome suffering, the remarkable revival of Jewish life, and, most importantly, continuity with the cultural world that had existed before. Though they were very popular across the world of transnational Yiddish before the Holocaust, their post-Holocaust performances made them into a beloved cultural institution that people took into their hearts far more than even the highest-quality entertainment in Yiddish. To understand how this came about, we need first to look a little more closely at their early careers.

Dzigan and Shumacher made their start in Łódź in central Poland in the late 1920s, in the *Kleinkunstbine* (cabaret theater). The company was called Ararat (an acronym for Artistisher revu teater or Artistisher revolutsyonerer teater) and was managed by the poet Moyshe Broderzon. One of the major companies in Yiddish that developed in Poland in the 1920s and 1930s, Ararat was influenced by both the modernist, avant-garde theater tradition of the European and Russian literary cabaret and the tradition of humoristic shows in Yiddish.[207]

Both Dzigan and Shumacher were born in Łódź, Poland's second-largest city, on the eve of World War II. Its Jews were known not only for the major role they played in developing the city's textile industry, which earned it the title the "Manchester of Poland," but also for their innovative and original Yiddish-language culture, which boasted a number of major writers and an active theatrical life. From after World War I until the late 1920s, no less than three Yiddish theaters operated in the city, including the Ararat company that nurtured the artistic growth of the comic duo.[208]

Ararat, an innovative and avant-garde company established in 1927, had its ups and downs. In the early 1930s, during a tour of Poland, it abandoned its artistic and experimental aspirations for humorous shows, skits, and sketches, satirical in nature and based on the Jews' life in Poland, together with songs that became enormous hits in Jewish society. The company also decided to abandon the dialect usually heard in Yiddish theater until then, from Volhyn, to use the authentic Łódź dialect of their daily lives. This was the moment when the Dzigan and Shumacher duo act was born, and Ararat performances provided the basis for their repertoire, which was mainly political and social satire.

Like other famous comic duos, such as Abbott and Costello and Laurel and Hardy, that of Dzigan and Shumacher was based on opposites. Dzigan was the simple guy, nervous, quick to react, funny, and always provoking the slow, intelligent, and well-educated Shumacher.[209] It was the contrast between the two that gave their sketches their energy.

The rise of Hitler and the increase of antisemitism in Poland pushed the duo to insert much more political material into their repertoire. In their shows, they reacted with growing acerbity to current events, while coming up with creative ways to fool the censor. Since their scripts were monitored, they used ad-lib jokes, physical gestures, their facial expressions, and even songs that they only hummed in order to say what the censor would not allow them to. It did not take long before they became enormously popular.

The pair continued to perform until August 25, 1939. In late September, about a month after the German occupation, they left Warsaw and fled to Bialystok. There, the Soviet authorities appointed them, together with Broderzon, managers of Der Bialystok Yidish miniatur teater (The Miniature Jewish Theater of Bialystok), which was founded with the support of the Minsk Regional Ministry of Culture. The theater existed until June 1941, during which time it staged two shows, which included familiar songs and sketches and pieces that reflected the realities of life for the Jewish refugees from Poland. Under the auspices of the Ministry of Culture, the company toured all the major Jewish towns in the Soviet Union, where it met with enormous success.

When the company disbanded following the Nazi invasion of June 1941, Dzigan and Shumacher tried to join the Polish military force known as the Anders Army but were arrested and imprisoned. Later they were sent to a labor camp in central Russia, from which they were liberated in August 1946. In July 1947, they returned to Poland.

When those Holocaust survivors who remained in Poland learned about the duo's return, many came to welcome them. The duo stayed in Poland for two years, during which time they staged four shows. The first, *Abi me'zet zikh* (Just as long as we meet again), was staged in Warsaw at the end of August 1947. It was a performance with profound symbolic significance for many Jews, signaling the possibility of revival and some kind of continuation of pre-Holocaust Jewish life.

In 1948 the two starred in one of the first films about the Holocaust, *Unzere kinder* (Our children), directed by Nathan Gross and produced in Poland.[210] In June 1949, they appeared in Paris in a performance attended by fifteen thousand people. From there they toured Europe and then made their way to Israel.

"They Are Performing in Yiddish": Dzigan and Shumacher in Israel

Dzigan and Shumacher arrived in Israel on March 15, 1950. When they disembarked at Haifa port, two receptions awaited them. The first was organized, a press conference and a brief toast in their honor. The second was spontaneous, warm, and moving, and it lasted much longer than planned. A crowd of police officers, firemen, sailors, and stevedores at the port surrounded the two and in an air of great excitement they reminisced about the duo's shows from prewar Poland.[211] The audience clearly loved Dzigan and Shumacher.

Their first performance in Israel was held the very next day at the Ohel Shem Theater on Balfour Street in Tel Aviv. The hall was packed to the rafters.[212] As the show began, the lights dimmed and Dzigan's hand came out from between the curtains waving a red kerchief—*Di royte fatsheyle*, his trademark. A hush fell over the audience and the curtain rose. The performance began with the sketch *Abi me'zet zikh* (Just as long as we meet again), which, as in Poland had enormous emotional power for the survivors. "Abi me'zet zikh," the two said to each other, as the audience rose to its feet in tears.

"Jews from all over the world have gathered here," Dzigan said to Shumacher.

"Yes, indeed," Shumacher replied, "Jews from Poland."

"Jews from Russia," Dzigan added.

And so they went through every part of the Yiddish-speaking Diaspora, until someone from the audience shouted out the name of one place that had not been mentioned. Dzigan responded at once with a stereotypical joke about the Jews of that country. The audience burst into laughter, and the show began.[213]

Abi me'zet zikh showcased every aspect of the duo's art: their use of a comic signature, Dzigan's red kerchief (which functioned like Charlie Chaplin's cane); their choice of familiar sketches from the past alongside the adoption of contemporary issues in their new material; their total fluency in all the nuances of contemporary Jewish humor; and, of course, their amazingly strong and direct emotional link with their audience, as well as the phenomenal comic virtuosity of each one individually and both together. Their success was immediate and enormous. The first show ran for eighty performances and was a total sellout.[214] The next, *Tate du lakhst* (Dad, are you laughing), ran from October 1950 until the end of March 1951 and was also a huge success.[215]

Though the duo left Israel in April 1951 after their two successful runs, they returned a year and a half later, at the end of 1952,[216] with a new show called *Di velt shoklt zikh* (The world is shaking).[217] The duo continued to appear in Israel until 1960, when they split up, ending a partnership that had lasted thirty-two years.[218]

Dzigan and Shumacher were a unique phenomenon in the world of Yiddish in Israel. Although they only became permanent residents in Israel in 1958, when each bought an apartment in Tel Aviv (until then they lived with their families at the Bristol Hotel in Tel Aviv, the residence of choice for Yiddish guest performers),[219] Israel was their center. It was the base from where they went on very long tours, in particular to Jewish communities in Latin America, usually starting with Buenos Aires, where they had had their own theater. Over the years they also appeared in the United States and in Western Europe.[220] In all, they put on ten shows in Israel during the 1950s, all outstanding box-office successes and highly acclaimed by the critics.[221]

In May 1961, a little over a year after they broke up,[222] Shumacher passed away.[223] Dzigan continued to appear on his own for another two decades, though with less success.

There can be no doubt that Dzigan and Shumacher were an extraordinary phenomenon in the world of Yiddish theater in Israel. Not only were they not Israeli citizens; they spent much of their time outside the country. Nonetheless, they received much greater coverage in the press than any other Yiddish performer, and when they—like all the other Yiddish performers—had to cope with censorship restrictions, leading journalists and public figures were always willing to come to their aid.

Such problems began on April 5, 1950, just two weeks after they had arrived in Israel for the first time. The duo applied to the Council for the Control of Films and Plays for a permit to put on a show in Yiddish. In the case of guest performers from abroad, the council usually gave them a permit for six weeks with the explicit caveat that it would not be extended.[224] In this case, the council gave a permit for a longer period, but only on condition that a third of the show would be in Hebrew.[225] In October of that year, the two were back with the council, applying for a second permit to put on their next show, which they described as bilingual. The permit was granted, but the duo was warned that this would have to be their last play before they left for abroad and that they would not be given another permit to appear with a program that was not entirely in Hebrew.[226]

However, while the Goldfaden Theater's struggle with the censor was barely covered in the media, and the Hebrew press was not generally supportive of the Yiddish theater, journalists hurried to help Dzigan and Shumacher. One of the first to do so was Ezriel Carlebach. Writing in May 1950, Carlebach published a long editorial devoted to the censorship of Yiddish theater in general and of Dzigan and Shumacher in particular. With sharp irony, he attacked the Ministry of the Interior over its policy of language censorship, as well as the attitude to Yiddish theater of the Council for the Control of Films and Plays. His main emphasis, though, was on the duo itself. He made much of their central role in pre-Holocaust Jewish culture in Poland, the miracle of their survival, and the enormous cultural importance of their shows for survivors in general, as well as for the broad Israeli audience.[227]

He was not alone. Several days earlier, Joseph Heftman, another leading journalist and chairman of the Journalists Association in Israel, had sent a letter to the minister of the interior, Moshe Shapira, asking him to rescind the language censorship of Israeli theater. Like Carlebach, he cited his objections in principle to the restrictions on Yiddish theater, but the major focus of his letter was the case of Dzigan and Shumacher, whose performance, he said, was heartwarming and gave expression to the very best of Jewish culture from prewar Poland.[228] Although the minister did not remove the restrictions and continued to express his hope that the pair would eventually introduce Hebrew into their performances, he did point out that he had attended their shows himself and enjoyed them very much—something definitely not typical for an official letter of that sort.[229]

In fact, Dzigan and Shumacher provided an exceptional theatrical experience that evoked waves of love for them from very different audiences. This they encouraged with radio broadcasts and voluntarily appearances in hospitals and even an army base.[230]

From the day that Dzigan and Shumacher first set foot on Israeli soil until the day they split up, they were lauded by the Hebrew press. Journalists of all political and cultural stripes sang their praises.[231] It was not only journalists who had connections to the world of Yiddish who raved about them; even critics who did not necessarily support Yiddish wrote that Dzigan and Shumacher were "elegant" performers, "a phenomenon unparalleled on our stage,"[232] and "virtuosos of Jewish humor."[233]

The Best Israeli Theatrical Satire: Dzigan and Shumacher's Success and the Development of Yiddish Theater in Israel

In many ways, Dzigan and Shumacher's act belongs to both the kinds of Yiddish performers we have discussed here. They started out as artists from abroad who performed in Israel as frequent guests but soon made Israel their base and came to be seen as part of Israeli cultural life.

Several questions follow: How did Dzigan and Shumacher manage to make the transition from visitors to permanent fixtures? And why were they so successful for an entire decade while all the other local Yiddish theater was such a dismal failure? Why were their shows treated differently from other theatrical performances in Yiddish in Israel? And what does that tell us about how Yiddish theater was viewed there during the 1950s?

The answer may seem simple. They had been celebrities throughout the Jewish world before the Holocaust. Of course, the same is true of Schwartz and Buloff. They had been—and still were—famous actors on the Yiddish stage and on the stage in general, who attracted audiences interested in quality Yiddish theater. They were not, however, from Eastern Europe. (Kaminska was, but as she came to Israel for only one brief tour, her case is not analogous.)

Not only did Dzigan and Shumacher come from Poland, where many then living in Israel had seen them perform, but they also symbolized Polish Jewry in the eyes of their audience. They had survived antisemitism in Poland, the Holocaust, and prison in the Soviet Union and then returned to Poland after the war. They thus, in the best possible way, represented survival and the continuation of Jewish life after the Holocaust. This gave them an emotional charge that was uniquely theirs and unquestionably played a major role in their success. That alone, however, probably cannot explain their decade-long success and the fact that their performances also attracted Israeli old-timers, who neither shared the duo's biography nor had any special interest in Yiddish.

One reason for their popularity was, of course, the sheer quality of their shows, their virtuoso performances, and the interaction between them, all of which created an unparalleled theatrical experience. In addition, there were the scripts, some of which they even wrote themselves, under the pen name "Shudzig"—Shu(macher) and Dzig(an).

Another reason for their success was the satirical nature of their shows. From the mid-1930s in Warsaw, the two had made the focus of their performances a satirical response to contemporary Jewish life. They had reacted not only to antisemitism and the economic crisis but also to the everyday life of Polish Jews, so their material had to be up-to-date, dynamic, and relevant to their audiences. This was also the hallmark of their shows in Israel.[234]

Although they did not live in Israel permanently, their ability to observe the realities of Israeli life and discern its nuances enabled them to present political and social satire that was precise, acute, and subversive. That was their great strength and perhaps the major reason for their huge success in Israel.

For example, in their first show, the duo performed a sketch reflecting the life of new immigrants in Israel in 1950: the lack of housing and employment, the difficulty of coping with the customs officers at the Haifa port, and Israeli bureaucracy in general that gave new immigrants a hard time. "Show me anywhere in the world another country like ours," Dzigan said to Shumacher in the sketch, "where there are so many hardships and you can laugh so much."[235]

The realities of Israeli life were the mainstay of the duo's shows throughout the 1950s. This is how Dzigan explained it in his memoirs, published in 1974:

> In my very first appearances in Israel, I was already looking for a new character for my monologues. I searched for a type that would have all the traits of the Israeli Jew, a persona in whose mouth I could put words relating to his everyday life. I wanted to find a substitute for my Polish Jew with the red kerchief. He had been murdered. I wanted to replant my Jew with his *kapote* and his little cap here on Israeli soil. I searched and I found. . . . I took off his *kapote* and dressed him in a khaki shirt and short pants. I put the famous Israeli *tembel* hat, round and shapeless, on his head. I left only the red kerchief in his hand as a symbol of continuity.[236]

And, as if to remove any doubt, Dzigan took his explanation and made it part of one of his monologues: "Shalom Tel Aviv, do you know me? I look like a sabra [a native Israeli] right? I've left the Diaspora behind. I no longer have a *kapote*. Only the [red] kerchief I cannot part with. It's been with me for twenty years. It served me as a handkerchief, later when the Nazis came—for my eyes. Oy, how many tears did that handkerchief soak up. In the Soviet Union I used it as a flag. Here in Israel I use it to wipe the sweat off my face."[237]

Dzigan was, of course, referring to himself. We have nothing comparable written by Shumacher, who died about a year after the two parted company, at the age of fifty-three. However, what Dzigan had to say undoubtedly referred to the duo as a whole—to its artistic trademark—and surely provides an explanation of its success.

Undoubtedly, for large segments of the Israeli public, Dzigan and Shumacher's theater was, in the words of the bilingual journalist Mordechai Halamish, "a familiar, precious world of characters and types drawn from Jewish life—that vibrant and productive Jewish milieu . . . Their comedy is rooted . . . in the works of the great humorists and writers, such as Sholem Aleichem, Y. L. Peretz, and others, who depicted Jewish life in Yiddish literature."[238]

But there were also many articles in the press that saw something new in Dzigan and Shumacher.[239] They were seen as archetypal purveyors of an inherently Israeli satire, following in the footsteps of contemporary Hebrew revue—such as the Matate, Li La Lo, and the entertainment troupe Batzal yarok.[240] Toward the end of the decade, an article in *Maariv* noted that "the best Israeli satire is [to be found in] the Yiddish shows of Dzigan and Shumacher."[241]

So Dzigan and Shumacher's popularity was based on the heady mixture of their status as survivors (representing the continuity of Jewish life), the quality of their humor and their satirical take on Israeli life, and, of course, their status as international Jewish celebrities. And though, like the local Yiddish theater, they too struggled against the restrictions of censorship and the hardships of taxation, they were somehow able to rise above it all and find their way to success.

The experience of the local Yiddish theater, from the days of the Goldfaden company to the lowbrow entertainment of the 1950s, was quite different. It found itself in a vicious circle. On the one hand, a lack of resources forced it to hold fewer rehearsals, reduce production values, and choose a low-level repertoire to attract undemanding audiences. On the other hand, such low-quality theater drove away more discriminating audiences and underscored the image of the Yiddish theater as *shund*. It did not take long before lovers of Yiddish in Israel stopped coming.

This made the local Yiddish theater, in particular the Goldfaden company, an immigrant theater. In fact, during the life of the Goldfaden, its major venue, Givat Aliya, became an "ethnic enclave"[242] of Yiddish-speaking Jews from Eastern Europe.[243] As a result, its chances of success were not very good.

Its potential audience was a small, static society of immigrants, for whom the processes of integration into society took place very quickly. This was due to both their desire to start a totally new life in the Jewish state and the cultural and linguistic policies developed by the state of Israel to encourage new immigrants to become part of the new Israeli Hebrew society and culture.

It was not, however, governmental policies that played the most important role in this development. More significant were the processes of cultural creation in Israel, many of which were encouraged by the government and by governmental agencies, particularly regarding Hebrew. These created a social climate that favored the transition to Hebrew and discouraged attachments to the old cultures that new immigrants brought from their "diasporic" homes." Yiddish light entertainment theater was representative of that culture and so it was little wonder that most found it unattractive.

Dzigan and Shumacher were different. They were not only outstanding comedians and actors, as well as international Jewish celebrities, they also touched a number of different audiences: Yiddish-speaking new immigrants for whom they represented survival, vitality, and continuity; veterans who had transitioned from Yiddish to Hebrew, but who saw in the shows a combination of their old and new cultures in the form of high quality satirical theater and, even more so, original Israeli satire in a traditional framework; and people who did not know Yiddish well but who wanted to see the performances of the famous comic duo and simply appreciated their contemporary satirical take on Israeli life.

Although Dzigan and Shumacher had not lived in Israel long, their repertoire was indeed genuinely Israeli in character. Their success, however, was cut short when they quarreled in 1960, and Shumacher died about a year later.

It would be a number years before a Yiddish production, staged this time by locals, would meet with success in Israel, and two decades before a permanent Yiddish theater would finally be established.

Notes

1. Nathan Wulfowitz, "Hershele Ostropolyer farn gerikht," *Letste nayes*, July 20, 1951. For an English translation, see "Hershele Takes the Stand," with an introduction by Rachel Rojanski, *Haaretz* (English ed.), April 11, 2004.
2. Wulfowitz, "Hershele Ostropolyer farn gerikht."
3. On Abraham Goldfaden, the father of the modern Yiddish theater, see Nahma Sandrow, *Vagabond Stars: A World History of Yiddish Theater* (Syracuse, NY: Syracuse University Press, 1996), 40–69. On the Broder singers, whom Goldfaden included in his troupe, see Sandrow, *Vagabond Stars*, 36–39.
4. See also Seth Wolitz, "Shulamis and Bar Kokhba: Renewed Jewish Role Models in Goldfaden and Halkin," in *Yiddish Theater: New Approaches*, ed. Joel Berkowitz (Oxford: Littman Library of Jewish Civilization, 2003), 87–96.
5. Joel Berkowitz and Barbara Henry, "Introduction," in *Inventing the Modern Yiddish Stage: Essays in Drama, Performance and Show Business*, ed. Joel Berkowitz and Barbara Henry (Detroit: Wayne State University Press, 2012), 5; Michael Steinlauf, "Jewish Theater in Poland," *Polin* 16 (2003): 71–92.
6. David E. Fishman, *The Rise of Modern Yiddish Culture* (Pittsburgh, PA: University of Pittsburgh Press, 2005), 25–29.
7. Sandrow, *Vagabond Stars*, 72–90. On Maurice Schwartz, see Edna Nahshon, "Maurice Schwartz and the Yiddish Art Theater Movement," in *New York's Yiddish Theater From Bowery to Broadway*, ed. Edna Nahshon (New York: Columbia University Press, 2016), 150–173.
8. David E. Fishman, *The Rise of Modern Yiddish Culture*, 29.
9. Ruth R. Wisse, *I. L. Peretz and the Making of Modern Jewish Culture* (London: University of Washington Press, 1991), 104–105; Ruth R. Wisse, "Yitskhok Leybush Peretz," *YIVO Encyclopedia of the Jews in Eastern Europe*, http://www.yivoencyclopedia.org/article.aspx/peretz_yitskhok_leybush. The word *shund* in German means the waste material created when skinning an animal's carcass, which gives rise to a powerful stench. The word was borrowed from German to describe something worthless, despicable, and corrupting, particularly in the fields of literature and culture, and made the transition from German to Yiddish. The term *shund* first appeared in Yiddish in a critical article published in a newspaper at the end of the nineteenth century and from then on became a name for literature that was addressed to an audience's lowest common denominator. See Nathan Cohen, "Sifrut ve'itonut shund," in *Zeman yehudi hadash* (Jerusalem: Keter, 2007), 1:314; Chone Shmeruk, "Le'toldot sifrut ha'shund be'Yidish," *Tarbitz* 52 (1983): 325–350.
10. Steinlauf, "Jewish Theater," 80–81.
11. On Yiddish theater in Poland see Ibid.
12. Letter from Yeshayahu Klibanov to the editor, *Maariv*, July 29, 1949, 6. In his letter Klibanov explains that the council consists of eight members: Y. Kisilov is the chair, and the other members are a teacher, an educator, the director of the municipality's social work

department, a writer/dramatist, a representative of women's organizations, and a representative of the Religious Front.

13. On this subject, see Glenda Abramson, "Theater Censorship in Israel," *Israel Studies* 2 (1)(1997): 111–135.

14. The fundamental decisions of the Council for the Control of Films and Plays, in the period from June 7, 1949, to August 25, 1949, State archives, GL-3881/14. (ISA-MOIN-InteriorFilm-Censor-oooooodlnq).

15. The fundamental decisions of the Council for the Control of Films and Plays of Films and Plays, in the period from September 15, 1949, to April 30, 1950, State archives, GL-3881/14. (ISA-MOIN-InteriorFilm-Censor-oooooodlnq).

16. Minutes of a meeting of the Council for the Control of Films and Plays, State archives, G-29/335.

17. Applying for a license involved a tax of 500 mils (0.5 Israeli pounds). The secretary of the Council for the Control of Films and Plays to the Police Station in East Jaffa, January 5, 1950, State archives, GL-3882/10 (ISA-MOIN-InteriorFilmCensor-oooe2xb). As Israeli citizens were forbidden to perform in Yiddish, there was no point in applying for a license, being refused, and thereby attracting the attention of the council members. The actors therefore preferred to ignore the process on the correct assumption that their play would not be stopped once it had begun. The fine for breaching the instruction was usually one Israeli pound.

18. Correspondence between the Council for the Control of Films and Plays and the Ministry of the Interior's legal advisor, December 19, 1949, to December 29, 1949, State archives, GL-3881/4 (ISA-MOIN-InteriorFilmCensor-ooodinq); Y. Kisilov, Chair of the Council for Control of Films and Plays, to the Ministry of the Interior's legal advisor, on the subject of changes to the Public Performances Ordinance, April 4, 1950, State archives, GL-3882/10 (ISA-MOIN-InteriorFilmCensor-oooe2xb); Attorney Dr. Menahem Kasbiner, assistant to the Ministry of the Interior's legal advisor, to the Council for the Control of Films and Plays, June 8, 1950, State archives, GL-3881/14 (ISA-MOIN-InteriorFilmCensor-ooodinq).

19. Notice to the National Police Headquarters/Criminal Investigations Branch, December 20, 1949, State archives, GL-3882/10 (ISA-MOIN-InteriorFilmCensor-oooe2xb); The Council for the Control of Films and Plays to the National Police Headquarters/Criminal Investigations Branch, State archives, GL-3882/10 (ISA-MOIN-InteriorFilmCensor-oooe2xb).

20. For more detail on this case, see the section on the Goldfaden Theater in this chapter.

21. According to the Public Entertainment Ordinance from the days of the British mandate, the state of Israel levied an entertainment tax on movie and theater tickets. The height of this tax was determined according to a table of tariffs that was planned according to the city or town in which the performance took place and applied mainly to movies, not to tickets for live performances, but also to non-Hebrew plays. In view of this, in 1958 Dzigan and Shumacher tried to enter a kind of partnership with Eliyahu Goldberger's Pargod Theater, in order to be considered as Hebrew theater. See Rotman, *Performans ke'bikoret tarbut*, 217–222. They even negotiated with the Ministry of Finance to reduce the tax levied on them, but in 1959 the commissioner for customs in the Ministry of Finance replied to their request for exemption from this tax by saying that the tax was about to be abolished. A. Gelden, Director of Customs and Excise to Dzigan and Shumacher, February 4, 1959, Yehuda Gabbay Theater archives, Dzigan and Shumacher file. In 1960 the entertainment tax on theater performances was indeed completely abolished. See Asher Arin, "Mas bulim ve'sha'ashuim," in *Hitpathut*

ha'misim be'Eretz Israel, ed. Avraham Mendel (Jerusalem: Museum of Taxes, 1968), 264–265. In 1960 when Maurice Schwartz performed in Israel, the government exempted him from this tax: "Maurice Schwartz rotze le'hakim te'atron idi kavu'a," *Davar*, February 1, 1960. In 1968 Dzigan told the *Davar* newspaper in an interview that a special tax was imposed on his performances that was not imposed on Hebrew theaters ("Ba'ayotav shel Dzigan," *Davar*, May 24, 1968), but at this time the entertainment tax no longer existed. The local authorities were permitted to collect an entertainment levy (Asher Arin, "Misei ha'rashuyot ha'mekomiyot," in *Hitpathut ha'misim be'Eretz Israel*, ed. Avraham Mendel [Jerusalem: Museum of Taxes, 1968], 296–297), but this subject belongs to another period and certainly does not reflect any policy toward Yiddish.

22. See chapter 1.

23. Minutes of the meeting of the Art and Theater Committee, April 24, 1952, State archives, GL-15/1086 (ISA-education-education-000hq40).

24. Permit no. 1935 for *Di froy numer tsvey* by G. Rubinstein, performed by the *Pupoler Yidish teater*, September 29, 1957, State archives, G-31/3591 (ISA-MOIN-InteriorFilmCensor-000jipp); Opinion of Haim Toren on the plays *Der zeyde geyt* and *A meydl fun Poyln*, June 1, 1952, State archives, G-3581/23 (ISA-MOIN-InteriorFilmCensor-000in9s); and permit no. 623 for the play *In hoykhe fentsters*, November 26, 1953, State archives, G-3584/2 (ISA-MOIN-InteriorFilmCensor-000jiqa).

25. Shmuel Atzmon, in *Bi'medinat ha'yehudim*, at https://vimeo.com/155535096.

26. In the case of Maxim Zakashansky, who told a joke in Yiddish during a performance in Hebrew, see "Mishpat pelili 1745/50" *Letste nayes*, August 24, 1951.

27. For advertisements for performances, see *Letste nayes*, December 9, 1949; on the new program *Lakhn on tsena*, see *Letste nayes*, January 6, 1950; Noah Klieger, "Ha'zameret she'simla tekufa," *Yedioth Aharonoth*, April 8, 1965; on Lola Folman, see *HaMashkif*, September 16, 1948; *Davar*, September 20, 1948; *Al HaMishmar*, October 14, 1948; *Maariv*, November 4, 1948; *Davar*, November 8, 1948; *Letste nayes*, January 26, 1950; *Davar*, February 2, 1949; March 31, 1949.

28. Y. Rosenberg, Second Inspector Tel Aviv Region HQ, May 28, 1950, State archives, G-3882/10; the above for Haifa District, June 2, 1950, State archives, G-3882/10 (ISA-MOIN-InteriorFilmCensor-000e2xb).

29. On Holzer, see the *Encyclopedia of Jewish Women*, http://jwa.org/encyclopedia/article/holzer-rokhl. On Weislitz, see "Weislitz gekumen keyn Yisroel," *Letste nayes*, August 11, 1950; "Ya'akov Weislitz (Vilna trupe) ha'erev," *Al HaMishmar*, December 14, 1950; "Higi'a bamai ha'vilner trupe le'Tel Aviv," *Al HaMishmar*, August 8, 1950; "Bamot—Rachel Holzer," *Davar*, March 23, 1951; "Hofa'ot Rachel Holzer," *Herut*, March 16, 1951.

30. Criminal file 16372/50, September 8, 1950, State archives, GL-3882/10 ((ISA-MOIN-InteriorFilmCensor-000e2xb).

31. Criminal file 16373/50, December 17, 1950, State archives, GL-3882/10; Criminal file 17881/50, October 8, 1950, State archives, GL-3882/10 (ISA-MOIN-InteriorFilmCensor-000e2xb); Criminal file 17882/50, January 7, 1951, State archives, GL-3882/10 (ISA-MOIN-InteriorFilmCensor-000e2xb).

32. Criminal file 16373/50, December 17, 1950, State archives, GL-3882/10 (ISA-MOIN-InteriorFilmCensor-000e2xb).

33. The National Headquarters of the Investigations Division, the Criminal Department, September 1, 1950, State archives, GL-3882/10 (ISA-MOIN-InteriorFilmCensor-000e2xb).

34. *Khasye di yesoyme* was a well-known play by Jacob Gordin.

35. "Divrei sifrut ve'omanut," *Yedioth Aharonoth*, September 7, 1951.

36. Victor Leibovitz from Transit Camp Hut 59 to the Ministry of the Interior, September 12, 1951, State archives, G-3579/59 (ISA-MOIN-InteriorFilmCensor-000k79e); permit no. 316, September 27, 1951, State archives, G-3579/59 (ISA-MOIN-InteriorFilmCensor-000k79e).

37. Dov Ber Malkin, "Zygmunt Turkow be'Israel," *Al HaMishmar*, March 2, 1950.

38. Zvi Levin, secretary of the Council for the Control of Films and Plays to the Criminal Investigation and Identification Department, National Headquarters, April 26, 1950, State archives, G-3882-10 (ISA-MOIN-InteriorFilmCensor-000e2xb); Rosenberg to the Council for the Control of Films and Plays, June 14, 1950 State archives, G-3882/10 (ISA-MOIN-InteriorFilmCensor-000e2xb).

39. At the beginning of the 1970s there was an attempt to establish a public Yiddish theater, but it did not succeed; this is discussed in chapter 7.

40. Appeal of the actors of the Goldfaden Theater to the High Court of Justice, State archives, High Court of Justice file 135/51; "Hukam te'atron al shem Goldfaden," *Al HaMishmar*, February 17, 1951.

41. "Wulfowitz in land," *Letste nayes*, October 9, 1950, 4; "David Hart," *Folksblat*, February 16, 1966; Letter of the Goldfaden Theater management on the matter of exemption from Entertainment Tax, February 20, 1952 (it is not clear to whom the letter was sent), Goldfaden Theater file, YIVO, RG 293.

42. Wulfowitz had a command of Hebrew before coming to Israel—interview with his son, Alexander Ze'evi, April 2003; Shin Tet [Shabtai Tevet], "Katri'elivka she'be'Yafo," *Ha'aretz*, November 2, 1951.

43. Goldfaden Theater to the Council for the Control of Films and Plays of Films and Plays, March 13, 1951, High Court of Justice file 135/51 *Hart and Others v. The Minister of the Interior and Others*, State archives.

44. "Antisemitizm un yidishkeyt," *Letste nayes*, May 10, 1951, and June 1, 1951.

45. "*Mirele Efros* in Goldfaden teater," *Letste nayes*, June 1, 1951.

46. Letter no. MB/425/152/15 from the Council for Control of Films and Plays to Aharon Stragovski, representative of the Goldfaden Theater, January 3, 1951 (the letter mentions the theater members' request of December 27, 1950), High Court of Justice file 135/51, State archives. The reason given for the negative answer was that such a permit was given only to guest artists visiting Israel. Copies of the answer were also sent to the Israel police, to the Criminal Department in the National Headquarters, and to the commander of the Tel Aviv region.

47. "A nay Yidish teater," *Letste nayes*, February 19, 1951.

48. Pesach Gutmark (member of the Goldfaden troupe) to the Council for Control of Films and Plays, March 13, 1951, High Court of Justice file 135/51, State archives. (Gutmark's signature is missing from the letter, but there is a letter to him that confirms receiving this letter from him dated March 27, 1951, High Court of Justice file 135/51, State archives.)

49. Ibid.

50. The Council for the Control of Films and Plays to Pesach Gutmark, March 23, 1951, High Court of Justice File 135/51, ibid.

51. Petition to the Supreme Court in its capacity as High Court of Justice file 135/51, *Hart and others v. The Minister of the Interior and others*, State archives.

52. Ibid.

53. "*Mirele Efros* in Goldfaden teater," *Letste nayes*, June 1, 1951.

54. Goldfaden Theater file, YIVO, RG 293.

55. Yehuda Gabbai, ed., *Te'atron "Ohel"—sipur ha'ma'ase* (Tel Aviv: Mifalei tarbut ve'hinuch, 1983), 144.

56. Emanuel Levy, *Ha'te'atron ha'le'umi Habima, korot ha'te'atron ba'shanim 1919–1979* (Tel Aviv: Eked, 1981), 44–45. See also Shelly Zer-Zion, "Ha'vilner trupe'—prolog la'historya shel Habima," *Bikoret u'parshanut* 41 (2009): 65–92.

57. Levy, *Ha'te'atron ha'le'umi*, appendix B.

58. Advertisement for "A forsaken corner" at the Ohel Theater, *Davar*, January 25, 1952; advertisement for *Grine felder* on July 20, 21, and 24, 1951, in Migdal Or Garden, *Letste nayes*, July 20, 1951.

59. Advertisements in *Letste nayes*, June 1, 2015; *Letste nayes*, January 29, 1951.

60. "Antisemitizm un yidishkeyt," *Letste nayes*, May 5, 1951, and receipts for payments of fines to the police in the name of the Goldfaden Theater. On May 28, 1951, a sum of two Israeli pounds was paid by Hanna Korski, and on June 22, 1951, a sum of ten Israeli pounds was paid by Wulfowitz. Receipts for payments in the Goldfaden Theater file, YIVO, RG 293.

61. Nathan Wulfowitz, "Hershele Ostropolyer farn gerikht," *Letste nayes*, July 20, 1951; see also "Hershele Ostropolyer Takes the Stand," trans. and intro. Rachel Rojanski, *Haaretz* (English edition), April 2, 2004.

62. Petition to the High Court of Justice, High Court of Justice file 135/51, State archives.

63. Ibid. The actors were represented by Reuven Nuhimowski.

64. Ibid.

65. Ibid.

66. Ibid.

67. Order *nisi*, July 1, 1951, High Court of Justice file 135/51, State archives.

68. Minutes of the High Court of Justice session, July 26, 1951.

69. Order of the Supreme Court, sitting as a High Court of Justice, July 26, 1951, High Court of Justice file 135/51, State archives.

70. Minutes of the government meeting, July 18, 1951. Theatrical plays in Yiddish.

71. Ibid.

72. Ibid.

73. Letter of the Council for the Control of Films and Plays, which confirms receiving the request, July 17, 1951; Letter of the Council for the Control of Films and Plays that confirms receiving the letter, July 25, 1951, Goldfaden Theater file, YIVO RG 293. See also program of the play *Er kumt haynt bay nakht*, ibid.; "*Er kumt haynt bay nakht* in Goldfaden teater," *Letste nayes*, September 21, 1951; Program of *Er kumt haynt bay nakht*, translation of the French play *Un ami viendra ce soir*, Goldfaden Theater file, YIVO RG 293.

74. Radio interview with Israel Segal, February 1952, transcript in the Goldfaden Theater file, YIVO RG 293.

75. The report states that in the seven months from April to October 1951 the number of people who attended all of the theater's 123 performances was only 35,000, of which 22,250 were in Jaffa in 94 performances, that is, an average audience of 234 at each of the performances that took place in Jaffa. See "Din vekhezhbn fun tetikeyt," April 21 to October 22, 1951, Goldfaden Theater file, YIVO RG 293. The plan of the theater hall in Jaffa indicates 350 seats, which means that about a third of the tickets were not sold. Plan of the theater, including an exact drawing of the stage and the location of the seats, Goldfaden Theater file, YIVO RG 293.

76. Yitzhak Perlov, "Tsigl far a Yidish kultur hoyz in Tel Aviv," *Lebns-fragn*, August 1951, 8. (The home of the Association of Yiddish Writers and Journalists was at 13 Tłomackie Street

and 2 Leszno Street was that of the Association of Polish Writers.) On this see Cohen, *Sefer sofer ve'iton*, 17–31.

77. The letter mentions that this is an answer to a letter of November 21, 1951; Letter from Ohel Shem to the Goldfaden Theater, December 6, 1951. Goldfaden Theater file, YIVO RG 293; Refusal by the management of Habima to a request by the Goldfaden Theater for assistance in acquiring a hall for a performance in Rehovot; Goldfaden Theater file, YIVO RG 293.

78. The evening's program, Goldfaden Theater file, YIVO RG 293; The seating plan in the hall and details of the tickets that were sent to invitees, Goldfaden Theater file, YIVO RG 293; The Goldfaden Theater to the management of Ohel Shem, February 17, 1951, YIVO RG 293; Authorization of the Council for the Control of Films and Plays to stage the play: the Council for the Control of Films and Plays (Y. Kisilov–Av-Razi) to the Goldfaden Theater, March 3, 1952, YIVO RG 293.

79. Financial report on the performance of *Got, mentsh un tayvl* in Hadera, July 17, 1952, Goldfaden Theater file, YIVO RG 293; division of roles in *The Dybbuk*, June 20, 1952, YIVO RG 293.

80. Goldfaden Theater management to Hapoel management, June 3, 1952, Goldfaden Theater file, YIVO RG 293.

81. Oystsug fun protokol num. 10, July 29, 1952, Goldfaden Theater file, YIVO RG 293. The sale agreement also stated that each actor who did not join another troupe within a month of July 30 would receive a sum of fifty Israeli pounds. On the Goldfaden Theater's financial state and its collapse, see also Herman Yablokoff, *Arum der velt mit Yidish teater* (New York: Herman Yablokoff, 1969), 2:590–591.

82. Radio interview with Yisrael Segal, February 1952, transcript in the Goldfaden Theater file, YIVO RG 293.

83. Sikron, *Ha'aliya ha'hamonit*, 25.

84. Ibid., 24.

85. In his novel *Jabalia*, the author Yitzhak Perlov describes Jabalia as a microcosmos of the immigrants from among the Holocaust survivors who settled in it. On Perlov and Jabalia as an area of immigrants from Eastern Europe, see Rojanski, "Yiddish Shtetl," 65–85.

86. Moshe Grossman, "Di libe provints in Yisroel," *Der yidisher kemfer*, February 16, 1951. On Grossman, see *Yidish literatur in Medines-Yisroel* [no author] (Tel Aviv: H. Leivick farlag, 1991), 236.

87. On Jaffa and particularly Givat Aliya as a neighborhood of people from eastern Europe and on Yiddish theater there, see Rachel Rojanski, "Yiddish Shtetl."

88. Y. D. Mittelpunkt, "Givat Aliya—tsores alie," *Letste nayes*, January 6, 1950.

89. Bronya Lev, "Yidish teater in Dzhebelie," *Letste nayes*, October 9, 1950, 4

90. Shin Tet [Shabtai Tevet], "Katri'elivka she'be'Yafo," *Haaretz*, November 2, 1951.

91. Ibid.

92. Pierre Bourdieu, *Distinction: A Social Critique of the Judgement of Taste*, trans. Richard Nice (Cambridge: Cambridge University Press, 1984), 53–54.

93. "Eilat koret," *Maariv*, May 6, 1951.

94. Goldfaden Theater management to Pinsky, February 17, 1952, Goldfaden Theater file, YIVO RG 293.

95. This is stated specifically in an article in *Letste nayes*, "Mirele Efros in Goldfaden teater," *Letste nayes*, June 1, 1951.

96. "*Mirele Efros* in Goldfaden teater," *Letste nayes*, June 1, 1951.

97. Letter of the professional organization of the Yiddish actors to the interministerial committee for approving visits of artists from abroad, June 28, 1959, State archives, GL-1427/8 (ISA-education-education-000a4yw).

98. "Yidish be'chol ha'ulam," *Maariv*, May 20, 1954 (on the performances of the Burstein family and Max Perlman).

99. "Nimshechet ha'nehira le'te'atrot ha'Yidish," *Maariv*, December 23, 1954.

100. Yitzhak Turkow-Grodberg, *Zygmunt Turkow* (Tel Aviv: Orly Press, 1970), 109–118.

101. For an announcement of the theater's festive opening, see *Letste nayes*, April 15, 1952; Raphael Bashan, "Monolog shel Zygmunt Turkow," *Maariv*, December 10, 1965.

102. Turkow-Grodberg, *Zygmunt Turkow*, 120.

103. Ibid., 72, 82; on Varshever yidisher kunst teater, see Steinlauf, "Jewish Theater."

104. Turkow-Grodberg, *Zygmunt Turkow*, 7–118.

105. Y. M. Neiman, "Zygmunt Turkow ba'monodrama le'hayim hadashim," *Davar*, February 22, 1952.

106. Before migrating to Israel, Zygmunt Turkow had already purchased an apartment in Tel Aviv. Turkow-Grodberg, *Zygmunt Turkow*, 120.

107. "Mahaze be'gimel ma'arachot ve'sahkan ehad ve'yahid," *Al HaMishmar*, February 9, 1952.

108. Asher Nahor, "Shuv le'hayim hadashim," *Davar*, February 15, 1952; Y. M. Neiman, "Zygmunt Turkow be'monodrama le'hayim hadashim," *Davar*, February 22, 1952.

109. Ibid.; see also *Letste nayes*, April 11, 1952; Yosef Lapid, "Ha'lashon ha'hamishit shel Zygmunt Turkow," *Maariv*, May 31, 1963; Turkow-Grodberg, *Zygmunt Turkow*, 120.

110. Raphael Bashan, "Monolog shel Zygmunt Turkow," *Maariv*, December 10, 1965.

111. Asher Nahor, "Onkl Mozes," *Herut*, April 18, 1952.

112. Asher Nahor, "Ha'te'atron ha'amami yatzig be'Ivrit," *Herut*, March 12, 1953.

113. "Te'atron zuta shel Turkow yatzig be'Tel Aviv," *Davar*, January 15, 1957.

114. "Yidishn operetn teater," *Davar*, July 30, 1954, 20; a *kuplet* in Yiddish theater was someone who presented light interludes, sometimes comic-satirical between serious pieces, sometimes even within the play. On the *kuplet* in Yiddish theater, see Sandrow, *Vagabond Stars*, 126–127, 390–391.

115. "Zehirut ha'derech be'tikun," *Davar*, October 25, 1953.

116. Azaria Rappaport, "Ha'gazlan ha'yehudi—Perlman," *Maariv*, January 12, 1956; permit no. 1557, March 24, 1961, State archives, 3596/7 (ISA--MOIN-InteriorFilmCensor-000l7ch), such as *Der Galitsyaner fun Meksike* [The Galician from Mexico] that was staged in Tel Aviv in 1967; see a poster of the play at the website of the Israel National Library: http://web.nli.org.il/sites/nli/hebrew/digitallibrary/pages/viewer.aspx?presentorid=NNL_Ephemera&DocID=NNL_Ephemera700102873. The list of plays Perlman and Galina performed included *Der groyser fardiner, Shlimazl; Motl Mayers glikn; Der yidisher gazlen; Alts tsulib parnose*; Ruth Bondi, "Bamot ha'la'az shel dor ha'midbar," *Davar*, July 30, 1954; for advertisements, see *Maariv*, January 27, 1953; *Herut*, February 3, 1954; *Maariv*, April 20, 1954.

117. Such as *Yashke zukht a kale*, permit no. 1500, the Council for the Control of Films and Plays, November 21, 1960, State archives, G-3595/38 (ISA-MOIN-InteriorFilmCensor-000kto5).

118. On this subject, see Sandrow, *Vagabond Stars*, 372, 374, 382.

119. For information about the hotel, see the website of the National Library of Israel: http://web.nli.org.il/sites/NLI/Hebrew/digitallibrary/pages/viewer.aspx?presentorid=NNL_Ephemera&DocID=NNL_Ephemera70033580.

120. Pesach Burstein, *Geshpilt a lebn* (Tel Aviv: no publisher, 1980), 327–332. Published in English as *What a Life! The Autobiography of Pesachke Burstein* (Syracuse, NY: Syracuse University Press, 2003); Azaria Rappaport, "Yom huledet le'Motele ve'Zisele," *Maariv*, June 28, 1954.

121. Blumenfeld had initially married Zygmunt Turkow but divorced him and married his brother, Jonas.

122. The play *Ver iz ver*, by H. Leivick. "Erev omanuti mi'ta'am hitahdut olei Polin be'hishtatfut Diana Blumfeld ve'Yonas Turkow," *Maariv*, January 11, 1955; Letter from the chair of the council to Moshe Yerushalmi, February 22, 1955, State archives, G-3586/49 (ISA-MOIN-InteriorFilmCensor-000jvez); Requesting a license, January 16, 1955, State archives, G-3586/49 (ISA-MOIN-InteriorFilmCensor-000jvez).

123. The repertoire of Witler-Lerer included *Yankel der shmid*, *Gelt, libe un shande*, and *Zayn groyse libe*; *Maariv*, March 26, 1956; Azaria Rappaport, "Laila, Laila," *Maariv*, February 16, 1956; "Ha'zarim nisharu ve'shelanu barhu," *Davar*, November 8, 1956.

124. *Herut*, June 5, 1958.

125. The plays were *Fishl zukht a vayb* and *Mit ofene oygn*. *Maariv*, March 30, 1956.

126. "Te'atron yidi yatzig et ha'ma'avak ba'britim," *Herut*, February 11, 1958; "Ha'mahteret ha'le'umit be'hatzaga idit," *Herut*, March 7, 1958.

127. Yablokoff, *Arum der velt*, 645–663, "Herman Yablokoff be'hatzagat ha'bechora Papirosn," *Herut*, June 15, 1959.

128. In addition to *A khasene in shtetl*, they performed *Di freylekhe kabtsonim / Di eybike kale* and *Der komediant*. Burstein, *Geshpilt a lebn*.

129. The plays they performed included *Khasye di yesoyme*, *Hot a yid a vaybele*, and more. *Maariv* and *Davar*, May 17, 1963; *Herut*, February 18, 1964; *Davar*, January 1, 1963 (advertisement); *Herut*, July 14, 1964 (advertisement); *Maariv*, April 23, 1962.

130. License no. 1407, March 3, 1960, State archives, G47/-3594 (ISA-MOIN-InteriorFilmCensor-000jvez); License no. 1337, State archives, G-26/3594 (ISA-MOIN-InteriorFilmCensor-000kjxu); License no. 1372, State archives, G-35/3594 (ISA-MOIN-InteriorFilmCensor-000kjy4).

131. License no. 1654, October 25, 1961, State archives, G-3597/8 (ISA-MOIN-InteriorFilmCensor-000l862); Permit no. 41595, June 19, 1961, State archives, G-3596/21 (ISA-MOIN-InteriorFilmCensor-000l7cv); *A khasene in tfise* by P. Freiman, permit no. 1337, October 29, 1959, State archives, G-3594/26 (ISA-MOIN-InteriorFilmCensor-000kjxu); *Heym zise heym*, permit no. 1372, December 14, 1959, State archives, G-3594/35 (ISA-MOIN-InteriorFilmCensor-000kjy4).

132. Nili Friedlander, "Natalia Lipman," *Maariv*, August 14, 1969.

133. Dov Ber Malkin, *"Mir froyen,"* *Maariv*, February 20, 1962; also, an advertisement for the play in *Maariv*, February 19, 1962.

134. Sh. Kalai, "Anu ha'nashim," *Herut*, August 3, 1962.

135. Dov Ber Malkin, "Eni Liton ve'te'atron Yidish be'Israel," *Maariv*, September 7, 1962.

136. "Bimot u'badim," *Herut*, October 13, 1962.

137. Tamar Avidar, "Masach u'masecha," *Maariv*, January 10, 1963.

138. "Mener in mayn lebn" [a short news item], *Maariv*, May 26, 1964; "Heseg nosaf le'Eni Liton," advertisement in *Maariv*, July 12, 1965.

139. Shraga Har-Gil, "Ma ha'lashon? Mameloshn," *Maariv*, November 29, 1963.

140. Z. Berachia, "Ha'mahaze, ha'kahal ve'hamevaker ve'hakupa," *Davar*, September 17, 1952.

141. N. Kh. Shin, "Der soyne shund," *Letste nayes*, January 18, 1952.

142. "Nimshechet ha'nehira le'te'atraot ha'Yidish," *Maariv*, December 23, 1953; "Ha'vilkomirskim be'kontzert nosaf," *Maariv*, February 16, 1956.

143. S. Gelbert, "Migdal Bavel te'atrali," *Al HaMishmar*, April 12, 1955; Moshe Ben-Shahar, "Orot ha'kerach," *Herut*, February 18, 1958.

144. D. L. [David Lazar], "Shund ve'la'az," *Maariv*, July 2, 1954: 8; *Khinke pinke* was a derogatory nickname for the *shund* theater in Yiddish.

145. Dov Ber Malkin, "Al ha'hatzaga *Mir froyen*," *Maariv*, February 20, 1962.

146. D. B. Malkin speaking on the Kol Israel radio station, *Al HaMishmar*, September 7, 1962.

147. Tamar Avidar, "Nashim bli gever," *Maariv*, January 30, 1962; Uri Hefer, "Anu ha'nashim be'te'atron Yidish," *Herut*, February 1, 1962; S. Kalai, "Anu ha'nashim," *Herut*, August 2, 1962.

148. Uri Kesari, "Motele Burstein—ha'ilui," *Maariv*, June 28, 1965.

149. Shraga Har-Gil, "Ma halashon? mameloshen," *Maariv*, November 29, 1963.

150. Nahum Barne'a, "Hamatzav adin, al timshechu oti ba'lashon," *Davar*, July 22, 1977. The article discussed the pathetic behavior of a politician (without mentioning his name), and Barne'a notes that the politician behaved as if he was playing a scene taken from Yiddish theater.

151. Abraham Goflat," Oyfn yidishn teater yarid," *Lebns-fragn*, March 1964, 10.

152. The Jewish communities in South Africa were also a destination for such visits, but since most of the Jews there came from Lithuania, and spoke and understood their own Lithuanian dialect in Yiddish, they did not invite artists such as the Burstyn family or Dzigan and Shumacher, because they found the Yiddish dialects of the latter difficult to understand.

153. A. H. Bialin, *Moris Shvarts un der yidisher kunst teater* (New York: Farlag Biderman, 1934), 105–125. See also Edna Nahshon, "Maurice Schwartz and the Yiddish Art Theater Movement," in *New York's Yiddish Theater From Bowery to Broadway*, ed. Edna Nahshon (New York: Columbia University Press, 2016), 150–173.

154. David Vardi, "Maurice Schwartz le'vo'o le'Israel," *Davar*, May 13, 1937; "Maurice Schwartz la'aretz," *HaTzofe*, July 31, 1938.

155. Y. Yatziv, "Maurice Schwartz," *Davar*, July 19, 1938; V. Latzki Bartoldi, "Maurice Schwartz, mi'toch ne'um bi'msibat Habima li'chevodo," *Davar*, June 4, 1937; "Yehe Maurice Schwartz baruch be'tzeto u'varuch be'vo'o!" *Davar*, August 28, 1938.

156. "U'Maurice Schwartz ba la'aretz," *Davar*, April 6, 1951, "Ba'tzibur," *Davar*, April 24, 1951; "Avayem kama hatzagot be'Israel, amar Maurice Schwartz be'siha meyuhedet le'Yedioth Aharonoth," *Yedioth Aharonoth*, April 6, 1951.

157. See the posters for Maurice Schwartz's performances placed by his agent, Sh. Cahane, during April–May 1951, Israel Goor Theater Archives and Museum in Jerusalem, Maurice Schwartz file. These performances, especially in the Habima Theater in Tel Aviv, drew a particularly large audience who knew Schwartz from his previous visits and applauded loudly as soon as he appeared on the stage. He also appeared, apparently on a voluntary basis, at performances held on Israel's day of independence, organized by the Association for the Well-Being of the Israeli Soldier (Ha'aguda le'ma'an ha'hayal). A letter to Maurice Schwartz from the chairman of the Assn. M. Bedolah, May 11, 1951, Israel Goor Theater Archives and Museum, Maurice Schwartz file.

158. See, for example, Y. M. Neiman, "Yaakov Weislitz, le'hofa'otav ba'aretz," *Devar Ha'shavua*, October 6, 1950. The article expresses an objection in principle to Yiddish theater in Israel.

159. Y. M. Neiman, "Maurice Schwartz, le'hofa'ato ba'aretz," *Davar*, May 10, 1951.

160. Asher Nahor, "*Pina nidahat* ba'Ohel," *Herut*, July 6, 1951; Nora, *Realms of Memory*, 1–20.

161. "Maurice Schwartz ba le'vikur memushach," *Davar*, March 5, 1956.

162. "Maurice Schwartz be'iton ha'itonai'im'," *Davar*, February 21, 1960.

163. Aharon Dolev, "Daisa delila u'tefisa primitivit," *Maariv*, March 3, 1960; "Hatzagat *Yoshe kalb* shel te'atron M. Schwartz," *Davar*, March 3, 1960; "Maurice Schwartz be*Yoshe kalb*," *Herut*, March 11, 1960.

164. "Hatzagat *Yoshe kalb* shel te'atron M. Schwartz," *Davar*, March 3, 1960. Only one writer opposed it, the revisionist leader Abba Ahimeir, under a pen name, as part of his political views that identified Yiddish with non-Zionist socialists. Abba Sikra [Ahimeir's pen name], "Hem megalim telafeihem," *Herut*, March 11, 1960.

165. "Maurice Schwartz rotze le'hakim ba'aretz te'atron idi kavu'a," *Davar*, February 3, 1960.

166. For example, the poet Ezra Zusman described it as "a theater of the poor, of wanderers . . . that fought for its uniqueness, even when it is pointless. A theater that never has the time to prepare a play as it should be." E. Z. [Ezra Zusman], "Halomo shel Maurice Schwartz," *Davar*, March 18, 1960.

167. "Maurice Schwartz eineno," *Maariv*, May 11, 1960; "Maurice Schwartz huva li'menuhot bi'New York," *Davar*, May 18, 1960.

168. "Met Maurice Schwartz," *Davar*, May 11, 1960.

169. On *Toyt fun a saylsman* (the Yiddish translation of Miller's *Death of a Salesman*) and its production in New York, Buenos Aires, and Tel Aviv, see Debra Caplan, "Attention Must Be Paid—Death of a Salesman Counter Adapted Yiddish Homecoming," *Modern Drama* 58, no. 2 (Summer 2015): 194–217.

170. "Yosef Buloff yatzig ba'aretz," *Maariv*, March 11, 1953; "Ha'erev - bechora shel Buloff," *Al HaMishmar*, March 19, 1953.

171. See, for example, "Kabalat panim nilhevet la'sahkan Buloff," *Herut*, March 17, 1953; "Mesiba la'sahkan Buloff be'mo'adon Milo," *HaTzofe*, March 18, 1953; "Mesiba la'sahkan ve'la'bamai Y. Buloff," *Davar*, March 20, 1953.

172. Buloff's performances included works originally written in Yiddish (by Y. L. Peretz, Moshe Leib Halpern, A Lutski), as well as a sketch translated from a work by Anton Chekhov. "Ha'erev bechora shel Buloff," *Al HaMishmar*, March 20, 1953; "Ha'erev—Yosef Buloff be'Ohel Shem im Fela Feld ve'David Hart," *Al HaMishmar*, April 13, 1953; "Erev rishon im Buloff," *Al HaMishmar*, March 23, 1953.

173. R. Azaria, "Yosef Buloff hulya mekasheret," *Maariv*, March 13, 1953.

174. "Yosef Buloff," *Davar*, April 10, 1953 [signed by YM"N].

175. R. Y., "Erev rishon im Buloff," *Al HaMishmar*, March 23, 1953.

176. "Kosovitzki ve'Buloff higi'u," *Maariv*, June 20, 1956.

177. R.Azaria, "Bikuro ha'sheni shel sahkan dagul, Yosef Buloff," *Maariv*, June 29, 1956.

178. Azaria Rappaport, "Ore'ah ratzu'i ve'rav yecholet," *Maariv*, August 28, 1956.

179. Dr. Emil Feuerstein, "Yosef Buloff," *HaTzofe*, July 13, 1956.

180. Asher Nahor, "Yosef Buloff," *Herut*, July 13, 1956.

181. "Yosef Buloff le'Israel," *Herut*, January 13, 1958; "Laila, laila," *Maariv*, February 6, 1958.

182. Ezra Zusman, "Mot ha'sochen im Buloff," *Davar*, February 14, 1958; R. Azaria, "Buloff hai be'*Mot ha'sochen*'," *Maariv*, February 10, 1958.

183. "Buloff sho'ef le'hakim te'atron keva ba'aretz," *Davar*, May 6, 1958.

184. Shlomo Shava, "Buloff rotze te'atron," *Davar*, May 15, 1958.

185. "Tzav ha'poter mi'mas bulim," *Davar*, May 15, 1958.

186. Arin, "Mas bulim ve'shashu'im," 264–270.

187. See note 21 above.

188. "Maurice Schwartz rotze le'hakim te'atron idi kavu'a," *Davar*, February 1, 1960.

189. Buloff arrived in Israel on April 15, 1961. "Yehid ve'tzibur," *Maariv*, April, 26, 1961; "Buloff bi'shetei hatzagot," *Maariv*, May, 19, 1961.

190. A. Ben Meir, "Yosef Buloff be*Tuvya ve'sheva benotav*," *Herut*, June 2, 1961; Uri Kesari, "Buloff," *Maariv*, June 8, 1961.

191. See chapter 6.

192. Nahman Ben-Ami, "Ore'ah beruch kisharon, Yosef Buloff be'hatzaga *Tuvya ve'sheva benotav*," *Maariv*, May 28, 1961.

193. Nahman Ben-Ami, "Ha'shalit al ha'bama," *Maariv*, March 15, 1966.

194. Michael C. Steinlauf, "The Kaminski Family," *YIVO Encyclopedia of Jews in Eastern Europe*, http://www.yivoencyclopedia.org/article.aspx/Kaminski_Family; Steinlauf, "Jewish Theater," 75–89.

195. Speech by Anshel Reiss, chairman of the Association of Polish Jewry in Israel, in "Ha'te'atron ha'yehudi be'Polin yavo la'aretz," *Davar*, August 1, 1957; Shlomo Nakdimon, "Ida Kaminska ba'a," *Herut*, November 17, 1959.

196. "Ida Kaminska magi'a hayom," *Maariv*, July 21, 1957; "Ida Kaminska; anu rotzim lavo le'Israel," *Davar*, July 23, 1957; "Ha'te'atron ha'yehudi be'Polin yavo la'aretz," *Davar*, August 1, 1957; "Ida Kaminska no'emet," *Davar*, August 11, 1957; "Ida Kaminska mevi'a et devar ha'seridim al tilei hurban yahadut Polin," *HaTzofe*, August 16, 1957; "Ha'te'atron ha'yehudi mi'Polin yavo la'aretz be'Mars 1958," *Davar*, August 23, 1957.

197. "Te'atron Kaminska yagi'a ba'aviv," *Herut*, August 23, 1957

198. Y. Mendelbaum from the office of impresario K. Ginzburg to Avner Israeli of the interministerial committee (the stationary lists the names of the artists represented by the agency), June 24, 1959, State archives, GL-1427/8; Y. Mendelbaum to the minister of education, June 26, 1959, State archives, GL-127/8 (ISA-education-education-000a4yw); Avner Yisraeli, deputy director general in the Ministry of Education to Rehavam Amir, Israeli consul in Warsaw, August 6, 1959, State archives, GL-1427/8 (ISA-education-education-000a4yw).

199. "Hatzagat Ida Kaminska," *Davar*, November 27, 1959; "Lahakat Ida Kaminska hofi'a be'hatzlaha be'Tel Aviv," *Davar*, November 29, 1959.

200. A *Maariv* journalist, "Bechora mefo'eret ve'nirgeshet la'te'atron ha'yehudi mi'Polin," *Maariv*, November 29, 1959; Ezra Zusman, "*Ha'etzim metim zekufim* ba'te'atron ha'yehudi be'Polin'," *Davar*, December 4, 1959; A. Ben-Meir, "Ida Kaminska ve'ha'tea'tron shela," *Herut*, December 4, 1959.

201. *Sender Blank*, Ba'te'atron shel Ida Kaminska," *Davar*, December 18, 1959; "Hatzagat bechora shel *Mirele Efrat* be'Ohel Shem," *Herut*, December 27, 1959; Ben-Meir, "*Melech sameach* ba'te'atron ha'yehudi mi'Polin," *Herut*, January 8, 1959.

202. A. Ben Meir, "Ida Kaminska be'*Mirele Efrat*'," *Herut*, January 1, 1960; "Lahakat Ida Kaminska hofi'a be'hatzlaha be'Tel Aviv," *Davar*, November 29, 1959.

203. Z. Shek, first secretary, Israeli Embassy in London to the foreign minister (Golda Meir), June 18, 1957, State archives, 10/508 (ISA-mfa-IsraeliMissionPolnd-000rvwq).

204. Katriel Katz, *Yoman Varsha*, July 20, 1957, State archives, 6/3118 (ISA-mfa-Political-000kfre).

205. Dov Satat, East European desk at the Foreign Office to Israeli consul in Warsaw, October 9, 1957, State archives, 10/508 (ISA-mfa-Political-000kfre).

206. "Ida Kaminska orahat Davar," *Davar*, December 28, 1959.

207. On Dzigan and Shumacher's career before they came to Israel and on their biographical background, see Rotman, *Performans ke'bikoret tarbut*, 19, 38–44, 73–188; Shimen Dzigan, *Der koyekh fun yidishn humor* (Tel Aviv: no publisher, 1974); Nathan Gross, *YIVO Encyclopedia of the Jews in Eastern Europe*, http://www.yivoencyclopedia.org/article.aspx/Dzigan_and_Shumacher.

208. Among the authors who lived and worked in Łódź were Yisroel Rabon and Yitskhok Katsenelson. Shimen Dzigan (1905–1980) was discovered by accident by Broderzon, who invited him to join Ararat and took him under his wing. Yisroel Shumacher (1908–1961) joined Ararat after completing his studies at the Hebrew Gymnasium in the city. They were members of the company from its very first day in 1927.

209. In fact, the duo retained some of the sketches from their prewar repertoire and adapted them to the new realities of the 1950s.

210. Gross, "Dzigan and Shumacher."

211. Dzigan, *Der koyekh fun yidishn humor*.

212. "Dzigan ve'Shumacher mitlotzetzim," *Herut*, March 19, 1950.

213. Conversation with Yitzhak Luden and another with Shmuel Atzmon. Atzmon repeated the story in the documentary film made by Anat Zeltser and Modi Bar-On, *Bi'medinat ha'yehudim*, in the second episode, "Be'Yidish ze nishma yoter tov," https://vimeo.com/155535096.

214. "Ha'sibuv ha'sheni shel Dzigan ve'Shumacher," "Safra ve'saifa," [signed by G"L] *Maariv*, October 13, 1950.

215. "Ha'sipuk ve'ha'mahma'a, sihot Maariv," *Maariv*, January 24, 1951.

216. "Dzigan ve'Shumacher hazru la'aretz," *Davar*, December 26, 1952.

217. "Hem mesapkim mitzrach hiyuni—tzehok," *Devar Ha'shavu'a*, February 5, 1953.

218. Letter from the attorney Raphael Lutz to Shumacher, regarding the cessation of the partnership with Dzigan, January 13, 1960, Yehuda Gabbay Theater Archive, Dzigan and Shumacher file.

219. The Bristol Hotel was at 75 Ben Yehuda Street in Tel Aviv.

220. Azaria Rappport, "Tov lir'ot yehudim tzohakim," *Maariv*, December 26, 1952.

221. In April 1953 the two left for a tour lasting a year and a half, which included Latin America, the United States, and Western Europe. On their return in February 1955, they put on a new show, *Na-dir un veyn nisht* (Here you are and don't cry), followed by *Toyznt un eyn lakh* (A thousand and one laughs). Early in May 1956, they left the country to return a year later with the show *Yom tov indervokhn* (A holiday on a weekday) and then *Nayn mos gelekhter* (Nine measures of laughter). After another tour abroad, they returned in 1958 with *Ze vi du geyst* (Look where you're going) and afterward put on *Feter me'ken aykh* (Uncle, we know you). In December 1959, they appeared in their last show, *S'blaybt baym altn* (It stays as it once was); "Matos ha'omanim," *Maariv*, April 14, 1953; "Dzigan ve'Shumacher higi'u la'aretz," *Al HaMishmar*, February 20, 1955; R. Azaria, "Dzigan ve'Shumacher ke'yom etmol," *Maariv*,

October 5, 1955; N. Asher [Asher Nahor], "Le'darkam shel "Dzigan ve'Shumacher," *Herut*, April 19, 1957; "Laila, laila," *Maariv*, December 10, 1957; Ezra Zusman, "Tish'a kabin," *Davar*, January 11, 1957; A. Ben-Meir, "Dzigan ve'Shumacher be'tochnit hadasha," *Herut*, October 17, 1958; Y. Gilboa, "Hem holchim be'darkam," *Maariv*, October 2, 1958; A. Ben-Meir, "Makirim otcha dod, be'tochnit hadasha shel Dzigan ve'Shumacher," *Herut*, May 20, 1959; "Dod, makirim othcha," *Maariv*, June 17, 1959; Ran Zeev, "S'blaybt baym altn," *Davar*, December 25, 1959.

222. Y. Lapid, "Dzigan ve'Shumacher al saf perud," *Maariv*, January 20, 1960; "Dzigan ve'Shumacher, preidah," *Davar*, January 27, 1960.

223. "Met ha'sahkan Israel Shumacher," *Davar*, May 22, 1961; "Israel Shumacher huva li'menuhot," *Davar*, May 23, 1961.

224. Permit no. 78, signed by Y. Kiselov, chairman of the Council for the Control of Films and Plays, to Dzigan and Shumacher, April 9, 1950, Yehuda Gabbay Theater Archive, Dzigan and Shumacher file.

225. Council for the Control of Films and Plays, to Dzigan and Shumacher, May 15, 1950, extension of permit no. 78, Yehuda Gabbay Theater Archive, Dzigan and Shumacher file.

226. Permit no. 139, signed by the chairman of the Council for the Control of Films and Plays, sent to P. Gornstein, Dzigan and Shumacher's impresario, October 19, 1950, Yehuda Gabbay Theater Archive, Dzigan and Shumacher file.

227. Ezriel Carlebach, "Yoman, Dzigan ve'Shumacher," *Maariv*, May 2, 1950.

228. Joseph Heftman to the Minister of the Interior, April 25, 1950, Yehuda Gabbay Theater Archive, Dzigan and Shumacher file.

229. Minister of the Interior Shapira to Joseph Heftman, May 10, 1950, Yehuda Gabbay Theater Archive, Dzigan and Shumacher file.

230. The director of the medical wing in the Malben Institution (a senior community), Gadera, to Dzigan and Shumacher, March 16, 1951, Yehuda Gabbay Theater Archive, Dzigan and Shumacher file; Letter from Col. Moshe Shein, commander of Brigade 933, to Journalists Association, July 27, 1950, Yehuda Gabbay Theater Archive, Dzigan and Shumacher file; Bella Bar'am (Office of Broadcast Authority, Tel Aviv) to Dzigan and Shumacher, January 26, 1951, Yehuda Gabbay Theater Archive, Dzigan and Shumacher file.

231. These ranged from Mordechai Halamish, the bilingual journalist, who called them "gifted actors," "possessed of a rare talent" (H. Mordechai, " Omanei ha'humor ha'amami," *Al HaMishmar*, February 6, 1953), to writers who were usually opposed to Yiddish, such as Y. M. Neiman of *Davar*, who devoted an extensive article to the duo in *Devar Ha'shavua*, giving vent to his harsh criticism of the censor that had placed obstacles in their way and describing them as "talented," "beloved of the audiences," and "bringing gaiety to Israel" (Y. M. Neiman, "Dzigan ve'Shumacher," *Devar Ha'shavu'a*, June 2, 1950). David Lazar, also not favorably inclined toward Yiddish, noted in an article opposed to the development of Yiddish in Israel that "Dzigan and Shumacher brought the very best Jewish humor in a cultured and attractive manner." D. L. [David Lazar], "La'az ve'shund," *Maariv*, July 2, 1954.

232. R. Azaria, "Dzigan ve'Shumacher ke'yom etmol," *Maariv*, October 5, 1955.

233. R. Azaria, "Laila, laila," *Maariv*, October 7, 1957.

234. On the satirical character of the Dzigan and Shumacher theater, see Rotman, *Performans ke'bikoret tarbut*, 87–93, 199–202.

235. Dzigan, *Der koyekh fun yidishn humor*, 306–310.

236. Ibid., 310.

237. Ibid., 313.

238. Mordechai Halamish, "Anshei ha'humor ha'amami," *Al HaMishmar*, February 6, 1953. Descriptions of this sort also appeared in articles by other writers, such as Asher Nahor, "Ha'te'atron ha'satiri 'Sambatyon'," *Herut*, July 12, 1957; Ezra Zusman, "Tisha'a kabin," *Davar*, November 1, 1957.

239. R. Azaria, "Dzigan ve'Shumacher osim tzehok," *Maariv*, March 2, 1955.

240. Asher Nahor, "Erev im Dzigan ve'Shumacher," *Herut*, January 9, 1953; Asher Nahor, "Dzigan ve'Shumacher ve'ha'humor ha'israeli," *Herut*, October 14, 1955. On the Li La Lo Theater, see Dan Laor, *Alterman, biyografya* (Tel Aviv: Am Oved, 2013), 426–428.

241. Yitzhak Avrahami, "Ha'omanim ha'tzalafim," *Maariv*, May 5, 1959.

242. On ethnic enclaves, see Mark Abrahamson, *Urban Enclaves: Identity and Place in America* (New York: St. Martin's, 1996).

243. On Givat Aliya as a Yiddish-speaking ethnic enclave, see Rojanski, "Yiddish Shtetl."

4

"TO ASSEMBLE THE SCATTERED SPIRIT OF ISRAEL"

High Yiddish Culture—Di goldene keyt *and the* Yiddish Chair at the Hebrew University

At the end of August 1948, the second truce in Israel's war of independence was in effect. The morning newspapers reported Israel's request for membership to the United Nations and the establishment of an academy of the Hebrew language. However, despite the fact that they were dealing these weighty matters, they also found a little space for another item announcing the forthcoming publication of a journal of Yiddish literature: "A quarterly in Yiddish, on culture, literature and society, to be called *Di goldene keyt*," announced *Davar*, "[is] soon to be published by the Histadrut (the General Federation of Jewish Labor). Editor—Abraham Sutzkever."[1]

Several days later a similar news item appeared in *Al HaMishmar*, which noted that in addition to Sutzkever, the quarterly would also be edited by Abraham Levinson, a representative of the Histadrut. It continued that the goal of the journal was "to bring Jews from all parts of the world closer to the Hebrew literature and culture being created in Israel, and to serve as a forum for the works of Jewish writers, artists and thinkers wherever they may be."[2] Over the next few days, more items of this sort appeared in the daily press, all of them noting the coeditorship of Sutzkever and Levinson and stressing the Histadrut's role as publisher.[3]

Di goldene keyt came out regularly for forty-six years from 1949 to 1995—a total of 141 issues. And despite the initial appointment of Levinson, it was a one-man show, totally identified with Abraham Sutzkever, the renowned Yiddish poet and ghetto resistance fighter. He shaped the quarterly in his own image and made it the most important Yiddish literary journal in the post-Holocaust world. *Di goldene keyt* had no peer, either in quality or in prestige.

Although Sutzkever was *Di goldene keyt*, the journal was owned by the Histadrut, which not only financed its publication but also provided its editorial offices and employed its staff throughout the nearly fifty years of its publication.[4] The Histadrut was essentially a labor organization, but in practice it had also served as the organizational base and major focus of power in the political system of the Jewish Yishuv during the British mandate. The transition from Yishuv to state was made possible by the web of organizations and institutions it had created, and once the state had been established, the government made the Histadrut its executive arm, charging it with furthering national aims.[5] In the late 1940s, the Histadrut owned a daily newspaper, two publishing houses, and a theater, and this made it the most appropriate public body to back the project of a literary journal in Yiddish.[6]

What lay behind the Histadrut's decision to publish a literary quarterly in Yiddish, and what was its significance for the development of highbrow Yiddish-language culture in Israel?

I will start this chapter by analyzing the political background to the establishment of the Yiddish quarterly, the development of the journal itself, Sutzkever's work as its editor, and his role in attempting to reestablish high Yiddish-language culture after the Holocaust. I will then examine Israel's policy in the first decade of its existence toward the treasures of Jewish culture, secular and religious, created in the Diaspora. In addition to examining *Di goldene keyt*, this chapter will involve a discussion of the establishment of the chair in Yiddish at The Hebrew University of Jerusalem, as well as of the government's attitude toward the yeshiva world, largely destroyed in the Holocaust, and its links with high Yiddish-language culture in general.

My major claim will be that the state of Israel under Ben-Gurion's leadership was interested in preserving—to some extent, even fostering—the high culture of the Jewish people that had developed in the Diaspora. With this in mind, small centers of diasporic Jewish culture, both secular and religious, were created under government auspices, or with the support of the government, and these became, in a sense, preserves for this culture. Because of their limited scope, and particularly in light of the small audience they attracted, these centers were not perceived as an obstacle to the development of the new Israeli Hebrew culture, certainly not to the project of inculcating the Hebrew language. At the same time, however, their existence and official support helped bolster Israel's status as the world center of Jewish culture, which, in turn, allowed it to spread its cultural hegemony across the Jewish world. As the decision to publish *Di goldene keyt* shows, Yiddish played a major role in this development.

The Background to *Di goldene keyt*: "The Publication of a Yiddish Quarterly—Approved"

The full background to the establishment of *Di goldene keyt* is not entirely clear. Existing documentation is minimal and fragmented, and the secondary sources are also partial, largely based on fragmentary memories, some rather tendentious. Sutzkever himself, in an article published on the quarterly's tenth anniversary, credited Yosef Sprinzak, secretary of the Histadrut from 1944 to 1949, with its founding. Sutzkever called Sprinzak "a lover of Yiddish" and a "friend of Yiddish" and repeated these sentiments at a party held in Tel Aviv in 1962 to mark the quarterly's "bar mitzva."[7] In fact, Sprinzak did have a warm feeling for Yiddish. He wrote books in Yiddish and often used Yiddish words when he spoke.[8] Nonetheless, his status had been in decline even before the foundation of the state, and he simply would not have had enough clout on his own to have the Histadrut set up and fund a Yiddish literary journal under its name. So, although he clearly had some influence on the decision to found *Di goldene keyt*, we must assume that other factors were in play.[9]

The archival record is not helpful. The first documented discussion on the possibility of publishing a Yiddish journal was held by the Central Committee of the Histadrut on May 9, 1948. The brief minutes of the meeting read only: "Publication of a quarterly in Yiddish—A. Levinson and Sutzkever—agreed to discuss it at the next meeting." The next meeting took place on May 16, just two days after the declaration of the state. Again, the minutes mention the subject only briefly: "Publication of a quarterly in Yiddish—approved."[10] No additional details were given.

The fact that the minutes of the meetings are so laconic suggests that the main discussions about the journal probably did not take place in the Central Committee at all. To judge from the fact that there is no mention at all of *Di goldene keyt* in the minutes of the Histadrut's Culture Committee, it was probably not discussed there either. It seems most likely that the decision was taken informally, perhaps even behind closed doors. It was a controversial move that seemed to run counter to the policy of encouraging Hebrew and was openly criticized in the press,[11] so it is hard to believe that it was taken without the blessing, or at least the silent approval, of the heads of the government in the making. If that was the case, the Histadrut, even if its leaders were interested in a Yiddish literary journal, served mainly in an executive function.[12]

The first notice on *Di goldene keyt* in *Davar*, with which I opened this chapter, holds another clue to understanding the decision to establish the new journal. When it mentioned the name of the editor, it wrote just Sutzkever, giving no explanation. Sutzkever, a major poet and hero of the Vilna ghetto, was a well-known personality in the Jewish world, familiar to the readers of *Davar*, and a self-evident choice as editor of a Yiddish quarterly. That being so, his prestate biography and eventual decision to move to Israel must have been major factors in the decision to set up *Di goldene keyt* with public financing, particularly because it was meant to serve as a sort of focal point for Yiddish high culture in Israel.

Abraham Sutzkever: "The Poet and the Hero"

Abraham Sutzkever was born in 1913 in Smorgon and died in 2010 in Tel Aviv. He was one of the foremost Jewish writers of the twentieth century and one of Israel's greatest poets. Benjamin Harshav, a professor of literature at Yale University, wrote about him in 2005 that "to the ears of anyone who knows the language [i.e., Yiddish] with all its secrets, its wrinkles and its hidden treasures, Sutzkever is one of the most preeminent poets of the twentieth century."[13] Dan Miron, a professor of literature at Columbia, described him in a heartrending article written on Sutzkever's death as "one of the foundations" of Israeli culture.[14]

In the late 1940s, when the establishment of *Di goldene keyt* was being discussed, Sutzkever was still a young man, though he already had an excellent reputation as a Yiddish poet, and was a well-known figure internationally in the Jewish world and beyond. Since the story of his life, as well as his literary and wartime achievements, played a pivotal role in the decision to create the Yiddish quarterly as a platform for his literary and cultural activity, this is a good place to take stock of them.

Born in Smorgon, a small city southeast of Vilna, Sutzkever moved with his family to Siberia in 1915, before finally settling in Vilna in 1920.[15] He spent his youth there, receiving a traditional Jewish education before attending a Polish Jewish gymnasium. In about 1927, he began to write poetry, initially in Hebrew, which, together with Polish, he considered a true language of culture.

He first encountered Yiddish literature in 1930 at the age of seventeen, when he joined the youth movement Bin (Bee), which combined scouting with the ideology of promoting Yiddish.[16] In 1933 he became part of the writers' group Yung Vilne, which had been active in the city since 1929.[17] However, as a lyrical poet, he did not really fit into the group, since some of its members were engaged in political poetry. In order to gain recognition for his work he had to go to Warsaw.[18]

His first Yiddish poem was published in January 1934 in Warsaw; the second was published in Vilna in May in the newspaper *Vilner tog*.[19] It did not take long before a poem of his was printed in *Yung Vilne*, the journal of the writers' group. Starting in 1935 he published his work in *In zikh*, the journal of the introspectivist group in New York that became a major venue for his poetry in the years to come.[20] His first volume of poetry, *Lider*, (Poems) was published in 1937 by the PEN Club in Warsaw; the second, *Valdiks* (Woodlore), in 1940 by the PEN Club in Vilna.[21] His work was hailed throughout the Jewish literary world, and he was depicted as a new star in the firmament of Yiddish literature.[22]

However, the readers of Israeli newspapers learned about Sutzkever only after he had managed to flee from the Nazi occupation. They got to know him not just as an important author but also as a hero who had borne arms against the enemies of the Jewish people during the Holocaust.

The Germans occupied Vilna on June 24, 1941. Sutzkever's attempts to flee with his wife failed, and, with the exception of several short periods during which they managed to hide in various places, they were forced to live in the ghetto from June 1941 to September 1943. During this time, his mother and his infant son were murdered. Unlike other poets, Sutzkever continued to write—at times feverishly. Some of his poems were copied and distributed in the ghetto, but not all survived.[23] During this time, his public profile changed. Formerly a poet who shied away from public activity, he soon became very active in the ghetto's cultural life. He joined a group of Jewish intellectuals whom the Germans appointed to pick out treasures of Jewish culture—precious books from libraries and synagogues. Most of this material was destined for destruction, but a part of it was to be transferred to the Nazi Institute for Research into the Jewish Problem in Germany.

At great risk to their lives, Sutzkever and the others in the group did whatever they could to save from destruction hundreds of rare manuscripts and valuable books, which they either smuggled into the ghetto or hid outside it.[24] Sutzkever himself also organized reading clubs for young people, where they could discuss the work of Yiddish poets. In 1942 he was awarded the belles lettres prize by the ghetto's writers association.

He was also a member of the underground organization FPO (Fareynikte partizaner orgnizatsye-United partisans organization), which made contact with groups organized by Soviet partisans in the region, whose representatives had actually managed to get into the ghetto. Sutzkever gave one of these partisans a manuscript of his poetry, including his poem "Kol nidre," to take to Moscow. It was a unique poem, built around an unexpected meeting between a soldier in the Russian army held prisoner by the Germans and a group of Jews in the ghetto, one of whom was the soldier's father. The poem was based on a true event that occurred during the Yom Kippur *aktions* (deportations) in 1941. The manuscript did in fact reach its destination, where it was read aloud at a gathering of writers, though without any mention of its author, then in the German occupied region.[25]

On September 12, 1943, several days before the liquidation of the ghetto, Sutzkever and his wife, together with a group of partisans, fled to the Narocz forests. It was a fateful choice, despite the many hardships they suffered. It turned out that the poems he had sent to Moscow, in particular "Kol nidre," had made a huge impression there. Russian intellectuals together with the Soviet Jewish Anti-Fascist Committee, tried to convince the authorities to smuggle Sutzkever out from behind the enemy lines.[26]

In March 1944, a special Soviet airplane was sent to rescue Sutzkever and his wife from the forest and bring them to Moscow. There he made his first public appearance at the third conference of the Jewish Anti-Fascist Committee. Another speaker at the conference was Ilya Ehrenburg, the Jewish Russian author and journalist, perhaps the most widely read writer in the Soviet Union at the time.[27] On April 29, Ehrenburg published in *Pravda*—the official newspaper of the Soviet regime—an article about Sutzkever, entitled "The Victory of a Man."[28]

"The impact of this article can hardly be overestimated," wrote David Roskies, "both on account of Ehrenburg's enormous popularity and prestige, and also because it spoke virtually for the first time in Soviet Russia about the singular fate of the Jewish people. . . . Sutzkever [was perceived as] the living symbol of Jewish consciousness and continuity."[29]

The first mention of Sutzkever in the Hebrew press in prestate Israel appeared on April 19, 1944, in the daily *Al HaMishmar*. That day the paper printed an article, cabled to it from the AP news agency, under the headline, "The Annihilation of the Jews of Vilna." The author's name was Abraham Sutzkever, and the paper added a subtitle, "The Tribulations of a Jewish Partisan Poet," without noting that the text was in fact Sutzkever's first speech to the Jewish Anti-Fascist Committee in Moscow. It contained a very moving description of the suffering of Vilna Jewry under Nazi occupation, which laid great emphasis on their determined stand against the Nazis and in particular the armed resistance of the partisans. The text ended with a call "to take revenge against the Germans for the murder of our brethern."

Above the text, the paper's editor added an opening statement about the author: "A. Sutzkever, gentle in form and clear in meter, a member of the well-known writers' group, *Yung Vilne*."[30] So, from the very start, Sutzkever was presented in the Hebrew press in two ways: as an intellectual and a hero—a poet-warrior avenging the wrongs of his people.

About a month and a half later, *Al HaMishmar* also published a translation of Ilya Ehrenburg's famous article from *Pravda*. It opened with a few words of praise for Sutzkever's poetry and a description of his role in saving from the Nazis cultural treasures, Jewish and non-Jewish (including a letter by Maxim Gorky). It's main focus, however, was the cruelty of the Nazis, the Jews' suffering, and the Jewish resistance—both armed and, in particular, cultural, as seen in the rescue of the precious manuscripts and books.

Referring to the poem "Kol nidre," Ehrenburg concluded: "This is the poet Sutzkever, with a machine gun in his hand, poetry in his head, and Gorky's letter on his heart [in his pocket] . . . the poet and soldier from the Vilna ghetto [who] saved Gorky's letter."[31]

Al HaMishmar chose to replace the article's original title, calling it instead: "Abraham Sutzkever, the Poet and the Hero." So, while the Russian original celebrated the victory of the human spirit over the Nazi beast, the Hebrew-language version foregrounded the victory of the Jew as both an intellectual and a hero. In this way, the two facets of Sutzkever's image as it was being created in prestate Israel were clearly stated at the very outset.

In the coming months, the Hebrew press continued to print items that enhanced the image. "A Partisan Poet to the Friend of a Partisan Poet" was the headline of a small item about a letter that Sutzkever received from another poet and partisan from Vilna, Abba Kovner, informing him of three actions carried out successfully by the partisans.[32] A year later *HaMashkif* reported, "The Jewish poet, Abraham Sutzkever, who fought with the partisans, was awarded the 'Red Star' medal (by the Soviet Union) for acts of heroism."[33] From then on, every time Sutzkever was mentioned in the Hebrew press, he was described as "partisan," "fighter," "hero," and the like.

Following the liberation of Vilna by the Red Army in the summer of 1944, Sutzkever returned there and, together with other survivors, began to retrieve the cultural treasures he and his comrades had hidden. He then returned to Moscow to become a member of the literary commission collecting material for the publication of the *Black Book* that documented the horrors perpetrated by the Nazis and was edited by Ilya Ehrenburg and Vasili Grossman.

Early in 1946 he appeared as a witness on behalf of the Soviet prosecution at the Nuremberg trials, where his testimony aroused a great deal of interest.[34] The Hebrew press in Palestine described his appearance at Nuremberg as a heroic act. "Sutzkever made an enormous impression," wrote the revisionist *HaMashkif*. He hurled accusations at the men on trial until "the accused did not dare put on the earphones to hear what he had to say."[35] All this reporting, then, depicted Sutzkever as a kind of New Jew—a fighter and a hero, a man bearing arms and facing his enemies—a description much in accord with the Zionist ethos at the time.

After two years in Moscow, Sutzkever and his family returned to Poland.[36] At this point he had to decide on his final destination. Though he failed to receive a visa to the US, he might have consoled himself with the difficulty of earning a living there, in a relatively large community of Yiddish journalists and writers whose readership was dwindling.[37] In the end, he decided on Israel.

In December 1946 Sutzkever participated in the Twenty-Second Zionist Congress at Basel. There he met Golda Meir, then head of the political department of the Jewish Agency. She helped him obtain forged British passports for himself, his wife, and his baby daughter, who had been born in Moscow. In September 1947, he and his family arrived in Israel.[38]

Moving to Israel was not without its problems. After all, Yiddish was at the center of his cultural universe and Israel's less-than-positive attitude to the language and the culture was well known.[39] In the absence of any Israeli educational or research institutions in Yiddish, and with a very curtailed Yiddish press, the prospects of publishing in Yiddish and even more so of making a living by writing Yiddish must have seemed bleak. This might have been the reason why he initially thought of the United States, but still settling in Israel did have some attractions.[40]

However, Sutzkever himself, from his earliest days in Israel, claimed that the decision to move there had not been determined by practical considerations. He would describe how his mother, murdered by the Nazis, had always kept a small bag with earth from the Holy Land and told him to settle there.[41] Although the story seems apocryphal, it may have had a grain of truth to it. Given all the hardships he had undergone and the fact that his brother was living in Israel, Sutzkever may have felt that moving there was a good option regardless of all the financial (and other) considerations.[42] It is also likely that he had already conceived the idea of setting up a Yiddish literary journal and had perhaps even raised it in his meeting with Golda Meir.

Why, however, did the Yishuv leadership want to bring Sutzkever and his family to Israel even before the establishment of the state? Golda Meir, then head of the Jewish Agency's political department, is usually given credit for organizing things, though it was almost certainly not simply an individual initiative on her part.[43] Clearly, the Yishuv was interested in bringing Jews—in particular, displaced Jews—to Palestine. Sutzkever, however, was no ordinary Jew. He was an extraordinary figure in every sense. An esteemed Yiddish poet, whose literary work had led the non-Jewish Soviet authorities to airlift him from the German occupation zone in a dramatic operation, he had gained international recognition, as a Jew who had risked his life to save not just people but the treasures of Jewish culture. In addition, he was one of the first Jews to bear witness to the horrors of the Holocaust, both in his testimony—given at great emotional cost—at the Nuremberg trials and in his book *Vilner geto*, which described his life under Nazi rule and was published in Yiddish in Paris and Moscow in 1946, in Buenos Aires in 1947, and in Hebrew translation in Tel Aviv in the same year.[44]

So, when the leadership of the Yishuv encouraged Sutzkever to settle in Israel, their goal was to show the Jewish world that not just the ordinary refugees but highly esteemed Jews chose the new country as their home. Beyond that, as was the case when they attempted to persuade great Yiddish actors to settle in Israel, they wanted to strengthen Israel's status not just as the nation-state of the Jewish people but as the cultural center of the Jewish world.

If an author of Sutzkever's eminence was to be brought to Israel, he had to be provided with a suitable literary environment, where he could continue his literary work and maintain or even enhance his international standing. From the earliest days of modern Yiddish culture, one of the main characteristics of a major Yiddish center was the literary journals produced there.[45] Setting up such a literary journal for Sutzkever in Israel was, then, the obvious thing to do.

I would like to argue that the leadership of the Yishuv, and later of the state, that supported the founding of *Di goldene keyt*, either openly or behind the scenes, understood this, at least intuitively. For them, there was no essential difference between bringing Sutzkever to Israel and setting up the journal for him to edit. In retrospect, it seems clear that *Di goldene keyt* had no raison d'être without Sutzkever, but at the time it was probably equally clear that without a literary forum or the possibility of creating a literary milieu for himself, Sutzkever would not have been able to live and work in Israel.

The Founding of *Di goldene keyt*: "The Histadrut Decides to Publish a Literary Journal in Yiddish"

When Sutzkever and his family arrived in Israel in September 1947, he was received with open arms by the literary and journalistic communities, both Hebrew and Yiddish. "Welcome to Sutzkever the poet, who also carried his poetry into the campaigns of the Jewish war, the likes of which has never existed before—the war of the ghetto," was the message that appeared on page 2 of *Al HaMishmar* in October 1947.[46] Various organizations, including the journalists' association in Tel Aviv, held emotional and moving receptions in his honor, attended by hundreds. The speakers at all these events repeated the hope that Sutzkever would find his place in Israel and not leave it—a fact reinforcing my assumption that *Di goldene keyt* was really founded to enable him to settle in Israel.[47]

It did not take long before rumors began to circulate about a literary journal in Yiddish, to be edited by Sutzkever and funded publicly. Not all the rumors were positive: "The partisan poet," wrote *Maariv*, "is planning a partisan action. . . . [He] is going to found a literary journal here in Yiddish."[48]

The scant archival documentation concerning the founding of *Di goldene keyt* can be filled out by the journal itself, which, over the years, published a number of articles describing its establishment.[49] However, these were all chosen for publication by Sutzkever himself, and some were even written by him. While this supports the view that Sutzkever regarded *Di goldene keyt* as a platform meant for him to revive Yiddish literary life after the Holocaust, the articles themselves reflect not so much what happened in real time but his own take on it.

The only article that did deal with the journal's founding from the point of view of the Histadrut was written by Yosef Sprinzak, then speaker of the Knesset, who at the time the decision was taken to found *Di goldene keyt* was the secretary of the Histadrut. It was the article chosen to open the very first issue that came out in January 1949.

"The Histadrut has seen fit to publish a literary journal in Yiddish to be called *Di goldene keyt*," were the first words of the article and in fact of the new journal as a whole. However, it neither discussed how the journal was established nor presented any kind of program. Instead it launched into a series of apologetic arguments to justify the decision to publish the journal, which suggests that the idea had met with some opposition.

Hebrew, Sprinzak wrote, is the language of the country and also the language of Zionist pioneering and the national renaissance. Nonetheless, the publication of a journal in Yiddish by an organization that has been in the forefront of the battle to make Hebrew the dominant language in all spheres of life (i.e., the Histadrut) is in no way a contradictory move. Sprinzak maintained that the "language war" had been won, which meant that Yiddish could have a role to play in the cultural life of Israel. He pointed out that many Yiddish writers were very popular and that theaters in Israel regularly staged plays translated from the Yiddish. It was only natural, he concluded, for a literary forum to be set up in which Yiddish "would gain inspiration from the pioneering spirit of the labor movement in Eretz Israel."[50]

In fact, Sprinzak's article was probably meant more to placate those opposed to the journal's publication than to give an accurate reflection of the cultural reality in Israel. It also failed to explain the motivations for founding *Di goldene keyt*. The only allusion to those may be found in the article's final paragraph: "At the heart of the present [decision to] found *Di goldene keyt*," Sprinzak wrote, "is the idea that in the Jewish nation-state, all the creative forces of the Jewish people should feel at home. This will naturally draw them closer to the Hebrew culture being created in Israel and its achievements."⁵¹ In other words, what Sprinzak seemed to be saying was that the real aim for founding the Yiddish journal was to make leading Yiddish writers feel comfortable enough in Israel to settle there and, in so doing, establish Israel as the natural home for the Jewish cultural elite and the world center of Jewish culture. So, rather than Sutzkever being brought to Israel to edit *Di goldene keyt*, *Di goldene keyt* was set up to bring Sutzkever to Israel.

"A Quarterly on Literature and Social Problems": The Nature of *Di goldene keyt*

As an elitist, high-quality journal, *Di goldene keyt* attracted a small, highly educated readership of intellectuals and scholars. Its elitism was such that in 1968, at a celebration to mark the journal's sixtieth issue, Mordechai Tsanin claimed that its high cultural approach was actually driving away many Yiddish speakers.⁵²

Di goldene keyt did not, therefore, pose any threat to Hebrew's hegemonic status. Nonetheless, the Histadrut does seem to have anticipated—correctly as it turned out—that the publication of a journal in Yiddish with public funding would arouse opposition. Its response was to suggest, as Sprinzak did, that the journal would form a bridge between Yiddish and Hebrew culture.⁵³ That was also the reason why it appointed Abraham Levinson as coeditor with Sutzkever.

A native of Poland, Levinson was head of the Histadrut's Cultural Center and was a well-known Hebrew writer, editor, and translator from Yiddish, Russian, and Polish.⁵⁴ There is no way of knowing whether he was supposed to play a real role in the journal or whether his appointment was just a way to shut down any opposition. Whatever the case might have been, Levinson's poor health prevented him from doing any actual editorial work, and he died in 1955.⁵⁵ The Histadrut did not replace him with a new coeditor and did not even nominate anyone else to take his place on the editorial board. Instead, Eliezer Pines, an editor and Yiddish journalist who had moved to Israel in 1949, was appointed assistant editor, a position he held for thirty years.⁵⁶

In this way, Sutzkever remained the sole editor, and *Di goldene keyt* became his exclusive province. He made it the worldwide center of Yiddish culture, largely by the force of his personality, his editorial skill, and his status as a foremost Yiddish author. He was helped in no small measure by the fact that the journal was financed by a public organization of the Jewish state.

For its entire forty-six years of existence, *Di goldene keyt* carried a subtitle: *Fertl yorshrift far literatur un gezelshaftlekhe problemen* (Quarterly for literature and social issues).[57] The reason for its addition is unclear. The Histadrut may have wanted to avoid presenting *Di goldene keyt* as a journal devoted solely to Yiddish literature. But by the same token, Sutzkever may have wanted to add it in the tradition of the nineteenth-century Russian "thick journals" that combined literary pieces with literary criticism and essays on social issues. This had been done by other Yiddish periodicals, in particular the New York–based *Di tsukunft*.[58]

The shape the quarterly would take in its early years was apparent in its first issue. It appeared in January 1949 and contained four major kinds of material. The first was the relationship between Hebrew and Yiddish; the second, articles on current events in Israel; the third, translations from Hebrew literature; and the fourth, the greater part of the issue, original Yiddish literature.

The first was highlighted in an article by the poet Yaakov Fichman entitled "Between Hebrew and Yiddish: The Pursuit of *Di goldene keyt*." Fichman discussed the benefits of a Yiddish influence on Israeli Hebrew, arguing that *Di goldene keyt*'s primary mission should be to help break down the dichotomy between Hebrew and Yiddish and to create an atmosphere that would put an end to any antagonism between the two languages.[59] He was not alone in his opinion. A. Boskovitch wrote similarly about "The Popular Poem in Yiddish and Hebrew." Herzl Berger, a member of the Knesset and bilingual journalist, followed the same line in his article entitled "The New Center," as did Ya'akov Zerubavel and Abraham Levinson in their contributions too. Finally, the famous New York–based literary critic Shmuel Niger gave a panoramic view of the history of Yiddish and its links with Hebrew in his piece, "Yiddish, the Language of a Wandering People."

Among the pieces that addressed current events was one by Bracha Habas describing the new immigrants to Israel and another by Raphael Lev, who surveyed Israel's military situation. Israel Galili, formerly the chief commander of the Haganah, wrote an article about David Marcus, the Jewish colonel in the US Army who had volunteered to fight in Israel's War of 1948 and been appointed the first major general of the IDF.

In addition, there were a few articles on Hebrew literature and translations of Hebrew poetry, including "The Silver Platter," written by Nathan Alterman, the consummate representative of modern Hebrew Israeli poetry—a poem that would become an icon of Israeli culture. However, the largest part of the issue was devoted to the Yiddish poetry of the past and the present, with a look toward the future.

There was a meticulously chosen selection of the work of important Yiddish writers: Sholem Asch, Aaron Zeitlin, H. Leivick, Yosef Opatoshu, Menakhem Boreysho, and Aaron Glantz-Leyeles from the United States; Yosef Papyernikov and Aryeh Shamri (whose poetry was discussed in an article in that same issue) from Eretz Israel; Yeshayahu Spiegel, then still in Poland; Moshe Shulshteyn from Paris; and Melech Ravitch from Montreal. Yiddish writers behind the iron curtain were not represented though some of their previously published writing did appear in later issues.[60] In addition, a story by Sholem Aleichem was published with an introduction by Y. D. Berkowitz, as well as poems by young Yiddish poets, new immigrants to Israel, which were printed in a separate section under the heading "Poems of Young Yiddish Poets in Israel." These will be discussed in the next chapter.

This model was repeated in subsequent issues: around a core of original Yiddish literary texts were some translations of the latest original Hebrew literature dealing with controversial issues related to the 1948 war such as S. Yizhar's controversial story "The Captive."[61] There were also articles on current affairs: the liberation of the Galilee in the War of 1948 (by Major General Moshe Carmel), Israel's foreign policy (by Ephraim Breude), Israel's economy (by Peretz Naphtali), the Palmach (by Yitzhak Sadeh), and even an article by Ben-Gurion, "The Struggle for a Jewish State."

However, this structure did not last long. Over the years, the number of articles on current affairs dwindled, and *Di goldene keyt* began to focus much more on Yiddish culture. In its first years, it still contained translations of contemporary Hebrew literature, particularly works identified with the establishment of the state, but the number of these also fell away. Though the subtitle, "A Quarterly for Literature and Social Issues," remained on the masthead until the journal's last issue in 1995, the words "social issues" were just a dead letter. *Di goldene keyt* became a periodical for Yiddish culture and especially Yiddish literature.

How did this come about? In his memoirs, Noah Gris, a member of the quarterly's editorial board from its very first issue, explains that the editorial policy on covering topical issues was not adopted in order to please the Histadrut but was an expression of a genuine desire that the quarterly contribute to Israel's social life. To this end, prominent public figures were invited to write for it. Gris writes about his efforts to convince people such as Yitzhak Sadeh, the founder of the Palmach, and Major General Yigael Yadin, the IDF chief of staff, among others, to write articles of contemporary relevance.[62]

It seems that this aspect of the quarterly reflected, more than anything else, the search of the editors for an editorial policy that would make *Di goldene keyt* an influential force in both the post-Holocaust Yiddish world and the nascent Jewish state. Current affairs—in particular, those connected with the establishment of the state or the role of new immigrants in the new society being built in Israel—were thought to be of great interest to Yiddish readers. (They were also discussed at great length in other Yiddish publications.) The participation of military commanders and leading public figures in *Di goldene keyt* was probably intended to lend it gravitas.

Over the years, Sutzkever built it gradually and astutely into the basis for a new center of Jewish post-Holocaust culture, which he wanted to see founded under his leadership in the state of Israel. However, this was not an easy process, and, particularly in the journal's early years, he struggled to find the right path and to develop the necessary editorial policy. These problems were given explicit expression in letters that Sutzkever wrote to Shmuel Niger, then considered the greatest critic of Yiddish literature, concerning his contribution to the first issue of *Di goldene keyt*.

Sutzkever was very interested in including articles by Niger in the first issues of the new periodical, and Niger offered him two, one of which was about the writing of H. Leivick, which he was planning.[63] The second was a very long paper on the history of Yiddish, its place in traditional society, and its links with *loshn koydesh* (the Sacred Tongue), entitled "Yidish: di shprakh fun a vander folk" (Yiddish—the language of a wandering people). Niger was working on this paper at the time and was interested in publishing it at once.

Sutzkever expressed his preference to publish the article on Leivick first and to leave the article on Yiddish for a future opportunity. A correspondence on the issue developed between the two men.[64]

"I still lack experience as an editor," Sutzkever wrote to Niger. "That's why I had my doubts, but perhaps it *actually is* a good idea to publish something like [the paper on Yiddish] in a journal like this, and so take the opportunity to say everything [that needs to be said] outright."[65] However, when Niger finished writing the article and sent it in, Sutzkever was hesitant to print such a long piece on the development of Yiddish in the very first issue of the journal and asked Niger to shorten it. "The attitude to Yiddish in this country is not yet clear to me," he wrote to Niger, in a letter explaining why he had shortened his article by almost half. "Neither of us [i.e., Niger and Sutzkever] has any interest in inflaming the atmosphere.... [This] is after all a publication of the Histadrut and I have to tread carefully."[66]

Despite what he wrote, there is no evidence either that Sutzkever was apprehensive about the Histadrut's reaction to what he published or that the Histadrut had the intention to interfere in his editorial decisions. What did concern him, however, was the possibility of a hostile public response to the appearance of a periodical in Yiddish. It was not long in coming.

"A Process Leading to a Turning Point": The Reception of *Di goldene keyt*, 1948–1952

The reports in the Hebrew press of the summer of 1948 about the Histadrut's intention to publish a periodical in Yiddish led to a small-scale public debate not only on the publication of *Di goldene keyt* itself but also on the place of

Yiddish in Israel in general.⁶⁷ Some articles in the Hebrew press responded favorably to the idea of a literary quarterly in Yiddish. Others took a more complex line. There were those who expressed surprise at the need to publish a journal in Yiddish with public financing at that particular time.⁶⁸ Several writers mentioned the issue in the course of articles on the inculcation of the Hebrew language, finding the publication of a Yiddish journal with Histadrut financing objectionable in that context. One of these articles was even printed in the Histadrut daily, *Davar*. ⁶⁹

However, the greatest hostility to publishing such a journal with Histadrut financing—and to the existence of Yiddish in Israel in general—came from the camp of those opposed to the socialist-Zionist hegemony in Israel. These views, which were printed in newspapers of the revisionist movement, interpreted the intention to foster Yiddish-language culture as support for the Yiddish-speaking socialist circles of the past, some of which were anti-Zionist.⁷⁰ "It is not only socialism that has taken control of Zionism and the State of Israel, but Yiddish also," wrote Abba Ahimeir, a leading figure in the movement, on the first anniversary of *Di goldene keyt*.⁷¹

In the midst of this sometimes heated debate, several articles appeared that expressed balanced positions, arguing that the two languages could and should coexist in the new reality of the state of Israel and held that *Di goldene keyt* had a place in that reality. The line most often taken had two elements: first, that Yiddish was no longer a rival to Hebrew; second, and perhaps more importantly, that the Hebrew culture had deep roots in Yiddish, which should be integrated into the new Hebrew culture. This could be done by both translating Yiddish literature into Hebrew and by nurturing original Yiddish writers in Israel.⁷²

Some of these pieces also identified another goal for *Di goldene keyt*. It was to serve as a link between Israel and the Yiddish world of the Diaspora and so make Israel the center of that world.⁷³ This was discussed in some detail by Y. M. Neiman of *Davar*, who had been a senior journalist of the Warsaw Yiddish newspaper *Haynt* before the Holocaust. "This is more than simply a quarterly for literature," he wrote in a long article on the controversy over the new Yiddish periodical. "We are now facing . . . a process leading to a turning point. . . . The appearance of *Di goldene keyt* is not a simple matter. A struggle awaits us, but not in relation to the language." Every culture has gained from contact with other cultures, he maintained, and the struggle between opinions and views diversifies and enriches it. *Di goldene keyt*, Neiman said, is a connecting link between Jewish communities, but "the primacy, the right of the 'first-born,' belongs to the *State of Israel*, whose function is also to be a center shining forth to the entire people."⁷⁴

The controversy in the press over *Di goldene keyt* lasted about a year. Starting in 1951, the quarterly became a permanent feature on the Israeli literary scene and so was unremarkable. It did occasionally receive some coverage, when, with the appearance of a new issue, the literary supplements of the Hebrew press noted that fact with a news item that sometimes even included a review of its contents.[75] The public debate over the Yiddish journal's right to exist had drawn to a close.

Of its two dominant motifs—the quarterly's contribution to enriching Israeli culture and the role it could fill in emphasizing the place of Israel as the leader of world Jewish culture—only the second came to anything. The quarterly very soon distanced itself from discussions of Israeli life and from 1952 focused almost exclusively on Yiddish literature—written in Israel and outside it—as well as various matters linked to Yiddish culture. Beginning in that year, *Di goldene keyt* also published—as *Di tsukunft* had in the past—symposia that discussed issues relating to the contemporary world of Yiddish.[76] However, the journal directed its energies in two main directions: the first was to encourage the creation of original Israeli Yiddish literature in general and those young Yiddish writers who had embarked on their literary lives in Israel in particular. The second was to make the journal the center of worldwide Yiddish culture in the second half of the twentieth century.

"The Future Historian": *Di goldene keyt* and the Aspiration to Reestablish Yiddish Culture after the Holocaust

From the outset *Di goldene keyt* enjoyed a special status in the transnational world of Yiddish periodicals. As we have seen, this was due in no small measure to Sutzkever's personality and his reputation as a leading Yiddish author, as well as the journal's literary quality. It was also due to the fact that the quarterly was almost the only one in Yiddish that had ever been published with public money and was the only one supported by the Jewish nation-state. This not only gave *Di goldene keyt* economic stability but also earned it respect in the Yiddish world.[77] However, it seems that Sutzkever's aspirations did not end there. While the leaders of the state, as well as some journalists, saw *Di goldene keyt* as a way of establishing Israel as the world center of Jewish culture and so spreading its cultural hegemony beyond its borders, Sutzkever viewed it as a crucial tool for the revival and development of Yiddish literature and culture in the post-Holocaust world.

Di goldene keyt never published a systematic manifesto or program. However, in its first issue, and then in various anniversary issues, it did publish pieces that discussed the journal's aims. A close examination of these texts can help reveal not only Sutzkever's vision for the quarterly but perhaps also the way he viewed his achievements over the years.

The first expression of the quarterly's vision was made even before it was fully established, in its choice of name. The title *Di goldene keyt* (The golden chain) did not simply allude to the link between the past and the present. It was also the name of a well-known play by Y. L. Peretz, the "father" of Jewish modernism. It was considered Peretz's most important, if not his best, work and had been very influential on the development of modern Yiddish culture.[78] Taking the name of a famous play that dealt with the tensions between continuity and break, renewal and tradition, was in many senses a fitting choice.[79] However, beyond that it created a subtle yet close affinity between Sutzkever and Peretz. After all, Peretz had made Warsaw the Yiddish literary capital of eastern Europe, if not the world.[80] And after his death, he had been eulogized with the words: "With Peretz, Yiddish literature began its true life."[81]

Sutzkever expressed the great importance he ascribed to Peretz in his farewell ode, "Tsu Poyln" (To Poland), which he wrote before he left the country. In the poem, the narrator wanders through Poland's abandoned streets and arrives at Peretz's *ohel*, his mausoleum, in the Warsaw Jewish cemetery. There he imagines himself lifting the tombstone onto his shoulders and carrying it away.[82] The poem ends with a quotation from Peretz's *Di goldene keyt*. Justin Cammy has noted rightly that the choice of the name *Di goldene keyt* for the journal symbolized that act of loading the destroyed culture of Polish Jewry onto Sutzkever's shoulders and bringing it to Israel.[83]

But it seems Sutzkever was not content just with that. He wanted to establish a center in Israel whose importance in the post-Holocaust Jewish reality would be equal to that of Peretz's center in early twentieth-century Warsaw. To do this, he understood that the new center of Yiddish literature around *Di goldene keyt* would have to form an integral part of the reconstruction and revival of the Jewish people after the Holocaust. It is therefore perhaps no surprise that the first issue of the quarterly contained a brief text, in bold type, with no context or signature, that described with great pathos the key role that Yiddish and its culture would play in the great historical events then unfolding. The text also characterized Yiddish as a link in a golden chain that connects between the Jewish past and its present in Israel. However, using the words "golden chain"—*di goldene keyt*, in Yiddish—also alluded to the role that the quarterly *Di goldene keyt* would have to play in all this.[84] Perhaps feeling that leaving the text anonymous would give it greater impact, it took Sutzkever thirty years to admit to being its author.[85]

Sutzkever gave even clearer expression to his vision in a speech he delivered at a party marking the quarterly's second anniversary. In it, he clearly linked the Yiddish periodical's founding to the establishment of the state of Israel and gave voice to his aspiration to make the journal part of the state-building process. "When future historians mention *Di goldene keyt*, they will probably see its major significance in the fact that it was forged in the fire of the Jewish war, in the days of our third revival," he said. Then, after mentioning the personal sacrifices made by his friends, particularly Yosef Sprinzak, who had lost his son in the 1948 war, he added: "It is my innermost belief that alongside the revival of the nation and its resettlement on its ancient homeland, the tones of the Yiddish language must also be heard." Since "the resurrection [*tkhies-hameysim*] of the Jewish people on its land cannot be physical alone, ... we must also bring about ... the resurrection of the Jewish spirit, the cultural treasures of our great people that have been shattered and scattered in all directions." He went on to thank the Histadrut for its support of the journal in the name of its writers and readers all over the world, "from Kibbutz Yagur to Los Angeles," and concluded by saying: "*Di goldene keyt* does not just want merely to be proud of its name, the title that we borrowed from Peretz. It wants to be *worthy of it*."[86]

So two years after *Di goldene keyt* began to appear, Sutzkever had given a very clear vision of what he thought he was doing. He was creating a journal that would not just be dedicated to Yiddish literature but would form an integral part of the great project of rebuilding the Jewish nation wherever it might be. He wanted this moment of creation to be equal in its intensity and importance to that made by Peretz in his time. That is why he felt that "a future historian," who would write the history of the Jewish people's reconstruction, would cite his journal as an inseparable part of it.

However, Jewish life after the Holocaust in Israel—and elsewhere—was very different from that in Peretz's day. So, though Sutzkever's vision of creating a Yiddish cultural center would indeed come to pass, it would not, tragically, have a significant role to play in Israel's rebirth.

After the journal's first few issues, articles dealing with the current matters became fewer and more of them dealt with issues significant to Israel's revival.[87] The journal began to narrow its focus mostly to the world of Yiddish literature, showcasing matters of high Yiddish culture and of the culture of east European Jewry in general. The layout of the issues soon took on their final shape, comprising a main block of literary articles, followed by reviews of literature and summaries of books. In the spirit of the journal's transnational character, the contributors came from both Israel and the whole Jewish world.

The second half of each issue was devoted to Yiddish culture more broadly understood. Faithful to his vision of bringing the treasures of Jewish culture to Israel, Sutzkever published a whole range of primary sources on the history of Yiddish literature and culture, including letters and articles by major figures and important documents.[88] He also gave space to research papers on Yiddish studies by various scholars, including some from the Hebrew University. In that way, he made a connection between the journal and the newly founded chair in Yiddish at the university, linking them both in the creation of the Israeli center for high Yiddish culture.

His aspiration to give the periodical a central role in the process of nation building was expressed first and foremost in his promotion of young Israeli Yiddish writers, in particular members of the Yung Yisroel group (to be discussed in the next chapter). Sutzkever saw the members of the group as the future of an original Israeli Yiddish literature and as a new stage in the development of post-Holocaust Jewish culture. His publication of translations of Hebrew literature and reviews of Hebrew literature were also meant to bring Hebrew and Yiddish culture into closer contact.[89]

Of course, Sutzkever's own poetry was published in the quarterly and added to its prestige, as were reproductions of works by such artists as Marc Chagall, Yossel Bergner, and others.

So, in *Di goldene keyt*, Sutzkever succeeded in harnessing what he called "all the creative forces in Yiddish in the world," to make the journal the most important center of Yiddish literature in the post-Holocaust world, as well as to put Israel at the head of the transnational network of Yiddish literature.[90] He had much to be proud of. However, in 1964, when the fiftieth issue came out, Sutzkever not only returned to his vision for the journal but also voiced some doubts.

"I am the man," Sutzkever wrote in the festive introduction to the issue, "who saw the destruction of my people in all its horror, who felt that we, the small handful of survivors, Yiddish writers, could not avenge with our pens the blood of Ponar, of Auschwitz. But we could avenge the incineration of our language . . . by helping it rise again, renewed . . . in the land of our rebirth." He asked: "Did we achieve our goal? Were our actions successful?" But he found it difficult to reply. Many who were present at the birth of *Di goldene keyt*, such as Sprinzak and Levinson, had already passed away, as had many of its staunchest supporters from across the Jewish world, such as Leivick, Opatoshu, Niger, Asch, and many others. Sutzkever chose to end his piece on a supposedly optimistic tone, anticipating a flowering of Yiddish literature, but in his lyrical language he describes it as "a flowering resurrection of the dead." It is hard not to sense the tone of disappointment.[91]

By then, about a decade and a half after the establishment of the state, *Di goldene keyt*'s target audience—Yiddish-speaking intellectuals in Israel and elsewhere, as well as an educated lay audience immersed in Yiddish culture—was dwindling. Though it remained the major forum for Yiddish literature in the world until its very last issue, the journal's loyal supporters were never more than a small elitist group.

Figure 4.1. Abraham Sutzkever and President Zalman Shazar. Courtesy of Rina Sutzkever.

Sutzkever's original aspiration, to make *Di goldene keyt* an integral part of the nation-building process, had also come to nothing. In its place was an attempt to see the journal integrated into the narrative of Jewish history to be written by future historians. This was seen nowhere more clearly than in the issue that marked the state of Israel's thirtieth anniversary. "Two dates," it announced on its very first page. "One [is] of great historical significance—the revival of Jewish independence—and the second, of great literary and sociocultural importance. The State of Israel has existed for thirty years and so has *Di goldene keyt*."[92]

Now the Yiddish quarterly had yet another aim—to integrate the history of twentieth-century Yiddish culture, including *Di goldene keyt*, into the history of the revival of Israel and into Jewish history in general, and to make a significant contribution to Yiddish scholarship. This led to an intensified cooperation with the chair, later the department, of Yiddish at the Hebrew University, whose importance in the worldwide revival of Yiddish Sutzkever saw as crucial.[93]

The Chair in Yiddish at the Hebrew University

The chair in Yiddish at the Hebrew University was inaugurated on September 4, 1951. This was not the first attempt to establish a chair in Yiddish at the Hebrew University. As far back as 1927, two years after the founding of the university, the editor of the New York Yiddish daily *Der tog* offered the university a donation to finance the establishment of a chair in Yiddish. The proposal aroused fierce opposition among professors at the university and led to a public debate about the place of Yiddish in the Yishuv. It was finally rejected.[94]

In 1951, too, it was a financial contribution by Jews in the United States that underpinned the establishment of the chair. However, this time, the creation of the chair and its approval by the university authorities was, like the establishment of *Di goldene keyt*, a part both of a much broader processes of state building then underway in Israel and Ben-Gurion's policy to make Israel the world center of Jewish culture.[95]

The seed of the idea was planted at the same Twenty-Second Zionist Congress in Basel, in 1946, where the founding of *Di goldene keyt* and Sutzkever's move to Israel were first mooted. In this case, it was Dr. Marc (Meir) Dvorjetski, a physician and survivor of the Vilna ghetto, who proposed the establishment of this chair.[96] It did not prove popular, so Dvorjetski withdrew it.[97] He tried a second time, making the proposal part of the congress's decision to allocate funds to the Hebrew University. This too he had to withdraw.[98] In the end, the congress referred the proposal to the Zionist Executive Committee, which ruled: "In order to build a bridge between Eretz Israel and the diaspora, and to enable the younger generation in the country, as well as the public activists and emissaries sent to work in the diaspora, to learn about the treasures of Yiddish culture, the University is called upon to establish a chair in Yiddish language and literature."[99] Although this was only a declaration, it was extremely important. No less than the Zionist Congress, the body representing the Zionist movement that supported Hebrew over Yiddish, had now declared Yiddish as a Jewish cultural treasure.

The first practical step toward establishing the chair was taken in March 1947. At a meeting of the university's board of trustees in the United States, the heads of Idish natsyonaler arbeter farband in the United States offered to finance not only the establishment of a chair in Yiddish at the Hebrew University but also the first few years of its activity.[100]

The Idish natsyonaler arbeter farband was a fraternal order associated with Poalei-Zion, the Labor Zionist movement of America. It offered its members social and cultural activities in the spirit of Labor Zionism and actively participated in fund-raising campaigns for Eretz Israel. However, though it was a

Zionist organization, the Labor Zionist movement of America saw Hebrew and Yiddish of equal importance. As an immigrant organization, it defined Hebrew as the language of the Jewish future in Eretz Israel and Yiddish as the language of the Diaspora present. It therefore invested great effort in promoting Yiddish through education and publishing.[101] In the late 1940s, the organization tried to boost its Zionist activity by supporting new educational projects in Israel.[102] The Yiddish chair at the Hebrew University fit the bill exactly.

The university's executive committee discussed the Farband's offer at its meeting of March 1947 and decided to accept it. The Institute for Jewish Studies and the Faculty of Humanities at their meetings in May and June of that year, respectively, also voted to accept the donation but added, that alongside the establishment of the chair in Yiddish, the study of Judeo-Spanish (Ladino) should also be introduced. The discussion at the humanities meeting dealt with the issue broadly and in depth, finally agreeing to the proposal on the grounds that the establishment of the chair would be an important step in saving the vestiges of Jewish popular culture and that Yiddish, which had once been spoken by so many Jews, was now in danger of extinction.[103] So, if in 1927 the idea of a chair in Yiddish had been rejected from fear that it would endanger the acceptance of Hebrew, in 1951 it was accepted because Yiddish was seen as a weak language in danger of disappearing that had to be saved.

Due to the outbreak of the war of independence in November 1947, the university had to stop its discussions of the chair in Yiddish. In January 1948, the university senate voted with a large majority to include in the university's curriculum the study of "Diaspora Jewish languages," namely Yiddish and Ladino.[104] This marked the beginning of a complicated process of organizing the funding for the chair in Yiddish and finding a candidate to fill it. The first people considered for the position were all from outside Israel. Though the search committee put academic excellence as its major criterion, two other considerations intervened. One was the desire to find a candidate working in popular culture rather than philology, and the second was to choose someone whose allegiance to Zionism left no room for doubt.[105] After considering several possibilities, the members of the search committee unanimously agreed to offer the post to the well-known Yiddish scholar Dr. Max Weinreich. They recommended, however, that his position on ideological Yiddishism first be clarified, to make sure that that he would not use his appointment to spread anti-Hebrew propaganda.[106]

Though willing to come for a period as a visiting professor, Weinreich turned down the university's offer.[107] Following that, the committee, in consultation with the donors, decided to look for a candidate in Israel. The choice fell upon Dov Sadan.[108] Although he was an autodidact, Sadan (formerly Berl

Stock) had impressive credentials. He edited the literary supplement of *Davar* and was a member of the editorial board of the Am Oved publishing house, as well as a well-known literary critic and scholar of Jewish popular culture.[109] Sadan, who was already teaching at the university, was also a member of the Knesset for Mapai, the Israeli Labor Party. Little wonder that Chaim Greenberg, the charismatic leader of the Labor-Zionist movement in the United States and a member of the university's board of governors, reacted enthusiastically to the idea of appointing him.[110] The question of financing was also resolved once the Farband undertook explicitly to support the chair for a few years to come.[111] On September 4, 1951, the Yiddish chair was inaugurated with Dov Sadan as the first incumbent.[112]

A number of speeches were delivered on that occasion, some of them very moving. Two are particularly relevant here. The first is Sadan's inaugural address. In addition to discussing its academic goals, Sadan described the Yiddish chair as a counterreaction to the idea of the negation the Diaspora and especially to the ideology of the historical leap discussed earlier. The second speaker was Professor Ben-Zion Dinaburg (Dinur). He described the chain of events that had led to the establishment of the chair and noted the historical importance of Yiddish culture. He then went on to put the founding of the Yiddish chair in the broader context of the state of Israel's responsibility toward the Jewish culture of the past. "It is our duty today," said Dinur, to set up "a large-scale project that will bring together all of Jewish creativity from across the generations," adding that "Yiddish is one of the foundations of our people's culture."[113]

Dinur was only appointed minister of education a few weeks later, but he was close to Prime Minister Ben-Gurion and shared his vision of what the new Israeli culture was to be. As a result, his description of the Yiddish chair as part of a large project encompassing Jewish cultural creativity from previous generations was probably not just his own view. From the university's side, this made the establishment of the Yiddish chair actually seem an act of cooperation with the political leadership, which was particularly important given that the university was then embroiled in a struggle with the government over its desire if not to totally nationalize the university, at least to make it a government agency that it could control.[114]

It would seem then that the idea of making Israel the repository for the historical treasures of Jewish culture was a guiding principle of the state's cultural policy in its early years. As we have seen, it found expression in the decision to set up *Di goldene keyt* and in the support given to establishing a chair in Yiddish at the Hebrew University. These were not, however, the only such projects that Ben-Gurion was willing to support for that reason.

Ben-Gurion and the Preservation of Diaspora Jewish Culture

One of the most important preservation projects was that to ensure the survival of historical Hebrew manuscripts. In March 1950, while on vacation in Tiberias, Ben-Gurion sent a long letter to the minister of finance, asking him to allocate a large budget to found, under the auspices of the Ministry of Education, an institute to collect photocopies of Hebrew manuscripts from across the world. "Before all else, we have an urgent duty to rescue Hebrew literature," he wrote in the letter. "There are thousands of Hebrew manuscripts in various libraries and they just lie there, useless. . . . Many of them have been lost in the darkness of the past or destroyed by the wrath of oppressors. Who knows how many manuscripts were destroyed in World War II. . . . The State of Israel has the responsibility to assemble the scattered spirit of Israel."[115]

So, a year after the first issue of *Di goldene keyt* and a year before the inauguration of the Yiddish chair at the Hebrew University, Ben-Gurion gave explicit expression to his view that the collection and preservation of Jewish cultural treasures was an important duty of the nation-state of the Jewish people. Although he defined the goal as preserving Hebrew manuscripts, his intention was to save any text written in Hebrew letters (which would include, among others, Judeo-Spanish, Judeo-Arabic, and, of course, Yiddish).[116]

The Institute for Hebrew Manuscripts was founded in 1952 as part of the Ministry of Education, and its director started traveling all over Europe to look for lost manuscripts and make copies to bring back to Israel.[117] In 1963, the institute was transferred to the National Library of Israel (then the Jewish National and University Library), where its name was changed to the Institute of Microfilmed Hebrew Manuscripts. By that time, the size of the collection had already reached fifteen thousand microfilms. The work of searching out and copying Hebrew manuscripts did not end there, and by the beginning of the twenty-first century, the collection contained more than seventy-six thousand microfilms.[118]

This initiative was all of a piece with the decisions to create a literary journal in Yiddish and establish a chair for Yiddish at the Hebrew University. All of them reflected the sense of responsibility felt by the Israeli leadership to preserve Jewish Diaspora culture and, at the same time, to make the Jewish nation-state the cultural center of the Jewish people as a whole.

This found expression in yet another of Ben-Gurion's decisions on cultural policy. On this occasion, it had nothing to do with Yiddish but rather orthodox Jewish religious culture. For this, too, the state of Israel felt responsible and acted for its preservation.

In 1948, Ben-Gurion decided to grant lengthy postponements, even exemptions, from military service to a small group of yeshiva students. It is true that in the reality of twenty-first-century Israel, when the question of military service for yeshiva students has become a major political issue, connecting it with cultural policy sounds strange. However, the political aspect only became a problem in the late 1970s. At the end of the 1940s, the exemption was very much a cultural issue, part of a broader policy on the preservation of Jewish culture in all its forms—including Yiddish.

In March 1948—during the war of independence—the Haganah chief of staff, Israel Galili, issued an order exempting a clearly defined number of yeshiva students from military service. In the order, he stated that its purpose was to avoid interrupting the studies of these students, whose names had been approved ahead of time. It was to be valid for just one year (September 1947 to September 1948).

In October 1948, at a meeting of the Security Committee of the State Council, Ben-Gurion justified the order, saying, "There are 400 yeshiva students, all young, and if they are forced to serve in the army, we will have to close the yeshivot."[119] That was not the end of the story. A year later, ostensibly at the request of representatives of the religious parties, he agreed to a long-term exemption. Unusually for him, he wrote at length in his diary about his meeting with the rabbis, making it clear that this was not, in fact, the case: "A delegation of heads of yeshivot came to see me—came to request an exemption from military service for yeshiva students; and though I told them at once that their request had already been answered, they insisted on giving the reasons for it."[120]

Ben-Gurion's accession to the wishes of the religious public has been interpreted as a move made out of political considerations. However, Ben-Gurion was acting as minister of defense, and his decision did not form part of any coalition negotiations. He made this clear a few years later in a letter to then Minister of Defense Pinhas Lavon: "I never made an agreement with any of the religious parties on the exemption of yeshiva students. I did so of my own free will.... In contrast to what I have seen in the press, the exemption was not the outcome of a coalition agreement."[121]

The background to the decision can be seen in the conditions of the time. After the Holocaust, the situation of orthodoxy in general, and of ultraorthodox society in particular, was at its lowest ebb. In the ultraorthodox world, there was a sense that an entire rabbinical and scholarly elite had been destroyed and that there was no way either to rehabilitate or to replace it. The political leadership of ultraorthodox and religious society was embroiled in internal political conflict, and many young people were abandoning orthodoxy.[122] As a result, Israel's political and academic leadership, as well as scholars of Jewish society the world over, believed that the days of Jewish orthodoxy were numbered and that the world of the yeshivot was coming to its end.[123]

Ben-Gurion's decision to exempt a limited number of yeshiva students from military service was, therefore, yet another expression of the responsibility felt by the state of Israel toward the Jewish culture of the past. Its goal was to preserve the remnants of a cultural—in this case, religious—treasure that had played a major role in Jewish life before the Holocaust but was now in danger of extinction.[124]

On the face of it, there seems little connection between Israel's support of the yeshivot, its collecting Hebrew manuscripts from around the world, its establishment of a chair in Yiddish at the Hebrew University, and its publishing *Di goldene keyt*. Nonetheless, all of these reflect the fact that the cultural policy of Israel's leadership under Ben-Gurion went far beyond the invention of a new Hebrew culture. Of course, in anything that might be considered daily life, the emphasis was very much on creating a new Israeli Hebrew culture cut off from the Jews' diasporic past. But the leadership of the nascent state also invested a great deal of thought in what to do with the cultural treasures of the Jews' historical past. It felt that it was Israel's responsibility to preserve them for future generations—a policy that they understood would have the added benefit of making the country the cultural center of the entire Jewish world.

What made this all the more palatable was that these acts of cultural preservation would, for the most part, touch only very small numbers of people—the contributors to and readers of *Di goldene keyt*, the professors and students of Yiddish at the Hebrew University, and the just four hundred yeshiva students who would be exempted from military service. All these groups could be supported without posing any threat to the development and general acceptance of the new Israeli Hebrew culture, which remained the apple of the government's eye.

Notes

1. "Riv'on be'Yidish," *Davar*, August 22, 1948.
2. "*Di goldene keyt*," *Al HaMishmar*, September 3, 1948.
3. "Iton yomi be'Yidish," *HaMashkif*, November 10, 1948.
4. The editorial offices were first housed at 113 Allenby Street in Tel Aviv, in the office that had previously been the editorial office of the Histadrut daily, *Davar*, and later moved to other buildings owned by the Histadrut.
5. Yosef Gorny, Avi Bareli, and Yitzhak Greenberg, "Introduction," in *Me'hevrat avoda le'irgun ovdim*, ed. Yosef Gorny, Avi Bareli, and Yitzhak Greenberg (Sede-Boker: Ben-Gurion University of the Negev Press, 2000), 1–2; Lev Greenberg, "Ovdim hazakim, ovdim halashim, zeramim ba'kalkala ha'politit ha'isra'elit, 1967–1994," *Te'orya u'bikoret* 9 (Winter 1996): 61–80.

Zeev Sternhell has written at length about the power of the Histadrut and how it became a vehicle of the leadership of prestate Israel. See Zeev Sternhell *Binyan uma o tikun hevra, le'umiyut ve'sotzyalism bi'tenu'at ha'avoda ha'isra'elit 1904–1940* (Tel Aviv: Am Oved, 1995), 226–230.

6. The Histadrut daily, *Davar*, Davar and Am Oved publishing houses, and the Ohel Theater.

7. A. Sutzkever, "Der yidishfraynd," *Di goldene keyt* 33 (1959): 20–27; "Bar mitzva la'riv'on *Di goldene keyt*," *Davar*, May 20, 1962.

8. Yosef Sprinzak, *Unzer zorg farn goles: unzer flikht far der tsyonistesher organizatsye* (Tel Aviv: Ihud Olami Poalei-Zion—Hitahdut, 1939); and Yosef Sprinzak, *In vort un in shrift* (Buenos Aires: Kiem, 1954); D. Dyokanai, "Roshim be'Israel: Yosef Sprinzak, o: min ha'temuna mabit Herzl," *Maariv*, May 22, 1953.

9. Melekh Noy Noyshtatt, a senior official in the Histadrut and a writer and journalist, wrote that Sprinzak had some influence on the decision to establish *Di goldene keyt*. Melekh Noy, "Ha'ish ve'yihudo" *Davar*, February 6, 1959; on the leadership of Mapai, including Sprinzak's weakened status at the time, see Avi Bareli, "Politika miflagtit u'politika shel mimshal: hanhagat Mapai ba'ma'avar mi'yishuv le'medina," *Israel* 5 (2004): 31–60.

10. Minutes of Central Committee of the Histadrut, May 16, 1948, Pinhas Lavon Institute for Labor Movement Research.

11. On opposition to a Yiddish literary organ in the press, see, for example, "Hovevei sefat Yidish," *HaMashkif*, August 9, 1948; "Bli lo'azit u'bli Yidish," *HaMashkif*, September 15, 1948.

12. Benjamin Harshav, himself a native of Vilna and an associate of Sutzkever, wrote in an introduction to a selection of Sutzkever's poetry that was published in Hebrew in 2005 that Manya Shochat and Zalman Shazar, a future president of Israel, were also among the supporters of a journal in Yiddish.

13. Benjamin Harshav, "Avraham Sutzkever, shira ve'hayim," in *Kinus dumiyot, mivhar shirei Avraham Sutzkever*, ed. Nitza Drori-Pereman, trans. into the Hebrew by Benjamin Harshav et al. (Tel Aviv: Am Oved, 2005), 11–30. The introduction is based on a previous version that appeared as the introduction to a collection of Sutzkever's poetry in English. Benjamin Harshav, "Sutzkever: Life and Poetry," in *A. Sutzkever, Selected Poetry and Prose*, trans. from the Yiddish by Barbara Harshav and Benjamin Harshav (Berkeley: University of California Press, 1991), 3–23. This poetic definition of the treasures of Yiddish appears in the Hebrew version only and not in the English original of the introduction about Sutzkever's life, which I will refer to later.

14. Dan Miron, "Laila tov, nasich matok," *Ha'aretz*, January 29, 2010.

15. The biographical survey of Sutzkever's early life is based mainly on the entry "Sutzkever" in *Leksikon fun der nayer yidisher literatur*, as well as on Benjamin Harshav's introduction to a selection of Sutzkever's poems in Hebrew, which is an expansion on the introduction to the selection of poems in English. See note 13 above; Ruth Wisse, "Avrom Sutzkever," *YIVO Encyclopedia of the Jews in Eastern Europe*, http://www.yivoencyclopedia.org/article.aspx/Sutzkever_Avrom.

16. Harshav, "Sutzkever: Life and Poetry," 23. The person who made him pledge allegiance to Bin was Dr. Max Weinrich, the great renowned Yiddish linguist and the founder of YIVO.

17. On Yung Vilne, see Avraham Novershtern, "Sifrut u'politika bi'yetzirata shel kevutzat 'Yung Vilne'," in *Bein shetei milhamot olam*, ed. Chone Shmeruk and Shmuel Verses, 169–181 (Jerusalem: Magnes, 1996). See Avraham Novershtern, *Avrom Sutzkever, tsu zayn vern a ben*

shivim, catalogue of an exhibition at the Jewish National Library (Jerusalem: no publisher's name, 1983), 9.

18. On the relations between Sutzkever and the members of Yung Vilne, see Justin Cammy, "Tsevorfene bleter: The Emergence of Yung Vilne," *Polin* 14 (2001): 170–191.

19. The first poem appeared in the literary weekly *Vokhnshrift far literatur, kunst un kultur*. Novershtern, *Avrom Sutzkever, tsu zayn vern*, 13; Abraham Novershtern, "Walk through Words as through Minefields: Abraham Sutzkever z"l," *Yad Vashem Studies* 38, no. 1 (2010): 47–59, 31; Wisse, "Avrom Sutzkever."

20. Novershtern, *Avrom Sutzkever, tsu zayn vern*, 15.

21. Novershtern, "Walk through Words," 41; Novershtern, *Avrom Sutzkever, tsu zayn vern*, 18.

22. See, for example, S. Lev, "Der dikhter fun 'Zeungen zunik gezen'," *Literarishe bleter*, April 30, 1937, 8. On Sutzkever's wartime poetry, see Roskies, *Against the Apocalypse*, 227–257; Harshav, "Sutzkever: Life and Poetry"; Novershtern, *Avrom Sutzkever, tsu zayn vern*; Ruth R. Wisse, "Introduction: The Ghetto Poems of Abraham Sutzkever," in *Abraham Sutzkever, Burnt Pearls: Ghetto Poems of Abraham Sutzkever*, ed. Ruth Wisse, trans. Seymour Mayne (Oakville, ON: Mosaic, 1981), 1–18.

23. Novershtern, *Avrom Sutzkever, tsu zayn vern*, 32–34.

24. On this, see David E. Fishman, *The Book Smugglers: Partisans, Poets, and the Race to Save Jewish Treasures from the Nazis* (Lebanon, NH: ForeEdge, 2017).

25. Justin Cammy, "Abraham Sutzkever," in *Writers in Yiddish*, ed. Joseph Sherman (Detroit: Thomson Gale, 2007), 303–313; Novershtern, "Walk through Words."

26. Novershtern, *Avrom Sutzkever, tsu zayn vern*, 147; Benjamin Harshav, "Avraham Sutzkever, shira ve'hayim," in *Kinus dumiyot, mivhar shirei Avraham Sutzkever*, ed. Nitza Drori-Pereman, trans. into the Hebrew by Benjamin Harshav et al. (Tel Aviv: Am Oved, 2005), 11–30.

27. See Novershtern, *Avrom Sutzkever, tsu zayn vern*; Harshav, "Abraham Sutzkever." On the meeting between Sutzkever and Ehrenburg, see Joshua Rubinstein, *Tangled Loyalties: The Life and Time of Ilya Ehrenburg* (London: I. B. Tauris, 1996).

28. Ilya Ehrenburg, "Torzhestvo cheloveka," *Pravda*, April 29, 1944, 1.

29. Roskies, *Against the Apocalypse*, 247–248.

30. See "Hashmadat yehudei Vilna," *Al HaMishmar*, April 16, 1944; Novershtern, *Avrom Sutzkever, tsu zayn vern*, 50.

31. Ilya Ehrenburg, "Avraham Sutzkever, ha'meshorer ve'ha'gibor," *Al HaMishmar*, May 26, 1944.

32. "Meshorer partizan le'haver meshorer partisan," *Al HaMishmar*, July 3, 1944.

33. "Ot hitztaynut la'meshorer Sutzkever," *HaMashkif*, September 12, 1945.

34. Novershtern, *Avrom Sutzkever, tsu zayn vern*, 60–61.

35. Marian Zhid, "'Ha'yom ha'yehudi' shel ha'tevi'a ha'sovyetit be'Nuremberg," *HaMashkif*, March 22, 1946.

36. "Ha'meshorer ha'yadu'a Avraham Sutzkever—bein ha'shavim mi'Rusya le'Polin," *HaTzofe*, May 29, 1946; "Dash mi'sofrim ve'itona'im be'Polin," *Al HaMishmar*, June 23, 1946.

37. See correspondence between Max Weinreich and Sutzkever about the unsuccessful attempts to help Sutzkever get a visa to the United States. Weinreich's letters, August 15, 1946, and September 12, 1946. Sutzkever archives, Jewish National Library, ARC* 1565 1 670 1. In a letter to Sutzkever, Zalman Shneur drew a rather gloomy picture of the situation of Yiddish

writers in the United States and of the possibility of earning a living there by writing in Yiddish. Novershtern, *Avrom Sutzkever, tsu zayn vern*, 68.

38. Novershtern, *Avrom Sutzkever, tsu zayn vern*, 69. On the forged passports that Golda Meir sent to Sutzkever and his family so that they could enter Mandatory Palestine, see an interview with Sutzkever by Uri Keisari, "Sharsheret ha'zahav ve'ha'atzvut shel Avraham Sutzkever," *Maariv*, April 3, 1969.

39. Rachel Rojanski, "The Final Chapter in the Struggle for Cultural Autonomy: Palestine, Israel, and Yiddish Writers in the Diaspora, 1946–1951," *Journal of Modern Jewish Studies* 6 no. 2 (2007): 185–204.

40. On this problem, see: Alexander Spiegelblatt, *Durkh farreykherte shayblekh* (Tel Aviv: Leivick farlag, 2007), 244–245.

41. "Erev im ha'meshorer Sutzkever," *HaTzofe*, November 20, 1947.

42. Novershtern, *Avrom Sutzkever, tsu zayn vern*, 29.

43. Novershtern, *Avrom Sutzkever, tsu zayn vern*, 69. Meir was the acting head of the political committee of the Jewish Agency from the time of Moshe Sharett's arrest on Black Shabbat on June 29, 1946, until the declaration of the state of Israel. See Moshe Yeger, *Toldot ha'mahlaka ha'medinit shel ha'sochnut* (Jerusalem: Mossad Bialik, 2010).

44. Abraham Sutzkever, *Vilner geto 1941–1944* (Paris: Farband fun di vilner in Frankraykh, 1946); Abraham Sutzkever, *Fun vilner geto* (Moscow: Melukhe farlag der emes, 1946); Abraham Sutzkever, *Vilner geto 1941–1944* (Buenos Aires: Ikuf farlag, 1947); Abraham Sutzkever, *Geto vilna*, trans. from the Yiddish by Nathan Livne (Tel Aviv: Sechvi, 1947).

45. On the literary center in Warsaw, see Cohen, *Sefer sofer ve'iton*, 39–51. On the literary groups and their journals in New York, see Howe, *World of Our Fathers*, 428–444.

46. "Le'A. Sutzkever be'vo'o artza," *Al HaMishmar*, October 20, 1947.

47. "Kabalat panim be'Haifa la'meshorer Sutzkever," *Al HaMishmar*, October 27, 1947; "Haifa ha'ivrit mekabelet et penei A. Sutzkever," *Davar*, October 28, 1947; "Erev im ha'meshorer Sutzkever," *HaTzofe*, November 20, 1947; "Tel Aviv," *Al HaMishmar*, November 21, 1947; "Tel Aviv," *Davar*, November 24, 1947. Dan Miron tells in an article in *Ha'aretz* that Nathan Alterman suggested to Sutzkever more than once to leave Israel and move to the United States. Dan Miron, "Laila tov nasich matok," *Ha'aretz*, January 29, 2010.

48. "Shamanu she'ha'partizan omed la'asot pe'ula partizanit ve'lehotzi yarhon be'Yidish," "Etzel sofreinu al ha'ovnayim," *Maariv*, March 5, 1948.

49. In Sutzkever's archives there are a few more documents linked to the allocation of funds for the production of the journal, but they do not provide any insights into the process that led to its establishment.

50. Yosef Sprinzak, "Di goldene keyt," *Di goldene keyt* 1 (Winter 1949): 5–6.

51. Ibid., 6.

52. "Fayerung lekoved zekhtsig bend *Di goldene keyt*" [Tsanin's speech], *Di goldene keyt* 62, no. 3 (1968): 335–337.

53. On the opposition to *Di goldene keyt*, see Isaac Rambah, "Mi'yomano shel itonai," *HaMashkif*, December 24, 1948.

54. One of the many books he translated was the ideological work of the historian Shimon Dubnow, *Letters on Old and New Judaism*, published in 1936 in Hebrew as *Michtavim al ha'yahadut ha'yeshana ve'ha'hadasha* (Tel Aviv: Ha'hoker, 1936). The Ha'hoker publishing house belonged to the Histadrut's Davar publishing house. The book presented Dubnow's national autonomistic views, but two chapters opposing Zionism are missing from the Hebrew translation, presumably because they were regarded as not exactly right for the readers in Eretz Israel.

55. On Levinson's role on the editorial board of *Di goldene keyt*, see Pinsky's words at a symposium marking the journal's second anniversary. *Di goldene keyt* 9 (1951): 213. Noah Gris, who worked on the editorial board of the quarterly from its founding and from the third issue was officially the secretary of the board, wrote in his memoirs that when Levinson was appointed coeditor he was already very ill, and although he wanted to be involved in the work of the journal, his poor health prevented him from doing so. Noah Gris, "Dos ershte yor *Di goldene keyt*," *Di goldene keyt* 71 (1970): 167. On Levinson's death, see "Avraham Levinson," *Davar*, July 20, 1955; "Avraham Levinson li'menuhot," *Davar*, July 21, 1955.

56. Niger and Shatzky, *Leksikon*, vol. 7. On Eliezer Pines in Sutzkever's view, see Abraham Sutzkever, "Eliezer Pines 1883–1984," in *Baym leyenen penemer, dertseylungen, dermonungen, eseyen* (Jerusalem: The Hebrew University of Jerusalem, 1993), 228–231.

57. See note 1 ("Riv'on be'Yidish," *Davar*, August 22, 1948).

58. On this, see Steven Cassedy, *Building the Future: Jewish Immigrant Intellectuals and the Making of the Tsukunft* (New York: Holmes and Meier, 1999), 10–11; Kenneth B. Moss, *Jewish Renaissance in the Russian Revolution* (Cambridge, MA: Harvard University Press, 2009), 76–77.

59. Yaakov Fichman, "Tsvishn Hebreish un Yidish," *Di goldene keyt*, 1 (1949): 7–9.

60. Noah Gris, "Dos ershte yor *Di goldene keyt*," *Di goldene keyt*, 71 (1970): 174. He eventually immigrated to Israel in 1970.

61. S. Yizhar, "Der gefangener," *Di goldene keyt* 2 (Spring 1949): 154–171; Moshe Carmael, "Di bafrayung fun mayrev-Galil," *Di goldene keyt* 2 (Spring 1949): 9–29; Ephraim Breude, "Di oysern politik fun Medines-Yisroel," *Di goldene keyt* 2 (Spring 1949): 35–41; Peretz Naftali, "Di arbeter virtshaft un ire oyfgabes in Yisroel," *Di goldene keyt* 2 (Spring 1949): 64–69; Yitzhak Sade, "Vegn Palmach," *Di goldene keyt* 2 (Spring 1949); David Ben-Gurion, "In kamf far a yidishe medine," *Di goldene keyt* 2 (Spring 1949): 5.

62. Noah Gris's name as secretary of the editorial board appears in the journal only from issue 3. His memoirs, which were published twenty years later, should be read carefully because they have chronological inaccuracies, such as the mention of Yigael Yadin as chief of the General Staff of the IDF prior to January 1949, while he in fact was appointed to the position only in November 1949. Noah Gris, "Dos ershte yor *Di goldene keyt*," *Di goldene keyt* 71 (1970): 172.

63. On Leivick's leading status in Yiddish literature at the time, see Noverstern, *Kesem ha'dimdumim*, 214.

64. See the correspondence between Niger and Sutzkever, Sutzkever archives, Jewish National Library, ARC* 4 1565.

65. Sutzkever to Niger, probably September 6, 1948 (the date in the original is unclear), Jewish National Library, ARC* 4 1565, emphasis in the original.

66. Sutzkever to Niger, no full date on the letter, and it is also missing from the Sutzkever archives at the Jewish National Library. The source used here is Novershtern, *Avrom Sutzkever, tsu zayn vern*, 181.

67. "Riv'on be'Yidish," *Davar*, August 22, 1948 (brief item).

68. Moshe Gorady, "Sharsheret ha'zahav ve'sin'at tzyon," *Davar*, June 2, 1949; David Pinsky, "Al michtav me'Amerika," *Davar*, June 24, 1949.

69. Avraham Sharon, "Filoglotizmus," *Davar*, February 16, 1949; Yehoshua Manoah, "Petah hatat," *Davar*, April 1, 1949; Yitzhak Domiel, "Be'havlei ha'ratzon," *Davar*, April 19, 1949; A. Shectman, "Sakanat Bavel," *Davar*, March 3, 1949; D. L. [David Lazar], "Me'et le'et" ("Tora hozeret la'achsanya shela," "Mi'tzyon tetze tora be'Yidish"—two excerpts in the same column), *Maariv*, December 31, 1948.

70. "Hovevei sefat Yidish," *HaMashkif,* August 9, 1948; "Beli lo'azit u'veli Yidish," *HaMashkif,* August 15, 1951; Isaac Rambah, "Miyomano shel itonai," *HaMashkif,* December 24, 1948; Asher Nahor, "Leveinim, lo. Gedud meginei ha'safa—ken!" *HaMashkif,* December 24, 1948; "Davar ve'hipucho," *Herut,* November 20, 1949; David Zakai, "Hutra ha'retzu'a," *HaTzofe,* October 29, 1948.

71. Abba Ahimeir, "Yudaika," *Herut,* September 29, 1950. Some writers reacted derisively to these ideological claims. See D. L. [David Lazar], note 69.

72. D. Ahiyosef, *"Di goldene keyt," Al HaMishmar,* February 4, 1949; Pesach Ben-Amram (Lipovtzki), "Shalshelet ha'zahav," *Davar,* January 12, 1950.

73. See Pesach Ben-Amram (Lipovtzki), "Shalshelet ha'zahav," *Davar,* January 12, 1950; Y. M. Neiman, "Mi'saviv le'shalshelet ha'zahav," *Davar,* March 4, 1949.

74. Y. M. Neiman, "Mi'saviv le'shalshelet ha'zahav," *Davar,* March 4, 1949, emphasis in original.

75. For example, "Ba'sifrut u'va'omanut," *Davar,* January 1, 1954; B. Y. Michali, "Mi'pilei ha'di'alektika ha'sherirutit," *Davar,* May 31, 1957.

76. For example, Abraham Golomb, "Di brokhes un di kloles fun goles," *Di goldene keyt* 14 (1952): 30–41.

77. Another Yiddish periodical with public financing was *Sovetish heymland,* which served the political aims of the communist leadership in the Soviet Union for thirty years from 1961 and also was useful in anti-Zionist indoctrination. On this, see Gennady Estraikh, "Sovetish heymland," *YIVO Encyclopedia of the Jews in Eastern Europe,* http://www.yivoencyclopedia.org/article.aspx/Sovetish_Heymland.

78. Noverstern, *Kesem ha'dimdumim,* 34–36. On the previous versions of the play in Yiddish and in Hebrew and on Peretz's attitude to Hasidism as expressed in the play, see Chone Shmeruk, "Ha'mahaze ha' 'hasidi' shel Y. L. Peretz," in *Ha'keri'a la'navi: Mehkarei historya ve'sifrut* (Jerusalem: Merkaz Shazar, 1999), 343–368. On the play and its implications, see Wisse, *I. L. Peretz,* 62–67.

79. Shmeruk, "Ha'mahaze ha' 'hasidi' shel Y. L. Peretz," 343–368; Wisse, *I .L. Peretz,* 62–67.

80. Avraham Noverstern, "Modernizm yidi be'mizrah Eiropa," in *Zeman yehudi hadash* (Jerusalem: Keter, 2007), 3: 166–167.

81. Cohen, *Sefer sofer ve'iton,* 13–14.

82. On the poem and its connection to the *Di goldene keyt,* see Cammy, "Vision and Redemption."

83. Cammy, "Tsevorfene," 141–142. Alexander Spiegelblatt, the last secretary of the editorial board of the quarterly, who immigrated to Israel in 1964 and joined *Di goldene keyt* in 1971, also related a similar version that he heard from Sutzkever. A collection of his articles, *Durkh farreykherte shayblekh* (Through a glass darkly), published in 2007, also contained a chapter on *Di goldene keyt.* In it, Spiegelblatt settles a score with the people who were connected to the publications of Mapai in the 1970s and describes at length the history of the journal, the tribulations surrounding its establishment, and its aims and achievements. "Sutzkever told me," Spiegelblatt wrote in an article published seventeen years earlier, "that he conceived the idea of publishing a journal in Yiddish called *Di goldene keyt* in 1946, in Warsaw, in the cemetery, when he stood before Peretz's grave and again read the inscription taken from Peretz's drama *Di goldene keyt:* 'Proud and glorious Jews.' This idea was the basis for his revival in the Jewish state." Alexander Spiegelblatt, *"Di goldene keyt* un ir melukhisher maymed," *Yidishe kultur* 52, no. 1 (1990): 39; Spiegelblatt, *Durkh farreykherte shayblekh,* 229.

84. *Di goldene keyt* 1 (1949): 9.

85. *Di goldene keyt* 100 (1979): 3.

86. *Di goldene keyt* 9 (1951): 214–215, emphasis in the original.

87. For example, the section of issue 27 from 1957 that was devoted to the war of 1956 and included Prime Minister Ben-Gurion's speech to the Knesset about the war, alongside a cycle of poems by Sutzkever, "In midber Sinai" [In the Sinai Desert], *Di goldene keyt* 27 (1957): 23–25.

88. For example, S. Niger, "Finf briv fun Moyshe Kulbak," *Di goldene keyt* 13 (1952): 235–240; "Finf briv fun Frishman tsu Sholem Aleichem," *Di goldene keyt* 14 (1952): 222–227; "A briv fun Bialik tsu Dr. Chaim Zhitlovsky," *Di goldene keyt* 17 (1953): 256; and many others.

89. Among the translations from Hebrew were works of such major writers as Nathan Alterman, Asher Barash, Haim Gouri Leah Goldberg, S. Y. Agnon, Avraham Shlonsky, Moshe Shamir, and others. The reviews of Hebrew literature were usually also translated from Hebrew. Reviews on Israeli Hebrew literature that were written originally in Yiddish were very rare in the quarterly.

90. Sutzkever's speech, "Barmitsve fayerungen fun *Di goldene keyt*," *Di goldene keyt* 43 (1962): 245; Eliezer Pines, "A vort tsum yoyvl numer," *Di goldene keyt* 50 (1962): 5.

91. *Di goldene keyt* 50 (1964): 4–5.

92. Eliezer Pines, "Tsvey dates," *Di goldene keyt* 95–96 (1978): n.p.

93. See greetings by the editorial board of *Di goldene keyt* to the Yiddish chair at its induction, *Di goldene keyt* 11 (1952): 202

94. On the attempt to establish a chair in Yiddish at the Hebrew University in the 1920s, see Pilowsky, *Tsvishn yo un neyn*, 91–141. See also Myers, *Re-inventing the Jewish Past*, 76–81.

95. On this, see Rachel Rojanski, "Ben-Gurion and Yiddish after the Holocaust," in *The Politics of Yiddish*, ed. Shlomo Berger (Amsterdam: Menasseh Ben Israel, 2010), 25–40. See also Charles S. Liebman, "Diaspora Influence on Israel: The Ben-Gurion Blaustin 'Exchange' and Its Aftermath," *Jewish Social Studies* 36 (July–October 1974): 274–275.

96. Dr. Dvorjetski settled in France after the war and came to the Congress as a delegate on behalf of the movement Poalei-Zion Hitahdut in France. Conversation with his daughter, Zvia Balshan. March 2017.

97. "Ha'kongres isher reva milyon le'Eretz Israel le'hinuch ha'ivri le'shenat 1946," *HaTzofe*, December 24, 1946. On Marc Dvorjetski, see Mordechai Eliav, "Meir Dvorjetski z"l ha'ish, ha'hoker ve'hamore," in *Iyunim bi'tekufat ha'sho'a* (Ramat Gan: Bar-Ilan University, 1979), 11–18; Conversation with Zvia Balshan, Marc Dvorjetski's daughter. For a survey of the establishment of the chair in Yiddish in 1951, see Noverstern, "Between Town and Gown."

98. "Ha'haktzavot le'hinuch u'le'tarbut," *Davar*, December 24, 1946.

99. *The 22nd Zionist Congress, Basel, December 9–24, 1946*, stenographic transcript, Jerusalem, publication of the directorate of the Zionist Histadrut [no name of printing house]: section 118, p. 604.

100. Minutes of the Executive Committee, March 26, 1947, Central Archive of the Hebrew University, Jerusalem, file 22730, 1948; Letter of V. Y. Noimung, administrative assistant, to members of the interim committee (of the university), April 12, 1948, Central Archive of the Hebrew University, Jerusalem, file 22730, 1948; Reminder re: chair in Yiddish (no date), Central Archive of the Hebrew University, Jerusalem, file 22730, 1950. See also M. Schneursohn (treasurer) to executive vice president, Dr. Senator, December 15, 1950, Central Archive of the Hebrew University, Jerusalem, file 22730, 1950.

101. On the attitude of Labor Zionism in the United States to Yiddish, see Rachel Rojanski, "Bein ideologya li'metzi'ut politit—Yahasam shel Poalei-Zion be'Amerika le'Yidish 1905–1933," *Yahadut zemanenu* 11–12 (1998): 51–71.

102. For an explanation of the establishment of the Farband, its aims and characteristics, see Rojanski, *Zehuyot nifgashot*, 104–116. On the fund-raising campaigns, see "Magbit ha'igudim ha'miktzo'iyim le'ma'an ha'histadrut u'Poalei-Zion be'Amerika," in *Me'hevrat avoda le'irgun ovdim*, ed. Yosef Gorny, Avi Bareli, Yitzhak Greenberg, 529–555 (Sede-Boker: Ben-Gurion University of the Negev Press, 2000); Louis Segal, "Der yidish-natsyonaler arbeter farband fun 1924 biz 1945," in *Yidish-natsyonaler arbeter farband 1910–1945—zamelbukh* (New York: no publisher, 1946), 263–338, 393–422; Pinhas Gingold, "Di role fun Yidish natsyonler arbeter farband in dem yidishn kultur lebn in Amerike," *Yidish-natsyonaler arbeter farband* (New York: no publisher, 1946), 339–385.

103. Memorandum, Teaching Languages of the Diaspora (Yiddish and Ladino), Archives of the Hebrew University.

104. Minutes of Senate meeting, January 14, 1948, Central Archive of the Hebrew University, Jerusalem, file 22730, 1948.

105. For this reason, Professor Gershon Scholem objected to the inclusion of the important literary critic Shmuel Niger on the list of candidates. Letter from Gershon Scholem, April 19, 1949, Central Archive of the Hebrew University, Jerusalem, file 22730, 1949.

106. Meeting of the committee on Yiddish, November 1, 1949, Central Archive of the Hebrew University, Jerusalem, file 22730, 1949. The chairman of the committee, Ben-Zion Dinaburg, also wrote a letter to him to clarify the matter. See Minutes of meeting of humanities faculty, November 16, 1949, Central Archive of the Hebrew University, Jerusalem, file 22730, 1949.

107. Weinreich agreed to come for a limited period as a guest professor, but the search committee preferred to continue its search. Letter of the committee chairman, Professor Ben-Zion Dinaburg to Max Weinreich, August 3, 1950, Central Archive of the Hebrew University, Jerusalem, file 22730, 1950; Committee on Yiddish and Judeo-Spanish, July 27, 1950, Central Archive of the Hebrew University, Jerusalem, file 22730, 1950.

108. Louis Segal to M. Schneurson (treasurer), Hebrew University, July 20, 1950, Central Archive of the Hebrew University, Jerusalem, file 22730. On the recommendation of Sadan, see Committee on Yiddish and Judeo-Spanish, July 28, 1950, Central Archive of the Hebrew University, Jerusalem, file 22730, 1950.

109. On Dov Sadan, see Dan Laor, "Dov Sadan, ha'ma'avak al ha'zikaron ha'yehudi," in *Ha'ma'avak al ha'zikaron, masot al sifrut, hevra ve'tarbut*, 161–169 (Tel Aviv: Am Oved 2008).

110. Letter from Chaim Greenberg to Ben-Zion Dinaburg, October 25, 1950, Central Archive of the Hebrew University, Jerusalem, file 22730, 1950.

111. From Louis Segal, secretary of the Farband, to Schneurson, university treasurer, October 24, 1950, Central Archive of the Hebrew University, Jerusalem, file 22730.

112. Address by Moshe Schwabe, provost, Hebrew University, at the opening ceremony of the chair in Yiddish, *Di goldene keyt* 11 (1952): 189. On the offer of the position to Sadan, see Committee on Yiddish and Ladino, first meeting, November 12, 1948, Central Archive of the Hebrew University, Jerusalem, file 22730, 1948; Chaim Greenberg to Professor Ben-Zion Dinaburg, October 25, 1950, Central Archive of the Hebrew University, Jerusalem, file 22730, 1948; Louis Segal to M. Schneurson, October 24, 1950, Central Archive of the Hebrew University, Jerusalem, file 22730.

113. A description of the event and the complete text of all the speeches were published in *Di goldene keyt* 11 (1952): 187–210.

114. Uri Cohen, *Ha'har ve'ha'giva: ha'universita ha'ivrit bi'tekufat terom ha'atzma'ut ve'reishit ha'medina* (Tel Aviv: Am Oved, 2006), 123–154.

115. Letter from Prime Minister Ben-Gurion to the minister of finance, March 5, 1950, Ben-Gurion archives, file: correspondence, March 1950.

116. T. Dobrin [Ruth Bondi], "Keitzad megalim ketavim," *Devar Ha'shavua*, May 22, 1959.

117. "Anashim u'mosadot," *Davar*, November 9, 1952; "Nitzal ha'osef ha'mada'i shel professor David Kaufman be'Budapest," *Davar*, April 21, 1954; "Nigalu kitvei yad atikim," *Davar*, April 2, 1958.

118. See http://web.nli.org.il/sites/NLI/English/collections/jewish-collection/Pages/manuscripts.aspx.

119. Ben-Gurion archives, file: minutes of meetings, October 1, 1948.

120. Ben-Gurion's diary, February 2, 1950. In his letter to the director general of the Ministry of Defense and to the chief of staff, Ben-Gurion stated that the exemption was given only to yeshiva students who were actively studying and that anyone who stopped his studies would be drafted immediately. David Ben-Gurion to the director general of the Ministry of Defense, January 9, 1951, Ben-Gurion archive, file: correspondence, January 1951.

121. Ben-Gurion to Pinhas Lavon, March 16, 1954, Archives of the Ben-Gurion Heritage Institute, correspondence folder. On this, see also Daphna Barak-Erez, "Giyus bahurei yeshivot: mi'peshara le'mahloket," in *Tzematei hachra'ot u'farshiyot mafteah be'Israel*, ed. Dvora Hacohen and Moshe Lisk (Sede-Boker: Ben-Gurion Research Institute for the Study of Israel and Zionism, 2010), 15. In fact, the Israeli political reality of the time did not call for any concessions to the orthodox. In the 1949 and 1951 elections, Mapai gained forty-six and forty-seven seats in the Knesset, respectively, and despite some problems that arose in forming a coalition, the religious parties had no power in this process, since they were unable to tip the scales. On this, see Yechiam Weitz, "Bein mashak kanfei ha'historya le'vein yemei hulin: harkavat ha'memshala ha'rishona u'mashma'uta," in *Politika be'milhama: kovetz mehkarim al ha'hevra ha'ezrahit be'milhemet ha'atzma'ut*, ed. Mordechai Bar-On and Meir Chazan (Jerusalem: Yad Ben Zvi and the Chaim Weitazman Institute for Zionist Studies, 2014), 127–154.

122. On the state of ultraorthodox society in Israel in the mid-1940s, see Kimi Kaplan, "Mosedot hinuch ba'hevra ha'haredit be'mahatzit ha'shenya shel tekufat ha'mandat ha'briti u'mekomam be'shikuma le'ahar ha'sho'a," *Israel* 21 (Spring 2013): 196–200.

123. Kaplan, "Mosedot hinuch." Also Nathan Glazer, *American Judaism* (Chicago: University of Chicago Press, 1957), 142; Jonathan Sarna, *American Judaism* (New Haven, CT: Yale University Press, 2004), 278.

124. On this, see Zerah Warhaftig, *Huka le'Israel: dat u'medina* (Jerusalem: Mesilot, 1988), 232; Barak-Erez, "Giyus bahurei yeshivot"; Yechiam Weitz, "Hishtamtut ha'haredim," *Ynet*, February 23, 2012, https://www.ynet.co.il/articles/0,7340,L-4193753,00.html.

5

"WE ARE WRITING A NEW CHAPTER IN YIDDISH LITERATURE"

The Literary Group Yung Yisroel and the Zionist Master Narrative

ON THE LAST WEEKEND OF OCTOBER 1951, TEN young Yiddish writers, most of them in their late twenties, convened in Kibbutz Yagur, on the eastern slopes of Mount Carmel. They came to read their writing and discuss it. The gathering was the idea of the poet Abraham Sutzkever, who had already included in the first issue of *Di goldene keyt* poems by two members of the group—Rivka Basman and Moyshe Yungman. The section with these poems was given the title "Lider fun yunge dikhter in Yisroel" (Poems of young [Yiddish] poets in Israel). This was not the only time Sutzkever did this. Shortly before the meeting in Yagur, *Di goldene keyt* published another collection of writing by members of this group, entitling it "Fun der yunger yidisher literatur in Yisroel" (From the young Yiddish literature in Israel).[1] The Yagur meeting lasted two days, during which the name of the group was announced: Yung Yisroel (Young Israel).

A day before the meeting, Zvi Eisenman, a leading figure in the group and a member of Kibbutz Yagur, described the aims of the young Yiddish writers: "We must be an integral part of the fabric of Israeli life.... We have linked our fate with the blossoming fields and the wilderness yet to be redeemed.... We are writing a new chapter in Yiddish literature which is so much in need of an infusion of new blood, of new forces."[2] With these words, Eisenman first stressed the Israeli context of the young Yiddish writers' work, employing key terms from Zionist discourse: "blossoming fields" and "the redemption of the wilderness." He also presented the young writers' work as part of the modern Yiddish literature of the past, now in need of a transfusion of new blood. This he saw as "a new chapter in Yiddish literature."

The members of Yung Yisroel were not the only Yiddish writers to deal with Israel in their writing. There were others who wrote about the Israeli experience and gave it great importance in their work. "The theme of Israel," wrote Shmuel Rollansky, a teacher, scholar of Yiddish, and a leader of Yiddish-speaking society in Argentina, "has given Yiddish literature 'new horizons, new hopes.'"[3]

Yung Yisroel, however, was different. Almost all its members were Holocaust survivors, and all had a very strong commitment to Zionist ideology. More importantly, as young people at the very beginning of their literary careers, their writing developed and grew in Israel. In fact, their literature was an indigenous and original Israeli literature in Yiddish that examined the main tensions in the Israeli life of the time. This made it a new and unique phenomenon in Israeli culture, as well as in post-Holocaust Yiddish literature.

Furthermore, these writers organized themselves into a Yiddish literary group—one of many in the history of Yiddish literature but the only one in the state of Israel. As a group they published a short-lived periodical and a series of books—most of which were eventually translated into Hebrew—as well as trying to make some kind of connection with a contemporary literary group of young Hebrew writers, Likrat. But despite all this, the group as a whole, as well as its individual members, were almost totally ignored by the hegemonic Hebrew-speaking cultural sphere of the day.

It is this Israeli Yiddish literature of the 1950s that will form the focus of this chapter. The Yung Yisroel literary group will be central to the discussion not only because its members dedicated their early literary careers to Israeli and Zionist themes but also because they were fervent supporters of Zionist ideology in their personal lives.[4] The group also engaged in theoretical discussions dealing with the rationale behind and meaning of its writing though it never published an official manifesto nor aspired to reach any consensus on these issues.

A close reading of their writing, both theoretical and literary, shows that the members of Yung Yisroel were really writing about their own lives and that their major aspiration was to create a new chapter in Yiddish literature. However, since all of them wrote about their encounters with life in the nascent state of Israel, we can, in retrospect, identify in their texts a kind of Zionist narrative, quite different from the hegemonic Hebrew-speaking milieu, that they had created from their own experience as Yiddish-speaking immigrants.

The main argument of this chapter will be that Yiddish literature written in Israel and dealing with the Israeli experience actually presented a new Zionist master narrative, different from and even contradictory to the hegemonic one. It used Zionist language, including terms like "the flowering of the desert," "the redemption of the wilderness," and even the "redemption from the exile," but took it in an entirely different direction. Interpreting these terms in ways they had learned in the Zionist youth movements of eastern Europe, the members of the group did not introduce the New Jew cut off from the recent Jewish past but instead made the diasporic experience one of the forces that shaped life in Israel.[5] For them, their past was an integral part of their present. In this way, the Israeli Yiddish writers created a different Zionist narrative, which, though it was ignored at the time, not only contested the hegemonic version but even provided an alternative to it.

These young writers also employed images and ideas from the Yiddish literary tradition in their writing, making it not only a new genre of Israeli literature but a modern development of Yiddish literature, too. As a result, the question they grappled with was not so much how they should respond to a hegemonic Zionist master narrative with which they did not identify but rather, what does it mean to be a Yiddish writer in the Hebrew-speaking Jewish nation-state?

The chapter begins with a discussion of the group's ideological and sociological development and then continues with readings of various texts written by its members in order to understand their place in Israeli culture. The readings are not aesthetic or literary in nature but use the literary texts as sources for cultural history, reflecting states of mind and ways of thinking. The texts used here are typically prose, which is, generally speaking, more detailed and accessible than poetry.

Yiddish Literature and the Zionist Master Narrative

From its very beginnings, modern Yiddish literature addressed itself to the broad readership of the Jewish masses, the *folk*, and reflected the tension between traditional society and modernity.[6] That changed with immigration to the United States. "Yiddish poetry written in the United States," asserted Benjamin Harshav, "was consciously and effectively a cosmopolitan, even primarily an American literature, expressing the emotions and thoughts of the individual in the modern metropolis."[7] Yiddish writers in the United States were not writing for the *folk*, the Jewish masses, but for the elite. They were aware that they were appealing to a limited Yiddish readership, and in the 1940s some poets explicitly referred to that fact in their verse.[8]

Although it would have been the most natural thing for them, most Yiddish writers in Israel also did not write as if they were still part of the great Yiddish literary tradition of the Jewish masses of eastern Europe (though some did choose to do so). The majority of the Yiddish speakers in the world had perished in the Holocaust, and the life of the Jewish people had been transformed in a way that their literary work had to reflect. In addition, the experience of immigrating to the Jewish nation state and integrating into it, "immigrating home," had to be dealt with, too.

The land of Israel and Zionism had been rather marginal topics in Yiddish literature before 1948. Following the Holocaust and the foundation of the state, Yiddish intellectuals throughout the world began to look more closely at Israel, often taking a somewhat romantic attitude, though they also expressed concern about the country's development, particularly given the rumors of the negative attitude to Yiddish there.[9] Post-Holocaust Yiddish literature in general, therefore, and that written in Israel in particular had to find its own voice to express its attitude to Zionism. It would not do so in lockstep with Israeli Hebrew literature.

The Zionist myth as it developed in prestate Israel and was reflected in Hebrew literature and culture, explained the Israeli leading literary scholar Gershon Shaked, held that the land of Israel would redeem the Jews from a degenerate *galut* and that returning to the land of Israel would allow the Jewish people social and spiritual renewal. These ideas shaped the world view of young people in prestate Israel and underlay the Zionist master narrative of the state's early years. The Zionist master narrative spoke of redeeming the Jews from the *galut* and the land from the wilderness and defending the process of settlement from those who were attempting "to put a spoke in the wheels of history," in Shaked's words.[10]

Although Yiddish literature in Israel and especially the writings of *Yung Yisroel* dealt with the major tensions within Israeli society in the 1950s, including immigration, immigrants, settlement, and the redemption of the wilderness, their work was ignored by the Israeli Hebrew critics. The most important publishing houses would not publish even Hebrew translations of their work. This was not the result of a dismissive attitude to Yiddish in Israel. Quite the contrary. In these years, Hebrew translations of Yiddish books were issued by the major publishers affiliated with the hegemonic Labor Party. It was just that these were books of a very specific kind. In the 1950s and early 1960s, Yiddish literature in Israel was seen mainly as Holocaust literature and sometimes also as stories of pre–World War II Jewish life. "Yiddish literature," wrote the celebrated Israeli author Aharon Appelfeld, "is first and foremost memoir-writing that aspires more than anything else to commemorate ... Jewish life before the Holocaust."[11]

As early as 1954, Hakibbutz Hameuchad and Am Oved publishing houses published Hebrew translations of Rachel Auerbach's *Be'hutzot Varsha* (On the streets of Warsaw), which was translated from a manuscript in Yiddish written especially for Hebrew readers, and Yeshayahu Spiegel's *Malchut geto* (*Malkhes geto*, The ghetto kingdom). Both books dealt with the Holocaust and both authors, Auerbach and Spiegel, were Holocaust survivors and new immigrants in Israel.[12] Spiegel together with two other Yiddish writers, Leyb Rochman and Yehiel Hofer, also new immigrants, saw their work highlighted in the Hebrew press.[13] Rochman wrote unique and powerful texts on the Holocaust, while Hofer wrote about Jewish life in Warsaw before the war. Their writing, together with that of Spiegel, which dealt mainly with the Holocaust but also touched on interwar Łódź, was published in Hebrew translation not only by private publishing houses but also by Am Oved and Hakibbutz Hameuchad.[14]

The fact that these two presses, founded around 1940 in order to create a meaningful library for the Hebrew reader, chose to print these books at such an early time indicates that their editors viewed literature based on an authentic experience of the Holocaust as part of the national Zionist bookshelf. Moreover, in 1955 Am Oved launched its prestigious list, "Ha'sifriya la'am," for the purpose of providing high-quality books for a broad readership (*ish ha'am* was the term they used in Hebrew for the general public).[15] It brought out original works as well as translations of books, a few from Yiddish. However, all the translations from Yiddish dealt with Jewish life in the Diaspora. Until the late 1960s these included novels by renowned Yiddish writers, such as Chaim Grade and Isaac Bashevis Singer. In subsequent years, Yehiel Hofer and Yeshayahu Spiegel joined the list. By that time, Spiegel had already integrated the Israeli experience into some of his writing, but Am Oved chose to publish only translations of his Poland-themed work.

Yiddish writers who wrote about life in Israel did not appear on this list at all, the only exception being the novel by Mendl Mann *Bi'kefar natush* (*In a farvorloztn dorf*, In an abandoned village). However, this book that combined the story of the protagonist's life in Israel with his former life in Russia was presented on its back cover as a historical novel about Jewish life in Russia.[16] Most other presses adopted the same policy. Hebrew translations of Yiddish literature that dealt with Israeli reality were normally published only by small private publishers and sometimes even by Yiddish-language presses. Yiddish literature, then, was acceptable to Hebrew publishers when it focused on the Diaspora. Writing reflecting the Zionist narrative about life in Israel was the sole province of Hebrew writers who had been born or at least lived a long time in Israel.

According to Gershon Shaked, more than a decade after the establishment of the state, authors began to rebel and create a counter-Zionist narrative. "The role of [this] literature," he wrote, "was not to accept the master narrative literally. . . . Its entire strength was expressed in the way it coped with it and digressed from it, to the point of . . . detachment from it."[17] One of the prominent examples of this trend for him are the writers who had immigrated from Iraq, such as Sami Michael and Shimon Ballas.[18] However, their objection to the Zionist master narrative derived from the tension between the Ashkenazi and Mizrahi Jews in Israel, and it was expressed in Hebrew-language works written more than a decades after the establishment of the state. This came too late for the members of Yung Yisroel—who were anyway Ashkenazi Jews and did not write in Hebrew. Much of their work had been published ten or more years earlier, long before the new counternarrative emerged.

A Distinguished Poet Seeks Young Buds: Founding the Group

In the twentieth century, quite a few literary groups were founded by both Hebrew and Yiddish writers.[19] Most were set up by young people just embarking on their literary careers and were centered on one or two leading figures, as well as on a shared literary vision. In many cases, the group members challenged the writing of the previous generation and presented themselves as revolutionaries. Yung Yisroel was not a group of that sort; its aims and path of development were quite unique.

The person who started the group was, as we have already seen, Abraham Sutzkever, who was not a member. In 1982, thirty years after the event, the group member Moyshe Yungman wrote: "This is not an ordinary event, when an eminent poet, himself a survivor of the inferno, seeks, as soon as he arrives [to Israel], young buds, a natural continuation. . . . If Yung Yisroel was organized at the time . . . it is thanks to Abraham Sutzkever."[20]

Sutzkever seems to have understood that to realize his vision of founding an active literary scene in Yiddish in Israel, a fertile environment for the enthusiastic activity of young writers was required. Apparently, he saw Yung Yisroel as the vehicle for this. He envisaged it as a workshop for its members' writing and a place where they could get feedback from people their own age. He wanted to encourage them to dedicate themselves to Yiddish writing and perhaps also to establish additional forums to publicize work in Yiddish. However, this meant that the group did not form spontaneously at the wish of its members, did not produce its own leader or major figure, and did not set a clear poetic agenda.

The group's first meeting took place on the weekend of October 26–27, 1951, at Kibbutz Yagur, a location probably chosen with Zvi Eisenman's help. In the invitation sent by the organizers, the conference was described as the founding meeting of a group of young Yiddish writers in Israel. The weekend program included a public event on the Friday night, at which the young authors would read from their work, and closed sessions on the Saturday.[21]

The name Yung Yisroel immediately suggests some kind of connection with the well-known literary group Yung Vilne, which had been active in pre-war Vilna and with which Sutzkever had been associated. Some of those who attended the inaugural meeting of Yung Yisroel even reported that Sutzkever himself proposed the name then, drawing an explicit connection with Yung Vilne.[22]

Despite this, it seems that this name had already been decided on in advance; it was certainly mentioned at least twice in the newsletter of Kibbutz Yagur, *Yoman Yagur*, in the weeks before the group's first meeting.[23] And as to any literary or ideological connection to the famous literary group from Vilna, articles were published in subsequent years explaining that no such thing was intended.[24] This was made fully explicit in Moyshe Yungman's 1982 article, in which he wrote: "Most of the group's members accepted the fact that the name *Yung Yisroel* referred to the national biological aspect of the group, a kind of continuation of the old Israel."[25]

This makes sense when we remember that the members of the group wanted, with Sutzkever's help, to create a new framework for integrating Yiddish literature into Israeli life. They had no reason to refer back to literary groups of the past and their ideologies.

Ten members of the group attended that first meeting:[26] the poets Moyshe Yungman, H. Benyomin (Hrushovski-Harshav), Moyshe Gurin, and Abraham Rintzler, and the prose writers Shlomo Vorzoger, Yossel Birstein (who had begun his career as a poet), Zvi Eisenman, Abraham Karpinovitsh, Peysakh Binetzky, and Mendl Mann. They were nearly all in their twenties, and with the exception of Birstein, who came from Australia, they were all Holocaust survivors.[27] Two of them (Eisenman and Birstein) were members of kibbutzim in northern Israel, and three others (Yungman, Gurin, and Rintzler) also lived in the north. The poet Rivka Basman, also a Holocaust survivor, a member of Kibbutz Ha'ma'apil and a leading member of the group, missed the meeting due to illness.[28] Rokhl Fishman, another poet who later became an important member of the group, joined it in 1954, when she came to Israel from Philadelphia and settled in Kibbutz Bet Alpha.

In keeping with the program, a literary evening was held on the Friday night that attracted a very large audience from among the kibbutz members. A representative of the kibbutz's cultural committee delivered greetings, and then Sutzkever made the keynote speech. He analyzed several of the writers' works and praised them lavishly. The elderly David Pinsky, who had come to Israel two years earlier, also added his voice to the congratulations. Then the writers took to the stage and read from their work.[29] The following day, Saturday, the writers held a closed session for literary discussions and decided to establish a journal to be called, like the group itself, *Yung Yisroel*. The group did not formulate a program or manifesto. Certainly, Sutzkever was opposed to adopting a platform, arguing that a multiplicity of approaches would actually benefit the group.[30]

It is hard to ignore the dominant role played by Sutzkever in the group's founding meeting. He also bestowed his patronage on the group and acted as mentor for its members. Still, he took care not to overshadow them, enabling them to give three lectures of a programmatic nature at their first meeting. The poet Abraham Rintzler spoke about "the political-cultural mission of contemporary authors" ("di kultur politishe oyfgabe fun hayntike shrayber"); Moyshe Yungman spoke about "Jewish authors and Yiddish authors in Israel" ("Yidishe shrayber un Yidish shrayber in Yisroel"); and Yossel Birstein delivered a lecture entitled "A yidisher shrayber in kibuts" (A Jewish/Yiddish author in a kibbutz).[31] This last was printed verbatim in *Di goldene keyt* a few months later,[32] while the main ideas of the other two were given expression in essays published in *Yung Yisroel*, the group's journal.[33]

The members of the group had a great deal in common. They had similar backgrounds and all aspired to write Yiddish literature in the state of Israel, whose official policy favored Hebrew culture and so relegated them to the sidelines. Still, a number of other questions remain: First and foremost, what made them a group? Then, what was their literary agenda, and why were they important?[34]

"If We Do Not Hold Firmly to Life Here, the God of Yiddish Will Not Appear before Us": Some Theoretical Views

Though the group never put together a formal manifesto, some of its members published theoretical pieces that grappled with the most basic questions about writing in Yiddish in Israel: what kind of Yiddish literature should be written there, what should it deal with, and how should it relate to the broader Yiddish literary heritage. These were all individual texts, none of which dealt with poetic or aesthetic issues, focusing instead on the abstract questions. Nonetheless, taken together, they do form a kind of collective literary credo that expressed their attitude, in general terms at least, toward the Zionist narrative.

The first to put in writing his thoughts on Yiddish literature in Israel—albeit briefly—was Zvi Eisenman. They appeared in print in *Yoman Yagur* in connection to the group's conferences.[35]

On the eve of the first meeting, Eisenman wrote that it was the duty of Yiddish writers to become part of Israeli life, to go "into its innards" and "not to stand to one side." He talked of a commitment to write about "flowering

Figure 5.1. The first meeting of Yung Yisroel. *Standing from right to left*: Shlomo Vorzoger, Abraham Karpinovitsh, Abraham Sutzkever, Yitzhak Paner, Peysakh Binetzky, Mendl Mann, Abraham Rintzler. *Sitting right to left*: Moyshe Gurin, Benjamin Hrushovski (Harshav), Moyshe Yungman, Yossel Birstein, Zvi Eisenman. *Source:* Gnazim Institute.

fields" and "a wilderness not yet redeemed," "these mountains" and "this soil."[36] A year later he emphasized again his desire to become part of the "true land of Israel."[37] As we have seen, these were all key terms from the Zionist lexicon as used by the Zionist youth movements in interwar Poland. Eisenman, who would later win approval for his writing, preferred not to discuss the aesthetic aspects of the group's writing.[38] As for "perfection from the artistic standpoint—that is still a long way to go," wrote Eisenman before the second meeting of the group in 1952. He added that, in his view, what bound the group together was the common struggle to cope with life in Israel.[39]

Eisenman's close friend, Moyshe Yungman, a poet and teacher who lived in the town of Tiv'on, southeast of Haifa, took a broader, more nuanced view.[40] Like Eisenman, he addressed the link between Israeli Yiddish literature and the experience of life in Israel. But unlike him, he did not use terms taken from Zionist discourse. In an essay based on his lecture at the first conference of Yung Yisroel, Yungman asked whether literary work written in the young state had to be national in character and whether Jewish art in Israel had to be linked to the environment and life of the country. His answer was in the affirmative.[41] On the other hand, he explicitly described settling in Israel as a reaction to the Holocaust and used key terms from the world of Yiddish literature, referencing the three Yiddish classical authors (Mendele Moykher Sforim, Sholem Aleichem, and Y. L. Peretz), as well as famous characters from their work.[42]

Yossel Birstein was ostensibly different from the other members of the group. He was a little older, had already published a book of poetry before moving to Israel, and was the only one of them who was not a Holocaust survivor. (Rokhl Fishman, from the United States, joined later.) Despite this, he actually had a great deal in common with the others. Like them, he was originally from eastern Europe, born and raised in the Polish shtetl of Biale Podolsk, and there—as he said at that first conference and described later in his stories—his identity as an east European Jew and his feelings for Yiddish were shaped. In 1937, when he was seventeen, he left eastern Europe and emigrated to Australia. All the other members of his family, who remained behind, were killed in the Holocaust. He moved to Israel in 1950.[43]

These experiences—especially his double immigration—gave Birstein a much wider perspective on the place of Yiddish in the society where he lived. He seemingly focused on the fundamental question of whether it was even possible to write in Yiddish in the state of Israel, but what he said led to another question—how should Yiddish writers portray life in Israel? The title of his lecture, and the essay he wrote following it, was "A Yiddish author in a kibbutz," though Birstein was not referring to an actual kibbutz but using the term as a metonym for Israeli society.

Although he believed the time was not yet right to talk about either the content or the art of Yiddish literature in Israel, he did believe it important to discuss what it meant to choose to write Yiddish in an environment that was Jewish but not Yiddish-speaking in character. He argued that Yiddish should be used not because of what it had been in the past but as part of contemporary life. If we, young Yiddish writers—Birstein said—"create only for Jews in other countries, and do not hold firmly to [our] life [here] because it is not in Yiddish—then the God of Yiddish, the Jewish God, will not reveal Himself to us.... I know," he wrote, "that here in today's State of Israel they want to sever the connection with the Diaspora past ... but how can a Yiddish writer accept that[?] ... [How can he] not feel that the most important thing for him is to put an end to the forgetting of the past?"[44] In other words, Birstein also saw Yiddish literature in Israel as planted in the present but drawing on the past, and he understood the connection between the two as indivisible.

Not all the speakers at the first conference felt that the connection between life in Israel and Yiddish writing was the bedrock of their work as Yiddish writers. The poet Abraham Rintzler expressed an entirely different view, which was also published in a two-part essay in the second volume of *Yung Yisroel* under the heading "Randn" (Margins). In the first part, entitled "Vortshaft" (Wordiness), he argued resolutely that Yiddish literature does not need to take into account the situation of Yiddish as a spoken language, and nothing in the politics of culture should be allowed to influence its development. The center of gravity of Yiddish literature is the literature itself, he stated.[45] Rintzler was an original and highly regarded poet, but he was a controversial figure even among the members of Yung Yisroel. His entire corpus of poetry consisted of a little more than fifty poems, which were never collected into a single volume, and toward the end of the 1950s, he stopped writing. His views did not reflect those of the other members in the group at the time, and in fact the disagreements he caused finally led to his resignation as the editor of the group's journal and then his leaving the group as a whole.[46]

After the 1951 meeting, the group never discussed again the issues involved in being Yiddish writers in Israel, even though they held two more meetings at Yagur, in 1952 and 1956. These included just literary readings and friendly conversation without any theoretical discussion.[47]

After the second conference, the members of the group toyed with the idea of publishing an anthology of contemporary Hebrew poetry in Yiddish translation, to bridge the gap between Hebrew literature and Israeli literature in Yiddish. They also tried to establish contact with the young, innovative Hebrew poets, members of the Likrat literary group, among whose founders was a former member of Yung Yisroel, H. Benyomin (Benjamin Harshav), but the meeting between the two groups did not go well.[48]

The publication of their journal was also delayed, and the first issue of *Yung Yisroel: Literatur, kunst, kritik* (Literature, art, criticism) came out only in December 1954. It was a relatively slender volume, containing some poetry, prose, and one essay, based on Yungman's lecture at the first conference at Yagur. The editors chose to emphasize the nonperiodical character of the publication, and the back cover of the first issue bore the words in Hebrew: "one-off publication." Two additional numbers came out in 1956 and 1957, in the same form, and in the last, the random nature of the publication was emphasized still further with a new subheading: *Zamlung far literatur un kritik* (A collection of literature and criticism).[49]

No further issues of *Yung Yisroel* were published. This was not for financial reasons. On the contrary, the group had many supporters and donors, who also financed the printing of books by members of Yung Yisroel that were published

Figure 5.2. The third meeting of Yung Yisroel in Yagur. *From right to left*: Abraham Rintzler, Rokhl Fishman, Abraham Karpinovitsh, Yossel Birstein, Abraham Sutzkever, Rivka Basman, Moyshe Gurin, Moyshe Yungman, Zvi Eisenman. Source: Gnazim Institute.

as the Yung Yisroel book series.[50] Even Rintzler's resignation as editor does not seem to have been the main reason for its closing. That seems to have had more to do with the rather loose nature of the group itself. Most of its members went their own way, often preferring to publish in *Di goldene keyt*, where they could gain the prestige of appearing in an internationally acclaimed Yiddish periodical, as well as winning Sutzkever's support. "Sutzkever's emphasis was always on quality," Rivka Basman told me.[51] For a young Yiddish writer at the start of his or her career, nothing could have been more important than passing the most stringent poetic test of the time.

After the group's meeting in Yagur in 1956, it disbanded. The members remained in contact with each other, and some even formed close ties that lasted for the rest of their lives. However, much more than their official organization, it was the literary common denominator of these authors—their own special brand of Zionist narrative—that made them (particularly the prose writers among them) into a recognizable group within Israeli literature.

"The Israeli Motifs Are Imbued with the Spirit of Poland": The Zionist Narrative in the Work of Yung Yisroel

A number of Yiddish writers and scholars have attempted to define the ways in which the members of Yung Yisroel wrote about Israel, calling them *Erets*

Yisroel tematik or *Erets Yisroel motivn*.⁵² In the early 1970s Shmuel Rollansky wrote that the writings of Yung Yisroel gave expression to the "essence of Vilne, transported to the land of the kibbutz, the orchard and the moshav."⁵³ A short time later, David Roskies, in the first scholarly work written about the group, described their writing as a synthesis of the traditions and conventions of Yiddish literature and an Israeli thematic.⁵⁴ However, though this kind of writing was typical for the members of Yung Yisroel, what made them unique was the Zionist narrative that they presented.

In the new reading I propose here, the heart of their alternative vision is to be found in the way in which they understood the concept of redemption differently from the hegemonic Zionist narrative. The Israeli Hebrew writers of the "1948 generation" (also known as *Dor ba'aretz*, "the generation of the land") used the term in the sense of redeeming the wilderness and redeeming the Jews from the unproductive life of the *galut* (exile). The very act of settling in Israel, leaving the exile behind and starting a new life in Israel, was redemption itself.⁵⁵ The members of Yung Yisroel, however, had a different understanding. For them, redemption from the *galut* was not achieved merely by settling in Israel. The Israeli experience led to the healing of wounded souls, comfort, and closure. The memory of the *galut* was not to be abandoned but reworked and integrated into the present. This was the true redemption.

This can be seen perhaps most clearly in the work of Zvi Eisenman, a central member of the group.⁵⁶ He published his first book, *Di ban: dertseylungen fun Poyln, Rusland, Yisroel* (The railroad: stories from Poland, Russia, and Israel), a collection of twenty-six short stories, in 1956, as part of the Yung Yisroel book series. It won him the Zvi Kesel (Mexico) prize that year.⁵⁷ The stories were described by the Yiddish writer Melech Ravitch in his introduction to Eisenman's book as "still life paintings in words."⁵⁸ All the major themes of Eisenman's work are found there, with the book reflecting the course of his life and divided into sections: Poland, Russia, and Israel. Eight of the stories are set in Israel.

Most of the Israel stories in the collection bear out Ravitch's characterization. They are like moments frozen in time, with no events, no plot. All that they have are the protagonist's thoughts. Nonetheless, they all describe an encounter between the Israeli present, firmly grounded in the life of the new immigrants, and the east European past they carried with them. However, for Eisenman, the past determined the direction of the present and sometimes even overtook it.

A good example of this is the story "Er iz gekumen" (He has arrived). In a brief, frozen moment, through a half-open door, the nameless female protagonist notices a man asking to rent a room in the house where she lives. She instantly recognizes him as the man she loved in her youth: "It is him! Her knees began to shake.... He stood before the landlady and in a soft voice inquired about the small room he wanted to rent." He had been in her thoughts throughout all the years of separation, but she had never expected to see him like that, a broken and exhausted man.[59] Their gazes do not cross, and they do not actually meet one another. The entire story takes place in the protagonist's mind. Her life passes before her eyes: the parting at the train station when she left to pursue her medical studies, her Zionist father who pressured her to go to Israel, and her lonely life there—all this in the moment of her hesitation over whether to speak to the man. Then, finally, through a crack in the door, she notices the number tattooed on his right arm. "Now she understands everything.... She has only one request, that he disappear as suddenly as he appeared.... From the stairwell, she heard the sound of his steps fading away."[60]

The story is written in very sparse language and gives no details. Nonetheless, it contains a great deal of information. The reader understands that it is about an encounter between a woman who immigrated to Israel, leaving her past life behind, and a Holocaust survivor, a new immigrant. The encounter is supposed to be the point at which new life begins in the new home, the land of Israel. But it is not enough for a new beginning. The memory of the *galut* and of the Holocaust are fundamental elements in the protagonist's life, and it is they that determine her future.

Another story, "A zeung" (A date), is similar in character. Its protagonists are a man and woman, both nameless. From snippets of information in the text, the reader learns that they had had families in the past, and now they are meeting on a "date" (quotations marks in the original) from their desire to "build a new, complete home out of the two that had been destroyed."[61] The failure of their date is played down in the story simply as a misunderstanding. But here, too, it is clear that for a new beginning to take place, a complex effort involving coming to terms with the past is required.

This becomes even clearer in another of Eisenman's stories, "Arum besmedresh" (Around the study house), first published in *Di goldene keyt* in 1952.[62] The story takes place on a kibbutz at the foot of Mount Carmel. Hersh-Ber is a widower who lives in an old-people's home on the kibbutz where his daughter is a member. Against a typical backdrop of tall cypress trees and a view of Mount Carmel, loneliness and the yearning for the now-destroyed shtetl play a dominant role. The only good moments in the hero's life are when he eavesdrops on his neighbors' conversations: "They talked about people who died a long time ago, about things that nobody remembered, but in those conversations they were still alive. Hersh-Ber snuggled himself up in their conversations, snapping up all the leftovers."[63]

Hersh-Ber often visits the study house (*besmedresh*), set up in the kibbutz for the old people who live there, and it becomes a site of memory for him. "The air in the *besmedresh* gave off a fragrance of *amol iz geven* [once upon a time]. . . . Hersh-Ber also had his own '*amol*' [once], which he clings to as if it were a precious jewel. . . . Without it he cannot set one foot in his small, emptied world." He looks out of the window of the study house and sees a flowering almond tree—so typical of the Israeli landscape. The whiteness of the branches and the flowering almond blossoms are transformed in his mind into broad, snow-covered dirt roads, all of them leading to one place—the shtetl.[64]

Certainly, the choice of a protagonist who is an old man at the end of his life intensifies the presence of the past, but Eisenman also uses the landscape of Israel to strengthen it further. The tree viewed from his window is the almond tree, blossoming in all its Israeli glory, but in the eyes of the protagonist, it turns into a *mandl boym*, the almond tree that symbolized the yearning of eastern European Jewry for the land of Israel. The transformation of the white blossom into snow completes the take-over of the present by the past.

The snow-covered ground also makes an appearance in Eisenman's story, "A mayse vegn Nisim fun Har-Tuv, vegn a varshever hoyf un vegn a shpil foygl" (A tale about Nissim from Har-Tuv, a Warsaw backyard, and a songbird), which was first published in the second issue of *Yung Yisroel*.[65] The whole story is a fantasy, a combination of a Warsaw backyard, Nissim (an exotic young Yemenite Jew from the Har-Tuv transit camp [*ma'abara*]), and a songbird with colorful feathers, an allusion to the golden peacock (*di goldene pave*) that is the metaphor for Yiddish poetry. Here too the past overshadows the present, covering it completely.

All of Eisenman's stories mentioned here depict an encounter between the east European past and the Israeli present, and in all of them, in the final analysis, the present cannot exist on its own. If it does not contain the past, then the past defeats it. This message stands in total contradiction to the Zionist master narrative, which held that redemption could only be achieved by severing all ties with the *galut*, the Jews' diasporic past.

In 1960, Hakibbutz Hameuchad published a Hebrew version of *Di ban* under the title *Ha'mesila*.[66] The Hebrew translation included about half of the stories from the "Poland" section and a few stories from the "Russia" section. The number of stories in the "Israel" section was almost the same as that in the Yiddish original, but "Er iz gekumen" was replaced by another story, "A hoyf in Yafo" (A backyard in Jaffe), which had appeared for the first time in the third issue of *Yung Yisroel*.[67] This story, like the others described here, has no plot and revolves mainly around neighborly relations between immigrants from various diasporas in the yard of an abandoned Arab house in Jaffa, where they all live. The story reaches its climax in a dinner shared by all the residents of the yard, during which they talk about simple day-to-day matters. This dinner is the embodiment of the Zionist idea of *kibutz galuyot* (ingathering of the exiles). In this story, the past is mentioned only in passing and does not interfere with the Israeli present. No wonder, then, that the Kibbutz Hameuchad Hebrew publishing house preferred this story to "Er iz gekumen," which was entirely caught up in the web of the *galut* and the Jewish past, especially the Holocaust.

A year after the publication of *Di ban*, David Cananni, senior editor at Sifriat Poalim, another major publishing house of the time, wrote to Eisenman: "[Your stories] flit between prose and poetry, and the latter wins out. . . . You know only the quiet sadness, the desperation that has reached reconciliation and the disappointment that does not rebel. The Israeli motifs are imbued with the spirit of Poland."[68] The Israeli literary scholar Hillel Barzel wrote similarly about *Ha'mesila*: "His [Eisenman's] main strength is revealed in the description of the past. Even when his stories are planted firmly in Israeli reality he draws his motifs from the world that has vanished."[69]

Abraham Karpinovitsh was among the oldest members in the group, one of the eight whose work was published in the seventh issue of *Di goldene keyt*.[70] Like Eisenman, Karpinovitsh published work in all three issues of *Yung Yisroel*. His first collection of stories, *Der veg keyn Sdom* (The road to Sodom) was published by the Y. L. Peretz publishing house in 1959 as part of the Yung Yisroel book series. The stories were mainly concerned with the experience of migrating to Israel, but the viewpoints they presented were quite different from those of Eisenman. While in Eisenman's work the traumatic past was dominant, Karpinovitsh's stories had a much more optimistic tone. Two of them won prizes, the first for Yiddish writing and the other for Hebrew writing, and they share a common theme in their relation to the Zionist narrative.

Karpinovitsh's story "Di mame vet nokh spondzshe makhen" (Mom will still be washing floors)[71] won the prize given by *Letste nayes* in 1954 for the best story written in Yiddish about Israel.[72] This is a remarkable text, told from a child's viewpoint. The protagonist is a boy called Shloymele, who is forced one day to give up on a day trip with his class so that he can go to Tel Aviv and let the lady who employs his mother as a cleaning lady know that his mother will be missing work because she is sick. If he doesn't, the "lady" will hire another woman, and his mother will lose the job and the income that she desperately needs. The reader learns that Shloymele is not yet ten years old and lives in poverty; his father has recently passed away; and his mother, a Yiddish-speaking new immigrant, has to earn her livelihood by cleaning houses in Tel Aviv. The boy narrator also helps out by selling popsicles at the movie theater.

Like Eisenman, Karpinovitsh is telling of an encounter between the immigrant and the new country. However, because the narrator is a child, the presence of the past is diminished, and the reader's attention is directed at the future. The boy's great ambition is to play the piano—an impossible dream due to his family's poverty. When he tries to practice on the piano at the movie theater, the other employees turn hostile and injure his hands. Nonetheless, Shloymele does not lose hope. "Mom will get well," he says at the end of the story. "She'll wash floors again. . . . She'll earn some money. She'll buy me a piano. And I'll play; for sure I'll play."[73]

Of course, this story raises an immediate association with the archetypal orphan in Yiddish literature—Motl the Cantor's Son, from Sholem Aleichem's famous story. But these two literary characters differ greatly. Motl is a classic immigrant. He continues to speak Yiddish, his knowledge of English is little more than basic, and life in the United States seems utterly foreign to him; he remains an outside observer.[74] Karpinovitsh's Shloymele is completely different. His knowledge of Yiddish is only passive. "When Mama feels ill," he says at the beginning of the story, "she speaks Yiddish, but I can understand."[75]

Not only is Hebrew his first language; Israeli life and its natural surroundings provide him his world of images. When he describes a well-groomed woman, he says her fingernails are as red as a *kalanit* (anemone), the common Zionist praxis of using a Hebrew term and an image from the nature of the land of Israel.[76] At the same time, Shloymele's aspiration to play the piano is drawn straight from the cultural conventions of east European Jewry. It is perhaps not surprising, then, that a story based on a Zionist message of overcoming hardships and integrating into Israeli society while preserving the cultural values of east European Jewry earned its author a prize from *Letste nayes*.

Karpinovitsh had won his Hebrew-language prize a couple of years earlier in a competition for stories by new immigrants held by the Am Oved publishing house in 1952. About eighty manuscripts in various languages were submitted, the best twenty-seven of which were translated into Hebrew and published in a book, called *Shevatim* (Tribes), which came out in 1953.[77] One of the winning stories was "Ganavim" (*Ganovim*, Thieves), by Karpinovitsh, which had been translated from Yiddish.[78]

Its protagonist is Haim, a new immigrant from Eastern Europe, who lives with his wife and baby daughter in an abandoned Arab house in Jaffe. The house is dilapidated, damp, and full of leaks, but Haim is too poor to fix it up. This heightens the tension between him and his wife, which is already high due to their very different backgrounds, and Haim is afraid the family will fall apart. The reader learns that Haim had met his wife during the war when, as a partisan in the forest, he had saved her life. Although she came from a respectable family and was well educated, while he was a thief, a man of the underworld, she fell in love with him and they married. Now they live in Israel, and Haim makes an honest living as a longshoreman at the port. Buddies from his past try to tempt him back into crime so he can make a quick fortune and buy a nice home for his family. He almost gives in and joins them, but just before he does, he thinks about his new life and his new family, his entire world. He turns his back on his friends from the past and goes back to his family and his job at the port.[79]

It is little wonder that this story was among those chosen to be included in the collection, which was put out by Am Oved, a publishing house affiliated to the ruling Mapai party. In fact, all the stories in *Shevatim* were consistent with the hegemonic Zionist narrative and contained the motifs of immigration and absorption, settlement in the country and cultivation of the land.

In Karpinovitsh's tale, life in Israel offers the hero dual redemption. First, he is saved from the suffering and persecution of the *galut* and not only makes a family for himself but fathers a new generation of young Israeli-born children. Beyond that, he also escapes the criminal underworld, which has a constant presence in modern Yiddish literature and is described as an integral part of Eastern European Jewish life.[80] The plot thus gives the hero redemption not only from the *galut* but also from its darker, degenerate side—and allows him to achieve it through his productive labor at the port, a clear metaphor for rebuilding the country and realizing the Zionist dream. So, while Karpinovitsh's previous story discussed above conveys a Zionist narrative close to the hegemonic one, the narrative of "Ganovim" conforms almost perfectly to it.

For this very reason, another of his stories, "Farges nisht" (Do not forget), is of great interest. It was first published in 1951 as part of the special section for young Yiddish writers in the seventh issue of *Di goldene keyt* and is also the opening story of Karpinovitsh's collection *Der veg keyn Sdom* (The road to Sodom).[81]

It describes an encounter between an Israeli soldier and a captive he has taken during the War of 1948. The soldier, a new immigrant and Holocaust survivor, had arrived in Israel only a few days beforehand. While participating in a battle, he gets cut off from his unit and then finds himself alone facing an enemy soldier. He manages to capture him and, proud of himself, takes pleasure in the thought that when he gets back to his unit with the prisoner, his comrades, all native-born Israelis, will accept him as one of their own. Suddenly, however, the prisoner tries to escape, and so the soldier trains his gun on him. Until that moment, the prisoner has been silent, and the soldier thinks that he has captured a senior officer from one of the Arab armies. But then the prisoner says a few words in German, the sound of which transports the soldier back to his past. He remembers the Nazi soldier who murdered his mother as he watched and her last words to him: "*Farges nisht!*" ("Do not forget!"). These terrible memories—described in great detail in the story—overwhelm him, and he kills the prisoner without mercy. But his revenge gives him no sense of satisfaction; the sight of the blood and the flesh on the ground only disgusts him. Then it begins to rain; the blood is washed from the rocks, and the soldier is calmed: "The dark skies embraced him warmly like a mother's kerchief. He looked around. The rocks, with their wizened, twisted walls, greeted him like friends. Consoled and encouraged by each stone of his homeland, he came down from the mountain with confident steps."[82]

Though the story seems to depict the killing of a prisoner of war in a positive light, its message is quite different. It opens with many elements from the hegemonic Zionist narrative. It is set "among biblical mountains," and the soldier, the protagonist, is described as a hero who has escaped a detention camp in Cyprus, come to Israel as an illegal immigrant, and joined the forces fighting the enemy. (The mountainous landscape may also suggest battles in the Jerusalem hills, perhaps even the battle at Latrun in which many new immigrants participated.)[83] His greatest wish is to be accepted by his comrades, native Israelis, as one of them. He hopes that his success in capturing the prisoner will do that for him and that he will no longer be a stranger or outsider. This is quite surprising, taking into account that a translation of the 1948 story "Ha'shavui" (The captive), by S. Yizhar, which addresses these issues in wartime and is considered one of the formative texts of Israeli literature, was published in the second issue of *Di goldene keyt* and was known to Yiddish readers.[84]

However, when the plot of Karpinovitsh's story shifts dramatically, once the prisoner starts to speak in German and the hero becomes convinced that he is not a Palestinian Arab but a German soldier who has joined the Palestinians to fight the Jews, it is only then that he shoots him (though whether or not the prisoner was actually a German soldier is never made clear).[85] This plot device makes the story not just about the 1948 war but about immigrants coping with the open wounds of the Holocaust by exacting revenge, real or imagined. That, of course, is the significance of the title, "Farges nisht" (Do not forget). In terms of the underlying narrative, the protagonist achieves redemption and the possibility to be part of the new homeland not by his heroism in capturing an Arab soldier and becoming part of the native Israeli society but by working through his post-Holocaust trauma within the Israeli reality.

The fact that this story was published in *Di goldene keyt* shows how much the Yiddish writers of the day, especially Sutzkever, valued it. Karpinovitsh himself also thought it his most important story and so chose it to open *Der veg keyn Sdom*. This suggests that the narrative of redemption in the Jewish state not through integration alone but through the experience of life there—experience that helped them cope with the wounds of the Holocaust—was the Zionist narrative they preferred, not least because it represented their own lives.

Two other writers from Yung Yisroel whose work carries a similar message are Mendl Mann and Yossel Birstein. Mann gained much esteem at an early stage of his literary career.[86] He immigrated to Israel in 1948, and within five years a collection of his Yiddish stories, *Oyfgevakhte erd* (Awakened Earth), had appeared as part of a small book series published by the editorial management of *Di goldene keyt* and financed by the Yiddish PEN Club in New York. That same year (1953), Am Oved published a Hebrew version of the collection as part of a special reworked and vocalized book series for new immigrants.[87] A few months later Hakibbutz Hameuchad published a Hebrew translation of his as yet unpublished novel *In a farvorloztn dorf* (In an abandoned village) entitled *Bi'kefar natush*.[88] The Yiddish original only came out a little later in Buenos Aires.[89] In 1956, a second Hebrew edition of *Bi'kefar natush* came out, this time with the Am Oved imprint.

Clearly Mann was very well regarded by editors, publishers, and literary critics in Israel. However, the relatively large number of Hebrew translations of his work put out by the major publishing houses also suggests that his writing was perceived as conforming to the accepted Zionist narrative.

In a farvorloztn dorf is, on the surface at least, about the life of new immigrants in Israel. The novel relates events in the life of Moyne, a new immigrant from Eastern Europe who has settled, together with other new immigrants, in an abandoned Arab village called Givat Ha'misgad (Hill of the Mosque). There, he tries to strike roots, build a home, and set up a family. He also works in agriculture, a typical occupation for the New Jew. However, despite this image of a Zionist idyll, the story that the novel has to tell is much more complex. It deals with the refugee experience, immigration, the nature of the Jewish family, and intergenerational tension, particularly that between the protagonist's life in Russia in the past and his Israeli present. The chapters alternate between the two, with the transitions between the times and the places creating the dramatic tension.

A scene of special importance here involves an encounter between the immigrants living in the village and an old Arab, presumably a refugee, who had lived there before and suddenly appears in the center of the village. The new residents of the village—refugees themselves—surround the Arab and discuss why he has come. One of them, a woman, recalls a day when she had been standing in a market in Poland and an angry mob had tried to attack her because she was Jewish. Another, this time a man, wonders if the house he lives in might have belonged to the stranger. A third, also a man, scornfully suggests they drive the Arab away, though he is the only person to do so. After the encounter, the residents return to their homes, "a heavy sadness in their hearts, anxiety aroused by silent memories . . . a house still standing, destruction, alienation, distances, ships on the ocean."[90]

This description of a meeting between an Arab refugee and a group of Jewish new immigrants is set in the context of the 1948 war and could have gone in many different directions. One is the expulsion of Arabs from their villages. That is indeed part of the novel and especially of the scene we are looking at here. However, it is not the central point. The conversation that develops between the new residents of the village and the range of emotions it arouses are not connected with what was happening in 1948. What is brought to the surface are the Jews' memories of their past in the *galut*, their suffering as a persecuted minority, and their fears when they were expelled from their homes and became refugees. Moreover, the fact that only one Jew suggests that the man should be driven out of the village serves to emphasize the nonaggressive tone of the conversation. The new immigrants know that what was done to the Arab was wrong, but they are caught up in their own experiences. For them, the encounter with the stranger brings them face to face with their past, reflecting their own experience of expulsion, their struggles as refugees and their difficulties as new immigrants.

Though Yossel Birstein dealt with the Zionist experience in a different way, the encounter between the Jewish past and the Israeli present was at the center of his writing, too. This can be seen very clearly in his novel *Oyf shmole trotuarn* (On narrow sidewalks), perhaps the most important of Birstein's writings of the 1950s. This novel about kibbutz life was published in Yiddish in 1958 and in Hebrew in 1959 (by a small private publisher).[91]

Birstein himself was very familiar with kibbutz life. After he came to Israel in 1950, he settled in Kibbutz Gvat in Jezreel Valley in northern Israel and lived there for about ten years. Nonetheless, his take on the kibbutz and kibbutz life is quite unique. *Oyf shmule trotuarn* has almost no plot but is a collection of snapshots of characters and events in the life of a fictional kibbutz called Yalon. In fact, it is constructed as a series of hasty meetings, conversations, and bits of conversation between the various characters.

Most of these are not native-born Israelis and belong to a kind of social hierarchy, unstated yet very clear, that underlies kibbutz life. The main protagonists are old-timers, Ze'ev, Menuha, and Hasia. They were born in eastern Europe and had been among the first to settle in the kibbutz, after its foundation a number of decades before the novel's action. In addition to them, there is the couple Daniel and Lottie, who joined the kibbutz at a later stage. Daniel had come "from the English-speaking lands," "in the early days of the war."[92] Lottie had come with an agricultural training group.⁹³ Daniel is a writer and Lottie an English teacher—occupations not typical for kibbutz members but still giving them a respectable place in its social hierarchy. Lottie and Ze'ev are lovers, though Udi, Ze'ev's son, also fancies Lottie. Still, it is not this love triangle that drives the plot, and there is also a third group on the kibbutz, Holocaust survivors from Eastern Europe. They are described as a separate group of far lower status. The established members regard them as "inferior creatures ... wandering around the kibbutz like poor people in a foreign city, popping up and then vanishing."⁹⁴

Ostensibly, the novel looks into the very heart of the Zionist ethos—the kibbutz, secular society, cooperative life, agricultural labor, the field, the plough, personal commitment to building the country. "Let's run away, you and me, for at least a week or two," Lottie says to Ze'ev. "How can we," he replies. "I have to plough tomorrow."⁹⁵ And yet, on closer examination the novel does not present its readers with the hegemonic Zionist narrative but a message all its own.

Critics who reviewed the novel in the Hebrew press tried to see how it presented the collective ideal underlying the kibbutz.⁹⁶ However, Birstein does not depict the kibbutz as a Zionist space but an arena for social interaction. The novel conspicuously ignores the ideological aspects of kibbutz life. There is no mention at all of the dramatic events that shook the kibbutz movement in the 1950s, and the values that underpin the kibbutz do not form part of the lives of its characters.⁹⁷

Even the kibbutz general meeting, the main institution of its communal life, is only indirectly described, through the eyes of Daniel—Birstein's alter ego in the novel—who thinks it boring and purposeless: "He sat at the meetings, those crammed with participants, the hall crowded, hot and full of everyone's breath, and the smaller ones with fewer participants.... Someone talks about a house and children, about cows and rain. Outside the walls, the world is full of night. Dark fields, the sky sown with stars. And between the stars—solitude."⁹⁸ This last sentence moves the focus of the novel from the kibbutz to the human experience. The members' general meeting—the very heart of communal life—evokes in the hero's mind only thoughts of solitude.

The author's Zionist experience was one of immigration and integration into Israel, and in his novel, the kibbutz provides the setting that reflects this. Birstein's imagined kibbutz, Assaf Inbary wrote, "suddenly looks like Biale Podolska [the shtetl where he grew up]."⁹⁹ Still, in the story, it is not Birstein's shtetl that is being built by the waves of immigration but Zionist Israel, in just the way that Birstein had experienced it himself.

So, beneath the sketchy events of the story, something else is being discussed, something far more relevant to our discussion—the place of the different generations of east European Jews in Zionist Israel. The protagonists of the novel, the founders of the kibbutz, immigrants themselves, remain connected to their personal histories and do not turn their backs on their eastern European experiences, trying to find a place for their past in the lives that they were building in Israel. "You surely know the fate of [your grandfather in the Eastern European shtetl]?" Hasia asks Udi, Ze'ev's son. Typically, of course, the young generation of native Israelis is not interested. "Udi didn't know. . . . He was not interested and had never asked. It was a far-off world that was not connected to him."[100]

However, when it comes to the Holocaust survivors, even those previous immigrants who want to preserve their ties with the past view them as inferior and alien: Haim, Hasia's husband, describes them as "a mixed bag of people, who do not know what a kibbutz is."[101] Udi, whose mother, Menuha, becomes close to a family of Holocaust survivors, also does not like her new friends. "I don't like them. . . . They sit there every evening making noise. They speak Yiddish, an incomprehensible language that I find hateful."[102]

The prevalent attitude of rejecting Yiddish was part of how Birstein saw life in Israel. About twenty years later, he expressed it in two stories in the first collection he published in Hebrew.[103] In his novel about the kibbutz Birstein preferred to underscore the attitude toward Yiddish rather than the idea of the kibbutz.

Yung Yisroel in Israeli Culture

The Hebrew press in Israel scarcely reacted to Yung Yisroel. A few articles appeared at different times making brief mention of the meetings at Yagur and then the publication of the group's journal, *Yung Yisroel*,[104] with one going so far as to stress the Israeli content of the first issue.[105]

In contrast, the Yiddish press, both in Israel and elsewhere—in the United States, Europe, and Latin America—gave wide coverage to the group's founding, the first publications of its work in *Di goldene keyt*, and the first issues of the journal *Yung Yisroel*.[106] This is perhaps not surprising given the transnational nature of Yiddish literature, but it also reflected a new understanding of the post-Holocaust literary world. With the disappearance of the Yiddish center in Eastern Europe and the dramatic decline in the status of Yiddish in the United States, Israel—even despite the attitude toward Yiddish there—now stood at the head of the transnational network of Yiddish literature. This made it a matter of great interest to all the centers of Yiddish throughout the world when young Israeli Yiddish writers organized into a group.

Most of the critics viewed with favor the fact that young authors in Israel were writing in Yiddish. Some even reviewed their work. However, the question that almost all of them asked—either openly or between the lines—was, what was the principle that led these young people to organize as a literary group? For the lack of a clear answer, some argued that Yung Yisroel was not a literary group at all but a kind of sociopolitical organization.[107]

Three major figures in the Yiddish world of New York, the literary critic Shmuel Niger and the writers Jacob Glatstein and Aaron Leyeles, agreed.[108] Glatstein even wrote a very favorable review of the second collection of work by members of the group, published in *Di goldene keyt* number 13, noting the high quality of the writing.[109] He also discussed at length the group's contribution to the continuation of Yiddish literature after the Holocaust, particular in the conditions of the state of Israel. However, he made the point, in no uncertain terms, that all of this was not enough to define Yung Yisroel as a literary group or a new voice in Yiddish literature. For that, they needed a clear "theoretical voice."[110]

The issue of Yung Yisroel's raison d'être as a literary group was also at the heart of the reactions in the Yiddish press in Israel. Several critics criticized the authors' work harshly, going so far as to deny that it had any literary value.[111] Others approved highly of the fact that young writers, Holocaust survivors, nearly all of them members of kibbutzim and moshavim, who worked in the fields and villages, were creating in Yiddish. But the question of what united the members of Yung Yisroel, what made them into a literary group, remained unanswered.[112] Daniel Leybl, the editor of *Nayvelt*, wrote explicitly: "I do not believe there is a substantive . . . link between the members of Yung Yisroel."[113]

The responses of Yung Yisroel to these critiques shed a great deal of light on how they saw themselves and their place as Yiddish writers in the state of Israel. Shlomo Vorzoger, a member of Yung Yisroel, was unequivocal. "What connects us?" he asked. "We are connected by one fate, the fate of a generation born between two world wars . . . whose youth was one of expulsion and flight. . . . And what else connects us? An organic link with everything around us . . . a plentitude of the joy of creation . . . the belief that the darkness from which we came is merely the absence of light—the light of the sun . . . that a beam of light will penetrate the fog of the chaos . . . until the great day arises."[114] Moyshe Yungman responded similarly that the role of a Yiddish author in Israel was to artistically depict the experiences of their new life, in all of its splendor, its ugliness, and its tragic nature, and to give expression to the destruction of the Jewish people and its revival.[115] So, in their own eyes, what united the members of the group was the fact that they were giving artistic expression to the experience of the Holocaust and the Jewish revival in Israel.[116]

In this context, the group's connection with Kibbutz Yagur seems to take on a special significance. The choice of Yagur was probably a result of the efforts of Zvi Eisenman, who was a member of Yagur, and was also influenced by the fact that five of the members lived in the north of Israel.[117] But it was Tel Aviv, not Yagur, that was the natural place for these meetings.[118] However, on the eve of the second conference, Eisenman wrote: "It was no coincidence that we chose a kibbutz. It was an expression of our fierce desire to strike roots in the country, and what else can symbolize the real Israel if not the kibbutz?"[119] But it seems that in actual fact there was another reason.

In Yagur—one of the strongest, most well-established kibbutzim in Israel—many of the members, though they belonged to different generations, came from eastern Europe and shared the linguistic and cultural capital of the members of Yung Yisroel.[120] These eastern European Jews often expressed their interest in events centered on Yiddish, which they called on one occasion "the mother tongue of hundreds of us."[121] "In the heart of Eastern European Jews," the *Yoman Yagur* wrote, "many of whom live among us—the embers of the love of Yiddish, the language of their childhood, still burn."[122] So the members of Yagur were not interested in Yung Yisroel as such; their interest was in Yiddish generally. It was not only the young authors whom they hosted but also other Yiddish writers, including H. Leivick and Itzik Manger, two of the best-known Yiddish poets of the day, when they come on visits from the United States.[123]

Bearing in mind the fact that its conferences were held so rarely and that the group did not hold frequent, informal meetings, of the sort typical of literary groups, Yung Yisroel cannot really be viewed as a literary group in the usual sense of the term. Yungman and Eisenman were basically right when they wrote that what united the group was its members' desire to overcome the experience of the Holocaust and to build new lives in Israel. It is probably true to say that more than being a literary group, Yung Yisroel was a kind of supportive framework for the young authors' literary development and for their lives in general, since most of them were grappling with post-Holocaust trauma, and all were writing in a language that their new country had rejected. This also explains their choice to hold their meetings at Yagur, a place that both represented the very heart of the Zionist ethos, Israeliness at its best, and contained a society of eastern European Jews, in touch with their past and still willing to show their love of Yiddish, even if only out of nostalgia.

"A Dividing Line between the Yiddish and Hebrew Writers": The Yiddish Writer's Zionist Master Narrative and Hebrew Literature

Nonetheless, even if they never explicitly formulated it, the members of Yung Yisroel, or at least the prose writers among them, did share a common literary platform and understanding of the Zionist narrative. This should have earned them an important place in the history of Israeli literature had it received the attention it merits.

The question that needs to be discussed here, then, is the relationship between the Zionist narrative as given by the Yiddish writers and the hegemonic narrative of Hebrew literature of the 1950s. To do that we need to look first at the ways Hebrew writers dealt with the immigration and absorption experience of the east European Jews in Israel, in comparison to Israeli Yiddish literature of the day.

Some scholars have discussed the question whether Yiddish literature was a "minor literature," in the sense that it was written in the shadow of or in opposition to a dominant literature in the hegemonic language.[124] However, I should like to argue here that if the members of Yung Yisroel did write in the shadow of a dominant literature, it was Yiddish literature, not Hebrew. Though Hebrew literature was indeed the hegemonic language in the state of Israel, the members of Yung Yisroel wrote neither in its shadow nor in opposition to it.

A more helpful theoretical framework here would probably be transnationalism. Yiddish literature flourished throughout the world because it was a transnational phenomenon, which developed in each new place where the Jews settled, against the background of the society there, and whose creative force was drawn in no small measure from the new realities in which the Jews found themselves. In the case of Yiddish writers in Israel, issues of majority and minority had little significance since Yiddish writers did not perceive themselves as a minority. This brings us back to the question of the Zionist narrative in the literature of Yung Yisroel. As these authors reworked the Israeli experience through their Yiddish writing, how, if at all, did their Zionist narrative relate to the hegemonic version?

To answer this question I will compare the works of the group members we have looked at to two of the very important works about the lives of the new immigrants in Israel written by writers of the 1948 generation—Moshe Shamir's *He Walked in the Fields* (*Hu halach ba'sadot*) and Hanoch Bartov's *Each One Had Six Wings* (*Shesh kenafayim la'ehad*).[125] The first, published in 1947, became one of the mainstays of the Israeli Zionist myth. The second, published in 1954, was the first Hebrew novel about the life and experience of the new immigrants—especially those from Eastern Europe. Both were extremely influential books that left their mark on Israeli culture. Both won literary prizes on their publication, and both were dramatized and staged by the Habima Theater.[126] Both are also considered classics of modern Hebrew literature.[127] As we will see, in both character and plot, these two novels conformed closely to the hegemonic Zionist narrative. As a matter of fact, *He Walked in the Fields* actually played a role in shaping it.

He Walked in the Fields, Moshe Shamir's first novel, is a bildungsroman about Uri, the first child born to his kibbutz and son of its leading members.[128] Uri returns to the kibbutz after completing his studies at an agricultural school and meets Mika, an orphan Holocaust survivor, who bears his child. The novel follows Uri from his young manhood, to his work in the kibbutz, his service in the Palmach, and his untimely death in a military training accident.

The novel contains many elements of the hegemonic Zionist narrative of the time, but for the purposes of this discussion, I will discuss only the way the characters were shaped. Uri, who is depicted in detail in the novel, is the definitive Israeli-born young man. He is handsome, strong, and capable of hard physical work; he joins the Palmach and gives building the national home priority over building his own. Mika is the opposite. She is a Holocaust survivor and has no parents or other family members; the reader does not know her background, what happened to her family, or anything about her personality. As opposed to Uri, she is depicted as a person without roots in the past or a vision for the future. While Uri is immersed in the future of the kibbutz and is not sure whether he should continue his work in the vineyard or move to another agricultural branch, Mika is focused on getting herself her own place to live. Uri and the rest of the kibbutz members do not understand her choices. They expect her to forget her past and to start afresh.

The novel reaches its climax with the death of Uri and Mika giving birth to his son. Finally, Mika, the Holocaust survivor, fulfills her Zionist duty by giving birth to an Israeli-born baby boy, a grandson to the founders of the kibbutz, who will follow in his father's footsteps.[129]

The desire to ignore the past of Holocaust survivors, to erase it, is also evident in Hanoch Bartov's book *Each One Had Six Wings* (1954).[130] This multicharacter panoramic novel was the first written by a native-born Israeli and describes the hardships of the new immigrants. It tells the story of a Jerusalem neighborhood whose Arab residents had fled during the War of 1948 and is now populated by new immigrants from various countries, most of whom are Holocaust survivors.

The novel describes how the immigrants face a whole range of difficulties, including bureaucratic hurdles put up by government agencies, as they attempt to acclimatize to their new home. Although the new immigrants in the novel are rather stereotypical, they are not described as weak or passive; some are strong, militant, and opinionated. The new Israeli is represented by Rakefet, a young Israeli-born teacher who lost her fiancée in the 1948 war and now lives in the neighborhood and teaches in the local school.

The climax of the novel comes when the people of the neighborhood join together to help the baker Mr. Glick, a weary, elderly Holocaust survivor who is struggling with the Israeli bureaucracy, which refuses to grant him a license to open a bakery. Eventually he is successful, and at the end of the novel, a baby daughter is born to him and his young wife, Manya—both the only survivors of their families. A baby-naming ceremony is held in the local synagogue and is attended by the whole neighborhood.

> The *gabbai* [the beadle of the synagogue] turned to Glick and asked the name of the newborn child.
> "Rakefet," Glick whispered in excitement. The ceremony goes wrong. [The beadle] hesitated, surprised, as if he had not heard correctly or did not believe what he had heard: "Rakefet?"[131]

When the ceremony is over, Glick explains:

> How did we think of that [name]? It was Manya, my wife, who said, ". . . The truth is, what name can we give her?" We have so many to remember, she and I, and we only have the one baby. . . . And then Manya, that's my wife, said, "Let's give her a new name, something different, one that will not remind us of anyone, so that she won't have to carry all that on her shoulders . . ." We were also seeking a name from here, from this land.[132]

So, the climax of the novel and its conclusion redeem the characters from the *galut*. The act of giving a new, Israeli name, the name of a typical Israeli flower that has been celebrated in Israeli songs for many years, to the infant instead of one that would commemorate those who had died in the Holocaust symbolizes their complete turn away from the Diaspora past and severing any connection with it.

The very essence of Israeliness was represented in the opening sentence of another of Shamir's novels—*With His Own Hands* (*Be'mo yadav*). Published in 1951, this is also a bildungsroman telling the story of the life of Elik, Shamir's brother, and his death in the War of 1948. The novel opens with the words "Elik was born from the sea," presented as a single sentence before the first paragraph.[133] This phrase became the quintessential representation of the new Israeli, connected to the land and its landscape and cut off from previous generations.

For Yiddish writers, this approach was impossible. Their protagonists were not "born from the sea." They were the heirs to many generations of Jews who had lived in the Diaspora—to their lives, their achievements, their sufferings, and their deaths. The members of Yung Yisroel were simply unable to turn their backs on them and on the *galut* where they had made their lives.

But beyond that, for the writers of Yung Yisroel, whose work we have discussed here, the Diaspora played a major role in their very Israeliness. They all viewed their lives in Israel and their lives in the Diaspora as somehow intertwined. For some of them life in Israel could enable a *tikun*, a rectification, an acceptance of their past and a continuation of it. Others viewed a selective memory of the past as a consolation for the hardships of the present. Without the presence of the Diaspora past, life in Israel had no meaning for them.

However, for many the connection was much stronger. For them the Israeli experience itself was a reflection of the experiences of the past, sometimes with the possibility of *tikun* or working through them. This can be seen in Mann's novel but is even more prominent in Karpinovitsh's story about the new immigrant who took a prisoner of war. When he kills the Palestinian/German soldier, the immigrant from Eastern Europe is not murdering a prisoner, and the act is not connected to the war Israel is fighting. It is the character working through a traumatic experience from his past by fighting for Israel's independence. That is his redemption.

And yet, there is no sign that the Yung Yisroel writers were rebelling against the hegemonic narrative. They were simply writing their unique Israeliness as they felt it, with no connection to how it was presented in contemporary Hebrew literature. In creating their own narrative, they were not grappling with the hegemonic version, not rebelling against it, and not subverting it. They were writing in parallel to it.

It would take thirty years before David Grossman, the celebrated Israeli author writing in Hebrew, would make the struggle to come to terms with the memory of the Holocaust central to his novel *See: Under Love*, which is now considered one of the most important Israeli novels.[134]

The writers of Yung Yisroel had understood that in the 1950s and had made it a key part of their writing. "It may sound like a paradox," Mendl Mann wrote in 1959, "but you can find the new Israel in Yiddish literature.... The day will come when [S.] Yizhar, [Moshe] Shamir and [Aharon] Megged will have to learn Yiddish in order to understand their own country." He added: "[But] in the meantime, there is a dividing line separating the Yiddish writer and the Hebrew writer in Israel."[135]

Notes

1. *Di goldene keyt* 1 (1949): 77; "Fun yunger yidisher literatur in Israel," *Di goldene keyt* 7 (1951): 135–149. After the 1951 meeting, Sutzkever went on to publish more work by these young writers in *Di goldene keyt* in separate sections.

2. Zvi Eisenman, "Kama milim al pegishat sofrei yidish ha'tze'irim," *Yoman meshek Yagur*, October 24, 1951, 2, Kibbutz Yagur archives.

3. Shmuel Rollansky, "Medines Yisroel in der yidisher literatur," *Yidishe literatur— Yidish lebn: shraybers, bashraybers un vizyonern in unzer literatur-geshikhte*, 2:2 (Buenos

Aires: A grupe fraynd fun der literatur-gezelshaft baym YIVO, 1973) 619. The name is pronounced Rozhansky and spelled in Argentinian Spanish "Rollansky."

4. Their main life goals at that time seem to have been to become what they perceived as "real" Israelis living in kibbutzim and the small towns of northern Israel.

5. On the youth movements in interwar Poland, see Ido Bassok, "Tenu'ot ha'no'ar ha'yehudiyot be'Polin bein shetei milhamot ha'olam," in *Alilot ne'urim: Otobiografyot shel benei no'ar yehudim mi'Polin bein shetei milhamot olam*, ed. Ido Bassok and Avraham Novershtern (Tel Aviv: Tel Aviv University Press, 2011), 769–792.

6. On this tension, see Dan Miron, *A Traveller in Disguise: The Rise of Modern Yiddish Fiction in the Nineteenth Century* (Syracuse, NY: Syracuse University Press, 1996), 1–33; Ruth Wisse, ed., *A Shtetl and Other Yiddish Novellas* (Detroit: Wayne State University Press, 1973), 4–5; Mikhail Krutikov, "Yiddish Literature: Yiddish Literature after 1880," *YIVO Encyclopedia of the Jews in Eastern Europe*, http://www.yivoencyclopedia.org/article.aspx/Yiddish_literature_after_1800.

7. Benjamin Harshav, *The Meaning of Yiddish* (Berkeley: University of California Press, 1990), 163.

8. See, for example, A. Glantz-Leyeles, "Nyu yorker nekht" and "Tsu aykh yidishe dikhter," in *Amerike un ikh*, ed. A. Glanz-Leyeles (New York: Der kval, 1963), 71–74, 79–80.

9. Rachel Rojanski, ""The Final Chapter in the Struggle for Cultural Autonomy: Palestine, Israel, and Yiddish Writers in the Diaspora, 1946–1951," *Journal of Modern Jewish Studies* 6, no. 2 (2007): 185–204.

10. Gershon Shaked, *Ha'siporet ha'ivrit 1880–1980*, vol. 4, *Be'havelei ha'zeman— Ha're'alism ha'isra'eli 1880–1980* (Tel Aviv: Hakibbutz Hameuchad and Keter, 1993), 15–16.

11. Aharon Appelferd, *Masot be'guf rishon* (Jerusalem: Ha'sifrya ha'tzyonit, 1979), 84.

12. Rachel Auerbach, *Be'hutzot Varsha*, trans. Mordechai Halamish (Tel Aviv: Am Oved, 1954). On the history of this book see *Be'hutzot Varsha*, 7–8. See also Yeshayahu Spiegel, *Malchut geto*, trans. A. D. Shafir, intro. Dov Sadan (Tel Aviv: Hakibbutz Hameuchad, 1952). At the time, Spiegel's book, first published in Warsaw in 1947 from a manuscript that the author had hidden in the ground before he was sent from the Łódź ghetto to Auschwitz, was regarded as the first Yiddish book published in Poland after the Holocaust. Spiegel, *Malchut geto*, 1–3. Today, some argue that the first Yiddish book published in Poland after the Holocaust was Mendl Mann's *Di shtilkeyt mont*. See Haim Kazshdan, *Der kinstler un dertseyler Mendl Mann* (Paris: Undzer kiem, 1965), 5.

13. On Spiegel, see Rivka Katznelson, "Sofrei Yidish ha'aharonim anahnu," *Maariv*, December 27, 1957; A. Volf Yasni, "Meshorer ha'kilayon ha'yehudi," *Davar*, March 9, 1951. See also a large collection of reviews of his work printed over the years in Charlotte Spiegel, *Dyokano shel sofer: Yeshayahu Spiegel: mivhar bikorot al yetzirato* (Tel Aviv: self-published, 1985). On Rochman, see B. Tz. Tzangen, *"Be'damayich hayi—*be'shulei sifro shel Leyb Rochman," *HaTzofe*, July 28, 1950; Yaakov Rabi, "Nitzotzot shel hesed, al *Be'damayich hayi* me'et Leyb Rochman," *Al HaMishmar*, December 22, 1961. On Hofer, see M. Grossman, "Sifrut beli yoreshim," *Davar*, January 19, 1951.

14. Yeshaya Spiegel, *Madregot el ha'shamayim*, trans. A. D. Shafir (Tel Aviv: Am Oved, 1970); Yeshaya Spiegel, *Arumim be'terem shahar*, trans. A. D. Shafir (Tel Aviv: Sifriat Poalim, 1968).

15. Address of Moshe Sharett, former prime minister and director of the Am Oved publishing house at the time. "Moshe Sharett—Yurhav hekefa shel ha'sifriya la'am shel Am Oved," *Davar*, June 19, 1960.

16. The back cover states that it is a book about the life of Jews in villages in Russia. Also, in 1961, Sifriya la'am published a translation from the Yiddish of *Ha'harariyim* (The people from the mountains), a novel by Joseph Erlich, who immigrated to Israel in 1933. It was the first translation from Yiddish published by that list, and I tend to believe that the editors chose it because it was about the journey of immigrants from Kurdistan to Palestine and their settlement in the Sha'ar Aliya transit camp and that it was not thought to represent Yiddish literature.

17. Shaked, *Ha'siporet ha'ivrit*, 16.

18. Ibid., 166–169.

19. In Hebrew literature in the land of Israel, literary groups have existed from the end of the nineteenth century until the present day. In Yiddish literature, they were a familiar phenomenon both in eastern Europe and in the United States. On such groups in the United States, see Harshav, *The Meaning of Yiddish*, 185–189.

20. Moyshe Yungman, "Draysik yor Yung Yisroel," *Di goldene keyt* 108 (1982): 59–66.

21. Invitation to the founding meeting of Yung Yisroel, Yagur, October 26, 1951, National Library, Yossel Birstein archives, box 5.

22. Yitzhak Paner, "Yung Yisroel in Yisroel, tsum grindungs-tsunoyftruf fun di yunge shrayber in Yagur," *Nayvelt*, November 16, 1951.

23. "Yung Yisroel," *Yoman meshek Yagur*, October 14, 1951. See also an article by Zvi Eisenman on the eve of the first conference, with a note from the newsletter's editor: "Kama milim al pegishat sofrei Yidish ha'tze'irim," *Yoman meshek Yagur*, October 24, 1951.

24. *Yoman meshek Yagur*, February 3, 1956. See also Y. N. Melekh, "Yung Israel, be'shulei kinus shel sofrim olim," *Ha'dor*, November 7, 1952.

25. Moyshe Yungman, "Draysik yor," 63.

26. "Ha'neshef ha'sifruti shel sofrei Yidish ha'tze'irim," *Yoman Kibbutz Yagur*, November 2, 1951.

27. "Tsuzamenkunft fun yunge yidishe dikhter un prozayiker in Yisroel," *Nayvelt*, November 2, 1951.

28. Pinsker, "Choosing Yiddish in Israel."

29. "Ha'neshef ha'sifruti shel sofrei Yidish ha'teze'irim," *Yoman meshek Yagur*, November 2, 1951.

30. Moyshe Yungman, "Draysik yor Yung Yisroel," *Di goldene keyt* 108 (1982): 62.

31. Yitzhak Paner, "Yung Yisroel in Yisroel, tsum grindungs-tsunoyftruf fun di yunge shrayber in Yagur," *Nayvelt*, November 16, 1951.

32. Yossel Birstein, "A yidisher shrayber in kibuts," *Di goldene keyt* 11: 162–167. A note at the top stated that it was the lecture delivered at the group's first meeting.

33. Moyshe Yungman, "Shtrikhn," in *Yung Yisroel, literatur, kunst, kritik* (Haifa: 1954), 35–36; Abraham Rintzler, "Randn," in *Yung Yisroel, zamlung far literatur un kritik* (Haifa: 1956), 58–59.

34. As Abraham Liss put it, "It is very interesting to know what are the aspirations of these young people. What makes them a group and what will be their collective activity." Abraham Liss, "Vegn di shafungen fun Yung Yisroel," *Unzer veg*, October 15, 1952, 14.

35. Eisenman was born in Warsaw in 1920; during the Holocaust, he was in labor camps in Siberia, and he arrived in Yagur in 1949.

36. Zvi Eisenman, "Kama milim."

37. "Likrat ha'pegisha ha'shenatit shel Yung Yisroel," *Yoman meshek Yagur*, October 24, 1952.

38. David Canaani to Eisenman, March 3, 1957, Eisenman archives, Gnazim—Archive of Hebrew Literature, Israel, 394, 5370/13.

39. "Likrat ha'pegisha ha'shenatit shel Yung Yisroel," *Yoman meshek Yagur*, October 24, 1952.

40. Moyshe Yungman was born in Chodorov, Galicia, in 1922 and spent the war years in Siberia. Nava Gonen, ed., *Asufa le'zichro shel Moshe Yungman* (Tivon: self-published, 1985), 1. On Eisenman and Yungman's close friendship, see Yehudit Eisenman, "Moshe lo yelech bi'shevil ha'yedidut," *Asufa le'zichro*, 71–80; Zvi Eisenman, "Ahi Moshe," ibid., 41–82.

41. In his 1982 article, Yungman noted that the essay entitled "Shtrikhn" was the essence of his lecture at the first conference of the Yung Yisroel group. *Di goldene keyt* 108 (1982): 63.

42. Yungman, "Shtrikhn," 35.

43. *Yidish literatur in medinas Yisroel*, Tel Aviv 1991: 132

44. Ibid., 165.

45. Rintzler, "Randn," 58.

46. On Rintzler, see Shachar Pinsker, "Ata, marvad me'ofef, eincha yoter me'hazaya shel am te'atrali," *Ha'aretz*, December 11, 2009; Pinsker, "Choosing Yiddish in Israel."

47. Participating at the second meeting, in addition to Sutzkever, were David Pinsky, Yitzhak Paner, Dov-Ber Malkin, and Mendl Zinger. *Yoman meshek Yagur*, October 24, 1952. The last conference was held in February 1956 and was attended by Sutzkever and the group members, plus Leyb Rochman, Melech Ravitch, and the poet Arye Shamari, from Kibbutz Ein Shemer, *Yoman meshek Yagur*, February 10, 1956. According to reports in *Yoman meshek Yagur*, that was the fourth conference. But since Yungman and Paner speak specifically about three meetings, and in *Yoman meshek Yagur* itself only three are described, that was probably the number of meetings held. Moreover, *Yoman meshek Yagur* contained many typographical errors, in particular numbers, as well as corrections of these errors.

48. Yungman, "Draysik yor," 60–61. On the Likrat group, see Amos Levin, *Le'darka shel havurat "Likrat"* (Tel Aviv: Hakibbutz Hameuchad, 1984); Shaked, *Ha'siporet ha'ivrit*, 192.

49. *Yung Yisroel, Zamlung far literatur un kritik* (Haifa: publication of a group of young Yiddish writers), December 1954; *Yung Yisroel* (Haifa, publication of a group of young Yiddish writers, 1956); *Yung Yisroel, Zamlung far literatur un kritik* (Haifa: publication of a group of young Yiddish writers, 1957).

50. In his memoirs Yungman explained that the group's publication did not cease due to economic reasons; on the contrary, the group had many supporters and donors, beginning with the authors N. B. Minkov, Jacob Glatstein, and A. Leyeles from New York and Aaron Meydanik from Paris, and ending with Max Holtzman, from Palm Springs, who was Eisenman's supporter. Max Holtzman also financed the publication of Eisenman's book, *Di ban*. See Eisenman's acknowledgments to Rose and Max Holtzman from Palm Springs. Zvi Eisenman, *Di ban: Dertseylungen fun Poyln, Rusland, Yisroel* (Yagur: Yung Yisroel series, 1956), n.p.

51. Conversation with Rivka Basman-Ben Haim, October 2007.

52. "Neshef sifruti shel Yung Yisroel," *Yoman meshek Yagur*, October 24, 1952.

53. Rollansky, "Medines Yisroel," 612.

54. David Roskies, "Di shrayber grupe Yung Yisroel," *Yugntruf* 28–29 (1973): 7–12; 33 (1975): 7–8; 34 (1976) 4–7; 28–29: 7.

55. "Dor ha'medina" or "Dor ba'aretz" are terms that connote the writing of authors born in the second and third decades of the twentieth century, who were born in Israel or at least grew up there, whose first tongue was Hebrew, and who wrote about life in Israel in the 1940s

and 1950s. On "Dor ba'aretz," see Anita Shapira, "Dor ba'aretz," *Alpayim* 2 (1989): 173–203; Avner Holtzman, "Ha'sipurim shel dor ba'aretz," in *Ha'asor ha'rishon 1948-49*, ed. Zvi Zameret and Hanna Yablonka (Jerusalem: Yad Ben Zvi, 1995), 263–280.

56. Eisenman was the only one from his family to survive the Holocaust. After the war he ended up in Italy and from there, in March 1947 came to Palestine on the *Moledet*, a ship carrying illegal immigrants, which was expelled from the shores of Haifa to Cyprus. In 1949 he immigrated to Israel alone. He began to write in the transit camps in Cyprus. Niger and Shatzky, *Leksikon*, 1:63. Eisenman's story "Der alter antikvar" was published in *Di goldene keyt* 7: 169–173.

57. Letter from Zvi Eisenman to the Zvi Kesel prize committee in Mexico after being informed that he had received the prize, January 2, 1956, Eisenman archives, Gnazim—Archive of Hebrew Literature, Israel 394-370167/4.

58. Melech Ravitch, "A vort fun an eltern khaver," in Zvi Eisenman, *Di ban: dertseylungen fun Poyln, Rusland, Yisroel* (Yagur: Yung Yisroel series, 1956), 8–9.

59. Ibid., 123.

60. All quotations from Eisenman, *Di ban*, 123–126.

61. Eisenman, "A zeung," *Di ban*, 34.

62. Zvi Eisenman, "Arum besmedresh," *Di goldene keyt* 13, (1952): 221–225.

63. Eisenman, "Arum besmedresh," *Di ban*, 146.

64. Ibid., 148.

65. Zvi Eisenman, "A mayse vegn Nisim fun Har-Tuv, vegn a varshever hoyf un vegn a shpil-foygel," *Yung Yisroel*, 1956: 14–16.

66. Zvi Eisenman, *Ha'mesila* (Tel Aviv: Hakibbutz Hameuchad, 1960).

67. Zvi Eisenman, "A hoyf in Yafo," *Yung Yisroel*, 1957: 44–49. Another of the Yiddish Israel stories, dropped from *Ha'mesila*, was "Di froy fun barg" (The woman from the mountain), which focused on an Arab woman.

68. David Canaani to Eisenman, March 3, 1957, Eisenman archives, Gnazim—Archive of Hebrew Literature, Israel, 394 5370/13.

69. Hillel Barzel, "Ha'mesila," *Moznayim*, December 14, 1961, 61.

70. Karpinovitsh was born in 1918 in Vilna and came to Israel in 1949. For more than thirty years, he was the administrative director of the Israeli Philharmonic Orchestra. He published nine books written originally in Yiddish and one written in Hebrew. His books have been translated into several languages.

71. The story was first published in *Letste nayes*. Abraham Karpinovitsh, "Di mame vet nokh spondzshe makhen," *Letste nayes*, November 5, 1954.

72. The newspaper offered two prizes: one for a story and the other for a journalistic reportage. "Literatur premye fun *Letste nayes* yidishe tsaytung," *Letste nayes*, August 20, 1954, 1.

73. Ibid.

74. For example, he explains the meaning of the word *breakfast* as "breaking a fast." *Tsom* in Yiddish means "fast," and "break" sounds similar to *brekhn* (to break) in Yiddish.

75. Abraham Karpinovitsh, *Der veg keyn Sdom* (Tel Aviv: Y. L. Peretz, 1959), 51.

76. *Royte vi kalaniyot*: the *kalanit* (anemone) is a common flower in Israel; it appears in many songs and plays a role in Israeli culture.

77. On the announcement of the competition, see "Al penei ha'aretz: peras Am Oved," *Al HaMishmar*, February 26, 1952; "Hotza'at Am Oved machriza al perasim sifrutiyim le'olim hadashim," *Herut*, February 28, 1952. See also Beracha Habas, "Be'fetah ha'kovetz," in

Shevatim, kovetz sipurim u'reshimot shel olim hadashim, ed. Beracha Habas (Tel Aviv: Am Oved, 1953), 5.

78. The Yiddish version was published in the collection *Der veg keyn Sdom*, 35–50.

79. Marriage between educated women and men from a lower social class was common among Jews who survived as partisans in the forest. On this, see Nechama Tec, *Defiance: The Bielski Partisans* (New York: Oxford University Press, 1993).

80. On the underworld in Yiddish literature, see Avraham Novershtern, "Outcasts: Representations of the Underworld in Modern Yiddish Literature," in *Margins and Centers in Yiddish Culture and Literature*, ed. Shlomo Berger (Amsterdam: Menasse Ben Israel Institute, 2014), 33–64.

81. Abraham Karpinovitsh, "Farges nisht," *Der veg keyn Sdom* (Tel Aviv: Y. L. Peretz Bibliotek, 1959; Yung Yisroel series, no. 5), 11–22.

82. Abraham Karpinovitsh, "Farges nisht," *Di goldene keyt* 7 (1951): 179. ("Der fartunklter himl hot im varem arumgenumen, vi a mamesher koptukh. Er hot zikh umgekukt in ale zayten. Di feldzen hobn im frayndlekh tsugenoygt mit zeyere oysgeboygene tseruntselte vent. Getrayst un gemuntert fun yedn shteyn oyf der heymlendisher erd, iz er mit zikhere trit aropgeshtign fun barg.")

83. On the Latrun battle, see Shlomo Shamir, *Be'chol mehir—li'Yerushalyim* (Tel Aviv: Ma'akharot, 1994).

84. S. Yizhar, "Der gefangener," *Di goldene keyt* 2 (1949): 154–171. It is a story about an IDF force during the 1948 war that takes an innocent Palestinian shepherd prisoner and subjects him to abusive interrogations to get information from him, which they all know he does not have. The story presents the dilemma of the soldier guarding him, who wants to and can release him but doesn't dare to do so. This story is considered one of the landmarks of 1948 Hebrew literature. Hannan Hever believes that the prisoner in the story is a metonym for the occupation and that it raises the question of the morality of the occupation. Hannan Hever, "Ahrayut u'merhav be'*Ha'shavui* me'et S. Yizhar," *Mehkarei Yerushalayim be'sifrut ivrit* 23 (2009): 273–278. I should note that this was not how it was understood in 1948.

85. During the 1948–1949 war, rumors were spread about German soldiers who allegedly joined Palestinians and sporadically organized into units fighting against the Israeli forces. These rumors were apparently baseless, but it turns out that a Yiddish writer saw fit to use them in his story. As far as is known, there is no evidence in the historical research of the truth of these rumors. I should thank Motti Golani for his assistance in this regard.

86. Niger and Shatzky, *Leksikon*, 5:432. Mordechai Halamish, in an introduction to Mann's story in an anthology of Yiddish writers in Israel, which he edited, wrote: "Mann is outstanding among young Yiddish writers in his exceptional descriptive skills and in his ability to reveal with a few deft strokes what is happening in the innermost soul of his characters." Mordechai Halamish, ed., *Mi'kan u'mi'karov: antologya shel sipurei Yidish be'Eretz Israel mi'reishit ha'me'a ve'ad yameinu* (Tel Aviv: Sifriat Poalim, 1996), 403.

87. Mendl Mann, *Oyfgevakhte erd* (Tel Aviv: Di goldene keyt, 1953); Mendl Mann, *Adam be'ohel*, trans. from the Yiddish by Yaakov Eliav (Tel Aviv: Am Oved, 1953).

88. Mendl Mann, *Bi'kefar natush: sipur*, trans. from the Yiddish manuscript by A. D. Shafir (Tel Aviv: Am Oved, 1954).

89. Mendl Mann, *In a farvorloztn dorf* (Buenos Aires: Kiem farlag, 1954).

90. Mann, *In a farvorloztn dorf*, 67.

91. Yossel Birstein, *Oyf shmole trotuarn* (Tel Aviv: Y. L. Peretz Bibliotek, 1958). Yossel Birstein, *Be'midrachot tzarot* (Safed: Ha'matmid, 1959). The Ha'matmid publishing house was

a private firm that owned a printing press in Safed. Parts of this book had been published earlier as stand-alone stories in *Di goldene keyt* and other Yiddish publications: "Der pastekh Khonen," *Di goldene keyt* 13 (1952): 195–202; "Der toyt fun an altn oks," *Di goldene keyt* 18 (1954): 129–132; "Baym akern in der nakht," *Di goldene keyt* 28 (1957): 81–85. Three were published in the periodical *Heymish*: "Onitses," *Heymish* (1956): 11; "Baginen," *Heymish* 22–23 (1958): 11; "S'vet regnen," *Heymish* 26–27 (1958): 9–10; and "Nakht" was published in *Yung Yisroel I* 3 (1957): 22–23.

92. Birstein, *Oyf shmole trotuarn*, 36.
93. Ibid., 38.
94. Ibid., 64.
95. Ibid., 218.
96. Moshe Grossman, "Hizaharu mi'penei sofrim," *Davar*, February 6, 1959.
97. In the early 1950s an ideological controversy raged in the kibbutz movement over the socialistic character of a kibbutz and the ties to the Soviet Union. In the end, this controversy led to a split in the kibbutz movement. Three kibbutzim broke into two parts, and from many others kibbutzim members left and founded new kibbutzim. The split rocked not only the kibbutzim but also caused many families to break apart for ideological reasons. Until today it is regarded as an extremely traumatic event. On the schism in the kibbutz movement, see Henry Near, *Crisis and Achievement, 1939–1995*, vol. 2 of *The Kibbutz Movement: A History* (Oxford: Published for the Littman Library by Oxford University Press, 1997).
98. Birstein, *Oyf shmole trotuarn*, 137.
99. Assaf Inbary, "Sipurei ha'kibbutz shel Yossel Birstein," *Keshet ha'hadasha* 21 (2007): 138–149.
100. Birstein, *Oyf shmole trotuarn*, 74; see also p. 191, where Zeev tells his son about the Passover customs in his parents' home.
101. Birstein, *Oyf shmole trotuarn*, 186.
102. Ibid., 161.
103. Yossel Birstein, "Ha'sofer A. M. Fuechs kevar haya zaken" and "Ke'she'bati le'beito shel ha'sofer A. M. Fuchs," in Birstein, *Ketem shel sheket*, 133–134, 135–136.
104. "Israel ha'tze'ira," *Davar*, November 8, 1951; "Sofrei Yung Yisroel be'kinusam," *Davar*, November 3, 1952; Yitzhak Paner, "Israel ha'tze'ira," *Omer*, May 4, 1956; "Ha'erev ha'sifruti mi'ta'am Yung Yisroel," *LaMerhav*, November 22, 1956.
105. Dibon, "Yung Yisroel," *Omer*, November 1, 1957.
106. Itzik Manger, "Yung Yisroel," *Der veker*, May 1, 1955, 21–22; Y. Horn, "Yung Yisroel un 'yunger dor'," *Yidishe tsaytung* (Buenos Aires), August 5, 1956; Yoel Gak, "Yung Yisroel, a brik far naye aspiratsyes," *Haynt* (Montevideo, Uruguay), April 15, 1958; Y. Horn, "In kibets Yagur," *Yidishe tsaytung* (Buenos Aires), April 8, 1956; Yitzhak Varshavsky, "Yung Yisroel," *Forverts*, January 28, 1958.
107. Yitzhak Yasnasovitch, "Yung Yisroel in Yidish-Yisroel," *Arbeter vort* (Paris), December 7, 1951. Yasnasovitch used the term "political" in the sense of internal politics among Yiddish writers in Israel.
108. A. Leyeles, "Yung Yisroel beletristik," *Der tog*, November 1, 1952; Leyeles, "Yung Yisroel zamlung," *Der Tog*, January 19, 1955; Leyeles, "Dertseylungen fun Yisroel lebn," *Der tog*, February 5, 1955; Leyeles, "Di proze fun Yung Yisroel," *Der tog*, November 1, 1952; Sh. Niger, "Yung Yisroel," *Der tog*, January 13, 1952; Sh. Niger, "Yung Yisroel," *Der tog*, February 17, 1952.

109. *Di goldene keyt* 13 (1952): 192–228. Recently a translation into English of Basman's poems has been published: Rivka Basman-Ben Haim, *The Thirteenth Hour*, trans. Zelda Kahan Newman (Woodstock, NY: Mayapple, 2016).

110. Jacob Glatstein, "Yung Yisroel," *Yidisher kemfer*, November 14, 1952, 12–13. Three years later, when the first volume of *Yung Yisroel* came out, Glatstein once again praised the work of several members of the group but even more firmly reiterated his reservations. Concerning a theoretical article written by Yungman in that issue, he argued that it did not suffice to serve as a platform for a literary group. In the absence of profound theoretical articles, dealing seriously with the broad issues of the acclimatization of Yiddish in Israel, he wrote that the publication of a separate journal was not justified; nor was there any significance to the existence of a separate literary group among Yiddish writers in Israel. Jacob Glatstein, "Yung Yisroel," *Yidisher kemfer*, February 11, 1955, 12–13

111. Moyshe Grossman, "Poetishe plaperay un ployderay," *Dos vort*, August 1952. Y. H. Biletzky, a bilingual journalist in Hebrew and Yiddish, wrote similar things in a brief article in *Al HaMishmar*, in which he which he characterized the work of members of the group as "empty verbiage." Y. H. Biletzky, "Shirat Yung Yisroel," *Al HaMishmar*, October 9, 1957.

112. Abraham Liss, a Yiddish essayist and literary critic, in a review of a collection of the members' works published in issue 13 of *Di goldene keyt*, asked what connected these young people in Yung Yisroel. A. Liss, "Vegn di shafungen fun Yung Yisroel," *Unzer veg*, October 15, 1952.

113. Daniel Leybl, "Etlekhe bamerkungen vegn Yung Yisroel," *Nayvelt*, October 17, 1952.

114. S. Vorzoger, "Yung Yisroel." *Oyf der vakh*. The article is in the Yossel Birstein archives in the National Library of Israel, as a newspaper clipping. The handwritten notation reads "Oyfn veg" and the year 1955. The content of the article, as well as its mention in articles published in 1952, indicate that the date is an error. Also the title of the publication that printed this article is unclear, and was handwritten in different ways. There was no way of finding the original, but because it is important, the article is cited without exact bibliographical details, and one can assume it was probably written in 1952.

115. Moyshe Yungman, "An entfer," *Nayvelt*, October 3, 1952.

116. Rivka Basman said similar things in a personal interview: "We came from the Holocaust and destruction; we were young and wanted to write," and Sutzkever "understood our souls." She described the meetings with him as a "psychological workshop." Interview with Rivka Basman, eve of Rosh Hashana, 2007.

117. Moyshe Yungman lived in Kiryat Tiv'on, Yossel Birstein in Kibbutz Gvat, Moyshe Gurin in Acre and Abraham Rintzler in Haifa.

118. The center of the Yiddish scene in Israel was of course Tel Aviv. The office of *Di goldene keyt*, the offices of *Letste nayes*, and other Yiddish newspapers were there, as well as the Y. L. Peretz publishing house, founded in 1956, and the Bristol Hotel, where Yiddish actors and guests from abroad stayed.

119. "Likrat ha'pegisha ha'shenatit shel Yung Yisroel," *Yoman meshek Yagur*, no. 2457, October 24, 1952, Kibbutz Yagur Archive.

120. Some of these were members of the kibbutz, from the Ahva group, who were connected to Poalei-Zion in the United States and were active in promoting Yiddish; some arrived from eastern Europe before World War II; and some were members of the core group that founded Kibbutz Lohamei HaGeta'ot. On Ahva, see Rojanski, *Zehuyot nifgashot*, 84–97, 223–229; Zeev Rimon, ed., *Sefer Yagur* (Tel Aviv: Kibbutz Yagur and Hakibbutz Hameuchad, 1965), 236–273, 281–325, 331–347, 372–387.

121. "Ha'erev al ha'deshe shel beit Bat-sheva, pegisha im ha'meshorer Itzik Manger," *Yoman meshek Yagur*, no. 2838, June 27, 1958, Kibbutz Yagur Archive.

122. *Yoman meshek Yagur*, no. 27, February 3, 1956, Kibbutz Yagur Archive.

123. His first visit was in 1936, his second in 1951. On the second visit, see Rachel Rojanski, "Ta'aru lahem et rabi Nahman mi'Braslav hoger herev—al bikuro shel H. Leivick be'Israel be'1950," *Ha'aretz*, April 19, 2010; "Im ha'meshorer Leivick," *Yoman meshek Yagur*, no. 2775, September 13, 1957, Kibbutz Yagur Archive; "Erev leil shabbat im Leivick," *Yoman meshek Yagur*, no. 2775, September 13, 1957, Kibbutz Yagur Archive. See Rimon, *Sefer Yagur*, 512.

124. Gilles Deleuze and Felix Guattari, who coined the term, state that minor literature uses the language of the majority after it has been deterritorialized. They add that minor literature also has a strong political character. Gilles Deleuze and Felix Guattari, *Kafka—Toward a Minor Literature*, trans. Dana Polan (Minneapolis: University of Minnesota Press, 1986), 23. Ruth Wisse, Chana Kronfeld, and Michael Gluzman have argued that a literature can be defined as "minor" if it is written in a national language like Hebrew or Yiddish, especially if it was written in the shadow of a dominant literature and expresses the experience of a weak or marginal culture. Ruth Wisse, *The Modern Jewish Canon—A Journey through Language and Culture* (New York: Free Press, 2000), 85–87; Chana Kronfeld, *On the Margins of Modernism* (Berkeley: University of California Press, 1966), 1–17.

125. Moshe Shamir, *Hu halach ba'sadot* (Tel Aviv: Sifriat Poalim, 1947); Hanoch Bartov, *Shesh kenafayim la'ehad* (Tel Aviv: Sifriat Poalim, 1954).

126. *He Walked in the Fields* was reworked into a movie in 1967. The story was changed a little and adapted to the 1967 Israeli reality.

127. Other writers that published novels or novellas between 1947 and 1955 that centered on an encounter between native-born Israelis and Holocaust survivors were Yehudith Hendel and Yigal Mossinsohn. On Holocaust survivors in Israeli literature, see Avner Holtzman, "They Are Different People: Holocaust Survivors as Reflected in the Literature of the Generation of 1948," *Yad Vashem Studies* 30 (2002): 337–368.

128. The novel won a number of prizes and was dramatized and staged at the Habima Theater in May 1948, the first play to be performed after the establishment of the state of Israel.

129. Shamir, *Hu halach ba'sadot*. On Moshe Shamir and this novel, see Dan Miron, "Al sipurei Moshe Shamir," in *Arba panim la'sifrut ha'ivrit bat yameinu*, Dan Miron (Jerusalem: Schocken 1962), 343–374; Michal Arbel, "Gavryut ve'nostalgya: Keri'a be'*Hu halach ba'sadot* shel Moshe Shamir al reka benei doro," *Mada'ei ha'yahadut* 39 (1999): 53–66; Gershon Shaked, "Sofer basar va'dam," in *Ha'siporet ha'ivrit 1880–1980*, 230–268; Yigal Schwartz, *Ha'yadata et ha'aretz sham ha'limon pore'ah, handasat adam u'mahshevet merhav ba'sifrut ha'ivrit ha'hadasha* (Or Yehuda: Kineret and Dvir 2007), 239–366.

130. On *Shesh kenafayim la'ehad*, see Dan Laor, "Bein metzi'ut le'hazon, al hishtakfuta shel ha'aliya ha'hamonit ba'roman ha'isra'eli," in *Olim u ma'abarot 1948–1952*, ed. Mordechai Naor (Jerusalem: Yad Yitzhak Ben-Zvi, 1987), 205–220; Nurit Gertz, *Makhela aheret: nitzolei sho'a, zarim ve'aherim ba'kolno'a u'va'sifrut ha'isra'elim* (Tel Aviv: Am Oved, 2004), 121–137; Avner Holtzman, *Mafteah ha'lev, omanut ha'sipur shel Hanoch Bartov* (Jerusalem: Mosad Bialik, 2015).

131. Bartov, *Shesh kenafayim le'ahad*, 244–245.

132. Ibid., 225.

133. Shamir, *Bemo yadav*, 1. Translated by Joseph Shachter as *With His Own Hands* (Jerusalem: Israel Universities Press, 1970), 1.

134. David Grossman, *Ayen erekh ahava* (Jerusalem: Keter, 1986). Translated by Betsy Rosenberg as *See Under: Love* (New York: Picador, 1989).

135. Mendl Mann, "Der yidisher shrayber in Yisroel," *Di tsukunft* 64 (1959): 287.

6

"YOU NO LONGER NEED TO BE AFRAID TO LOVE YIDDISH"

1965, the Production of Di megile, and the Return of Eastern Europe to Israel's Collective Memory

THE SHOW *DI MEGILE* PREMIERED AT THE HAMAM Theater in Jaffa in June 1965. It was a musical comedy in Yiddish, based on the cycle of poems *Di megile lider*, by Itzik Manger, which was modeled on a traditional *purimshpil* and presented the heroes of the biblical book of Esther as poor Jews in the shtetl.[1] The cast featured the Burstein family—Pesach; his wife, Lillian Lux; and their son, Motele, later known as Mike Burstyn—along with Perele Mager, Zishe Gold, and Bruno Fink, a veteran of Ida Kaminska's troupe in Poland.[2] In the annals of Israeli cultural history, this production of *Di megile* appears as an extraordinary and moving hit.[3] The Israeli press, both at the time and for some years later, saw the staging of the show at the Hamam Theater in Jaffa and its enthusiastic reception as marking a transformation in the attitude toward Yiddish and Yiddish culture in Israeli society. So what was the nature of this change, and was it really caused just by the production of *Di megile*? These are the questions that stand at the heart of this chapter.

In "Whatever Became of Negating Exile," Anita Shapira maintains that over the course of 1960s and 1970s Israel witnessed a slow retreat from the dominant ideology of negating the exile—and particularly from the idea that there was no continuity between the Jews' past in eastern Europe and their present in the state of Israel that had previously been so dominant.[4] But as Shapira herself notes, even before the founding of the state, leaders of the Yishuv had been uneasy with the "negation of exile" and sometimes even expressed affection for the Eastern European Jewish past.[5]

As we have seen, the attitude toward Yiddish among the leaders of Israel as well as public figures was complex and included both rejection on ideological grounds as well as affection. This attitude was typical not only for public figures but also for the public at large, a feeling of longing for the old home that was lost in the catastrophe. However, while various objections to Yiddish and eastern European Jewish culture found open expression, the nostalgic yearning for them remained beneath the surface. This was "a longing for a world hidden in a dream," in the apt phrase of Moshe Bernstein, one of the first Israeli painters to depict Jewish life in eastern Europe.[6]

It was only in the early 1960s, mainly in response to the Eichmann trial, that these deep feelings began to bubble to the surface. In fact, as the eastern European Jewish past resurfaced in popular consciousness, it started to find its place in the Israeli historical memory from which it had previously been excluded. This was not a simple process. For it to happen, the past had to take on a new guise and become, once again in the words of Moshe Bernstein, an "enchanted garden."[7] To put this another way, it had to become a usable past, one whose disappearance could—and should—be regretted. So it was that in the 1960s a romantic image of the shtetl became an emblem of the lost world of eastern European Jewry, of which Yiddish was an integral part. This new nostalgia for Yiddish differed from the complex attitudes of previous years, because it looked back to a culture and language whose power lay in its simplicity and folksiness—in its very lack of depth. Yiddish high culture was largely forgotten, replaced in the public mind by a cocktail of folk aphorisms, colorful expressions, and jokes.

To understand how all this came about, we need to turn our attention to four important issues. We will begin with the decision to stage *Di megile* at the Hamam Theater and ask both why the Israeli theatrical world was open to such an idea and why it caused such enthusiasm in bohemian circles. Next, we will look at Manger himself, particularly the ways in which he was viewed by the Israeli political, cultural, and literary elites. Our question here will deal with the reasons for the special treatment he received. Then we will focus on the Israeli audiences for the *Di megile* production, examining their responses to it and how these changed over time. Finally we will turn to the key question at the heart of the whole discussion: How did the production of *Di megile* fit into the changing patterns of Israeli collective memory of and nostalgia for the Jewish eastern European past that developed during the 1960s?

Venue: "The Warmth of the Shtetl between the Walls of the Hamam"

The Hamam production of *Di megile* was unusual—unlike any Yiddish show that had been staged in the country before. It was a musical comedy based on twenty poems and excerpts of poems drawn from Itzik Manger's cycle *Di megile lider* (The poems of the biblical book of Esther). To give the show a narrative, Haim Hefer, a famous lyricist, wrote a series of texts in rhymed Hebrew that framed the Yiddish poems and so created a bridge between Manger and the Israeli audience. The score was written by Dubi Seltzer—a very popular composer of the day. According to the playbill, "the melodies and segues are based on the motifs and sounds of conventional Jewish music—but the composer's intent is to present this material from the perspective of an Israeli composer."[8] Clearly *Di megile* was meant to be a Yiddish show presented in a Hebrew setting, embedded in the Israeli sensibilities of the 1960s. But what gave the play its extraordinary pull was the venue.

The opening of the Hamam Theater in Jaffa in May 1961 had marked a milestone in the history of Israeli entertainment.[9] The new establishment, which billed itself as "a satirical theater," was the first in a series of new or revamped such venues to open during the decade. It was located in a large, multidomed Turkish bathhouse (*hamam*) from Ottoman days, which had been renovated, redesigned, and even furnished with footstools in an effort to play up the exotic atmosphere; it attracted the upper echelons of Israeli society—among them military officers, senior civil servants, and prominent businessmen. But what really gave the Hamam its special flavor and made it so central to the world of Israeli culture and entertainment were its charismatic owners: Haim Hefer and Dan Ben-Amotz.[10]

Hefer, a songwriter, poet, and writer, and Ben-Amotz, a journalist and satirist, were cultural icons during the state's first two decades—both played a pivotal role in forging the concept of the sabra, the new Israeli Jew, eventually becoming models of the type. As veterans of the Palmach (the elite fighting force of the underground army in prestate Israel),[11] they formed part of a postindependence cultural milieu that had grown out of military experience and would now define Israel's self-image. The Chizbatron, the IDF entertainment troupe that Hefer established in 1948 and commanded until 1950, exerted an influence far beyond the entertainment world, putting its stamp on the very notion of the sabra. The hundreds of songs for which he wrote lyrics reflected—and to a great extent actually created—the Palmach cultural experience and especially its youthful brand of military humor.[12]

Dan Ben-Amotz had begun writing for the Hebrew press in 1945, contributing, among other things, to *Yalkut Ha're'im* (The friends' carry-all)—an annual anthology, published between 1942 and 1946, that opened the door to many of the writers who would later come to be known as the "1948 generation."[13] In 1953, Ben-Amotz joined forces with Hefer to produce *Yalkut Ha'kezavim* (Pack of lies), a highly popular section in *Masa*, the literary periodical of the Ahdut

Ha'avoda–Poalei-Zion party, where they published the stories and jokes of the Palmach.[14] In the mid-1950s, he became a regular on the popular humorous radio program *Shelosha be'sira ahat* (Three men in a boat), soon becoming its star. His renditions of sabra humor in an accent and diction rarely before heard on Israeli state radio became an important force in disseminating the image and the argot of the sabra.[15]

It came as no surprise, then, that the Hamam, managed by Hefer and Ben-Amotz, put on shows that expressed the Israeli-sabra experience and, initially at least, proved a commercial success.[16] Its very first performance in 1961 was *Mishlei arav* (Arabian proverbs), a satire about Jews and Arabs trying to live next door to each other.[17]

After its initial success, the Hamam's special appeal began to fade and some of its productions bombed.[18] According to Hefer, he and his partner were always on the lookout for something new and surprising and decided that they needed to make a splash in order to turn around the theater's declining popularity. In fact, in an interview given years later, he even hinted that this might have been the impetus for putting on *Di megile*.[19]

Staging a Yiddish play with a Diaspora setting in an institution seen as a stronghold of sabra identity could well be seen as a deliberate ploy to attract audiences. Yet, in reality, the decision to produce *Di megile* appears to have emerged from a rather more complex set of social and cultural factors connected with the place of Yiddish and Yiddish culture in Israel.

Neither Hefer nor Ben-Amotz was actually a sabra—a fact they never tried to hide. Hefer was born Haim Feiner in Poland in 1925 and came to Mandatory Palestine with his parents at age eleven.[20] Ben-Amotz, born Musia Tilimzoger in Poland in 1923, was brought to Palestine by Youth Aliyah at the age of fifteen and sent to the Ben Shemen youth village. He changed his name twice, finally settling on Dan Ben-Amotz, and inventing the persona of the quintessential sabra—a model emulated by many.[21] Both men had some fluency in Yiddish: Hefer was a student in the Yiddish Department at the Hebrew University in 1953/1954;[22] Ben-Amotz used to speak Yiddish with the painter Yossl Bergner on a number of occasions.[23]

All this would seem to undercut the idea that the decision to put a Yiddish play on a quintessentially Israeli stage was little more than a publicity stunt. Clearly, there were also deeper factors at work. To understand what these were, we need to look at the production in the broader context of Israeli society and culture in the 1960s, focusing particularly on its attitude toward Yiddish. The best place to start is with the author of *Di megile*, Itzik Manger, and the reception he and his work received in Israel.

Author: "The Poet of the *Khumesh lider* in the Land of the Bible"

Born in Czernowitz in 1901, Itzik Manger was one of the greatest Yiddish poets of his day. He was perceived both as a kind of "folk troubadour," who knew how to touch his audience very deeply, and also as a bold, even revolutionary modernist. He settled in the great Jewish literary center of Warsaw in 1928, where he soon became a kind of Jewish cultural icon.[24]

Itzik Manger based his poetry on Jewish sources, mainly the Bible, but molded them in a new creative, personal way that echoed the culture of his day. In 1935, he published the *Khumesh lider* (The Pentateuch poems), a series of poems that retold stories from the Torah, setting them and their heroes in the Jewish communities of the small towns of eastern Europe—the shtetls. The next year, he came out with another collection of poems called *Di megile lider* (The poems of the book of Esther) in which he gave that biblical story, retold every year during the Purim holiday, the same treatment. This poetic cycle was a compelling—and incredibly popular—combination of humor, folksiness, midrash, and the living tradition of the *purimshpil*. Manger left Poland in 1938, surviving the Holocaust years in England, before moving to New York in 1951.

Neither Manger nor his poetry was unknown in Israel. He was, like many other Yiddish writers, treated with appreciation in the literary columns of the Hebrew press.[25] However, his work had an emotional impact all its own and gave him a special place in Israeli culture.

As we have already noted, almost all of the leading Israeli cultural figures during the first two decades after independence, whether mainstream or bohemian, were Ashkenazi, and most had been born in eastern Europe. Some had arrived in Palestine as young children, others as teenagers or young adults. All of them had some degree of fluency in Yiddish. Under their sabra veneer, whether native or acquired, they were bound, consciously or unconsciously, by delicate, sometimes invisible, yet persistent ties to their parental or childhood culture. Manger's unmatched ability to evoke the world from which they came gave him enormous appeal to these Hebrew-speaking literati, who had ostensibly turned their back on the shtetl and the Yiddish culture that animated it.

Shmuel Bunim, who would direct *Di megile*, wrote in his memoirs of his meeting with Manger in Paris and of his growing fondness for the poet's work, which culminated in the Hamam production.[26] The journalist Uri Keisari, born in Jaffa in 1901 as Shmuel Keizerman, expressed his own bond with the past in moving fashion in an article inspired by the production of *Di megile*. "Every time I come into contact . . . with this world [of Yiddish culture], the grandfather of some long-ago ancestor, or a great-grandmother from some small town in the Kherson district, awakens somewhere deep inside me, and I live, if not the language and actual colors, at least the atmospheric hues of the background, in the soul and the blood."[27]

Manger's poetry was introduced to the Palmach generation by the poet Nathan Alterman.[28] Alterman, who had a great influence on the literature of the 1948 generation, held Manger in high regard; some believe that he was strongly influenced by Manger's work.[29] Tel Aviv bohemians, and especially former members of the Palmach among them, were influence by Alterman, who was their "undisputed leader," in the words of the poet Natan Zach.[30] At the legendary Kassit coffeehouse in Tel Aviv, the regular meeting place of writers, poets, actors, and other bohemians, Alterman's close friend Yosifon (Ze'ev Yoskowitz) would, with undisguised delight, read Manger's poems aloud from a notebook into which he had copied them.[31] "For thirty years he's been walking around with that thick notebook in his pocket," observed Shlomo Shva, the author and Tel Aviv bohemian. "He's the one who sold Manger in this country. The women of the Jezreel Valley still remember how he wooed them with Manger's love poems."[32]

Manger himself visited Kassit: in 1958, during his first visit to Israel, the Tel Aviv literati threw him a party there that was described by the journalist K. Shabtai as "Alterman's orgy of Manger's poetry."[33] Manger also visited Kassit during his second visit to Israel in 1961.[34] Manger was officially invited to come to Israel as part of the celebrations marking the tenth anniversary of the state.[35] He arrived on May 13 and stayed for three months.[36] As befitted an official guest and important Jewish poet, he was greeted with respect by the immigration and customs officers at the airport and invited to meet the president, Yitzhak Ben-Zvi.[37] Other special events organized for him included a press conference at Beit Sokolow, the press club in Tel Aviv, attended by journalists in both Hebrew and Yiddish; a reception given by the editor of the major daily, *Davar*, Haim Shurer, and other journalists; a reception thrown by the Tel Aviv Labor Council; and a gala reception at Ohel Shem Theater in Tel Aviv, open to the public at large.[38]

Of course Manger was not the first or the only Yiddish poet invited to visit Israel. H. Leivick had come in 1950, as the guest of the Histadrut and created a scandal.[39] Like Manger after him, Leivick had been feted at a number of receptions and had enjoyed extensive press coverage that went well beyond notices in the literary pages. Nevertheless, substantial differences marked the reception of these two Yiddish poets. While Leivick had been held up as the greatest Yiddish writer of his generation (some had even compared his place in Jewish literature to that of Bialik in his day),[40] Manger was not really celebrated for his literary significance. In his case the spotlight was on his folksiness.[41]

Even the writer in *Davar* who referred to him as "one of the most important Yiddish poets" went on to explain that Manger's poetry was marked by folk elements that drew on the Jewish world of eastern Europe and dealt with the simple Jews—the laborers, the poor, the tailors, the nomads, the hungry yeshiva students.⁴² In a long article devoted to Manger's visit to the *Davar* editorial offices, Shlomo Shva also called Manger "a great poet" and described his visit as a "festival" of "spiritual rapture," before writing at length about how Manger himself was the son of a tailor and a representative of the simple folk. Shva quoted the editor of *Davar*, Haim Shurer, who had compared Manger to the great painter Marc Chagall and said that if Chagall made the shtetl Jew float above the rooftops, Manger had brought the heroes of the Bible down to earth in the shtetl.⁴³

An unsigned piece in *Maariv* described Manger in the same way.⁴⁴ However, most of the press coverage of Manger's visit presented him simply as a folk poet, the representative of the simple Jews of the shtetl, noting that he had also written about the Holy Land and had now come to see it. Yaakov Zerubavel summed it up in the lead to his piece on Manger in *Masa*: "Itzik Manger, the author of the *Khumesh lider* and the *Megile lider*, has arrived in the land of the Bible and the Palmach."⁴⁵ In other words, Itzik Manger, who came from the world of the shtetl, had now come to visit the land of the sabra.

Manger returned to Israel in 1961 on the occasion of his sixtieth birthday. This visit was organized by a public committee set up especially for the purpose, whose members included Abba Eban (the minister of education), Zalman Shazar (then a member of Knesset and later the president of Israel), Ya'akov Zerubavel (the left-wing political activist), and the poet Avraham Shlonsky, among others.⁴⁶ As before, Manger was received very warmly. He spent most of his time with Yiddish writers and with Hebrew authors who knew Yiddish.⁴⁷ The highlight of this visit was a gala in his honor at Habima, the Israeli national theater, on the Sabbath eve—Friday night, November 10, which was attended by a galaxy of writers and intellectuals.⁴⁸

Manger came back to Israel for a third time in 1963 and once again spent most of the visit with leading Yiddish writers and their close associates.⁴⁹ By then, a gap seems to have opened between the way he was perceived in literary circles and his image among the public at large. The cultural elite seems to have had a genuine familiarity with Manger and his work and, on the whole, viewed him as one of the most important modern Yiddish poets. They identified his unique voice and understood the sophistication that lay behind the apparent simplicity of his work. In the rest of Israeli society, however, the view was profoundly different. For them, Manger was either a representative of the world of Yiddish, distinct and separate from Israeli culture, or a folk poet who spoke for the people—the simple, poor working Jew. If the first of these views goes some way toward explaining the choice of *Di megile* for staging at the Hamam, the second seems to have helped shape the public's response—first its initial indifference and then its enormous enthusiasm.

Reception: "Once a Year You're Allowed to Lose Control and Shout 'Hurrah!'"

In fact, the first performances of *Di megile* at the Hamam in Jaffa were a box-office failure. The official premiere had been preceded by a lukewarm short tour in early June 1965 and an evening symposium at Tzavta Center for Advanced Culture on June 8, with a panel consisting of Mordechai Tsanin, Yehiel Hofer, and the Burstein family.[50]

Nonetheless, the first performances received good reviews. "A burst of pleasure, like a shot of brandy," wrote Nahman Ben-Ami, the *Maariv* theater critic, in his review of June 24. He added, "It should be made clear from the outset that only those who understand Yiddish will enjoy the full delight of the evening." Ben-Ami went on to praise the staging, directing, and acting and concluded, "In the end, this production of *Di megile lider* . . . is not only an evening in the company of an effervescent and brilliant poet, but also an evening of fine theater."[51]

Ben-Ami was not alone. A few days later, Uri Keisari wrote about the show under the headline, "The Prodigy Motele Burstein." The article focused on the young Burstein, who costarred with his parents in "a presentation of life in a Diaspora biblical shtetl, written in the Yiddish language and inspired by a Yiddish poet." Keisari wrote, "He [Motele] is a prodigy of the Israeli theater, and if he happens to be located on the Yiddish side . . . people on the Hebrew side must make the effort to bring him across."[52] Similar praise appeared in *Davar*.[53]

In *Yedioth Aharonoth*, Yeshayahu Ben-Porat wrote that *Di megile* was "first of all an artistic experience . . . due to the remarkable excellence of Manger's poems, . . . the inventive direction of Shmuel Bunim, [so] full of emotion . . . the score, arranged and orchestrated by Dov Seltzer, . . . and, finally, the fine acting by the Burstein family, with son, Motele, in the lead."[54] Like Keisari in *Maariv*, Ben-Porat emphasized that the young Burstein would be well advised to switch to the Hebrew theater.

Ben-Porat was absolutely clear in describing the production as being in Yiddish. "A *Purimshpil* for Yiddish Speakers" read the title of his article, which began with an unambiguous statement: "The saddest thing about the production of Itzik Manger's *Di megile lider* at the Hamam is that our admiration for

"You No Longer Need to Be Afraid to Love Yiddish" | 233

Figure 6.1. A Hebrew poster marking 150 performances of *Di megile* at the Hamam Theater in Jaffa. Courtesy of Mike Burstyn.

it has to be accompanied by a serious reservation: this wonderful production is not intended for the public at large but only for that portion that speaks and understands Yiddish."⁵⁵

So, for all the praise the reviewers in the Hebrew press heaped on the production, they were also unanimous in insisting, in various ways, that the show was meant for Yiddish speakers and not for the general public. In fact, they even suggested that such fine actors and such an excellent play should really find their way to the Hebrew theater. In this way, they effectively tagged *Di megile* as lacking the cultural capital—more specifically, the linguistic capital—that it needed to be part of Israeli culture, to use Bourdieu's terms.[56]

It seems likely that the treatment of *Di megile* by the Israeli press put Hebrew speakers off.[57] The first performances of *Di megile* were a fiasco. The audience never exceeded two dozen or so, and it looked as if the run would have to end before it really got started.[58]

After about a month of treading water, however, there was a sudden and dramatic upsurge in ticket sales. Israeli patrons of the Yiddish theater and, even more, of the Hebrew theater began flocking to *Di megile*. The play went on to record some 250 performances, making it the most successful Yiddish production in Israeli history and an unprecedented box-office success.[59]

And the reason for this astonishing reversal of fortune? All of those associated with *Di megile* who expressed an opinion—most notably Haim Hefer, Shmuel Bunim, and Pesach Burstein—were unanimous in attributing it to the Hebrew press.[60] In particular, they saw a piece by Michael Ohad in the *Ha'aretz* weekend magazine as the game changer.[61]

A cultural authority, Ohad was the editor of the two most important regular radio programs about theater in the 1950s and 1960s (*Ha'masach ole* [Curtain going up] and *Bimot u'vadim* [Stages and fabrics]). He also wrote on culture, art, and theater in the *Davar* weekend supplement and later for *Ha'aretz*. In early July 1965, Ohad published an illustrated article in the *Ha'aretz* weekend magazine, which he called "One King, Two Queens, and Six Actors." He wrote: "The best performance of the end of the season is not being staged in Tel Aviv, but in Jaffa. Not at the Alhambra, but at the Hamam. And the Hamam is not full, because Yiddish-speaking audiences tend to frequent Ohel Shem and the Mugrabi [where simple Yiddish melodramas were performed], while the regular patrons of the Hamam are far from [being interested in] Yiddish.[62] There are grounds for fearing that a theatrical gem that should be a smash success will close prematurely."[63]

"If you're expecting a critical analysis," continued Ohad, "come back next week. Once a year you're allowed to lose control and shout 'hurrah!' There's no drama here, because what Itzik Manger wrote isn't a play but a collection of poems. The scenery is no more than a hint. . . . The language is not Hebrew but Yiddish, which, in the ears of a 'goy' like me, resonates like an Italian salad of Hebrew and German and Serbian. Nevertheless, it is the most magnificent theatrical experience I have had since [Goldoni's] *Servant of Two Masters* at the Piccolo Teatro di Milano."[64]

Ohad also lavished praise on the cast and the production. He began with Lillian Lux, who played both Vashti and Esther: "How many actresses do we have in the Hebrew theater who can go from romance to parody without batting an eye and enchant us in both?"[65] On the score, he wrote: "I am beginning to feel sorry for the wise men of Broadway. Why did they have to commission Jerry Bock to write the songs for *Fiddler on the Roof*, when our own Dubi Seltzer would have done the same work for half the price and twice as well?" He referred to Shmuel Bunim's direction as the "Bunim touch," on the model of the "Lubitsch touch" of the well-known Hollywood director Ernst Lubitsch, and added that even Berthold Brecht could have learned something from *Di megile*.[66] He reserved his highest praise for Motele Burstein, who had, in his words, "a fine voice, dancer's legs, and a phenomenal talent."[67]

If previous reviewers had depicted *Di megile* as lacking linguistic capital, Ohad's rave notice turned that upside down. He dismissed the linguistic issue as irrelevant. He described the show itself as an artistic experience that deserved to be part of Israeli culture and was, in fact, better than every other play running in Israel at the time. His insistence that *Di megile* was a theatrical masterpiece that met the highest universal standards of dramatic art thus shifted it from the province of Yiddish theater to the realm of high culture and gave its cultural capital an enormous boost.

This caused an immediate transformation. From a fringe production that could not draw an audience, *Di megile* became an overnight sensation that attracted the Israeli bon tons, including Prime Minister Levi Eshkol and President Zalman Shazar.[68] The owners of the Hamam decided to invite Manger to Israel and put on a gala performance for him.[69] Manger was received very warmly in all levels of society.[70] The Hebrew press reported widely on his visit,[71] with Raphael Bashan, a journalist well known for his in-depth and intimate style, interviewing him for *Maariv*.[72] All this caused a great deal of excitement, which may, in turn, have increased interest in the play.

Enthusiasm for the show in the press and among the public seemed to feed off of each other in the summer of 1965, but it is very difficult to believe that the play's enthusiastic reception by the Hebrew press, which lasted for only a month or so, would have been enough to keep the theater full for two whole years.[73] When we take into account the fact that 1965 saw the start of a huge recession in Israel, with unemployment reaching 11.4 percent, the level of ticket sales is even harder to understand.[74]

What, then, was *Di megile*'s attraction for Israeli audiences? To answer this question, we must now look at its success in the broader context of Israeli society and culture in the 1960s.

Collective Memory: "You No Longer Have to Be Afraid to Love Yiddish"

Di megile was a unique phenomenon not just because it was staged by one of what Mendel Kohansky has called Israel's "pathbreaking theaters,"[75] but because it was a Yiddish play performed in Yiddish as a part of the Hebrew repertoire. Still, the fact that it was truly a superb show or that it received rave reviews was probably not enough to make it such a smash hit. It must also have struck a chord with the Israeli culture of its day—and it was this that made so many people want to see it.

Biblically based plays with allusions to current affairs and politics were by no means unknown on the Israeli stage of the 1960s.[76] On one level, then, *Di megile*, which was also based on a biblical tale, the story of Esther, must have seemed familiar. On the other hand, it did not refer directly to the contemporary situation in Israel, presenting instead the lost world of the Jews of eastern Europe, or rather a nostalgic image of that world as had already coalesced in the Jewish cultural imagination in the United States and was now coming to Israel.[77]

The Eichmann trial (1961) had brought the Holocaust and the actual east European Jewish past to Israeli public discourse and so paved the way to the new attitudes and new images that began to appear in Israel. (I will discuss these in the next section.) The first expressions of this new development seem to have come directly from Broadway, in the form of the musical *Fiddler on the Roof*, in Hebrew translation, whose Israeli premiere was in June 1965, at the same time as *Di megile* opened.

Fiddler on the Roof was inspired by Sholem Aleichem's Tevye the Dairyman stories. But its creator, Joseph Stein, confessed that when he wrote the book for the musical, he had already forgotten the Yiddish he knew as a child and based the play on English translations of Sholem Aleichem's stories, which he adapted freely.[78] He drew further inspiration from observation of weddings and other celebrations in the Hasidic communities in New York, while the character of Golda, Tevye's wife, was based on his own mother—a "true *Yidishe mame*," in his words.[79] To put it another way, *Fiddler on the Roof* embodied (and to some extent even shaped) the memories of Jewish life in eastern Europe as imagined by Jews in the United States.

Its success on Broadway soon led to a Hebrew version being mounted in Tel Aviv. Although Israeli critics were not wild about the show, audiences flocked to the theater.[80] Six months after it opened at the monumental Alhambra Theater in Jaffa, some two hundred thousand Israelis (out of a population of 2.5 million) had gone to see it.[81]

It would seem, however, that even though *Fiddler on the Roof* was about eastern European Jews, it did not invoke memories of eastern Europe for Israelis. All of the critics who reviewed the musical emphasized how far it deviated from Sholem Aleichem's original.[82] Y. D. Berkowitz, Sholem Aleichem's son-in-law and at the time still his only Hebrew translator, described the play as a travesty of the original, full of "silly jokes."[83] In *Ha'aretz*, Haim Gamzu wrote that "instead of the wisdom of Sholem Aleichem's sad smile, what are served up to the audience are Dan Almagor's jokes."[84] "Is this Sholem Aleichem?" asked Nahman Ben Ami in *Maariv*. "Heaven forbid!"[85]

The magnetic attraction that the show had on Israeli audiences was probably based largely on the show's American cachet and the growing popularity of musicals in Israel in those years. In 1964 Giora Godik, the producer of *Fiddler on the Roof*, had put on a wildly popular production of *My Fair Lady*, and some observers attributed the success of *Fiddler on the Roof* to that of the earlier show.[86] In 1965, the Cameri Theater of Tel Aviv had a great hit with the musical *King Solomon and Shalmai the Shoemaker*, which described the life of King Solomon in a comic way.[87] Godik went on to bring *Oliver!* to Israel in 1966.

But while *Fiddler on the Roof*, which the critics insisted did not represent Sholem Aleichem's writing or his "spirit," was drawing huge audiences with great fanfare, productions of Sholem Aleichem's own plays were returning to the Hebrew theater, though slowly, quietly, and under the media radar.[88]

In late April 1964, the Ohel Theater put on Sholem Aleichem's comedy *Amcha*. At a press conference with the director Peter Frye and the star of the production, Meir Margalit, before the premiere, the latter said, "The most difficult, dangerous, and responsible role for a Hebrew actor is portraying the Exile."[89] The Ohel Theater was facing grave financial difficulties when it decided, with reservations, to put on *Amcha*.[90] The doubts stemmed in part from the fact that the play had already been produced at Habima, and some thought that a revival might fail, but mostly from the fear that the Diaspora theme would not speak to younger audiences in Israel. These anxieties proved to be unfounded, and *Amcha* became both an artistic and box-office success.[91] In late 1964, negotiations to film Abraham Goldfaden's *Two Kuni Lemel* began,[92] and in April 1965, just a few weeks before the premiere of *Di megile*, another Sholem Aleichem play in Hebrew, *It's Hard to Be a Jew*, opened at the Habima.[93]

The idea of staging *Di megile* had little to do with these other productions. As we have seen, it had been in the works for a number of years. The fact that its run overlapped several other productions based on Yiddish literature may have been a coincidence, but the simultaneity might help explain the Israeli public's reception of *Di megile*.

The proliferation of productions based on Yiddish originals did not escape the theater reviewers. As early as June 1965, even before *Di megile* became a hit, Rachel Oren wrote in *Davar*: "The most recent fad in theater is Yiddish plays: Itzik Manger's *Di megile*, *Fiddler on the Roof*, and *It's Hard to Be a Jew*, which was carried over to this season from last and is still a success. Note that three of the four productions on this list are based on plays by Sholem Aleichem. Sholem Aleichem means *laughter, lots of laughter, and a few tears*."[94]

Two things stand out here. The first is her characterization of Sholem Aleichem, to which we will return below. The second is that she lumped together all of these shows, including *Fiddler on the Roof*, as "Yiddish plays"—a sign of her feeling that the Jewish world of eastern Europe was beginning to make its presence felt on the Israeli stage. In fact, the list of these shows continued to grow over the next few years: *Itzik Wittenberg* (The ghetto bird), by the Yiddish writer Chava Rosenfarb, and Sholem Aleichem's *The Golddiggers* were staged at Habima in 1966 and 1968 respectively,[95] while the Haifa Municipal Theater put on a production of Sholem Aleichem's *Menakhem Mendl* in 1966.[96]

But among Israeli Hebrew speakers in 1965, very few drew a connection between the growing number of dramatic productions derived from Yiddish sources and a change in the Israeli attitude toward the eastern European Jewish past. Even the author of the article in *Davar* saw the spate of plays as just a fad, which she associated with changing fashions in the theatrical world. The other newspapers ignored the phenomenon altogether.

It was really only after the 1967 war and in the wake of another theatrical production, not in Yiddish but strongly connected to the Jewish east European past, that the Israeli Jews' eastern European—and so, Yiddish—heritage really became an issue in the consciousness of Hebrew-speaking Israelis.

On October 16, 1968, *There Was a Pious Man* premiered at the Bimot Theater and quickly became a huge success.[97] Young actors in blue jeans recounted Hasidic tales in contemporary Israeli Hebrew and sang Hasidic songs to the accompaniment of a guitar. The text had been adapted and edited by Dan Almagor. Yossi Yizre'eli had directed the play, and the musical director was Yohanan Zarai, a songwriter who composed for army entertainment troupes and was at the height of his popularity in the 1960s. *There Was a Pious Man* proved to be an even bigger hit than *Di megile*. More than a quarter million people attended its six hundred performances in Israel.

Contemporaries—and following them, scholars—viewed the play's great success as a reflection of the change in how secular Israelis related to Judaism in the wake of the Six-Day War. However, neither contemporaries nor scholars found it easy to put their finger on what that Judaism precisely was. Dan Urian, a scholar of Israeli theater, used the words "tradition" and "Yidishkeyt," which he defined as "an attitude towards social and cultural milieus that were associated with Jewish family life in the Diaspora."[98] The law professor and public intellectual Amnon Rubinstein was more explicit: "The rejection of the Diaspora was replaced ... by nostalgia for a world that had been destroyed.... The shtetl took on a new and positive meaning in the mind of Israelis."[99]

So, although they had obvious differences, there were enough similarities between *There Was a Pious Man* and *Di megile* to show the profound changes in the ways Israeli society related to eastern European Jewish culture and, ipso facto, to Yiddish. Whereas *Di megile* was essentially an original Yiddish text by Manger, even though it was given a Hebrew-language setting, *There Was a Pious Man* was originally written in contemporary Israeli Hebrew and reworked Hasidic tales and other sources (taken from the works of Martin Buber, Eliezer Steinman, Micha Josef Berdyczewski, the stories of Rabbi Nahman of Braslav, and others) into lyrics, written mainly by Dan Almagor. Although reviewers were not always happy with the choice of Hasidic texts or their treatment, the audiences filled the halls.[100]

Dan Urian, who wrote a book on the Jewish nature of Israeli theater and devoted an entire chapter to this play, saw it as "Judaism for the secular." He quoted theater critics who explained the play's reception by pointing to the public's "fervent nostalgia" for its lost past.[101] But what was the significance of that lost past? Was it really a substitute for religion? The common thematic thread running through all the lyrics of the show had to do with the shtetl, the villages, simple and pious Jews, Hasidic rebbes, and klezmers.[102]

There Was a Pious Man was not, then, just one more play about the Jewish past in eastern Europe. It highlighted the primal symbols of eastern European Jewish life, those that became the building blocks of the Israeli memory of that world. As Yohanan Zarai wrote in 1968, the show offered "Hasidic melodies ... that survived among a handful of Holocaust survivors and that we are singing, here and now, to pass them on to future coming generations as a wonderful legacy."[103] Even if *There Was a Pious Man* owed its extraordinary success, as scholars claim, to the exhilaration that followed the Six-Day War, it was also the high point of the process of the construction of a popular memory of eastern European Jewish life in Israel that had begun years previously.[104] Starting perhaps with the Eichmann trial, this process found its way into the Israeli theater around 1964, exploded into public view with the production of *Di megile*, and reached its high point after 1967 with *There Was a Pious Man*.

Writing about that play in *Davar*, under the headline "The Second Coming of the Baal Shem Tov," the Holocaust survivor and journalist Ruth Bondi tied all of these strands together, if in an acerbic vein:

> Slowly but surely, the Exile has returned from its exile to the bosom of those who dwell in Zion. Only ten years ago the young generation that grew up here thought of Yiddish as the language of exile, the language of the pitiable residents of the shtetl, of peddlers, of fishmongers, of beggars, of the Rebbe's disciples gesticulating while they talked. Today, however, you no longer have to be afraid to love Yiddish. . . . Today it detracts not a whit from your sabra identity

if you feel a fondness for Yiddish and what it represents: seven hundred years of Eastern European Jewish culture, including the Rabbi's songs and Hasidic stories.[105]

It would seem that alongside the ideology of the rejection of the Diaspora, which had dominated Israeli culture in the 1950s, there had also existed an underground current of nostalgia for the eastern European past. In the first half of the 1960s, thanks to the passage of time—but also in the wake of the Eichmann trial—this current began to bubble to the surface. A new and more acceptable form of memory was therefore needed—a usable past that could legitimize this nostalgia for the lost world of eastern Europe. *Di megile* would not only play a decisive role in its formation but also reap its rewards.

Nostalgia and the Restoration of Historical Continuity: "The Essence of the Symbolic Experience"

"Nostalgia," as Svetlana Boym has explained, "is the longing for a home that no longer exists—a sentiment of loss and displacement, but is also a romance with one's own fantasy."[106]

As we have seen in previous chapters, Ben-Gurion and the other leaders of the Yishuv and later of the infant state wanted to sever the continuous thread of the Jewish historical narrative and to erase the east European past. They aimed to create the image of the New Jew of the land of Israel as heroic, active, and in stark contrast to the old, suffering, and persecuted Jew of the Diaspora. "The remote past, when we lived in our land, is closer to me than the immediate past, because our life in exile was defective," wrote David Ben-Gurion in his diary in 1950, referring to the eastern European Diaspora. [107]

For many Israelis of the 1950s and 1960s, however, that "immediate past" was not a theoretical link in an abstract historical memory passed down from generation to generation; it was their own lives or those of their close relatives. This made it impossible for them to bracket out that chapter of Jewish history. It could be depicted in a negative light or rejected, in the hope that people would ignore or even repress it, but it had been something real and refused to go away. In order for that past to rise to the surface and reassert its place in the historical sequence, it had to be reinvented.

Examining a similar process in the development of the American Jewish imagination as early as the 1950s, Steven Zipperstein argued: "The European catastrophe, the search for identity and place in post-war America, the geographical dispersion of a previously urban American Jewry in the 1950s and beyond—all these had their impact on the perception of East European Jewish past that [makes it] . . . an American story, not a Russian [one]."[108] In Israel, too, the eastern European Jewish past had to be shown in a new way, given an image that could be part of the Israeli collective memory or, to paraphrase Zipperstein, to be written as "an Israeli story."

When the Eichmann trial opened in Jerusalem in April 1961, it marked, as Tom Segev has put it, "the beginning of a dramatic shift in the way Israelis related to the Holocaust. The terrifying stories that broke out from the depths of silence brought about a process of identification with the suffering of the victims and the survivors."[109] The Jewish past of eastern Europe, long held back and limited to the private sphere, or at most to the closed public sphere of eastern European immigrants—chiefly in meetings of Jews from specific cities and memorial services for communities that had been annihilated, which in practice constituted another type of private space—to overflow into the public domain.[110]

By then, almost two decades—nearly a generation—had passed since the Holocaust. The image of the past that now crystallized reworked elements of history and memory, turning them into a usable past for the present—"into a home that no longer exists," in Boym's words. It was what she called, "a reflective nostalgia"—which could be both ironic and humorous.[111]

The shtetl, or at least the image of the shtetl, provided excellent material. This was because, even before the Holocaust, Jewish writers, particularly those working in Yiddish, had treated it at some length. As Dan Miron and David Roskies[112] have shown, these authors often wrote about their imaginary return to the shtetl and, in so doing, created a satirical, mythical, nostalgic, and sentimental picture of these small towns that had almost nothing in common with the reality of Jewish life.[113] These images from Yiddish literature, both ironic and humorous, offered ideal material for creating a usable past that enabled a return the eastern European experience into the Israeli historical narrative in the early 1960s.

If we take another look at the many articles about *Di megile* that appeared in the Hebrew press, we find that, alongside the fulsome praise for the quality of the production, there are also references to its function as a sort of "realm of memory," to employ Pierre Nora's term—a place in which the shtetl, the preeminent symbol of the eastern European past, could be reborn.[114]

"The Warmth of the Shtetl between the Walls of the Hamam" was the title of the review in *LaMerhav*. It read: "The Hamam is emptying out now. Until a few minutes ago it was buzzing with Israelis who came to enjoy the richness of the Yiddish language, which they know only from talking with their grandparents and sometimes with their parents.... When they left [the theater] they took with them a full measure of *heymishkeyt*, that warm homelike atmosphere that made the Eastern European shtetl so special."[115] The *Herut* reviewer wrote that even people who could not understand Yiddish and so could not really enjoy the text should not miss the experience, in which "the shtetl is reborn in a *purimshpil*."[116]

The most focused reaction, however, which best homed in on the heart of the matter, was provided by the communist daily *Kol Ha'am*:

> A strange match ... the Yiddish language, Jewish melodies, the world of the shtetl under the oriental dome of the Hamam in Jaffa. A moving match of a past that was wiped out with such brutality with a present *that is searching for road signs to the treasures of the past*. The folk characters played by the *Purimshpil* actors, ... sons and daughters of common Jews, are walking about, reincarnated on the stage of a theater that is the Israeli present through and through. Jewish laughter, at once serious and witty, ... flows in abundance ... Go to the Hamam, and enjoy ... the essence of a symbolic experience.

"An Enjoyably Symbolic Experience" was also the title of the review, which seems to have captured all that was best about *Di megile* and the reason for its success.[117]

Di megile *in Retrospect: "A Wreath We Laid on the Tomb of Yiddish?"*

In December 1987, twenty-two years after the publication of his *Ha'aretz* article that held up *Di megile* as a masterpiece of the modern stage, Michael Ohad returned to the play. This time he did so in the context of a larger discussion of the fate of Yiddish, including his own attitude toward it: "My affair with Yiddish was long and unexpected. In my childhood I ran away from that Diaspora language. Yiddish struck me as a caricature of German, spiced with grotesque Hebrew—but it never let me go. *Mayn yidene* is what my father said in the grocery store when he spoke about my mother. The Yiddish plays that I saw, all of those ludicrous operettas, only made my revulsion greater.... I would have continued to despise Yiddish had I not found myself at a performance of Itzik Manger's *Di megile* at the Hamam in Jaffa.[118]

For Ohad, whose writing followed clear artistic criteria, *Di megile* was a watershed. It gave him the ultimate proof that a Yiddish play could meet the highest standards. In its wake, he claimed, his attitude toward Yiddish changed from scorn to esteem. But a closer look at his reconstruction of his encounter with *Di megile* in 1965 lays bare another layer of his attitude toward Yiddish, one that had remained hidden till then, perhaps even from himself: "In school, I was brought up on the shtetl of 'Brawny Aryeh' [Bialik's story] ... and was bored to death. Now, though, [the shtetl] took real shape. Paysachke Burstein put on the red nose of a drunk, and suddenly we had King Ahasuerus, enchanted by a starry night, deciding that 'it's *a mekhaye* to be alive!' ...

Laughter and tears, a tailors' rebellion, and the joy of a heart leap when Queen Esther emptied a chamber pot on the head of the wicked Haman."[119]

So even Michael Ohad, the paladin of high culture, who pursued the most rarified forms of art, turned out to be in need of a usable past compatible with his own values—and he found it in *Di megile*. "To its great surprise, the Israeli audience," he wrote, "discovered that the Yiddish theater it despised could produce sweet fruit."[120]

But the sweet fruit that appealed to Ohad's palate was not to the taste of the regular patrons of Yiddish theater. When *Di megile*'s success led to an attempt to found a national Yiddish theater, it failed. "The Yiddish-speaking public," Ohad wrote bitterly, "voted with its feet. It preferred [the sentimental song] *Mayn shtetele Belz*. Our calculations were wrong. *Di megile* was not the first swallow that heralded Yiddish's revival. *Di megile* was the wreath we laid on its grave."[121]

If the hope was that *Di megile* would pave the way for the Israeli public to become consumers of high Yiddish culture, it was indeed disappointed. The production of *Di megile* did not lead to a flowering of Yiddish culture in Israel. All that changed was the image of this culture and language in Israeli society.

No longer rejected, as Ohad wrote, Yiddish was soon converted into an important element of the usable past needed by a large section of the Israeli public. However, *Di megile* also blazed the way for Yiddish culture to penetrate the public consciousness by emphasizing its folksy side. As a result, many Israelis came to perceive Yiddish as the representative of a positive, attractive, and happy folk culture, accessible to all, at once amusing and moving—"laughter and tears," as Ohad wrote of *Di megile* in 1987. In fact, laughter and tears are the two words that best characterize the Israeli attitude toward Yiddish since the 1960s.

In May 1966, after more than five years of effort, Beit Sholem Aleichem, an institution intended to house the archives of the great Yiddish writer and to encourage public interest in him and his work, opened in Tel Aviv. At the dedication ceremony, the president of Israel, Zalman Shazar, officially proclaimed that year, the fiftieth anniversary of Sholem Aleichem's death, as "Sholem Aleichem Year." All the academics and literary figures who took part in the ceremony solemnly noted that Sholem Aleichem's work was a cornerstone of Jewish literature.[122] But the Hebrew press saw things differently. In a sympathetic and moving article, Uri Keisari referred to Sholem Aleichem as "the humorist of Jewish tears" and to his work as "the Jewish challah dough that was kneaded with Jewish tears."[123]

The Hebrew-speaking Israelis' view of Yiddish as a comic—even a ridiculous—language does not date just to the 1960s. It had been around for years before that. Dan Miron has noted how making fun of Yiddish had been part of the construction of a barrier between the Yiddish-speaking "others and the new Jewish society that evolved in the prestate Israel."[124] Starting in the mid-1960s, however, alongside this mockery arrived a more sympathetic laughter of affectionate nostalgia. Nonetheless, this new image of Yiddish came largely at the expense of its high culture. Sholem Aleichem, one of the greatest writers the Jewish people had ever known, came to be viewed in Israel as a simple humorist rather than the literary virtuoso he was.[125]

At first sight, then, *Di megile* let Yiddish out of the closet and quite literally put it center stage in Israeli society and culture. In practice, however, what it did was to help create new perceptions of the language and culture with which the public at large felt more at home.

Having said that, the show at the Hamam was not entirely without influence. Though Israel's cultural elite tended to view the production as a one-time artistic achievement, and not necessarily a reflection of Yiddish culture, its attitude began to shift.[126] It was true that after *Di megile*, Yiddish culture, especially high culture, still had to fight for its survival. But with the changing circumstances, the Israeli establishment sometimes even tried to help it along.

Notes

1. *Di megile* playbill, Israel Center for the Documentation of the Performing Arts. For the date of the first performance, see, inter alia, the listing for it in *Davar*, June 13, 1965.

2. Tamar Avidar, "Ha'megila shel Itzik," *Maariv*, June 4, 1965. See also the playbill.

3. Ora Achimeir and Haim Be'er, *Me'a shenot tarbut 1900-2000: ha'yetzira ha'ivrit be'Eretz Israel* (Tel Aviv: Miskal, 2000), 257.

4. Shapira, "Whatever Became of Negating Exile?"

5. Shapira notes that Berl Katznelson and Itzhak Tabenkin, each in his own way, had a soft spot for eastern European Jewry and its various elements. Shapira, "Whatever Became of Negating Exile?"

6. Moshe Bernstein, *Balada al ha'ayara* (Ramat Gan: Unknown publisher, 1966). On Bernstein's place in the history of Israeli art, see Gideon Ofrat, *Ha'shiva el ha'shtetl, ha'yahadut ke'dimui ba'omanut be'Israel* (Jerusalem: Mossad Bialik, 2011), 114–119.

7. Bernstein, quoted by Ofrat, *Ha'shiva el ha'shtetl*, 116.

8. *Di megile* playbill, n.p.

9. Ruth Bondi, "Ha'hamam tamam," *Davar*, May 26, 1961.

10. "In the presence of a large audience of celebrities, Messers Ben-Amotz and Hefer's outrageous Hamam opened this week in a modest ceremony," wrote Ruth Bondi in her satirical column in *Davar*. "Yihye tov," *Davar*, May 26, 1961. On the Hamam, see Mendel Kohansky, *The Hebrew Theater: Its First Fifty Years* (New York: Ktav, 1969), 251–256. On the special atmosphere of the Hamam, see Shmuel Bunim, *Kan Bunim* (Tel Aviv: Dvir, 1994), 69.

11. Ben-Amotz had served in its naval wing, the Palyam.

12. Almog, *The Sabra*, 11.

13. Ben-Amotz's first book, the story collection *Arba'a ve'arba'a* [Four and four] (Tel Aviv: Sifriat Poalim, 1950), included one story that would later appear in the classic collection *Dor ba'aretz*, ed. Azriel Uchmani, Shlomo Tanai, and Moshe Shamir (Merhavya: Sifriat Poalim, 1958). See Reuven Kritz, *Erev rav: al sefarim, sofrim ve'sugyot sifrut* (Tel Aviv: Pura, 1990), 101.

14. In 1956 the best of that material was collected in a book that became a best seller and served as the model for other humorists and influenced the development of Israeli slang.

15. Almog, *The Sabra*, 12–13.

16. Interview with Haim Hefer, April 7, 2005.

17. Sh. Kalay, "Bimot u'pargod," *Herut*, May 22, 1961. Bunim, *Kan Bunim*, 69–74.

18. Shmuel Bunim hints at problems in the management in the Hamam (Bunim, *Kan Bunim*, 76). Mendel Kohansky notes that the satire presented by the Hamam had a false ring to it, because the shows criticized the establishment, whose leaders were sitting in the audience (Kohansky, *Hebrew Theater*, 252). Amnon Dankner writes bluntly in the biography of Dan Ben-Amotz that two plays that aroused great hopes were stinging failures, and the relations between the two owners also became rocky. Amnon Dankner, *Dan Ben Amotz: biografya* (Jerusalem: Keter, 1992), 223.

19. Interview with Haim Hefer, April 7, 2005.

20. Ibid. See also "Sihot *Maariv*, ha'kena'ani mi'Sosnowiec," *Maariv*, July 27, 1965. The short report brings excerpts from Hefer's remarks at a party in honor of Manger, during which he said that he was born in Sosnowiec in Poland.

21. Interview with Dan Ben-Amotz, *HaOlam Haze*, April 24, 1968. Almog, *The Sabra*, 12–13.

22. Interview with Haim Hefer.

23. Dankner, *Dan Ben Amotz*, 230.

24. For a detailed biography of Manger, see Efrat Gal-Ed, *Niemandssprache—Itzik Manger—ein europaischer Dichter* (Berlin: Judischer Verlag im Surhrkamp Verlag, 2016).

25. Yitzhak Paner, "Itzik Manger, li'melot lo hamishim," *Davar*, June 15, 1951; Shimon Gan-Gans, "Im Itzik Manger," *Davar*, November 19, 1954.

26. Bunim, *Kan Bunim*.

27. Uri Keisari, "Motele Burstein, ha'ilui" *Maariv*, June 28, 1965.

28. Interview with Haim Hefer, April 7, 2005.

29. On Alterman's influence on the 1948 generation, see Chaya Shaham, *Hedim shel nigun, shirat dor ha'palmach ve'havurat Likrat be'zika le'shirat Alterman* (Tel Aviv: Hakibbutz Hameuchad, 1997). On Manger's influence on Alterman: some believe that the title of Alterman's first book, *Kochavim ba'hutz* (Stars outside), came directly from Manger's debut volume, *Shtern oyfn dakh* (Stars on the roof). Ben-Ami Feingold maintains that Alterman's play *Ester Ha'malka* (Queen Esther) was influenced by the *Megile lider*. See Ben-Ami Feingold, "Shenot ha'shishim ba'te'atron ha'isra'eli," *He'asor ha'sheni*, ed. Zvi Zameret and Hanna Yablonka (Jerusalem: Yad Ben-Zvi, 2000), 252. Also, Haim Hefer said in a personal interview, "A hidden thread ran from Alterman to Manger." Interview with Haim Hefer, April 7, 2005.

30. Natan Zach, *Mi'shana le'shana ze, pirkei biyografya sifrutit u'muvaot* (Tel Aviv: Hakibbutz Hameuchad, 2009), 32. Zach also described Alterman as "the most charismatic man I have ever met." Zach, *Mi'shana le'shana ze*, 39.

31. Kassit, located at the center of the "West Bank" of Dizengoff Street in Tel Aviv, was the bastion of the country's bohemians from the mid-1940s through the 1970s. For a description of the atmosphere in Kassit and Alterman's status there, see Zach *Mi'shana le'shana*, 35–36.

Ze'ev (Yoskowitz) Yosifon established the Transit Camp Theater, which later developed into Omanut La'am, a nonprofit that works to disseminate Israeli art and culture in immigrant communities and among the underprivileged. He was on intimate terms with the bohemian world and the regulars at Kassit. In a dedication to Yosifon, dating from September 1946, Alterman wrote to his "close friend and companion . . . from me, who never stops being fond of him" (*Yedioth Genazim* 74 [Nisan 1971]).

32. Shlomo Shva, "Devarim bi'zechut Vashti," *Davar*, May 27, 1958.
33. K. Shabtai, "Mitoch siha im meshorer" *Davar*, May 3, 1958.
34. "Im Manger be'Kassit," *Davar*, September 29, 1961.
35. "Itzik Manger ba'aretz," *Davar*, May 14, 1958.
36. "Sihot ba'pa'am ha'shenya," *Maariv*, May 14, 1958; "Itzik Manger nifrad mi'kora'av," *Davar*, August 1, 1958 (the article quotes from a farewell note written by Manger in July 1958).
37. Shlomo Shva, "Devarim bi'zechut Vashti," *Davar*, May 27, 1958.
38. Among the participants in the Beit Sokolow party were Yaakov Zerubavel and Mordechai Halamish. "Itzik Manger oreah itona'ei Tel Aviv," *Davar*, May 21, 1958; Shlomo Shva, "Devarim bi'zechut Vashti," *Davar*, May 27, 1958; "Kabalat panim le'Itzik Manger," *Davar*, June 1, 1958; "Sihot," *Maariv*, May 28, 1958.
39. Rachel Rojanski, "Ta'aru lachem et Rabi Nahman mi'Breslav hoger herev: bikuro shel H. Leivick be'Israel, 1950," *Ha'aretz*, April 19, 2010.
40. Novershtern, *Kesem ha'dimdumim*, 214.
41. "Itzik Manger ba'aretz," *Davar*, May 14, 1958.
42. Ibid.
43. Shlomo Shva, "Devarim bi'zechut Vashti," *Davar*, May 27, 1968.
44. "Meshorer be'artzo," *Maariv*, May 16, 1958.
45. Yaakov Zerubavel, "Itzik Manger be'Israel," *Massa*, May 30, 1958.
46. "Erev Manger be'Habima," *Davar*, November 8, 1961; "Erev hagigi le'Itzik Manger," *Davar*, November 12, 1961.
47. Notices in *Maariv*, November 6 and 7, 1961.
48. Including Professor Dov Sadan of the Yiddish Department at the Hebrew University, the Yiddish writer Yehiel Hoffer, the Hebrew poet Avraham Shlonsky, the Labor Zionist leader and writer Yaakov Zerubavel, and other prominent figures with links to Yiddish literature. "Erev hagigi le'Itzik Manger," *Davar*, November 12, 1961; [untitled], *Maariv*, November 12, 1961. A similar event, with the participation of Leah Goldberg, took place in Jerusalem on November 23. "Neshef Manger bi'Yerushalayim," *Maariv*, November 22, 1961.
49. "Kabalat panim la'meshorer Itzik Manger," *Davar*, August 19, 1963.
50. Tamar Avidar, "Ha'megila shel Itzik Manger," *Maariv*, June 4, 1965; notice in *Maariv*, June 8, 1965.
51. Nahman Ben-Ami, "Tzehok mi'tahat la'dema," *Maariv*, June 24, 1965, 12.
52. Keisari, "Motele Burstein, ha'ilui," *Maariv*, June 24, 1965.
53. "Yidish ve'Ivrit mi'tahat la'hupa," *Davar*, June 18, 1965.
54. I. B. F., "Purimshpil le'dovrei Yiddish," *Yedioth Aharonoth*, July 12, 1965.
55. Ibid.
56. A key component of Israeli cultural capital was what Bourdieu calls linguistic capital, which produces immediate profit as soon at its owners begin to speak, no matter the content of what they are saying, and which serves as a central element in determining the relations of linguistic control. Pierre Bourdieu, *Sociology in Question*, trans. Richard Nice (London: Sage, 1993), 80.

57. Shmuel Bunim in his memoirs conjectured that the depiction of the show as a Hebrew-Yiddish hybrid played a part in the low audience turnout. Bunim, *Kan Bunim*, 81.

58. Interview with Haim Hefer, April 2005.

59. Bunim, *Kan Bunim*, 82.

60. Interview with Haim Hefer, April 2005; Bunim, *Kan Bunim*, 81; Burstein, *Geshpilt a lebn*, 348.

61. Rafi Ilan writes the Hefer told him that it was the theater critic Haim Gamzu who made the difference. Rafi Ilan, "Nes ha'megila, 1965: hatzagat mofet be'Yidish be'te'atron ha'hamam be'Yafo," *Davka* 4 (2008): 46. In our interview, Hefer did mention Ohad, and his responsibility was also hinted at by Amnon Dankner in his biography of Dan Ben-Amotz. Dankner, *Dan Ben Amotz*, 242.

62. Most stagings of Yiddish plays were at Ohel Shem on Balfour Street in Tel Aviv. A few were at the Mugrabi Cinema on the corner of Allenby and Ben Yehuda Streets in Tel Aviv. There were occasional performances in the garden of the ZOA House on Iben Gabirol Street and also at an open-air theater in Jaffa. See Yablokoff, *Arum der velt*, 650–651.

63. Michael Ohad, "Melech ehad, malkot shetayim ve'sahkanim shisha," *Ha'aretz*, weekend supplement, July 2, 1965, 16–17.

64. Ibid., 16.

65. Ibid., 16.

66. Ibid., 17.

67. Ibid., 17.

68. *Maariv*, August 1, 1965; "Sihot Maariv," *Maariv*, August 18, 1965.

69. "Itzik Manger be'hatzagat ha'megila," *Maariv*, July 26, 1965.

70. "Higi'a Itzik Manger," *Maariv*, July 23, 1965.

71. For example, "Shirei ha'megila shel Itzik Manger—nosah Purimshpil," *Davar*, July 30, 1965.

72. "Ha'meshorer she'ba min ha'kahol: Raphael Bashan mesoheah im Itzik Manger," *Maariv*, July 30, 1965.

73. According to Shmuel Bunim's memoirs, there were 250 performances. To judge by the listings in the daily press, it ran for about two years. See, for example, *Maariv*, December 8 and 15, 1967. For the cast's tour abroad, see *Maariv*, February 9, 1966.

74. Nahum Gross, "Kalkalat Israel," in *Ha'asor hasheni 1958–1968*, ed. Zvi Zameret and Hanna Yablonka (Jerusalem: Yad Ben Zvi, 2000), 43–45.

75. Kohansky, *Ha'te'atron ha'ivri* (Jerusalem: Weidenfeld and Nicolson, 1974), 202. This paragraph appears in the Hebrew version only.

76. For a list of such plays, see Ben-Ami Feingold, "Shenot ha'shishim ba'te'atron ha'Israeli," in *He'asor ha'sheni*, ed. Zvi Zameret and Hanna Yablonka (Jerusalem: Yad Ben-Zvi, 2000), 244–245.

77. Steven J. Zipperstein, *Imagining Russian Jewry: Memory, History, Identity* (Seattle: University of Washington Press, 1999), 20.

78. Raphael Bashan, "Monolog shel Yosef Stein, mehaber ha'tamlil shel 'Kanar al ha'gag'," *Maariv*, May 21, 1965.

79. Ibid.

80. In their advertisements, the producers included snippets from reviews—naturally, only those that were favorable. This makes it hard to ignore how tepid they actually were. *Maariv* praised the size of the cast. Boaz Evron in *Yedioth Aharonoth* waxed enthusiastic about the outstanding choreography, imported from the United States. Haim Gamzu

in *Ha'aretz* noted that Bomba Zur as Tevye was blessed with a sense of humor. Yeshayahu Ben-Porat in *La'isha*, Ben-Ami Feingold in *HaBoker*, and Nahman Ben-Ami in *Maariv* all concentrated on the dancing. See the advertisements for the play, in *Davar*, June 24, 1965, and elsewhere.

81. "Yoter mi'ma'ataim elef ish ra'u et 'Kanar al ha'gag'," *Davar*, November 29, 1965.
82. "Anatevka, Broadway, Yafo," *Davar*, June 11, 1965.
83. "Ben ha'shemonim" *Davar*, November 26, 1965.
84. *Ha'aretz*, June 8, 1965.
85. Nahman Ben-Ami, "Hatzagat ha'mahazemer 'Kanar al ha'gag' be'te'atron Godik," *Maariv*, June 9, 1965.
86. See note 81 above.
87. The playwright was Sammy Gronemann, who lived in Tel Aviv and wrote in German, and Nathan Alterman translated it to beautiful Hebrew. Kohansky, *Ha'te'atron ha'ivri*, 185.
88. See note 85 above.
89. "*Amcha* le'Sholem Aleichem yu'ale al yedei ha'Ohel be 26 be'April," *Davar*, April 14, 1964.
90. Kohansky, *Ha'te'atron ha'ivri*, 187.
91. Talila Ben-Zakai, "*Amcha* higi'a le'hatzagat ha'me'a," *Maariv*, November 15, 1964.
92. Ibid.
93. Kohansky, *Ha'te'atron ha'ivri*, 249; Talila Ben-Zakai, "Masach u'masecha," *Davar*, June 23, 1965.
94. Rachel Oren, "Kashe li'hyot yehudi," *Davar*, July 2, 1965, emphasis added.
95. Habima online archives: http://habima.millenium.org.il/show_item.asp?levelId=64382&itemId=2818; http://habima.millenium.org.il/show_item.asp?levelId=64382&itemId=4599.
96. Kohansky, *Ha'te'atron ha'ivri*, 265.
97. The Bimot Theater, managed by Yaakov Agmon, made its debut in the Israeli theatrical world in 1966 with a production of Murray Schisgal's *Luv*; see Kohansky, *Ha'te'atron ha'ivri*, 216.
98. Dan Urian, *Yahaduto shel ha'te'atron ha'Israeli: pirkei mehkar* (Tel Aviv: Hakibbutz Hamehuchad, 1998), 38, 123n3.
99. Amnon Rubinstein, *The Zionist Dream Revisited: From Herzl to Gush Emunim and Back* (New York: Schocken, 1984), 69–70.
100. Urian, *Yahaduto*, 125n18.
101. Ibid., 47; Emil Feuerstein, "'Ish hasid haya be'Habima," *HaTzofe*, October 18, 1968.
102. All of the songs can be found on the Hebrew Nostalgia website: http://www.nostalgia.org.il/album_details.asp?id=14.
103. Ibid.
104. See Urian, *Yahaduto*; Rubinstein, *Zionist Dream*.
105. Ruth Bondi, "Hitgaluto ha'shenya shel ha'Besht," *Davar*, October 11, 1968.
106. Boym, *Future of Nostalgia*, xiii.
107. Rachel Rojanski, "Ha'omnam 'safa zara ve'tzoremet'? Li'she'elat yahaso shel Ben-Gurion le'Yidish aharei ha'sho'a," *Iyunim bi'tekumat Israel* 15 (2005): 466.
108. Zipperstein, *Imagining Russian Jewry*, 20.
109. Tom Segev, *The Seventh Million: The Israelis and the Holocaust* (New York: Henry Holt, 1991), 361.
110. Tom Segev has written about the meetings of those born in various cities in (mostly) Poland and memorials for towns that were wiped out during the Holocaust, as a space that

was based on the presence of the eastern European past; see Segev, *Seventh Million*, 458–462. Alongside the dominant convention of the survivors' silence about the horrors of the Holocaust, there is abundant evidence that, at home, many of those from eastern Europe cherished their memories of the past—not of the Holocaust, of course, but of the Jewish life that had preceded it. In many families, parents told their children stories of their own parents' homes, recollections of their childhood and youth, and memories of their grandparents. See Hanna Yablonka, *Medinat Israel neged Adolf Eichman* (Tel Aviv: Miskal, 2001), 200–201.

111. Boym defines two types of nostalgia: restorative and reflective. The second type cherishes shard fragments of memory and temporalized space. Boym, *Future of Nostalgia*, 49.

112. Dan Miron, "The Literary Image of the Shtetl," in *The Image of the Shtetl and Other Studies of Modern Jewish Literary Imagination* (Syracuse, NY: Syracuse University Press, 2000), 1–48; David G. Roskies, *The Jewish Search for a Usable Past* (Bloomington: Indiana University Press, 1999), 41–66.

113. Roskies, *The Jewish Search*, 49.

114. Nora, *Realms of Memory*, 1–20.

115. Zviya, "Hamimut ha'ayara bein kotlei ha'Hamam," *Lamerhav*, July 21, 1965.

116. Sara Frankel, "Ha'ayara kama li'tehiya be'purimshpil'," *Herut*, July 23, 1965.

117. Peter, "Havaya simlit mehana," *Kol Ha'am*, July 23, 1965, emphasis added.

118. Michael Ohad, "Ha'bat ha'ovedet," *Ha'aretz*, December 25, 1987.

119. Ibid.

120. Ibid.

121. Ibid.

122. "'Beit Sholem Aleichem' nehnach be'Tel Aviv," *Davar*, May 16, 1966.

123. Uri Keisari, "Zahav beli sigim," *Maariv*, July 7, 1966.

124. Dan Miron, *Ha'tzad ha'afel bi'tzehoko shel* Sholem *Aleichem, masot al hashivuta shel retzinut ba'yahas le'Yidish ve'sifruta* (Tel Aviv: Am Oved, 2004), 12.

125. Ibid., 19.

126. Over the years, the production of *Di megile* took on a life of its own. It was revived in Israel in 1967, again with the Bursteins. There were revivals by the Yiddishpiel Theater in 1988 and again in 2010. In that last year (2010), a bilingual edition of the play was published, with a new Hebrew translation. See Itzik Manger, *Shirei ha'megila, mahadura du-leshonit Ivrit ve'Yidish*, ed. Jonathan Nadav, trans. and notes David Assaf (Tel Aviv: Hargol, 2010). A new generation of critics reviewed this edition. All of them related to Manger's poetic art and the place of *Di megile* (and all of his work) in the honor roll of Jewish literature. Some of them mentioned Bunim's bravura production of 1965. But none of them connected *Di megile* with the contemporary status of Yiddish in Israel.

7

THE END OF THE TWENTIETH CENTURY

Private Memory, Collective Image, and the Retreat from the Melting Pot

Following the success of *Di megile* and the wave of nostalgia for the east European past, it seemed in the mid-1960s as if a way had opened for Yiddish to return to center stage in Israeli culture. Yiddish writers continued to write and publish, and there were no less than three active Yiddish presses: the Y. L. Peretz Farlag that was founded in 1955 and had already put out some two hundred books; Menora, founded in 1962; and Yisroel Bukh, founded in 1965.[1] *Di goldene keyt*, the jewel in the crown of Yiddish in Israel and around the world, also continued to print the finest Yiddish literature of the day—and of the past too. However, by the early 1970s, the presence of Yiddish in the Israeli public sphere had declined dramatically and the Yiddish scene seemed disconnected from the major developments in Israeli culture.

The situation of popular Yiddish culture was even more difficult. Yiddish theater and especially Yiddish light entertainment were still active and attracted a small audience. But the Yiddish press, the heart of the Yiddish cultural scene, had shrunken dramatically. Many Yiddish newspapers that were founded in the 1950s had already shut down. *Letste nayes* was still being published by the Mapai party, but *Ilustrirte velt vokh*, the private popular weekly that Mordechai Tsanin founded in 1957 and still owned, was forced to shut down in 1975— "A korbn fun der tsayt" (A victim of the time) was the title of Tsanin's farewell article.

This was not due to a lack of sympathy from Israel's leaders. Since the production of *Di megile*, many of them had demonstrated an open fondness toward Yiddish. As a result, writers, journalists, and activists in Yiddish had begun to hope that they might be able to recruit official support for various projects that would further improve the status of Yiddish in Israel. And, indeed, some public figures did support such projects, on occasion actively and on occasion just with fund-raising. However, despite this, little or nothing was achieved beyond the purely symbolic, such as the construction of both Beit Sholem Aleichem and Beit Leivick—two buildings that were added to the urban landscape of Tel Aviv in the late 1960s and designated to be centers of Yiddish culture in the first Hebrew city.

The first of the two was Beit Sholem Aleichem. Established on the initiative of Y. D. Berkowitz, the legendary author's Hebrew translator (and son-in-law), and built on a plot that had been donated by the Tel Aviv municipality,[2] its declared purpose was to hold the author's archives and serve as a library of books of folklore and humor in Hebrew and Yiddish as a way to encourage the Israeli public, particularly the younger generation, to take an interest in Sholem Aleichem and his works.[3] Its cornerstone was laid in April 1964 and its inauguration took place on May 15, 1966, in the presence of, among others, President Zalman Shazar, Zalman Aran (the minister of education), and Mordechai Namir (the mayor of Tel Aviv).[4] At the inaugural ceremony, President Shazar also announced the opening of Sholem Aleichem Year to mark the fiftieth anniversary of the author's death.[5] Four years later, on May 16, 1970, Beit Leivick (Leivick House) was also inaugurated at a very well-attended ceremony. Professor Dov Sadan said that Beit Leivick was "the missing link in the overall structure that includes *Di goldene keyt* and the department of Yiddish at the Hebrew University."[6] The keynote speaker, Prime Minister Golda Meir, said that one of the roles of the house was "to bring the youth of Israel closer to the Yiddish language and its literature."[7]

All the optimism was misplaced. Despite the support of the Israeli leadership, neither Beit Sholem Aleichem nor Beit Leivick managed to change popular attitudes toward Yiddish. The first became a center that commemorated the author whose name it bore but in fact remained unused for most of the year. The second did function as a venue for Yiddish writers and was even home to activity connected with Yiddish literature, but all its activities remained in the realm of Yiddish speakers, did not reach out to the younger generation, and had no influence on the status of Yiddish in Israeli culture. Articles in *Maariv* and *Davar* described both houses as "splendid and empty" and "empty palaces."[8] Yisokhor Aykhenboym (known by his pen name, Artusky), the editor of *Lebens-fragn*, maintained that Beit Leivick was only a demonstration of sentiment for the past, while the present already "belongs to Hebrew."[9] Yitzhak Luden commented in a similar way.[10]

What seems to have underlain both projects was the growing understanding of intellectuals, journalists, writers, and public figures in the Yiddish sphere—including such key individuals as Luden, Aykhenboym , and Tsanin—that

Yiddish would never be in general daily use in Israel and so would not be able to develop naturally. Instead, Yiddish activists turned their attention to encouraging writing in Yiddish, to creating possibilities for Yiddish publications, and to improving the status of Yiddish in the public eye. For them this meant boosting its cultural capital by presenting it as a serious, high culture and particularly as one esteemed and embraced by the Israeli establishment, the very opposite of its previous position as a shunned culture of the Jewish past.

This explains the importance ascribed to another of the projects of the late 1960s: the establishment of the Itzik Manger Prize for Yiddish literature, which was announced at a ceremony at the president's residence in October 1968 and was the highest financial literary award in Israel. Although the prize itself was a private initiative of the journalist Shalom Rosenfeld and Meyer Weisgal, the president of the Weizmann Institute for Science,[11] the members of its committee included Prime Minister Levi Eshkol, Minister of Education Zalman Aran, and Knesset member Golda Meir. This created the wrong impression that the prize was awarded by the state.[12] In fact, it had no impact on the status of Yiddish in Israel. "Does the prize reflect a revolutionary change in the attitude towards Yiddish in Israel?" asked Yitzhak Luden, almost rhetorically, in a long article in *Lebens-fragn*.[13] For the Israeli public at large the cultural capital of Yiddish remained very low, not rising much above an affection for "a folksy, and juicy language," in the words of Aykhenboym.[14]

By then it had become clear that, if it was to survive in Israel, Yiddish had to continue to function and grow as an active and dynamic culture. Monumental buildings, literary prizes, and words of support from the political elite were simply not enough. "We are not allowed," wrote Aykhenboym in another article, "to let Beit Leivick become a kind of Yad Vashem, a tombstone on the grave of Yiddish."[15] Social, cultural, and political developments in Israel in the 1970s and 1980s would prove a further challenge to its development.

This chapter will deal with the processes undergone by Yiddish in Israel during the last three decades of the twentieth century. It argues that two major developments can be seen in those years. First, during the 1970s and 1980s, Yiddish writers, journalists, and activists were trying to create a new process—the opposite of the process that occurred during the 1950s—and change the status and public image of Yiddish in Israel, reaching out for the help and public support of the leadership of the state. However, although they did get this help, Yiddish was pushed back to the margins of Israeli culture, and public interest dwindled. Nonetheless, the activity of these years, including the work of a small group of new-immigrant authors from the Soviet Union, did at least keep Yiddish culture alive and so helped prepare the ground for its renewed growth in the twenty-first century.

The seeds for this renewed growth were planted toward the end of the 1980s and particularly during the 1990s. In what was the second of the two major developments to be discussed in this chapter, the search for public support and legitimization of the previous decades was replaced by a series of private initiatives undertaken by a number of very determined people. Their success, though it would take a little time coming, was no longer based on the collective memory of the first generation of east European immigrants and Holocaust survivors but on their private memories of their childhood homes, and even more so on the private memories of the next generation of Israelis—those born after World War II. It was their memories of not the Old World they never knew but of their parents and their upbringing that would become the most powerful catalyst for nostalgia in the twenty-first century.

The 1970s: The Cultural Background to the Decline of Yiddish

Israel changed dramatically during the late 1960s and 1970s. Victory in the Six-Day War and then 1973 Arab-Israeli War transformed the social, cultural, and, of course, political landscape. Of particular importance for the discussion here was the outburst of renewed interest in Eretz Israel (the land of Israel) in all its aspects, which made it a hot topic in Israeli public discourse.[16] To take just one example, those years saw Israeli universities found departments and programs of Israel studies, which became enormously popular and attracted many students.[17]

Israeli popular culture also reflected the renewed centrality of Eretz Israel in the public imagination. Nowhere can this be better seen than in the world of Israeli popular music. In the early 1970s, influenced by what was happening in Europe and the United States, Israel saw the beginning of protest songs[18] and then the beginning of a local rock music scene that would continue to grow and develop for decades to come.[19] Tellingly, however, Arik Einstein, who was a leading figure in the emerging world of Israeli rock and would go on to become one of the greatest and most influential Israeli singers, decided at that time to bring out an album with classic Hebrew songs from the prestate years, as well as new songs in the same spirit. Entitled *Eretz Israel ha'yeshana ve'ha'tova* (The good old Eretz Israel), it appeared in 1973 and was an immediate best seller. Einstein followed up its success with three more albums in 1976–1980. The huge popularity of this music reflected a powerful new wave of nostalgia that was sweeping Israel following the post-1973 crisis, not for the pre–World War II Diaspora but for prestate Israel (and the state's early years).

The expression "good old Eretz Israel" became a popular catchphrase in Hebrew, one that was in keeping with the political discourse of the period. This was picked up by Channel One, then the sole TV channel in Israel, which, in 1974, began to broadcast a series of programs called *Sharti lach artzi* (I sang to you, my country), produced and presented by Dan Almagor and Eliyahu Hacohen. It presented Israeli songs from the beginning of the twentieth century until 1948, as well as stories about those songs and the time they were written.[20] The program was broadcast for four years in its initial format and for a few more in a slightly altered form. It was hugely successful.

Clearly, then, the window that had opened for Yiddish and the culture of east European Jewry in the memory and nostalgia of Israeli society was now closing. The land of Israel proved a much more powerful realm of memory than the east European shtetl. It appealed to much broader sections of the Israeli public, including the younger generation that was born after World War II and had taken part in the 1973 Arab-Israeli War. It was also consonant with Zionist ideology and, particularly, the increasingly significant ideas concerning the land of Israel in Israeli politics. Finally, as the 1970s drew to an end, the *mizrahim*, Jews who came from the Muslim countries, for whom the shtetl was an entirely foreign idea, became a much more important force in Israeli society. The east European Jewish past was well and truly pushed to the margins of Israeli collective memory.

"There Is No Room for Illusions": The Aliya of the 1970s and the Committee for Jewish Culture in Israel

This marginalization was a process that took time, and it was not always clear that it was happening. In fact, initially, at least, there still seemed to be reasons for optimism for the fate of Yiddish in Israel. The 1969 wave of immigration from the Soviet Union was one such reason. This wave of immigration grew significantly in 1971 and went on throughout the entire decade. About 150,000 new immigrants arrived in those years.[21] The overwhelming majority of them, more than 70 percent, came from the European Soviet republics and the Baltic countries, where Jews still spoke Yiddish.[22] Among them was a group of about twenty Yiddish writers, some very well known and highly respected, all of whom aspired to publish their work and to attract an Israeli readership. To the supporters of Yiddish, this seemed like a golden opportunity to reinvigorate the world of Yiddish.

But in fact, the immigration of the 1970s did little to improve either the world of Yiddish in Israel or its status in Israeli society. The processes of absorbing the new immigrants were by then very effective. The immigrants were housed in special "absorption centers," learned Hebrew relatively quickly, and so showed no special interest in Yiddish.[23] The Yiddish writers who had arrived in Israel "with joy beaming from their eyes," in the words of Mordechai Halamish, were soon forced to confront a constantly shrinking Yiddish readership. "There is no room for illusions about the potential size of Yiddish readers in our time," wrote Halamish in great sorrow.[24]

Nonetheless, as soon as these immigrants arrived, intensive activity in the field of Yiddish was planned, and the Committee for Jewish Culture in Israel (Komitet far yidisher kultur in Yisroel) was established in 1972. Although its founders stressed that it was a body for Jewish culture in both Hebrew and Yiddish and that the words *yidishe kultur* in its name meant Jewish rather than Yiddish culture, this was merely lip service.[25] In practice, its activity was tailored to meet the needs of the Yiddish writers newly arrived from the Soviet Union.

The driving spirit behind the committee was Yitzhak Coren, a veteran of public life in Israel and a member of the Knesset from the hegemonic Mapai party.[26] It is worth stressing that he was not acting on behalf of the ruling party as much as he was using his status and his connections to promote his aims.

The committee's main role, as Coren saw it, was "to change the atmosphere surrounding Yiddish" by encouraging cooperation between Hebrew and Yiddish in Israel.[27] He had raised the idea of establishing the committee in 1970 and had immediately received the support of the linguist and lexicographer Yudel Mark, as well as of Abraham Sutzkever and Dov Sadan, who would eventually chair the committee together with Coren. Although it was supposed to represent the worlds of both Yiddish and Hebrew, the committee's members were mainly people active in Yiddish in and outside Israel, such as the bilingual journalist Mordechai Halamish and Mordechai Tsanin, as well as Professor Joshua (Shikl) Fishman and the poet Aharon Zeitlin, both residents of the United States.[28] In July 1973, after he completed his term as president of Israel, Zalman Shazar was appointed the committee's honorary president.[29]

Though its stated aims were ambitious, its first practical act was to establish two new periodicals.[30] The first was the monthly *Folk un medine* (People and state), which first came out in September 1972 and intended to serve, among other things, as a source of information about the Jewish world for Jewish newspapers everywhere. The editors, whose names were not given, were careful to strike a balance between items about Israeli society and culture and those dealing with Yiddish.[31] From the thirtieth issue, the cultural department of the World Jewish Congress became copublisher, and the journal's name was changed to *Folk, velt un medine* (People, world, and state). Its content focused much more on Jewish communities in the Diaspora, on their links to Israel, and particularly on questions of Yiddish and Yiddish in Israel.[32]

The second periodical, a literary journal that came out at the very same time, was *Bay zikh: heftn far di shafungen fun shraybers, naye oylim* (At home— notebooks for the work of new immigrant writers). Yitzhak Yanasovitsh, a writer, journalist, and newspaper editor who had settled in Israel from Argentina and was close to Mapai circles, was appointed editor.[33] The first issues included only work by writers who had recently arrived, mainly from the Soviet Union, emphasizing that fact with the inclusion of either a note about their land of origin or a brief biography. The book review section also covered only books published in Israel by new immigrants.[34] The main contributors to *Bay zikh* were Hirsh Osherovitsh, Rokhl Boymvol, Ziyama Telesin, Yankl Yakir, Leyzer Podraytshik, David Markish, and David Sephard (who had come to Israel from Poland in 1969).

Coren and the other members of the committee regarded *Bay zikh* as their crowning glory. One reason was, of course, that it was a literary journal, a respected and prestigious genre. But even more important, the Yiddish writers who came to Israel in the 1970s had suffered from a lack of opportunities to publish their work, not to mention severe harassment, for many years. Finding them venues in which to publish their writing immediately on their arrival in Israel was a major, perhaps even the most significant, factor in their successful integration.

Like all Yiddish writers everywhere at that time, they wanted most of all to see their work on the pages of *Di goldene keyt*, the pinnacle of Yiddish literature. Some, such as Hersh Smolyer, Kalman Segal, Yankl Yakir, and Eli Shechtman, who was a highly respected author, did achieve that. Most of the new-immigrant writers, however, did not. From a practical standpoint, there was simply not enough space in *Di goldene keyt* to include all the writing produced by these new immigrants. Moreover, not everything that was written met Sutzkever's rigorous standards. Some authors became bitter and disillusioned with Israel.[35] It was, as much as anything, to help them that the Committee for Jewish Culture under Coren and Sadan's leadership offered them *Bay zikh* as a forum of their own.

It soon became clear, however, that it was not enough. Just a year after the first issue of *Bay zikh*, another periodical in Yiddish appeared. Called *Almanakh— tsaytshrift far literatur, kultur, shprakh un forshung* it was founded by Yosef Kerler, a poet and well-known figure in the world of Yiddish literature, who had settled in Israel in 1971. Even before he had arrived, he had published his work in both the New York daily *Forverts* and *Di goldene keyt*. *Almanakh*, which a year later changed its name to *Yerusholaymer almanakh*, was published in cooperation with the Jerusalem branch of the Association of Yiddish Writers and Journalists in Israel. It was not intended solely as a forum for new immigrants, and its first issue included work by veteran writers in Israel, as well as some from the United States, such as Gella Fishman and Sol Liptzin. However, the overwhelming majority of its contributors were the same as those in *Bay zikh*. Clearly, the new immigrants from the Soviet Union needed more than one venue in which to publish.

Bay zikh was important, then, for reasons that went beyond Yiddish literature. Its aim was "to enable immigrants from the Soviet Union to pitch their creative tents on the soil of their new-old home" and to integrate into Israeli culture.[36] It became a vehicle for the absorption of Yiddish writers from the Soviet Union and, along the way, also made a contribution to Israeli society and culture in general.

The committee helped immigrant writers finance the publication of their books with the Y. L. Peretz publishing house in Tel Aviv.[37] In the years 1973–1979 about a dozen books by writers from the Soviet Union were published, including two volumes of Shechtman's monumental novel *Erev* (The eve of) and the novel *A shlitn mit yishuvnikes* (A sled with village Jews), by Yankl Yakir, which came out in 1974.[38]

Not all of the committee's work was just for the new immigrants. For example, it reached an agreement with the Hebrew University concerning the joint publication of a series of ten Yiddish books of academic merit.[39] The first three volumes selected were collections of stories by Isaac Bashevis Singer,[40] Abraham Sutzkever,[41] and S. Y. Agnon, edited by Dov Sadan.[42] Another such initiative was the establishment of the prime minister's prize for Yiddish literature, which was initiated by the committee and personally promoted by Coren himself. The prize was founded by Prime Minister Golda Meir and was first awarded in 1973.[43] Unlike the Manger prize, this was an official state award, so its establishment marked the first time that the state of Israel established and financed an award for Yiddish literature.

The first recipient of the prize was Eli Shechtman, who had come to Israel from the Soviet Union a year earlier and was regarded as one of the most important Jewish writers of the twentieth century.[44] In 1974, Moyshe Yungman, a member of the Yung Yisroel group, won the prize; in 1975, the recipient was Leyb Rochman.[45] In 1976 Abraham Sutzkever was personally awarded the prize by the former prime minister Golda Meir at a widely attended ceremony held at the closing session of the World Congress for Yiddish and Jewish Culture.[46] In the following years, the winners of the prize were Yosef Papyernikov, Dov Sadan, Hirsh Osherovitsh, Abraham Karpinovitsh, and Yeshayahu Spiegel, as well as the Yiddish daily *Forward* and its editor Shimon Weber, who shared the prize with Abraham Liss, in 1982.[47]

Another cultural initiative in Yiddish that won official support was in the world of theater. Among the immigrants from the Soviet Union had been groups of Yiddish actors. One such group, Mir zaynen do (We are here), was a Jewish folklore company that had performed for more than a decade in Vilna, mainly in Yiddish, and also proved very successful in Israel.[48] Another company was the Iditron, a repertory theater in Yiddish that was set up in Israel but did not have much success.[49] From 1972, the Ministry of Absorption supported both these companies as part of its efforts to encourage immigrant artists. In fact, in 1974, the Public Council for Culture and Art, which was part of the Ministry of Education, together with the Ministry of Absorption and the Jewish Agency, went so far as to establish the Yidish kunst teater (Yiddish Art Theater), an artistic theater in Yiddish, and to allocate it a temporary budget to enable it to gain an audience and become self-sufficient.[50]

Shortly before the theater opened, Leah Porat, the director of the culture and art section of the Ministry of Education and chair of the Council for Culture and Art, explained that the reason why the Ministry of Absorption and the Jewish Agency were helping to finance the theater was because it was meant to serve as a first step for new immigrants just embarking on their careers in Israel. However, that was not the only reason. It was also supposed to make Israel the world center for Yiddish theater and attract Jewish actors from across the Diaspora.[51]

Following the policy of the 1960s, which favored bringing stars from abroad to breathe life into Yiddish theater in Israel,[52] Joseph Buloff was invited to manage the new theater in 1974. He accepted. Shmuel Bunim, who had directed *Di megile*, was appointed director, and a company was put together of new-immigrant actors from the Soviet Union, as well as veteran Israelis.[53] Finally, in March 1975, Ida Kaminska came to Israel, this time with the intention of settling there, and she too joined the new enterprise.[54]

Yet all this hope in the fields of literature and theater did not lead to much. The fact that the Committee for Jewish Culture itself was not funded by the state but through donations from Jewish philanthropists across the world was not an auspicious start.[55] And the committee did not even really achieve its major goal—the integration into Israeli society and culture of the Yiddish writers from the Soviet Union. *Bay zikh* and the *Yerusholaymer almanakh*, the journals in which they published, were soon pigeonholed as specialist forums for writers from the Soviet Union. Even the books by these writers that were published by the Y. L. Peretz publishing house came out in a separate series, not as part of the house's general list, and had to be financed by money from abroad.[56]

Though some of the group (Rokhl Boymvol, Yanasovitsh, Yakir, Kerler, Osherovitsh, and others) did succeed in having their work published in Hebrew translation, they were always seen as immigrants from the Soviet Union.[57] It should be noted that all these writers wrote in their works—poetry as well as prose—about their past experience in eastern Europe, and these topics were very far from the interests of the Israeli-Hebrew readership. In fact, Eli Shechtman was the only one that won the respect of the Israeli literary readership. His work was published by Sifriat Poalim and Hakibbutz Hameuchad, important public publishing houses, and was reviewed in the Hebrew press as Hebrew literature.[58] However, although Shechtman distanced himself from the group of Yiddish writers in Israel—so much so that his work was not included in the 1991 anthology of Yiddish literature in Israel brought out by the Association of Yiddish Writers—he too failed to win general acceptance.[59] His work continued to focus on eastern Europe, including his great novel *Erev*, which told the four-hundred-year story of a Jewish family from its flight from a blood libel in medieval Germany to its life in early twentieth-century Russia. While his oeuvre was highly appreciated in literary circles, it did not appeal to a broader readership.[60]

The Yidish kunst teater fared even worse. It opened in May 1975 with the play *Amkho*, by Sholem Aleichem. The production was both a critical and a box-office failure and closed after only one month.[61] The next production was *Glikl fun Hamel*, directed by and starring Ida Kaminska and featuring Eni Liton.[62] It failed too. Any plans to stage further plays in the theater were then abandoned, and it closed.[63] Ida Kaminska continued to perform in Israel for a while in other venues and then returned to New York.[64] The same Hebrew press that had given some coverage to the founding of the Yidish kunst teater entirely ignored its closure.

"*Yidn redt Yidish!*" (Speak Yiddish, Jews!): The World Congress of Yiddish and the World Council for Yiddish

The Committee for Jewish Culture's limited success in improving the status of Yiddish in Israel during the 1970s seems to have spurred it to try to establish a large, more comprehensive permanent organization to act on behalf of Yiddish. Its first step in this direction was to convene an international advisory group in Jerusalem to discuss the issue of the future of Yiddish. Activity began in earnest in 1974 and included the establishment of an executive committee in Jerusalem, as well as local committees in many places throughout the world.[65] Finally, after two years of preparation, the World Congress for Yiddish was held in Jerusalem on August 23, 1976. To the Israeli public at large, this event, which took place about a month after the IDF's heroic operation in Entebbe, must have seemed marginal indeed.

Nonetheless, for those who attended it, the opening session at the Jerusalem Theater was a moving event. A huge crowd from Israel and abroad filled the large hall, overflowing into the aisles and the stairways. The atmosphere was festive. "A festival of Yiddish in Jerusalem, the Capital" was how the organizers described it.[66] Unfortunately, beyond all the excitement, neither the opening session nor the days to follow brought any fresh hope for the future of Yiddish. Quite the reverse. On the first evening, Yitzhak Coren made a flowery oration;[67] the greetings of the president, Ephraim Katzir, were read out; and then a long series of speeches were delivered.[68] The session ended with an artistic performance marking the sixtieth anniversary of Sholem Aleichem's death.[69] There followed two days of discussions on Yiddish literature, education, and theater[70] at the Hebrew University campus on Givat Ram and a final session on the third day that culminated with former prime minister Golda Meir awarding the prime minister's prize for Yiddish literature to Abraham Sutzkever.[71] However, only one significant resolution was passed during those whole three days of discussion, and it was to establish another body to deal with Yiddish and its problems. This was the World Council for Yiddish and Jewish Culture (A velt rat far Yidish un yidisher kultur), which was meant to be a broad, permanent international organization whose leadership would be in Israel and whose role would be to strengthen the Yiddish language and culture in Israel, as well as in Jewish communities throughout the world.[72]

In real terms, this decision amounted only to an admission that the Committee for Jewish Culture had failed to achieve its goals and had had no significant impact on the state of Yiddish in Israel. While it had established new Yiddish periodicals and financed the publication of literary works in Yiddish, none of this had made a significant contribution to integrating Yiddish into the Israeli Hebrew culture. So, at the end of the day, the World Council for Yiddish was really nothing more than a replacement for the Committee for Jewish Culture.

The event marking the establishment of the council took place on July 31–August 4, 1978, in Tel Aviv with the participation of the same people who had spoken at the Yiddish conference in Jerusalem. Still, there were two significant differences between the two conferences, both signs of the real change in the status of Yiddish in Israel. The meeting in Tel Aviv was far smaller than its Jerusalem predecessor and lacked its sense of excitement. Also, and perhaps most importantly, no government representative came to deliver greetings.[73] The only official personality to do so was the chairman of the Jewish Agency, Arieh Dulzin.[74] The establishment of the council thus marked the decline of Yiddish in Israel rather than its expansion. The effort to expand the influence of

Yiddish in Israel and to make Israel a world center of Yiddish was now replaced by cooperation with the Jewish Agency with the major goal of strengthening Yiddish in the diasporic Jewish communities. This was clearly reflected in the two new publications that the council brought out. The first, an information bulletin, *Yidish yedies: informatsye buletin fun veltrat far Yidish un yidisher kultur*, appeared from 1978 to 1982 and from 1984 to 1992 in its later form *Yidish velt*. Both publications served as a channel of contact between communities of Yiddish lovers throughout the world.

The council was active until 1998, and its major achievements were in the sphere of publication and publicity. It continued to bring out the two publications of the Committee for Jewish Culture—*Folk, velt un medine* until 1982 and *Bay zikh* until 1989. In addition, between 1983 and 1985, the council also published three issues of a bilingual literary journal, *Gesharim-Brikn* (Bridges), which was financed by Jewish organizations or individuals outside of Israel.[75] It also supported the publication of a number of Yiddish books.[76] Finally, during its twenty years of existence, the council organized eight large international conferences on Yiddish, four of which were held in Israel.[77]

So, what did the committee and later the council accomplish for Yiddish in Israel? After the council had been active for a decade, some of its leaders, as well as Yiddish journalists, tried to draw up an interim summary of its achievements. The clearest and most reasonable voice was probably that of Mordechai Halamish. His work in both the Hebrew and the Yiddish press provided him with the broadest view of Yiddish in Israeli life. He emphasized the efforts made vis-à-vis the authorities as the most important achievement of the Committee for Jewish Culture and later the council. This greatest success in this field was, he claimed, the inclusion of Yiddish as a second foreign language in the curriculum of about twenty high schools in Israel and the appointment of a superintendent of Yiddish teaching by the Ministry of Education.

However, unlike other journalists, Halamish was prepared to admit openly, albeit with much regret, that Yiddish would never be able to regain the status it had had before the Holocaust as long as it was not a language of everyday speech. "To mark its tenth anniversary," he wrote, "the council should urgently issue a call to all its members and to all Yiddish speakers in general: Speak Yiddish, Jews! [*Yidn, redt Yidish*] Let us revive our *mame loshn* as a living language in our homes and in the public sphere!"[78] The introduction of Yiddish as a second foreign language in a small number of high schools might have seemed like an achievement, he added, but it actually emphasized how marginal Yiddish had become in Israeli culture and society. Nonetheless, he was the only person prepared to admit as much in public.

The Late 1980s and the 1990s: The Retreat from the Melting Pot

In 1977, a political upheaval took place in Israel, putting an end to twenty-nine years of rule by the Labor Party, which itself had followed more than forty years of socialist-Zionist control in the Jewish prestate Yishuv. The Likud party, which came into power, was a composite of the right-wing Herut party, the Liberal Party, and other groups with right-wing leanings, including the Movement for Greater Israel.

This dramatic political change had far-reaching implications that would transform Israeli society and culture. By reaching out to Mizrahi Jews, those who had immigrated to Israel from Muslim countries, especially in the 1950s and 1960s, Menachem Begin, the charismatic leader of the Likud, made his party their political home. A crucial part of his strategy was to exploit the sense of deprivation felt by those people who lived in development towns, in the distant periphery, far away from the good education, health services, and job opportunities to be found in the center. In this way, Begin was able to turn them even more strongly against the until-then hegemonic Labor Party, accusing it of every bad thing—real or imagined—that they had suffered. This not only widened the already existing rift in Israeli society between the Ashkenazi Jews (of European origin) and the Mizrahi/Sephardic Jews (mainly from the Muslim countries) but also created the stereotype of the Ashkenazi Jews as the alienated elite of the political center/left as opposed to the Mizrahi Jews, who were depicted as a kind of authentic group with deep connections to the real values of Jewish traditional culture. This led to further political developments that would have significant cultural ramifications in the years to come. In the 1981 elections, a party called Tami (Tenua'at masoret Israel [Movement for Jewish tradition]) appeared for the first time, representing mainly Jews from Morocco. Under the slogan "Standing Tall," its followers demanded equality of opportunities for all Israeli citizens and the granting of equal status in Israel for all past Jewish cultures. A short-lived party, Tami was soon followed by the Shas party (the association of orthodox Sephardi Jews), whose power in the Knesset grew in an unprecedented manner until the end of the twentieth century.[79]

Against this background, a discourse of individualism emerged in Israel that began to replace the discourse of unity that had underlain the melting pot ideology of the previous regime. The most prominent cultural consequence of this process was the explosion of the *muzika mizrahit* (Middle Eastern/Mediterranean music) into Israeli culture. In previous years, it had been perceived as marginal and had barely been played on Israeli radio and television, but during the 1980s, it started entering the mainstream of Israeli culture, becoming the most popular Israeli music at the turn of the twenty-first century and brushing aside the "good old land of Israel" songs.[80]

Multiculturalism was now not only permitted but desirable. Instead of a single Israeli Hebrew cultural identity, alternative identities emerged, and different groups in Israeli society demanded that the story of their past become part of the historical narrative of the Jewish people and Zionism.[81] This could not but have a significant impact on Israeli collective memory. Instead of one unified collective memory that had existed until then, space now had to be made for the collective memories of the many different groups that made up Israeli society. This also allowed for private and personal memory to become a factor in shaping Israeli culture.

As far as Yiddish was concerned, these developments had far-reaching consequences. By the 1980s most of those who had immigrated to Israel from Eastern Europe in the 1950s had long been part of Israeli Hebrew culture. The vast majority never spoke Yiddish to their Israeli-born or Israeli-raised children, and many stopped using Yiddish outside their homes altogether. However, the changes in Israeli culture, as well as their own advancing years, led many of them to look back at their personal experience and memories, a great deal of which were connected, in one way or another, with Yiddish. Though they may never have visited a Yiddish theater, either because they considered it *shund* or because they had been influenced by the Zionist attitude to Yiddish, these elderly people now felt the need to hear a little Yiddish—at least sometimes. The only place to do this in public, and sometimes at all, was the Yiddish theater.

No less significant for the development of Yiddish was the second generation. These were people who had been born after World War II and raised in Israel and so knew very little Yiddish if at all. For them, hearing the sound of spoken Yiddish became part of the very personal memory of their childhood homes in 1950s and even 1960s Israel.

The time was thus right for a new approach to finding a place for Yiddish in Israel. The organizations and committees of previous years began to be replaced in the late 1980s and 1990s by private initiatives started by individuals who had grown up in a Yiddish-speaking milieu. They were thus fluent in the language and familiar with the culture, though they had never been part of any public activity on behalf of Yiddish. They proved a real powerhouse.

The two main initiatives of this period were the founding of the Yiddishpiel, the first viable Yiddish theater in Israel, which was supported by public funds, and the adoption of the law establishing the National Authority for Yiddish Culture in Israel. The driving force behind both developments was one man—the actor Shmuel Atzmon-Wircer.

The Shift of 1987: The Yiddishpiel—A Permanent Yiddish Theater in Israel

Born in Poland in 1929, Atzmon received a Hebrew education as a child. He survived the Holocaust by fleeing eastward into territories of the Soviet Union and immigrated to Israel during the 1948 war. In Israel, he acted in the Ohel and Habima Theaters, and in 1958 he joined a group of young actors who founded the avant-garde Israeli theater Zavit. In the 1960s he became its artistic director and led it to impressive achievements.[82] Critics praised it as "a small theater that achieved great things."[83] In 1968, the Zavit Theater company was invited to join Habima.[84] In the 1970s Atzmon also worked with Shimon Dzigan, directing his one-man shows, which brought him into the world of Yiddish theater.[85]

His connection to it became even closer when, in 1976, the actor Eliyahu Goldenberg, a member of the trio of Yiddish actors who had staged Sholem Aleichem's play *Di kleyne mentshelekh* (The little people) with great success for some fifteen years, passed away. Atzmon was invited to join the other two members of the trio—Shmuel Rodensky and Shmuel Segal—to continue with the production. The trio was renamed "the three Shmuliks" and enjoyed enormous success during the 1970s and 1980s.

Within a few years, Atzmon began to look into the possibility of establishing a permanent Yiddish theater in Israel. He initially worked on the project with Israel Becker, a veteran actor and native of Bialystok, who had recently retired from a long career in the Habima Theater. Becker had also been the person who had introduced the idea of a permanent Yiddish theater at the Yiddish conference of 1976. Unfortunately, the cooperation between the two did not lead to much, and Atzmon continued alone.

Unlike those who had come before him, Atzmon did not seek the patronage of the state or its institutions. Also, instead of cooperating with people from the world of Yiddish, he looked for figures with leading positions in Israel's economy and financial world who were also Yiddish lovers. With the assistance and encouragement of the attorney David Rotlevi, formerly head of the Israel Bar Association and a member of the Tel Aviv city council, he put together an impressive group of people. These included the industrialist Israel Pollack; the director general of the Barclays-Discount Bank, Moshe Neudorfer; the head of the Clal concern, Aaron Dovrat; the accountant Eliezer Oren; and the deputy mayor of Tel Aviv, Nathan Wolloch. However, most important of all, Atzmon succeeded in winning the very enthusiastic support of the mayor of Tel Aviv, Shlomo Lahat (popularly known as "Chich"). Lahat's commitment and unreserved support was the key factor in the eventual establishment of the Yiddish theater.

Another important development came in November 1987, when UNESCO recognized Yiddish as a unique cultural heritage threatened with oblivion. This, together with the support of the board members, gave a significant boost to fund-raising efforts in Israel and abroad and provided the impetus for the establishment of the new Yiddish repertory theater in Israel in December 1987. It would soon become a permanent fixture in Israeli cultural life.[86]

The new company was set up as an independent nonprofit organization with Shlomo Lahat as its head and David Rotlevi chairman of its executive committee.[87] Other members of the organization included a number of actors, representatives of the Jewish Agency and the Histadrut, and the poet Abraham Sutzkever.[88] Shmuel Atzmon was appointed manager. It received public financing from the Tel Aviv municipality, as well as a grant from the government of Hessen, Germany. The theater's budget for its first year of operation was 1,150,000 new shekels (about $740,000 at that time), of which Tel Aviv contributed half a million shekels ($319,000) and Hessen 100,000. It had to raise the remainder itself. The Yad le'banim building in Tel Aviv was chosen as its temporary venue, and from there it moved to the ZOA (Zionist Organization of America) House, which became its permanent home.

The theater's aim, as laid down at the ceremony announcing its establishment, was "to preserve Yiddish culture, which has been a major building block in the creation of contemporary Israeli culture." It also had to take care "not to reconstruct past productions, but rather to adapt to the possibilities and vision of the contemporary stage." An additional aim was to bring the young generation that did not speak the language closer to the cultural world of Yiddish.[89]

The first production was *Shver tsu zayn a yid* (It is hard to be a Jew), by Sholem Aleichem. It premiered on January 24, 1988, in the presence of the prime minister, Yitzhak Shamir, Tel Aviv mayor Shlomo Lahat, and many invited guests.[90] The play was adapted and directed by the retired Habima actor Israel Becker, who also starred in it.[91] The renowned Yiddish actors Yankele Alperin and Ethel Kobinsky also performed.

The production was not well received by the critics. Quite the reverse. Some articles in the Hebrew press objected to the very establishment of the theater.[92] Others, which were prepared to support the idea of Yiddish theater in Israel, subjected to very harsh criticism not only the production itself but the management's choice of that particular play to open the first season. Becker's direction and acting were characterized as antiquated and kitsch, and the theater was told in no uncertain terms to adopt a modern approach.[93] The few Yiddish newspapers that were still in existence almost did not mention the event.

Nonetheless, the play ran to full houses for sixty performances, after which preparations began immediately for the next presentation, a new production

Figure 7.1. Shmulik Atzmon-Wircer in *Tevye der milkhiker*, 2004. Photograph: Gerard Allon.

of Itzik Manger's *Di megile*.[94] That same year the theater also staged Sholem Aleichem's *Di kleyne mentshelekh* (Little people), a production that had been performed to great success on stages across Israel for more than two decades.

After five years of successful activity, the management decided to change the name of the company, which had been until then, the Yiddish Theater in Israel. In 1994, with the help of people in the field of advertising, the name Yiddishpiel was chosen. The new brand name was an immediate success and made the theater itself the trademark for Yiddish in Israel.[95]

From its establishment until the year 2000, the theater staged thirty-seven productions. Seven were plays by Sholem Aleichem, there were two productions of Manger's *Di megile*, and others of classical Yiddish plays by Sholem Asch, Abraham Goldfaden, and Jacob Gordin.[96] It also put on translations of plays by contemporary Israeli playwrights, such as Aharon Megged, Ephraim Kishon, and Joshua Sobol, among others. It continued to grow and develop successfully into the twenty-first century.[97]

Unquestionably, the Yiddishpiel's success was possible due to the great changes that were sweeping Israeli culture and society at that time, in particular the emergence of the kind of discourse that encouraged individual initiative and the growing importance of private memory.[98] The role of the mayor of Tel Aviv, Shlomo Lahat, was of critical importance. As well as allocating a generous budget and providing a hall for the theater, he succeeded in making the Yiddish theater an integral part not only of the fabric of Tel Aviv, which during Lahat's tenure became Israel's "City That Never Sleeps," but also of its dynamic cultural life.[99] It was the first time since the establishment of the state that a Yiddish theater was included in municipal cultural initiatives. In fact, so strong was the impression that the Yiddish theater was a project of the Tel Aviv municipality that in 1988, Yitzhak Yanasovitsh, the editor of the journal of the World Jewish Council, mistakenly called it the "Tel Aviv Municipal Yiddish Theater" (Yidishn shtot teater in Tel Aviv).[100]

This notwithstanding, the decisive role in Yiddishpiel's success was played by Shmuel Atzmon. He was the driving force behind the theater and searched tirelessly for the types of innovation that would allow the theater to adapt to the zeitgeist. Atzmon was always conscious of the changes in Israeli society during those years, and he knew how to help the theater respond to them. Most importantly, he was able to identify new audiences for the Yiddish theater and was constantly looking for new ways to bring them in.

Perhaps from his own life experience, Atzmon understood that those Jews who had come to Israel from eastern Europe and lived for decades totally immersed in Israeli Hebrew culture, were now, in their advancing years, feeling nostalgia for their own personal past, when Yiddish had been spoken. And once they were in his auditorium, Atzmon knew how to engage them. At the beginning of every performance, he would come out on stage and speak to the audience in Yiddish and tell a few jokes. In doing so, he was giving them a sense of community as people who had once spoken Yiddish and had now come to the theater to reconnect to the language of their past.

He was also sensitive to the needs of the second generation. For the most part, they did not really know Yiddish but wanted to hear the voices of their childhood in their parental homes, to be in the atmosphere of their past and their memories of growing up. For them, the Yiddish theater was a way of accessing their personal realms of memory.[101] So, to make them feel comfortable in a show whose language they loved but did not understand, the management provided running translations of the text into Hebrew. And when, in the early twenty-first century, immigrants from the former Soviet Union, very few of whom knew Yiddish, also began to attend the theater, which they regarded as a kind of east European Jewish experience, the management also added running translations into Russian.

As the twentieth century drew to its end, then, the Yiddishpiel was at the height of its development. At the beginning of the twenty-first century, it was already an integral part of Tel Aviv's theatrical scene and also was receiving financial support from the Ministry of Culture. This was, to a great extent, a result of Atzmon's ongoing activity on behalf of Yiddish. One of his most significant accomplishments was his initiative in the 1990s to harness the Knesset for the support of Yiddish and to get legislation passed that would ensure permanent support for Yiddish culture in Israel.

Yiddish, Ladino, and the Commemoration of the Holocaust: The National Authority for Yiddish Culture

It was on March 7, 1996, very late at night, that the Knesset approved the second and third readings of a bill establishing a National Authority for Yiddish Culture, whose goal was to strengthen the knowledge of Yiddish in Israel, to encourage the creation of original works in the language, and to support institutions fostering its culture.[102] Nearly fifty years had passed since the government first discussed the place of Yiddish in Israel and encouraged the relevant offices to stop restricting performances in Yiddish as part of its melting pot policy. The events and debates leading up to the law establishing the National Authority for Yiddish reflected both the marginalization of Yiddish in Israel and the final abandonment of the melting pot policy, which had effectively come to an end twenty years earlier.

The driving force behind the efforts to enlist the Israeli parliament in favor of Yiddish was Shmuel Atzmon, whose initial goal was to strengthen his theater. He managed to persuade the Knesset to devote a special session to Yiddish, which was held on January 4, 1993. Yiddish activists in Israel described the session as an "event of historical importance," in which "the Knesset . . . the highest institution of Israeli democracy, honored the Yiddish language and its culture."[103] However, that was not the case. The event served only to emphasize the generally accepted stereotypical view of Yiddish, the widespread ignorance of its nature and history, and in particular its marginal status in Israeli society and culture.

About five hundred guests were invited to attend the Knesset on that day, to an event that culminated with a performance of several Yiddishpiel actors. Then Abraham Sutzkever read his poem "Yidish," written in 1947, and two high school students read excerpts from the works of Itzik Manger and Ka-Tzetnik. In the debate itself, five Knesset members delivered speeches. Two of them, Ovadia Eli, the deputy speaker of the Knesset, and the young Knesset member Avraham Burg demonstrated impressive knowledge of Yiddish literature and its history. Still, they both also spoke about Yiddish as a "folksy" or "piquant" language—a language of humor and jokes. "I was born in Iraq," said Eli, "and am not fluent in Yiddish, otherwise perhaps I would have opened with a good joke," one like those that people say about them, "'in Yiddish it sounds better.'"[104] And Burg said: many Israelis say that "in Yiddish it sounds funnier, and we ask ourselves, does that mean Yiddish is a funny language?"[105]

The motif of Yiddish as a language of jokes was used by some of the other speakers, but another aspect also came to the fore, particularly in the words of two of the more veteran and senior among them, Shevah Weiss, the speaker of the Knesset, and Dov Shilansky, the former speaker, both Holocaust survivors.[106] In their speeches, they referred to Yiddish in stereotypic terms as a "popular" or "soft" language but went on, each in his own way, describing it as the language of the Jews that had perished in the Holocaust.[107] The connection between Yiddish and the Holocaust they drew would prove particularly important in the process leading to the establishment of the National Yiddish Authority, and this is what also prompted Shilansky to act on behalf of Yiddish and the Yiddish theater in the Knesset.

On April 17, 1994, as part of a discussion on the support given by the Ministry of Arts and Science to small theaters, Shilansky raised the question of the support given to Yiddish theater in Israel and asked: "Why do so many begrudge the preservation of Yiddish, which also involves the commemoration of the Holocaust for many people? . . . Will the Minister [Shulamit Aloni] act in order . . . to commemorate Yiddish, so that it will remain, at the very least, like a specimen preserved in a museum?"[108] Significantly, however, Shilansky was not here talking about reviving Yiddish or even just helping it survive; all he proposed was to have it put in a museum.

Not long after that, Atzmon reached out to Shilansky, requesting his support in a further initiative: the passing of a law to create a new statutory public body—a National Authority for Yiddish Culture—whose budget would come from the state and whose structure and activity would be laid down in law.[109] The two men's remarkable success in achieving this goal seems, as much as anything else, to have been a result of their intuitive grasp of how the Israeli identity politics had developed since the late 1970s. By the time they began to cooperate on the new law, the new multicultural approach to identity, which did not privilege any one culture over any other, meant that Yiddish was being presented to the Israeli public not as the majority culture of the Jewish people before the Holocaust—which it had been—but rather as one of several Jewish cultures that had existed in the Diaspora, all similar to each other in size and influence.

Understanding that, they assumed (probably correctly) that the idea of passing a law for the establishment of a national authority for Yiddish would not be viewed by either the Knesset or the Israeli public as a purely cultural initiative but rather as an attempt to bolster the already privileged Ashkenazi culture. The strategy they adopted, therefore, was to expand the scope of the bill beyond Yiddish itself.[110] They contacted Yitzhak Navon, Israel's fifth president, who was very active in promoting Ladino (Judeo-Spanish), and suggested that he cooperate with them in establishing two parallel but separate statutory authorities, one for Yiddish and one for Ladino.[111]

This idea of establishing an authority for Ladino as an instrumental step to enable the establishment of one for Yiddish, and in particular the fact that it met with success, is the clearest possible reflection of how Yiddish was seen in Israel at the end of the twentieth century. It is true that Yiddish and Ladino have much in common. They are both Jewish languages created as fusion languages based on a non-Jewish language (medieval German or Castilian Spanish, respectively) but with a significant component of the "sacred tongue" (Hebrew and Aramaic). They both also became transregional languages of Jews who immigrated from the original country where the language was created to other countries, where the language became one of their defining features. In both, a cultural corpus was created, which played a role in the process of modernization of the Jewish societies that used these languages, and entire communities of speakers of both languages were annihilated in the Holocaust.[112]

They were also widely perceived as very similar. In 1969, Habima, Israel's national theater, staged the play *Bustan sepharadi* (Sephardic orchard), which depicted life in a Sephardic neighborhood in Jerusalem and was based on secular and sacred songs, as well as amusing stories, in Ladino with some Hebrew translation. The play, written by Yitzhak Navon, was extremely popular and successful. It was first performed several years after *Di megile* and was, for the lovers of the Judeo-Spanish language and culture, what *Di megile* had been for Yiddish lovers—a realm of memory and nostalgia.

The parallel was not lost on the Hebrew press: "This phenomenon has already become a feature of our theatrical life," wrote *Maariv*'s theater critic. "[I mean] plays in the form of a musical, with deep Jewish roots, drawn from folklore and the liturgy, 'acted and sung' in Hebrew with the addition of another popular language. It began with Itzik Manger's *Di megile* . . . and now another pearl has been added to the necklace, *Bustan sepharadi*, a popular musical from the life of the Sephardic community."[113] The play, which was filmed and screened in 1971 on Israeli television's Channel One (the only channel at the time), introduced Ladino to a public generally ignorant of it and in doing so deepened the feeling of similarity between the two languages in the public imagination. For years afterward, people would mention Yiddish and Ladino in the same breath or describe Ladino as "the Yiddish of the Sephardic Jews."[114]

Nonetheless, there also significant differences—cultural and historical—between Yiddish and Ladino.[115] These differences and especially their significance were never discussed. The fact that Yiddish—the language of the vast majority of the Jews before the Holocaust—alone, without the link to the Sephardic language, would not have been seen as worthy of the kind of body that was eventually set up makes it abundantly clear just how superficial the general public's understanding of Yiddish was at that time.

The two bills for the establishment of separate authorities for the Jewish languages and culture from the Diaspora were in fact submitted to the Knesset in tandem, with totally identical wording, apart from the names of the languages, Yiddish and Ladino.[116] The bill was discussed at the Knesset Committee on Education on December 14, 1994, and was brought for a first reading and a vote by the Knesset plenary on April 4, 1995, very late at night.[117] The importance with which it was viewed was made clear by the fact that only 8 of the 120 Knesset members bothered to turn up. None of the speakers showed any knowledge or understanding of the historical role of Yiddish in Jewish culture or of the part Yiddish played in the development of Israeli literary culture over the years. They seemed simply to be going through the motions and paying some kind of lip service to the new Israeli identity politics. Once again, both cultures were presented as "piquant" and "folksy" in a kind of derogatory way, and the fact that the establishment of the two authorities was another contribution to the commemoration of the victims of the Holocaust was also stressed.[118] There was also general agreement about the harmful nature of the melting pot policy of the 1950s. In other words, the Knesset members who voted for the bill saw it as part of an ongoing effort to commemorate the Holocaust rather than an Israeli cultural endeavor. The bill passed in its first reading that same night, with all those present, 8 members, voting in favor.[119]

On March 7, 1996, once again in the middle of the night with very few members present, the Knesset approved the Law for the National Authority for Yiddish Culture in its second and third readings.[120] The aims of the authority as defined in it were "(a) To deepen acquaintance of the Israeli public with Yiddish (or Ladino) culture in all of its forms and to foster research and instruction in this culture; (b) To promote and encourage the creation of contemporary works in Yiddish (or Ladino); (c) To assist in the establishment and preservation of institutions in which activity relating to this culture is carried out." The bill also stated that the authority (for Yiddish or Ladino) "will conduct long-term projects and cover diverse fields of activity, such as education, research, preservation, creation, culture and the arts."[121]

Almost fifty years had passed since the leaders of the state had sought ways to invent and create a new Israeli culture, based purely on Hebrew, and to ensure that it was completely cut off from the past cultures of the Diaspora Jews, including and perhaps particularly Yiddish. Now a step had been taken in something of an opposite direction—to bring Israeli Hebrew culture closer to the past Jewish cultures of the Diaspora that had been forgotten, or at least despised, in Israel.

The National Authority for Yiddish Culture finally came into being in 1999.[122] In addition to the rather small budget provided by the state through the Ministry of Science, Culture and Sport, the heads of the authority managed to raise various donations to help finance its activity for about five years. During that time, the authority supported a series of courses throughout the country in the Yiddish language (some quite successful), financed performances by artists in Yiddish (particularly outside central Israel), and encouraged the creation of original works in Yiddish. The authority's crowning achievement during this period was the publication of a journal in Yiddish, *Toplpunkt*. Its editor was the bilingual poet Yaakov Besser, who worked on it from 2000 until his death in 2006.[123] Ten issues were published, containing the work of various Yiddish writers active in Israel at the time.

All this, however, had no effect on the status of Yiddish in Israel, as its effects were mostly limited to just a small circle of Yiddish activists.[124] In some ways, little had changed since the 1950s. As we have seen, the status of Yiddish in Israel at that time was not shaped by legislation but rather by public opinion (though that was itself influenced to some extent by the attitude of the authorities). The same situation developed in the 1990s. The new legislation of those years was equally incapable of changing the status of Yiddish in Israel. It was the culture's public image rather than laws passed by the Knesset that did that. And that public image remained complex even at the end of the twentieth century.

A good sense of this public image can perhaps be found in the words of Amnon Rubinstein, a professor of Law at Tel Aviv University and also the minister of education who presented the bill for the national authorities to the Knesset for its second and third reading:

These two bills [Yiddish and Ladino] . . . fit remarkably well into our new language policy. In contrast to that of the fifties and sixties, the [new] policy does not want to eradicate [anyone's] mother culture or mother tongue. On the contrary, it aims to encourage the language of people's heritage. . . . We do not want an educational melting pot, which erases cultures of origin. . . .

[In relation to] Yiddish, I have to admit that a great mistake was made in the past. This law constitutes a 180 degree *volte face* . . . [from] completion of the policy that was pursued until a few years ago, and particularly in [Israel's] formative prestate years. For that was when a conscious attempt was made to erase the glorious culture of the Yiddish language, its literature, its poetry, its vast body of academic writing, and to depict it as an inferior language.[125]

Rubinstein was clearly being harshly critical of the melting pot policy, and he emphasized that the Law for the Authority for Yiddish Culture marked its official end. He did mention—albeit in a very superficial way—the former glories of Yiddish and the problems it had had to face, though he did not mention the restrictions imposed on Yiddish, the difficulties faced by the Yiddish theater, or the way it was portrayed in the press. In fact, he only mentioned one issue—the attempt to depict Yiddish as an inferior language. It was this image of Yiddish as an inferior and rejected language that had taken hold of the Israeli historical memory and overshadowed all its achievements and struggles and in particular the complex, dialectic attitude toward it of Israeli society and culture.

It was a multifaceted image, however. The flip side of Yiddish's inferiority was its folksiness or, put more positively, its authenticity. And that was expressed in its humor. Yiddish was widely perceived not only as a language of jokes but as a language whose very sound was funny.

Notes

1. Based on the catalog that Y. L. Peretz farlag published, it was founded in 1955. Other sources, including Yitzhak Coren's memoirs, mention 1956 (*Dos gerangl far Yidish in Yisroel* [Tel Aviv: Veltrat far Yidish un yidish kultur, 1982], 187). It seems to me that the publisher's catalog is the more reliable source. *Algemeyner katalog 1955-1995* (Tel Aviv: Y. L. Peretz farlag, 1995), 3.

2. "Beit Sholem Aleichem," *Herut* April 23, 1964.

3. "Ha'yom tunah even ha'pina le'beit Sholem Aleichem," *Maariv* April 27, 1964; "Beit Sholem Aleichem," *Davar*, May 16, 1966.

4. "Even pina le'beit Sholem Aleichem be'Tel Aviv," *Al HaMishmar*, April 8, 1964; "Derefnt Beit Sholem Aleichem," *Lebens- fragn*, May 31, 1966; "Beit Sholem Aleichem nehnach be'Tel Aviv," *Davar*, May 16, 1966.

5. "Shenat tashk"av tuchraz ki'shenat Shalom Aleichem'," *Davar*, August 10, 1964, 6.

6. Dov Sadan, "Grus fun nonte kroyvim," *Di goldene keyt* 69/70 (1970): 14.

7. "Khanukes habayis fun Leivick hoyz in Tel Aviv," the speech of Prime Minister Golda Meir, *Di goldene keyt* 69/70 (1970): 7.

8. Daniel Dagan, "Mefo'arim ve'reikim," *Maariv*, February 26, 1974, 54, 98; Nahum Barnea, "Armonot shomemim," *Davar*, July 10, 1970,

9. Y. Aykhenboym, "Nokh der farzamlung fun yidishn shrayber fareyn," *Lebens-fragn*, July 1, 1970, 11. Typically Aykhenboym used his pen name, Artusky.

10. Y. Luden "Der nayer maymed fun Yidish," *Lebens-fragn*, November 1, 1967, 1.

11. "Nosad peras Itzik Manger le'yetzira be'Yidish," *Davar*, October 30, 1968; "Peras al-shem Manger le'yetzira be'Yidish," *Davar*, October 22, 1968. The Manger Prize awarded each winner 5,000 Israeli pounds, which were in 1968 equivalent to 1,500 USD. On Shalom Rosenfeld, see Mordechai Naor, "Oman ha'milim," *Ha'ayin ha'shevi'it*, May 17, 2012, https://www.the7eye.org.il/6596.

12. David Lazar, "Gushpanka mamlachtit le'Yidish," *Maariv*, November 6, 1968.

13. Yitzhak Luden, "Di Itzik Manger-premye un der 'melukhisher' maymed fun Yidish," *Lebens-fragn*, November 1, 1968.

14. Y. Aykhenboym, "Tsu der derefenung fun Leivick hoyz," *Lebens-fragn*, March 1, 1970, 11.

15. Y. Aykhenboym "Nokh der farzamlung fun yidishn shrayber fareyn," *Lebens-fragn*, March 1, 1970, 11.

16. Rubinstein, *Zionist Dream*, 69–70.

17. Machon Avshalom, which opened in 1952 and had its offices in Beit Liesin, joined Tel Aviv University in 1970 and was associated with it for fifteen years. In this university, as well as in the University of Haifa and Bar-Ilan University, programs for Israel studies were opened, and many students enrolled in them.

18. The most important protest song was "Shir ha'shalom" (Song of peace) first performed in 1969.

19. On Israeli rock music, see Motti Regev and Edwin Saroussi, *Popular Music and National Culture in Israel* (Berkeley: University Press of California, 2004), 137–190; Nachumi Har-Tzion, "Nitzanei ha'rok ha'isra'eli," in *Ha'asor ha'sheni, 1948–1958*, ed. Zvi Zameret and Hanna Yablonka (Jerusalem: Yad Ben Zvi, 2000), 199–314; Nachumi Har-Tzion, "Mi'binyanei ha'uma ad holot Nu'eba: ha'zemer ha'ivri be'asor ha'shelishi," *Ha'asor ha'shelishi, 1958–1968*, ed. Zvi Zameret and Hanna Yablonka (Jerusalem: Yad Ben-Zvi, 2008), 217–230.

20. Conversations with the composer and conductor Shimon Cohen, April 2016. Also see Dan Almagor and Eliyahu Ha'kohen, an explanation of the series by its editors and presenters: https://www.youtube.com/watch?v=Jcpjlvk7kYM.

21. The Central Bureau of Statistics, various years, table 4.

22. Ephraim Yaar and Zeev Shavit, eds., *Megamot ba'hevra ha'isra'elit* (Ra'anana: Open University, 2001), 1:388–390.

23. Ibid., 1:390, 452–453.

24. Mordechai Halamish, "Tsar fun shrayber," *Yisroel shtime*, January 10, 1973.

25. Yitzhak Coren, "Komitet far yidisher kultur in Yisroel," *Folk un medine*, no. 1 (September 1972): 35–36.

26. Coren was a Knesset member from 1961 to 1965 and from 1969 to 1974.

27. See note 25 above.

28. Other members of the committee were Yitzhak Yanasovitsh, who had come to Israel in the 1970s and edited the committee's publications; Israel Stolarski, a member of Left

Poale-Zion, secretary of the committee; the journalist Yeshayahu Avrech; and the writer K. A. Bertini, Coren, *Dos gerangl*, 226–227; Yitzhak Yanasovitsh, "Tsvey yor komitet far yidisher kultur in Yisroel un tsvantsik numern *Folk un medine*," *Folk un medine* 20 (April 1974): 3.

29. "Shazar be'rosh ha'va'ad le'tarbut yehudit be'Israel," *Davar*, July 14, 1973.

30. Yitzhak Coren, "Komitet far yidisher kultur in Yisroel," *Folk un medine* 1 (September 1972): 35; Yanasovitsh "Tsvey yor komitet."

31. The journal contained many items by the bilingual writers Mordechai Halamish, Dov Sadan, and Yehuda Gothelf, the former editor of *Davar*.

32. *Folk, velt un medine* 30 (February 1975).

33. Yanasovitsh immigrated to Israel in 1972. Auerbach, Kharlash, Shtarkman, *Leksikon*, (1961) 4:191; Berl Cohen, *Leksikon fun Yidish shraybers* (New York: Raya Ilman Cohen, 1986), 293.

34. From the third issue, a section reviewing Yiddish literature was added, entitled "Bikher fun shrayber naye olim, dershinen in Yisroel" (Books that appeared in Israel by new immigrant authors).

35. Yitzhak Coren spoke at length about the disappointment, particularly the bitter feelings among those whose work was not accepted for publication in *Di goldene keyt*.

36. The introduction by the committee to the book: Yankl Yakir, *A shlitn mit yishuvnikes* (Tel Aviv: Y. L. Peretz farlag, 1974).

37. The committee was unsuccessful in its attempt to expand the public radio broadcasts in Yiddish on Kol Yisrael: Dr. Gershon Weiner, "Barikht vegn Yidish in yisroeldikn radio," *Folk un medine*, No. 24, (August, 1974).

38. Other books printed with the committee's financing: Hirsh Osherovitsh, *Tsvishn blits un duner, lider un poemes* [Between lighting and thunder—Songs and poems], 1973; Meir Kharats, *In fremdn gan-eyden* [In a foreign paradise], 1973; Yosef Lerner, *Fun khelmer pinkes* [From the Chelm record book], 1975; Motl Saksier, *Mit farbotenem blayer* [With a forbidden pencil], 1977; Leyzer Podriatshik, *In profil fun tsaytn*, 1978.

39. Yitzhak Yanasovitsh, "Tsvey yor komitet far yidisher kultur in Yisroel un tsvantsik numern *Folk un medine*," *Folk un medine* 4 (April 20, 1974): 4, 5; "Rosh ha'memshela yisda peras le'sifrut Yidish," *Davar*, April 18, 1973.

40. *Der spigl un andere dertseylungen* came out in 1979 with an introduction by Chone Shmeruk. See Isaac Bashevis Singer, *Der spigl un andere dertseylungen* (Jerusalem: The Hebrew University of Jerusalem, Yiddish Department, 1979).

41. *Griner akvarium* came out in 1975 with an introduction by Ruth Weiss. Abraham Sutzkever, *Griner akvarium* (Tel Aviv: Tsherikover, 1975).

42. "Velt konferents far Yidish kultur vet forkumen in 1976 in Yerusholayim," *Folk un medine* 6 (July 1975): 30.

43. "Yidish kultur gezelshaft in Yerusholayim, rezolutsyes ongenumen oyf der algemeyner farzamlung fun 5 Aug, 1954," *Folk un medine* 26 (October 1974): 27.

44. He was awarded the prize on the basis of the whole corpus of his work but in particular for his monumental novel *Erev* (The eve of).

45. "Peras rosh ha'memshala le'sifrut Yidish le'Leyb Rochman," *Davar*, July 1, 1975.

46. *Barikht fun velt konferents far Yidish un yidisher kultur* (Tel Aviv: Velt buro far Yidish un yidisher kultur, 1977), 217–222; "Ninal kenes ha'Yidish, A. Sutzkever kibel peras rosh ha'memshala," *Maariv*, August 27, 1976.

47. "Hirsh Osherovitsh hatan ha'peras le'sifrut Yidish," *Davar*, 21 December 1983.

48. On "We Are Here" (Anahnu kan), see Hava Novak, "Anahnu kan—lahakat olim mi'Brit Ha'mo'atzot," *Davar*, October 19, 1972. For a survey of the history of the company,

along with interviews with its founders, see http://www.we-are-here.net. Also see A. Kinarti, "Lahakat Anahnu kan, lahit be'Artzot Ha'brit," *Davar*, February 20, 1975.

49. Hava Novak, "Ho'alta hatzaga rishona shel ha'Iditron," *Davar*, May 8, 1975. See also Arye Kinarti, "Ha'bizayon be'Iditron," *Davar*, May 25, 1975; Arye Kinarti, "Lo kal li'hiyot sahkan ole," *Davar*, June 16, 1975. For a survey of the Iditron, see also Sandrow, *Vagabond Stars*, 384. She wrote this chapter of her book on Yiddish theater on the basis of interviews with actors when the theater was active, as well as on the basis of her impressions during her visit to Israel at the time.

50. Arye Kinarti, "Te'atron mamlachti be'Yidish," *Davar*, March 23, 1975.

51. A *Davar* journalist, "Nishlamot ha'hachanot le'*Amcha* be'te'atron ha'omanuti be'Yidish," *Davar*, March 17, 1975.

52. See chapter 3.

53. A *Davar* journalist, "Mekimim te'atron isra'eli kavu'a be'Yidish im Y. Buloff," *Davar*, October 6, 1974; Yaakov Ha'elyon, "Te'atron isra'eli bi'sefat ha'Yidish," *Maariv*, October 10, 1974.

54. Arye Kinarti, "Ida Kaminska hazra ke'ola," *Davar*, March 14, 1975.

55. L. Winograd, "Der komitet far yidisher kultur in Yisroel," *Lebens-fragn*, February 28, 1974, 16.

56. For example, Yankl Yakir's book *A shlitn mit yishuvnikes* was published with the aid of a donation by the cultural fund in the name of Chaim Rubinstein from Melbourne, Australia. See Yakir, *A shlitn mit yishuvnikes*, on an unnumbered page between 7 and 8; Poalei-Zion in the United States donated $500 for the publication of Rokhl Boymvol; Zahava Mendelson, "Hotza'at Y. L. Peretz metzayenet hofa'at sifra ha'shelosh me'ot," *Maariv*, February 17, 1972.

57. "Shiltonot Brit Ha'mo'etzot hitiru la'meshorer ha'idi Yosef Kerler la'alot la'aretz," *Al HaMishmar*, March 12, 1971; "Ha'meshorer ha'idi Yosef Kerler be'kevutzat ha'olim mi'Brit Ha'mo'etzot," *Davar*, March 28, 1971; "Erev al tarbut Yidish be'Brit Ha'mo'atzot," *Davar*, August 16, 1972; "Roman shel Alter Kacyzne," *Davar*, August 17, 1973 (the item also mentioned Hirsh Osherovitsh's book of poetry published by Y. L. Peretz); Yankl Yakir, "Valentina ha'mo'avia, korot Shike Driz ve'ishto ha'goya," *Maariv*, July 4, 1974; Yankl Yakir, "Itzik Kipnis sofer mi'lamed vav," *Maariv*, October 31, 1974.

58. Ehud Ben-ezer, "Taba'ot shel esh be'neshama yehudit, al yetzirato shel Eli Shechtman," *Maariv*, October 2, 1980. Shechtman's most important work, the seven-volume novel *Erev* was published in Yiddish in 1983, by Yisroel Bukh. A Hebrew translation of the first four volumes, by Zvi Arad, had been published already in 1975, by the Kibbutz Hameuchad.

59. *Yidish literatur in medines Yisroel* (Tel Aviv: H. Leivick Farlag, 1991).

60. Eli Shechtman, *Erev*, 7 vols. (Tel Aviv: Yisroel Bukh, 1983); Eli Shechtman, *Be'terem*, 4 vols., trans. from Yiddish into Hebrew by Zvi Arad (Tel Aviv: Hakibbutz Hameuchad, 1973).

61. Arye Kinarti, "La'Yidish kunst teater darush mazal," *Davar*, May 26, 1975.

62. "Ida kaminska hitztarfa la'Yidish kunst teater," *Davar*, April 24, 1975.

63. Sandrow, *Vagabond Stars*, 384.

64. "Hatzagot Mirele Efrat le'zecher Ester-Rokhl Kaminska," *Davar*, January 6, 1976; "Meta ha'sahkanit Ida Kaminska," *Davar*, May 22, 1980.

65. The committee included Dov Sadan, Yizhak Coren, Abraham Sutzkever, B. Y. Michali, K. Bertini, Yizhak Yanasovitsh, Israel Stolarski, and Mordechai Halamish. "Velt konferents fun Yidish shrayber, kinstler un kultur tuer vet forkumen in yuli 1975 in Yerusholayim," *Folk un medine* 26 (October, 1974): 25. The Committee that was founded in the United States

included Shimon Weber, Mordechai Shtrigler, Yoseph Mlotek, Chaim Bez, and others. Among committee members in Paris was Mendl Mann. Committees were also founded in Canada, Australia, and Argentina. Ibid.

66. "Der yontef fun Yidish in Yerusholayim habira, derefenung sesye," in *Barikht fun velt konferents*, 7. Among the attendees at the conference, there were four hundred representatives from Jewish communities around the world who came to Israel at their own expense. Ibid., 209.

67. *Barikht fun velt konferents*, 7–9.

68. Among the speakers were the mayor of Jerusalem, Teddy Kollek; the chairman of the Jewish Agency, Yosef Almogi; the minister of education, Aharon Yadlin; and the rabbi Dr. Arthur Herzberg, president of the World Jewish Congress. Mordechai Tsanin spoke on behalf of the Association of Yiddish Writers and Journalists in Israel, and Israel Cohen on behalf of the Association of Hebrew Writers. The last on the list of speakers was the Yiddish activist, educator, and editor from the United States Yoseph Mlotek, who spoke for the delegation from the United States.

69. *Barikht fun velt konferents*, 36–37.

70. Ibid., 137–200.

71. Ibid., 217–232.

72. Ibid., 234–235.

73. Report on the founding meeting of the Veltrat: "Di grindung zitsung fun Velt-rat far Yidish un yidisher kultur," *Folk un medine* 44 (September 1978): 23–29.

74. Ibid., 20.

75. The fourth issue, scheduled to appear in 1987, was never published. "Firter heft 'Gesharim-Brikn,'" *Yidish-velt*, August 1986, 11.

76. "Di ershte tsen bikher fun der serye vos der velt-rat vet aroysgebn," *Yidish yedies* no. 2, 4; "Naye serye yidishe bikher fun Velt-rat fun yidisher kultur," *Yidish yedies* 5 (May 1980): 28.

77. The first international conference took place in Tel Aviv on July 31–August 4, 1976. "Di grindung zitsung fun Velt-rat far Yidish un yidisher kultur," *Folk un medine* 44 (73) (September 1978): 23–29. The second took place in Tel Aviv on June 16–20, 1980. *Yidish yedies* 5 (May 1950): 1–2. The third was in Montreal, on May 19–24, 1982. *Yidish yedies* 7 (September 1981): 3. The fourth was held again in Tel Aviv on May 21, 1985. *Yidish velt* 2 (February 1985): 1–2, 13. The fifth took place in London on July 5–8, 1988. *Yidish velt* 55 (August 1988): 1–2. The sixth in Moscow, on May 27–30, 1991. *Yidish velt* 8 (December 1990): 1, 3. The seventh in Kiev, on August 24–31, 1994. *Lebens-fragn*, June 30, 1994. And the last one, again in Israel, this time in Ashkelon and Neve Ilan on June 9–12, 1998. *Lebens-fragn* April 30 1998; July 1, 1998.

78. Mordechai Halamish-Flint, "Tsen yor velt-rat far Yidish—un vos vayter?" *Yidishe velt* 28 (May 1986): 11.

79. On the connection between the political map and the social map in Israel, see Moshe Lissak, *Iyunim be'historya hevratit shel Israel* (Jerusalem: Mosad Bialik, 2009), 337–341; on the emergence of Shas and the politics of identities in Israel, see Aviezer Ravitzky, ed., *Shas: Hebetim tarbutiyim ve'rayoni'im* (Tel Aviv: Am Oved and Merkaz Yitzhak Rabin, 2006), 9.

80. Regev and Saroussi, *Popular Music*.

81. Anita Shapira, *Israel: A History* (Waltham, MA: Brandeis University Press, 2012), 391–421; Ravitzky, *Shas*.

82. About the Zavit Theater, see Kohansky, *Ha'te'atron ha'ivri*, 163–165.

83. Talila ben Zakai, "Te'atron katan she'hisig gedolot," *Maariv*, December 14, 1965. See also "Le'Zavit hayta ona shel zahav," *Davar*, September 12, 1965.

84. Tamar Avidar, *Masach u'masecha*; "Atzmon: ani mathil perek hadash ba'hayim," *Maariv*, March 26, 1969.

85. H. L. Fuchs, "S. Dzigan in a nayer teater-kreatsye," *Lebens-fragn*, December 21, 1971; Shraga Har-Gil, "Ha'erev im Shimon Dzigan," *Maariv*, December 25, 1972; Conversation with Shmuel Atzmon, Tel Aviv, November 2008.

86. On the UNESCO resolutions, see An announcement about the founding of the Yiddish theater written by the advertising firm Shira, Meir, Shuv-Ami, Shkolnik, December 20, 1987 (given to me by Shmuel Atzmon); Yoseph Mlotek, "Fun Czernowitz biz UNESCO," *Yidish velt* 55 (August 1988); "UNESCO letoyves Yidish," *Yidish velt* 77 (July 1990).

87. "Dos yidish teater in Yisroel," *Yidish velt* 48 (January 1988); and the advertising firm announcement, note 86 above.

88. Shmuel Rodensky, Miriam Zohar, and Shimon Finkel—press release from the Yiddish theater.

89. Announcement of the advertising firm, note 86 above.

90. "Kultur nayes," *Lebens-fragn*, January–February 1988, 24.

91. Imanuel Bar-Kadma, "Haya bayit," interview with Israel Becker, *Yedioth Aharonoth*, January 29, 1988 (Shiva leilot supplement), 20–21.

92. Michael Handelzalts, "Be'shivhei ha'tzyonut," *Ha'aretz*, February 14, 1988.

93. One outstanding critique was that by Dan Miron, who included it in an article that supported the very establishment of a Yiddish theater in Israel. Dan Miron, "Bechol zot tzarich et ze," *Yedioth Aharonoth*, February 26, 1988. See also Fayvl Zigelboym, "Arum dem nayem yidishn teater in Yisroel," *Yidish-velt* 50 (March 1988): 15.

94. "Di megile fun Itzik Manger," *Lebens-fragn*, August 31, 1988.

95. In a conversation, Atzmon explained that since the establishment of his theater, other groups have formed that call themselves "Israeli Yiddish Theater," and therefore the management of the theater decided to find a name that would be a unique brand name. By the end of 1993, the theater appeared in the press and in notices as the Israeli Yiddish Theater, and from 1994 as Yiddishpiel.

96. Sholem Aleichem's productions included two productions of *Shver tsu zayn a yid* (It's hard to be a Jew), two of *Di kleyne mentshelekh* (The little people), one of *Shimeles khoylem* (Shimele's dream), of *Sender Blank un zayne yorshim* (Sender Blank and his heirs), and *Der farkishefter shnayder* (The enchanted tailor).

97. Conversation with Shmuel Atzmon, April 2016. For a complete list of all the plays staged by Yiddishpiel from its establishment to the present, see http://www.yiddishpiel.co.il/en/from-then-till-now.html.

98. Another individual initiative in the field of Yiddish, which is not discussed in this book, is Yung Yidish, which has been active since 1993 but never attracted broad public attention.

99. "Dos yidish teater in Yisroel," *Yidish velt* 48 (January 1988).

100. Yitzhak Yanasovitsh, "Der yontef premye fun yidishn shtot teater in Tel Aviv," *Yidish velt* 49 (February 1988), 1–2.

101. This is based on my longtime observation of the audiences that come to Yiddishpiel performances and on conversations I have had with people in the audience of this theater.

102. The 430th session of the thirteenth Knesset, Thursday, May 7, 1996, *Divrei ha'knesset*, 146:8348.

103. Yitzhak Luden, ed., *A Homage to Yiddish* (Tel Aviv: World Council for Yiddish and Jewish Culture, Association of Yiddish Writers and Journalists in Israel, 1993), 3. The booklet also explicitly notes that the person initiating the event was Shmuel Atzmon. Ibid.

104. The forty-sixth session of the thirteenth Knesset (January 4, 1993), https://main.knesset.gov.il/Activity/plenum/Pages/Sessions.aspx.

105. Ibid. The texts also appear in Luden, *Homage*, 8.

106. Other speakers at the discussion were the minister of education, Shulamit Aloni; member of Knesset Abraham Burg; and member of knesset Ovadia Eli.

107. The 46th session of the thirteenth Knesset, January 4, 1993, *Divrei ha'knesset*, https://main.knesset.gov.il/Activity/plenum/Pages/Sessions.aspx.

108. The 246th session of the thirteenth Knesset, July 25, 1994, *Divrei ha'knesset*, https://main.knesset.gov.il/Activity/plenum/Pages/Sessions.aspx. Knesset member Dov Shilansky asked specifically about the Inbal Dance Theater and the Khan Theater in Jerusalem.

109. Conversation with Shmuel Atzmon, November 2008. See also Atzmon's words in a meeting with the Education and Immigration Committees of the Knesset, March 4, 2014, https://www.youtube.com/watch?v=pPXBEw9Br6c.

110. Conversation with Shmuel Atzmon, November 2008. Meeting of the Education, Sport and Culture Committee on March 4, 2014, https://www.youtube.com/watch?v=pPXBEw9Br6c.

111. Conversation with Yitzhak Navon, November 2008.

112. On this, see Sarah Abrevaya Stein, *Making Jews Modern: The Yiddish and Ladino Press in the Russian and Ottoman Empires* (Bloomington: Indiana University Press, 2004), 3–7.

113. Nachman ben Ami, "Od penina be'maharozet," *Maariv*, September 14, 1970.

114. David Lazar, "Gushpanka mamlachtit le'Yiddish," *Maariv*, November 6, 1968; Yehudah Gotthelf, "Ha'ma'avak al yihudeinu ha'le'umi," *Davar*, March 29, 1972.

115. On the history of Ladino, see Olga Borovaya, *Modern Ladino Culture: Press, Belles Lettres and Theater in the Late Ottoman Empire* (Bloomington: Indiana University Press, 2012). There were local attempts to use Ladino for purposes of developing a national consciousness, but they never actually bore fruit. See Margalit Mattityahu, "Ha'yetzira be'Ladino," *Moznayim* 87, no. 6 (2014): 28–30.

116. The bill for Law of National Authority for Yiddish Culture and the National Authority for Ladino 1994, submitted on May 19, 1994, http://fs.knesset.gov.il//13/law/13_ls1_291377.PDF. For the date of submission, see the footnote therein.

117. Meeting of the Committee on Education of the thirteenth Knesset, December 14, 1994, 13_ptv_473121.PDF; The 333rd plenary session of the thirteenth Knesset, April 4, 1995, *Divrei ha'knesset*, https://main.knesset.gov.il/Activity/plenum/Pages/SessionItem.aspx?itemID=160829.

118. Ibid.

119. Ibid.

120. The 430th plenary session of the thirteenth Knesset, Thursday, March 7, 1996, *Divrei ha'knesset*, https://main.knesset.gov.il/Activity/plenum/Pages/Sessions.aspx.

121. Ibid.

122. For less than a year, it was headed by the former Knesset member Abraham Melamed, who was replaced in 2000 by the retired colonel Dr. Asher Porat, a native of Argentina who was raised speaking Yiddish: "Dr. Asher Porat, der nayer forzitser fun der natsyonaler instants far yidisher kultur," *Lebens-fragn*, May 1, 2000.

123. Interview with Dr. Asher Porat, chairman of the National Authority for Yiddish, from 2000 to 2004, July 2012.

124. In the end, internal tensions among the members of the authority brought it to a standstill for several years. The efforts to revive it in 2008 revealed how marginal Yiddish had become in Israel and how meager public interest in it was. The author served as the head of the authority from 2008 to 2010 and was one of the people who tried to revive it.

125. The 430th session of the thirteenth Knesset, Thursday, March 7, 1996, *Divrei ha'knesset*, https://main.knesset.gov.il/Activity/plenum/Pages/Sessions.aspx.

EPILOGUE

THE IDEA FOR THIS BOOK MATURED SLOWLY. It was many years ago that the history of Yiddish in Israel began to fascinate me. I have since read accounts, impressions, and anecdotal stories and participated, both actively and as an observer, in discussions and debates on the topic. These have usually been of two types.

The first has involved individuals active in the Yiddish world for many years, mostly Holocaust survivors who immigrated to Israel between the second half of the 1940s and the 1950s, who felt the attitude toward Yiddish in Israel as a personal insult. Many of them argued fervently that Yiddish had fallen prey to the ideology of negating the Diaspora, which had led to discrimination against Yiddish, its marginalization within Israeli culture, and even to persecution. "The authorities in Israel not only killed Yiddish, they went on attacking it to ensure that it was really dead," said Yitzhak Luden, a leading Yiddish journalist, who died in 2017 after a long and very accomplished life.[1] Many others would cite, as proof for this contention, Ben-Gurion's 1945 description of Yiddish as "a foreign and grating language," even though it was a one-off observation that he never repeated.

The second type of conversation on Yiddish involved individuals born after the Holocaust who had grown up in Israel. These people usually regarded Yiddish as a "pleasant" and "folksy" language that creates a "warm atmosphere" and is essentially "funny," in the sense of being not only entertaining but also ludicrous.

The questions then remain: Was there indeed a consolidated, official attitude toward Yiddish in Israel? What motivated the attempts to restrict Yiddish during the early 1950s? How did Yiddish develop in Israel, and how did these restrictions affect its development? And finally, how did the perception of Yiddish as a "funny" language affect its place in Israel in the long run?

To answer these questions, particularly the last, it is necessary to go back to the conclusions we reached earlier.

A Foreign and Grating Language—The Attitude of the State of Israel toward Yiddish: Conclusion

This book has dealt with the history of Yiddish in Israel from the establishment of the state to the end of the twentieth century. Its main conclusion strongly contradicts the claims made by Yiddish activists that there was a deliberate anti-Yiddish policy in Israel, especially in the early years of the state. The state of Israel never formulated a definitive policy on Yiddish, certainly not one that negated it. It is true that high-ranking bureaucrats, as well as several governmental and public committees, attempted to limit the use of Yiddish. It is also true that the Yiddish theater and press were harassed by some government officials and even the police and that Yiddish cultural endeavors were often treated with disrespect and even rejection. Various interest groups also tried to push for measures against foreign languages, and especially Yiddish, including attempting to persuade members of the Knesset to introduce relevant legislation. None of these attempts bore fruit. Ultimately, in terms of policy, no government official or agency in Israel—the prime minister, the government, the Knesset, or individual members of the Knesset—ever took practical steps toward establishing a policy on Yiddish, and no law relating to Yiddish or to any language other than Hebrew was passed in Israel.[2]

The restrictions on Yiddish relied on the Israeli licensing regime for newspapers, movies, and theater shows, which was based on press and theater ordinances established during the British mandate. With the establishment of the state of Israel, these ordinances were absorbed into Israeli law and enabled the Ministry of the Interior and the newly created Council for the Control of Films and Plays to deny licenses to newspapers and theater shows that they felt to be against the public interest. It was this rather than any state legislation that led to limiting the licenses for Yiddish theaters, as well as to restricting the Yiddish press from appearing no more than three times a week.

Nonetheless, Yiddish had a significant presence in Israel during the state's first decade, mainly in the form of a vibrant Yiddish theater scene and an extensive Yiddish press with a large readership. This means that in practical terms, the restrictions had only limited success. Many Yiddish theater companies, facing difficulties in obtaining licenses for their performances, simply ignored the licensing process and put on performances without a license. The penalties for transgression of the regulations usually amounted to only a symbolic fine, which did not act as a deterrent.

Moreover, in July 1951, just over three years after the founding of the state, the Israeli government under Ben-Gurion explicitly instructed the minister of the interior not to deny licenses to non-Hebrew theaters, especially those performing Yiddish. From then on, all licensing requests to produce Yiddish plays were approved.

The licensing restrictions on Yiddish daily newspapers had a similar fate. Private publishers found creative ways to circumvent them. They were not alone. Even political parties, including the ruling Mapai, that were interested in promoting their political interests among Yiddish readers published their own Yiddish dailies and used the same tricks as other Yiddish publishers to work around the limitations. Thus, they too contributed to the creation of a vibrant Yiddish press in Israel.

So, despite all the limitations and hardships and the widespread view of Yiddish as a rejected language, a very active, popular Yiddish arena did exist in Israel. Beyond that, highbrow cultural endeavors in Yiddish would, on occasion, enjoy strong support from the authorities. Conceiving the state of Israel as belonging to the entire Jewish people and aspiring to make it their spiritual center, the Israeli leadership made efforts to include parts of Jewish cultures created in the Diaspora in Israeli Hebrew culture. Yiddish was central to those efforts. In this vein, attempts were made to convince famous Yiddish actors from abroad, several of whom were international stars, to settle in Israel and perform with public funding. These attempts failed. In the literary field, on the other hand, there was much more success. The arrival of Abraham Sutzkever, the world-renowned Yiddish poet, and the establishment of his literary quarterly *Di goldene keyt*, which was fully financed by public money for four and a half decades, made Israel not only the center of Yiddish literature in the post-Holocaust world but also a unique site of Yiddish literary excellence.

So why has the idea that Yiddish was persecuted and even banned in early Israel by the government become a kind of national consensus? How is it that even in the early twenty-first century, Yiddish activists, including actors and journalists, continue to propound the idea that the young state of Israel had a policy of persecuting Yiddish?

Promoting the Hebrew language was undoubtedly a very high priority for the Israeli leadership during the early years. For both ideological and practical reasons it was, perhaps, the highest priority. Ideologically, Hebrew was one of the mainstays of the Zionist world view, but it also played a crucial practical role. In a state one of whose major goals was to absorb immigrants from many countries speaking many different languages, including different Jewish languages and dialects, Hebrew was going to be made the unifying common language of the state and the basis for the new Israeli culture. This was a highly significant policy goal, and the state's attitude to all other languages derived from it.

Foreign languages, especially Jewish languages prevalent before 1948—foremost among them Yiddish—were considered a hurdle to this process because they were felt to inhibit the development of Hebrew. That was why governmental committees and officials dealing with the issues of Hebrew language and culture sought ways to minimize the impact of Yiddish, which they were afraid would stop new immigrants from learning Hebrew.

But Yiddish was not a "foreign" language. It was not just any Jewish language; it was the one used by most Jews in the pre-Holocaust world. The body of modern secular Jewish literature in Yiddish in the prestate years was significantly larger than that in Hebrew and included works considered Jewish classics by prominent authors. Not unnaturally, Yiddish had been in competition with Hebrew over the status of the national language of the Jewish people in the early twentieth century.

Moreover, it was not just the immigrants who came to Israel from eastern Europe with the establishment of the state that spoke Yiddish. Most Israeli leaders had themselves immigrated to prestate Israel from eastern Europe years previously and, like the new immigrants, knew Yiddish well. Many even loved the language. So, alongside their personal affection for Yiddish, they also remembered how strong its status had been among Jews in the past. As a result, they considered that its pervasive use in the state of Israel would inhibit the acceptance of Hebrew. This was the tension at the heart of the attitude toward Yiddish in Israel.

The Yiddish-speaking new immigrants from Eastern Europe—most of them Holocaust survivors—expected an entirely different attitude to their language and culture. They never thought that Yiddish would have a central place in Israel and obviously did not want it to compete with Hebrew. They understood, fully accepted, and even supported the idea that Hebrew should be the language of the state of Israel. However, they hoped that, following the destruction of the Holocaust, Israel would support, or at least not stand in the way of, some kind of renewal of Yiddish. They were looking for respect. Years later some would even use the word *compassion*. The efforts to develop highbrow, as opposed to popular, culture in Yiddish seemed to them far from sufficient. Some even perceived it as a sophisticated way to push Yiddish further to the margins, to make it an exhibit in a museum, something that belonged to the past.

All this leads to the conclusion that the authorities' attitude toward Yiddish was not the main factor in determining its fate in Israel. Much more significant were the social, political, and cultural developments that took place in Israel over the years.

The first were the processes of absorption and adaptation that the new immigrants underwent. Some were natural and typical for many immigrant societies; others were specific to the unique circumstances of the state of Israel, especially to the linguistic and cultural challenges it faced. The strong desire of many Holocaust survivors to integrate in their new home as fast as possible and to start a new normal life quite naturally encouraged the use of Hebrew in everyday life and reduced the use of foreign languages in general, and of

Yiddish in particular. Many Yiddish speakers continued to love the language for what it symbolized and went on using it in among themselves. However, and most importantly, many avoided speaking Yiddish with their children and thus did not pass on the language to the next generation.

Starting in the 1960s, a complex mix of political, social, and cultural developments began to determine the place of Yiddish in Israeli society. The Israeli public, which included Yiddish speakers and their children, as well as people who did not know Yiddish at all, began to see the place of Yiddish in Israeli culture in a new light. Their attitudes were shaped by dramatic events like the Eichmann trial and the Six-Day War, as well as by developments in Israeli culture in general, that affected trends of nostalgia and changes in collective and personal memory.

The early 1980s saw the rise of transformative social processes that were the direct opposite of those that had occurred in the state's first decade. Contrary to the government's melting pot policy, which ultimately did not prevent Yiddish from finding its place in Israel, a reverse, grassroots process gave rise to a new kind of identity politics. This influenced Israel's popular culture and reshaped its realms of memory. Space was made for the collective memories of specific subgroups within Israeli society, while personal and private memories began to act as culture-forming factors.

This process paved the way for the return of Yiddish to Israeli culture during the 1990s and thereafter, most prominently in the form of the privately initiated Yiddishpiel theater, which was embraced and to some extent also funded by the mayor of Tel Aviv. The next step took place in the Knesset when it passed the law establishing the National Authority for Yiddish Culture, which had also started as a private initiative.

So natural processes of social and cultural development had a much stronger and long-lasting influence on the place of Yiddish in Israeli culture than the administrative restrictions and harassment of Yiddish that occurred. What was left behind was the sense of insult felt by Yiddish speakers for many years that their language was not accepted as right for Israel and especially the long-lived perception of Yiddish as a diasporic and folksy language fit only for jokes and humorous stories. It is to the roles that these feelings and perceptions have played in the developing status of Yiddish in Israel that we now turn.

"Yiddish Is Softer, Warmer, More Intimate": How Yiddish Endured in Israel's Public Sphere

In 1987 Am Oved, a leading Israeli publisher, brought out Aharon Megged's novel *Foiglman*, which features a Yiddish poet. Unlike Birstein's story that opened this book, which reflected the image of a Yiddish writer in Israel through the eyes of a Yiddish author, Megged's novel reflected the image of the Yiddish author and Yiddish in general from the point of view of a leading Hebrew author—one of the generation of 1948 writers—who did not know Yiddish at all.[3]

In the encounter between an Israeli-born historian and a Yiddish poet, which is central to the novel, all the stereotypical attitudes toward Yiddish found in Israel are presented, including statements regarding Zionism's persecution of Yiddish. However, the book focuses mainly on the image of Yiddish as a folksy, warm, humorous, and often ludicrous language.

Scholars of Yiddish, as well as intellectuals and Hebrew and Yiddish journalists, perceived this image as degrading and belittling. Over the years, Dan Miron has argued that this ridiculing of Yiddish has in fact been the most long-lasting anti-Yiddish attitude, seeing as its purpose the creation of a sharp divide between Hebrew-speaking Zionists and Yiddish speakers. This ridiculing, in his opinion, could exist only among those who had some kind of daily contact with Yiddish. He made great play of the extent to which this attitude, often used in reference to Sholem Aleichem, did an injustice to the man and his stature as a modern Jewish writer, one of the greatest authors ever produced by the Jewish people.[4]

Miron is undoubtedly correct regarding the attitude to Yiddish in the prestate period and the first two decades of the state. It is also quite clear that the greater Israeli public—including graduates of Israel's school system who had been exposed to at least a little of Sholem Aleichem's writing through the translations of Y. D. Berkowitz—did not have the tools to appreciate the literary genius of Sholem Aleichem. Nonetheless, the question remains: Did the folksy image of Yiddish held by the Israeli public, especially their view of it as a humorous language with many comical elements, harm its status in Israel in the long run? The answer, based on an examination of the status of Yiddish in Israel from the 1970s to the present, is clearly no. In fact, quite the reverse is true.

Over the years, as live contact with Yiddish gradually decreased, the need to separate Yiddish speakers from Hebrew speakers, as well as to prove the superiority of Zionist over Diaspora values, disappeared. This did not, however, affect the image of Yiddish as a comic language, which was already deeply ingrained in Israeli public opinion. There were a number of reasons for this.

One was the Yiddish folk aphorisms and idioms that had been integrated in spoken Hebrew through paraphrase or translation and had become part of the Israeli way of speaking. These were largely perceived as humorous and entertaining. The second was the Yiddish theater, whether performed in Yiddish or Hebrew translation. Its greatest successes were in the field of popular and humorous presentations. People remembered (or had heard) about the renowned comic duo Dzigan and Shumacher, from the 1950s, as being sophisticated and hilarious. During the 1960s Yiddish readings of Sholem Aleichem's work featuring famous Israeli actors—Shmuel Rodensky, Shmulik Segal, and Eliyahu Goldenberg, who was later replaced by Shmuel Atzmon—proved highly successful. However, this too reinforced the image of Yiddish as funny and entertaining, ensuring that that was the way it would continue to be viewed.

It turns out, however, that that was not necessarily a bad thing because, in the long run, this image did not negatively affect the attitude of the Israeli public to Yiddish. For example, in a 1977 interview for the daily *Maariv*, a ninth grader from the town of Holon (outside Tel Aviv) told a reporter that he was studying Yiddish to better communicate with his grandparents, adding, "Yiddish is a 'juicy' [language] and has a humor all its own."[5] The image of Yiddish as folksy and humorous was, then, one of the aspects of the language that attracted an adolescent boy in the 1970s to choose Yiddish studies. And he was not the only one.

In 1989, two years after the publication of *Foiglman*, Aharon Megged returned to question of Yiddish, this time in two essays. "I have never spoken Yiddish, I have never learned it," he wrote, "and yet I still feel as if I understand much more than I know [i.e., of the language]. I feel it, I 'sense' its qualities. . . . I can read a poem by Manger, not understand most of its words and still understand the poem, 'feel' it. I am ignorant in Yiddish, but my heart longs for it. . . . It is softer, warmer, more intimate."[6] Similar perceptions of Yiddish were also voiced by members of the Knesset on different occasions.[7]

The fact that Yiddish was perceived as a folksy language that could be understood without really knowing it—to "feel it," as Megged wrote—encouraged many to become closer to it. In fact, there can be no doubt that one of the main forces that preserved Yiddish in Israeli society toward the end of the twentieth century was the second generation of Yiddish speakers, for whom Yiddish was a part of their personal memories. These individuals were attracted to expressions of Yiddish-language culture in the public sphere, making them into a kind of realm of memory of their own, even though their actual knowledge of the language might have been weak or even nonexistent.

For most of them, attending Yiddish theater was enough. A smaller group began attending various activities in Yiddish for the Israeli public that emerged in Israel at the turn of the twenty-first century. A few others, mainly of the third generation, have discovered Yiddish high culture and become deeply involved in its literature—poetry, prose, and drama.

Looking back, therefore, it would seem that the popular image of Yiddish as a humorous language, as for example in the superficial perceptions of Sholem

Aleichem's writing, made it paradoxically into something accessible and even attractive to the Israeli audience and so kept it alive in the public sphere. As the years passed, it also contributed to drawing the children of the Yiddish-speaking generation closer to the language and ultimately led some young people at the beginning of the twenty-first century to take a serious interest in the language and culture and, most particularly, in the popular Yiddish author who had died some hundred years earlier.

The Twenty-First Century—A New Cultural Process

Toward the end of the twentieth century, the Yiddishpiel Theater, which had just been founded, was the only place to find Yiddish-language culture in the Israeli public sphere. There were groups that conducted activities in Yiddish on a regular basis, the most important of which were held at the Bund-Brit Avoda House on Kalischer Street in Tel Aviv. But these were groups of veteran Yiddish speakers and were conducted by closed groups that operated far from the public eye.[8]

The change, when it came, began in Tel Aviv when the two veteran Yiddish houses, Beit Sholem Aleichem and Beit Leivick, which had not been active for years, had a transfer of leadership. These new leaders were people born after World War II who had a completely different perspective on Yiddish than that of the prior generation. Instead of focusing on creating frameworks and platforms for veteran Yiddish speakers, they turned their attention outward—to the Hebrew-speaking Israeli society. The new idea was to make sure that Yiddish became incorporated into Israeli culture and to draw the second and third generations of east European immigrants, as well as individuals for whom Yiddish was not part of their family's cultural biography, closer to Yiddish and the culture created in this language.

The first of these was Beit Sholem Aleichem, which, during the twenty-first century under the leadership of Professor Avraham Novershtern, has been transformed into a vivacious center for Yiddish culture and a defining factor in the revival of Yiddish in Israel. In the fall of 1999, following its change of management, Beit Sholem Aleichem began offering Yiddish-language classes to the general public. The response was surprising. Hundreds, mostly from the second generation of Yiddish speakers, flocked to Beit Sholem Aleichem to study Yiddish, to hear Yiddish spoken, and to reconnect with a language that for them was a realm of memory with a deep emotional context. Yiddish's folksy image, which had been rooted in the Israeli psyche for decades, proved a bonding rather than a belittling factor.

Very soon Beit Sholem Aleichem began offering an extensive curriculum, from beginner to advanced conversation levels, as well as Yiddish literature classes for those who knew the language. With a meticulously selected teaching faculty, and in cooperation with Israeli universities, the teaching curriculum at Beit Sholem Aleichem expanded continually and today includes collaboration with the Naomi Prawer Kadar International Yiddish Summer Program at Tel Aviv University.[9] It did not take long before Beit Sholem Aleichem began widening its range of activities to include lectures on topics related to Yiddish and east European Jewish culture and various cultural events, as well as theatrical and musical performances.

Beit Leivick underwent a similar process. In 2001, under the leadership of the composer Daniel Galay, it experienced a dramatic change when it turned its attention toward Israeli society at large and changed from being the home of the Yiddish Writers Association, as it had been in the first generation, into an organization with its face to the Israeli public. It began an intensive program of activities aimed at promoting Yiddish, doing so with a high level of social engagement. Beit Leivick hosts conferences on Yiddish-related topics, such as Yiddish theater and Yiddish translation, as well as on issues associated with Israeli and Jewish identity. It has even been successful in attracting young people.[10]

The Yiddishpiel theater, the largest and most stable institution in the world of Yiddish in Israel, has gone on expanding and developing. By accompanying all its plays with Hebrew and Russian subtitles, it also attracts an audience of non-Yiddish speakers. In addition to support received from private people and various organizations, the theater is subsidized by four government ministries and the Tel Aviv municipality. Although it performs throughout Israel, it has become an integral part of Tel Aviv's cultural landscape, like other Israeli theaters.[11]

The new atmosphere and the openness of young people—mostly members of the third generation of Yiddish speakers—have laid the groundwork for bridging the gap between Yiddish and Hebrew literature and its readers. This process is still in its early stages, but the steps taken so far are very significant.

The first was the public recognition of the Yiddish poet Abraham Sutzkever. Although he is generally regarded as one of the greatest Jewish writers of the twentieth century, and despite his being awarded the Israel Prize in 1985—the only time to date that the prize has been given in the Yiddish literature category—the Israeli public remained quite unaware of him. In 2005, fourteen years after a significant collection of his poems had been published in English translation by Benjamin and Barbara Harshav, another collection appeared in

Hebrew. Most of the poems in that collection, entitled *Kinus dumiyot* (A collection of silences), were—like in the English one, translated by Benjamin Harshav, who also wrote the introduction (as he had in the English collection of Sutzkever poems).

The Hebrew edition differed from the English one in a number of ways. It included works from all periods of Sutzkever's life. Several of the poems appeared in a number of different translations alongside the original in Yiddish. In addition to Harshav's erudite introduction, a brief, personal, and very moving epilogue by the book's editor, which in an understated and sensitive way reflected on the difficulties involved in the status of Yiddish in Israel during the 1950s, was also included.[12] This was not just another translation of Sutzkever; it was a tribute to a great Jewish poet and an attempt to gain for his work the acknowledgment of broader literary and intellectual circles in Israel. Indeed, the book was very well received, and a tribute event took place at Tzavta Theater in Tel Aviv.

Seven years later, in 2013, after Sutzkever's death, one of his poems ("The chopped-off hand belonged to me, my catch"),[13] which had appeared in both the Yiddish original and in two Hebrew translations in *Kinus dumiyot*, was introduced into the Israeli high school curriculum and even included in the state exam for graduating high school in Israel. It is true that the poem was included in the section "Post-Holocaust Poetry" and not as a part of Yiddish literature. Still, the fact that it was included in the curriculum was surely a practical step toward the recognition of Yiddish as an integral part of Israeli literature.

Since the beginning of the twenty-first century, several new Hebrew translations of Yiddish literature have appeared. New translations of the works of Isaac Bashevis Singer, with whom the Israeli public has long been familiar, have achieved an impressive circulation.[14] In addition, young translators have started demonstrating interest in Yiddish. The most active and productive of these is Benny Mer.[15] In 2005, Mer's Hebrew translation of short stories by Sholem Aleichem, a collection entitled *Iram shel ha'anashim Ha'ketanim* (The town of the little people), appeared. It formed another link in the long chain of translations of Sholem Aleichem into Hebrew. Refreshing and captivating, Mer's translation presented Sholem Aleichem to the Israeli reader in contemporary Hebrew and, in so doing, demonstrated the timelessness of this great Jewish writer. The book sold very well and was even adapted for the stage, in a production by the prestigious Jerusalem Khan Theatre. The Yiddish book translation project continues, and in the last decade new translations of Yiddish works have appeared, including further works by Sholem Aleichem and *Black Beads*, a collection of poems by Sutzkever.[16]

Alongside these activities, Yiddish has also been making its way into new Hebrew literature written in Israel. Since the beginning of the century, a number of young Israeli authors—all born after the mid-1960s—have published outstanding literary works whose content and style are associated with the world of Yiddish. The first was Yirmi Pinkus, who in 2008 published *Ha'kabaret ha'histori shel profesor Fabricant* (Professor Fabricant's historical cabaret), a novel about a Yiddish theater troupe and its travels across eastern Europe on the eve of World War II.[17]

In 2011 *Hebrew Publishing Company*, a novel by Matan Hermoni, which weaves its plot in the world of Yiddish speakers, came out. While Pinkus sets his story in the *shund* theater in eastern Europe—a major part the of Yiddish theater world—Hermoni positions the heroes in his novel (which is to a large extent reminiscent of *shund* literature) in a different Yiddish cultural arena: the world of literature and printing. Although Hermoni's heroes find themselves at the center of the Yiddish-speaking Jewish society in New York, his Hebrew, which evokes the Yiddish vernacular and its characteristic expressions, links them to Israel. This direct connection is reinforced in Hermoni's second novel, *Arba aratzot* (Four lands). It also deals with Yiddish literature and its authors but takes place in 2010 in Tel Aviv on Arba Aratzot (Four Lands) Street, which is named after the Council of Four Lands, the central body of Jewish authority in Poland between the sixteenth and eighteenth centuries.[18]

In 2017, another book dealing with the world of Yiddish was published. Written by the young author Ya'ad Biran, *Li'tzhok im leta'ot* (Laughing with lizards)—a Yiddish idiom referring to laughing while crying—is a collection of Yiddish-themed stories, some even dealing directly with the issue of Yiddish in Israel.[19]

Common to all these writers—apart from the fact that they are young and Israeli born—is that all their characters, in one way or another, elicit smiles, if not laughter, and therefore ostensibly validate Yiddish's image as a folksy and humorous language. However, these are not grotesque characters but rather, to some degree at least, tragic, heart-rending figures, and the works reflect not only a serious and respectful attitude toward Yiddish but also the sense that the language constitutes a part of the cultural language of young Israeli authors.

It is not only Hebrew literature that has witnessed this development. Since 1990 Israeli films too have started to feature scenes from the world of Yiddish, culminating with the 2008 film *Beit avi* (directed by Dani Rosenberg). With dialogue entirely in Yiddish, using the specific Łódź dialect, *Beit avi* explores in a very subtle and nuanced way the complex encounter between Yiddish and Hebrew in early Israel.

It would seem then that the long and winding story of Yiddish in Israel, its struggles and its successes, is not over. The ambivalence demonstrated by both state and society in Israel's first years, though often seen as simply destructive, provided Yiddish culture with a space in which it could not only survive but continue developing and creating in the Israeli environment. Today, the uniqueness of Yiddish, its history, and literature still attracts young Israelis. The last word of its story has not been said.

Notes

1. See https://www.youtube.com/watch?v=vQsN-aXiH2Q. Hadas Kalderon, the granddaughter of the great Yiddish poet Abraham Sutzkever, who accused the Israeli government of passing laws against Yiddish, expressed a similar view in March 2018. See https://www.youtube.com/watch?v=eYpm-ZTZWeE&feature=share.

2. Until July 2018 the state of Israel never had any legislation concerning its language policy. The only law that defined this policy was clause 82 of the King's Order-in-Council passed in 1922 by the British government based on the second clause of the British Mandate for Palestine. In July 2018 the Knesset passed the Nation State Bill, which defined for the first time Hebrew as the only official language in Israel.

3. Aharon Megged, *Foiglman* (Tel Aviv: Am Oved, 1987).

4. Dan Miron, *Ha'tzad ha'afel bi'tzehoko shel Sholem Aleichem, masot al hashivuta shel retzinut ba'yahas le'Yidish ve'sifruta* (Tel Aviv: Am Oved, 2004), 11–12. Miron repeated this position also in articles published in *Ha'aretz*; see Dan Miron, "Hem tzohakim ani boche," *Ha'aretz*, July 14, 2004; August 25, 2011.

5. Nurit Bartzky, "Ivri daber Yidish," *Ma'ariv* (Weekend Supplement, *Yamim ve'leilot*), October 7, 1977, 8–10.

6. Aharon Megged, *Shulhan ha'ketiva: kovetz ma'amarim be'inyenei sifrut* (Tel Aviv: Am Oved, 1989), 136–137.

7. See, for example, http://knesset.gov.il/tql/knesset_new/knesset13/HTML_27_03_2012_06-21-01-PM/19930104@19930104003@003.html.

8. Over the years the Bund-Brit Avoda has tried—unsuccessfully—to open up to new and younger members.

9. Beit Sholem Aleichem also collaborates with universities and individual scholars on academic research and publishing initiatives, supporting books and studies on topics related to Yiddish culture and east European Jewry.

10. There have also been smaller endeavors: in the early 1990s, Yung Yidish, a nonprofit organization whose purpose is to instill traditional Yiddish culture in Israeli society, especially among young people, was founded and, as of 2018, continues to exist. Its activities are held in centers in Tel Aviv and Jerusalem and include lectures, performances, klezmer music concerts, memorial ceremonies, and holiday events.

11. The Yiddishpiel is supported by the following ministries: Ministry of Culture and Sport, Ministry of Education, Ministry of Aliya and Immigrant Absorption, and Ministry for Senior Citizens.

12. Nitza Drori-Peremen, "Ne'ila," in *Kinus dumiyot: mivhar shirim*, ed. Nitza Drori-Pereman (Tel Aviv: Am Oved, 2005), 372–374.

13. English translation in *A. Sutzkever, Selected Poetry and Prose*, trans. Barbara Harshav and Benjamin Harshav (Los Angeles: University of California Press, 1991), 49.

14. Many of Bashevis's translations were done by Bilha Rubinstein (born in 1936), a retired teacher and literary scholar. Her recent translations of Bashevis Singer include *Beit ha'din shel abba* [In My Father's Court] (Tel Aviv: Sifriat Poalim, 2011); *Yarme ve'Keyle* (Tel Aviv: Yedioth Aharonoth, 2011), and a collection of his short stories, *Tishme'u sipur* (Tel Aviv: Am Oved, 2014).

15. Benny Mer (born in 1971) graduated from an orthodox high school in Bnei-Brak and holds a master's degree in Yiddish literature from The Hebrew University of Jerusalem. He is a writer, editor, and translator from Yiddish into Hebrew.

16. Sholem Aleichem, *Menakhem Mendl*, trans. with notes by Benny Mer (Tel Aviv: Olam Hadash, 2016); Avraham Sutzkever, *Haruzim shehorim*, trans. from the Yiddish by Benny Mer (Tel Aviv: Hakibbutz Hameuchad, 2015); Avraham Sutzkever, *Ghetto Vilna*, trans. from the Yiddish by Vicky Shifris (Tel Aviv: Am Oved, 2016). The book *Ghetto Vilna* first appeared in Hebrew translation in 1947. *Ghetto Vilna*, trans. from the Yiddish by Natan Livne (Tel Aviv: Sechvi, 1947).

17. Yirmi Pinkus, *Ha'kabaret ha'histori shel profesor Fabricant* (Tel Aviv: Am Oved, 2008).

18. Matan Hermoni, *Hebrew Publishing Company* (Or Yehuda: Kineret Zemora Bitan, 2011); Matan Hermoni, *Arba aratzot* (Tel Aviv: Kinneret Zemora Bitan, 2014).

19. Ya'ad Biran, *Li'tzhok im leta'ot* (Hevel Modi'in: Zmora Bitan, 2017).

BIBLIOGRAPHY

Primary Sources
Archival Sources
ARCHIVES OF THE ISRAELI LABOR PARTY, BEIT BERL
9/48/56; 9/49/56; 9/49/57; 9/49/58; 9/49/59

THE BEN-GURION ARCHIVES, SEDE-BOKER
Correspondence files: January 1950; March 1950
Minutes of meetings, October 1948
Ben-Gurion diary, 1950

THE CENTRAL ARCHIVE OF THE HEBREW UNIVERSITY OF JERUSALEM
22730 1948; 22730 1949; 22730 1950

GNAZIM—ARCHIVE OF HEBREW LITERATURE, ISRAEL, TEL AVIV
Zvi Eisenman 394 G
Mordechai Tsanin 504 G

ISRAEL STATE ARCHIVES, JERUSALEM
Meetings of Prime Minister Ben-Gurion with Hebrew writers, ISA-PMO-PMO-000wd15.
Supreme Council for Cultural Affairs, ISA-education-education-000hq4p;
    ISA-education-education-000ylbg; ISA-education-education-000ylbg;
    ISA-education-education-000hq40.
Foreign Language Press, ISA-MOIN-MOIN-0003p1s.
The Incalcation of the Hebrew Language, ISA-PMO-PMO-000v8gn;
    ISA-Privatecollections-BenZviRelations-000fm3z.
Hebrew Column in the Foreign Press, ISA-education-education-000fzw8.
Department of Information and Cinema, Tel Aviv Region, ISA-MOIN-Moin-000qlvr.
Printing Paper for the Press, ISA-MOIN-MOIN-00083z5.
Unauthorized Theater Performances and Movies, ISA-MOIN-InteriorFilmCensor-000e2xb.
Various Plays and Theater Shows, ISA-MOIN-InteriorFilmCensor-000jipp; ISA-MOIN-
    InteriorFilmCensor-000in9s; ISA-MOIN-InteriorFilmCensor-000in9s; ISA-
    MOIN-InteriorFilmCensor-000jiqa; ISA-MOIN-InteriorFilmCensor-000k79e;
    ISA-education-education-000a4yw; ISA-MOIN-InteriorFilmCensor-000l7ch;
    ISA-MOIN-InteriorFilmCensor-000kto5; ISA-MOIN-InteriorFilmCensor-000jvez;
    ISA-MOIN-InteriorFilmCensor-000jvez; ISA-MOIN-InteriorFilmCensor-000kjxu;
    ISA-MOIN-InteriorFilmCensor-000l862; ISA-MOIN-InteriorFilmCensor-000kjxu;
    ISA-MOIN-InteriorFilmCensor-000kjy4; ISA-education-education-000a4yw;
    ISA-education-education-000a4yw.

High Court of Justice file 135/51
High Court of Justice file 213/52

THE ISRAEL GOOR THEATRE ARCHIVES AND MUSEUM, JERUSALEM

Maurice Schwartz files

KIBBUTZ YAGUR ARCHIVE, YAGUR

Yoman meshek Yagur
Notes on visits of Yiddish writers to the kibbutz

THE NATIONAL LIBRARY OF ISRAEL, ARCHIVES DEPARTMENT, JERUSALEM

Papers of Yossel Birstein
ARC. 4* 1627 1 228; 1627 1 228.1; 1627 4 249
Papers of Abraham Sutzkever
ARC. 4* 1565 2 255; 1565 1 670.1

PINHAS LAVON INSTITUTE FOR LABOR MOVEMENT RESEARCH

Minutes of the Central Committee of the Histadrut

YEHUDA GABBAY THEATER ARCHIVE, TEL AVIV

Files of Dzigan and Shumacher

YIVO INSTITUTE, NEW YORK

Abraham Goldfaden Theater (Tel Aviv) 1951–1952 RG 293.

Hebrew Newspapers

Al HaMishmar
Davar
Devar Ha'shavua
Ha'aretz
HaBoker
Ha'dor
HaMashkif
HaTzofe
Herut
Kol Ha'am
LaMerhav
Maariv
Yedioth Aharonoth

Hebrew Periodicals

Ha'ayin ha'shvi'it
Sefer ha'shana shel ha'itonaim

Yiddish Newspapers and Periodicals

Published in Israel:
Bay zikh

Bleter far oylim—Alim la'olim
Di goldene keyt
Di tsayt
Di vokh
Dos vort
Folk, velt un medine
Fray Yisroel
Gesharim-Brikn
Haifa, yorbukh far literatur un kunst
Hayntike nayes
Heymish
Ilustrirter vokhnblat
Lebens-fragn
Letste nayes
Oyf der vakh
Tsanins yidishe ilustrirte velt (Ilustrirte velt vokh)
Unzer haynt
Unzer fraynt
Veltshpigl
Yerushalaymer almanakh
Yidishe prese
Yidishe tsaytung
Yidish-velt
Yidish yedies
Yisroel shtime
Yisroel tog ayn tog oys
Yung Yisroel

Published outside Israel:
Arbeter vort (Paris)
Der tog (New York)
Der veker (New York)
Der yidisher kemfer (New York)
Di tsukunft (New York)
Di yidishe tsaytung (Buenos Aires)
Forverts (Jewish Daily Forward, New York)
Haynt (Montevideo, Uruguay)
Yidishe kultur (New York)

Printed Sources

Barikht fun velt konferents far Yidish un yidisher kultur. Tel Aviv: Der Velt-buro far Yidish un yidisher kultur, 1977.
Divrei Ha'knesset
Divrei sofrim (Minutes of Ben-Gurion's meetings with Hebrew writers in 1949)
Luden, Yitzhak. *A Homage to Yiddish*. Tel Aviv: World Council for Yiddish and Jewish Culture, Association of Yiddish Writers and Journalists in Israel, 1993.

Minutes of the Israeli government 1950–1953
The 22nd Zionist Congress, Basel, December 9–24, 1946, stenographic transcript, Jerusalem, publication of the directorate of the Zionist Histadrut [no name of printing house]: section 118, p. 604.

Interview and Background Conversation Participants

Shmuel Atzmon-Wircer
Zvia Balshan
Rivka Basman-Ben Haim
Haim Hefer
Yitzhak Luden
Lydia Ophir
Asher Porat
Mordechai Tsanin
Ze'ev Tsanin
Shlomo Zeutouni

Hebrew and Yiddish Literature (in the original and in translation)

Auerbach, Rachel. *Be'hutzot Varsha*. Translated by Mordechai Halamish. Tel Aviv: Am Oved, 1954.
Bartov, Hanoch. *Shesh kenafayim la'ehad*. Tel Aviv: Sifriat Poalim, 1954.
Bashevis Singer, Isaac. *Beit ha'din shel aba*. Translated by Bilha Rubinstein. Tel Aviv: Sifriat Poalim, 2011.
———. *Der shpigl un andere dertseylungen*. Jerusalem: The Hebrew University of Jerusalem, Yiddish Department, 1979.
———. *Tishme'u sipur*. Translated and edited by Bilha Rubinstein. Tel Aviv: Am Oved, 2014.
———. *Yarme ve'Keyle*. Translated by Bilha Rubinstein. Tel Aviv: Yedioth Aharonoth, 2011.
Basman-Ben Haim, Rivka. *The Thirteenth Hour*. Translated by Zelda Kahan Newman. Woodstock, NY: Mayapple, 2016.
Ben-Amotz, Dan. *Arba'a ve'arba'a*. Tel Aviv: Sifriat Poalim, 1950.
Biran, Ya'ad. *Litzhok im leta'ot*. Hevel Modi'in: Zemora Bitan, 2017.
Birstein, Yossel. "Baginen." *Heymish* 22–23 (1958): 11.
———. "Baym akern in der nakht." *Di goldene keyt* 28 (1957): 81–85.
———. *Be'midrachot tzarot*. Safed: Ha'matmid, 1959.
———. "Der pastekh Khonen." *Di goldene keyt* 13 (1952): 195–202.
———. "Der toyt fun an altn oks." *Di goldene keyt* 18 (1954): 129–32.
———. *Ketem shel sheket*. Tel Aviv: Hakibbutz Hameuchad, 1986.
———. "Nakht." *Yung Yisroel* (1957): 3–22.
———. "Onitses." *Heymish* (1956): 11.
———. *Oyf shmole trotuarn*. Tel Aviv: Y. L. Peretz Bibliotek, 1958.
———. "S'vet regnen." *Heymish* 26–27 (1958): 9–10.
———. *Sipurim me'ezor ha'shalva*. Tel Aviv: Hakibbutz Hameuchad, 2004.
———. "A yidisher shrayber in kibutz." *Di goldene keyt* 11: 162–167.
Eisenman, Zvi. "A hoyf in Yafo." *Yung Yisroel*, 1957: 44–49.
———. "A mayse vegn Nisim fun Har-Tuv, vegn a Varshever hoyf un vegn a shpil-foygel." *Yung Yisroel*, 1956: 14–16.

———. "Arum besmedresh." *Di goldene keyt* 13 (1952): 221–225.
———. "Der alter antikvar." *Di goldene keyt* 7 (1950): 169–173.
———. *Di ban: dertseylungen fun Poyln, Rusland, Yisroel.* Yagur: Yung Yisroel series, 1956.
———. *Ha'mesila.* Tel Aviv: Hakibbutz Hameuchad, 1960.
Glantz-Leyeles, A. *Amerike un ikh.* New York: Der kval, 1963.
Grossman, David. *Ayen erekh ahava.* Jerusalem: Keter, 1986. Translated by Betsy Rosenberg as *See Under: Love* (New York: Picador, 1989).
Habas, Beracha, ed. *Shevatim, kovetz sipurim u'reshimot shel olim hadashim.* Tel Aviv: Am Oved, 1953.
Halamish, Mordechai, ed. *Mi'kan u'mikarov: antologya shel sipurei Yidish be'Eretz Israel.* Tel Aviv: Sifriat Poalim, 1966.
Haratz, Meir. *In fremdn gan-eyden.* Tel Aviv: Y. L. Peretz farlag, 1973.
Hermoni, Matan. *Arba aratzot.* Or Yehuda: Kineret Zemora Bitan, 2014.
———. *Hebrew Publishing Company.* Or Yehuda: Kineret Zemora Bitan, 2011.
Karpinovitsh, Abraham. *Der veg keyn Sdom.* Tel Aviv: Y. L. Peretz, 1959.
———. "Di mame vet nokh spondzshe makhen." *Letste nayes,* November 5, 1954.
———. "Farges nisht." *Di goldene keyt* 7 (150): 174–179.
Lerner, Yossel. *Fun khelmer pinkes.* Tel Aviv: Y. L. Peretz farlag, 1975.
Manger, Itzik. *Megile-lider.* Varshe: Aleynenyu, 1936.
———. *Shirei ha'megila, Mahadura du-leshonit Ivrit ve'Yidish.* Edited by Jonathan Nadav. Translated and notes by David Assaf. Tel Aviv: Hargol, 2010.
Mann, Mendl. *Adam be'ohel.* Translasted from the Yiddish by Yaakov Eliav. Tel Aviv: Am Oved, 1953.
———. *Bi'kefar natush: sipur.* Translated from the Yiddish manuscript by A. D. Shafir. Tel Aviv: Am Oved, 1954.
———. "Der yidisher shrayber in Yisroel." *Di tsukunft* 64 (1959): 287.
———. *In a farvorloztn dorf.* Buenos Aires: Kiem farlag, 1954.
———. *Oyfgevakhte erd.* Tel Aviv: Di goldene keyt, 1953.
Megged, Aharon. *Foiglman.* Tel Aviv: Am Oved, 1987.
Osherovitsh, Hirsh. *Tsvishn blits un duner, lider un poemes.* Tel Aviv: Y. L. Peretz farlag, 1973.
Pinkus Yirmi. *Ha'kabaret ha'histori shel profesor Fabricant* Tel Aviv: Am Oved, 2008.
Podriatshik, Leyzer. *In profil fun tsaytn.* Tel Aviv: Y. L. Peretz farlag, 1978.
Saksier, Motl. *Mit farbotenem blayer.* Tel Aviv: Y. L. Peretz farlag, 1977.
Shamir, Moshe. *Bemo yadav.* Tel Aviv: Am Oved, 1951. Translated by Joseph Shachter as *With His Own Hands.* Jerusalem: Israel Universities Press, 1970.
———. *Hu halach ba'sadot.* Tel Aviv: Sifriat Poalim, 1947.
Shechtman, Eli. *Be'terem.* 4 vols. Translated from Yiddish into Hebrew by Zvi Arad. Tel Aviv: Hakibbutz Hameuchad, 1973.
———. *Erev.* 7 volumes. Tel Aviv: Yisroel Bukh, 1983.
Sholem Aleichem. *Menakhem Mendl.* Translated with notes by Benny Mer. Tel Aviv: Olam Hadash, 2016.
Spiegel, Yeshayahu. *Arumim be'terem shahar.* Translated by A. D. Shafir. Tel Aviv: Sifriat Poalim, 1968.
———. *Madregot el ha'shamaim.* Translated by A. D. Shafir. Tel Aviv: Am Oved, 1970.
———. *Malchut geto.* Translated by A. D. Shafir, with an introduction by Dov Sadan. Tel Aviv: Hakibbutz Hameuchad, 1952.
Sutzkever, Abraham. *Fun vilner geto.* Moscow: Melukhe farlag der emes, 1946.
———. *Geto Vilna.* Translated from the Yiddish by Nathan Livne. Tel Aviv: Sechvi, 1947.

———. *Geto Vilna*. Translated from the Yiddish by Vicky Shifris. Tel Aviv: Am Oved, 2016.
———. *Griner akvarium*. Tel Aviv: Tsherikover, 1975.
———. *Haruzim shehorim*. Translated from the Yiddish by Benny Mer. Tel Aviv: Hakibbutz Hameuchad, 2015.
———. *Kinus dumiyot, mivhar shirim* (various translators). Tel Aviv: Am Oved, 2005.
———. *Vilner geto 1941–1944*. Paris: Farband fun di vilner in Frankraykh, 1946.
———. *Vilner geto 1941–1944*. Buenos Aires: Ikuf farlag, 1947.
Uchmani, Azriel, Shlomo Tanai, and Moshe Shamir, eds. *Dor ba'aretz*. Merhavia: Sifriat Poalim, 1958.
Yakir, Yankl. *A shlitn mit yishuvnikes*. Tel Aviv: Y. L. Peretz farlag, 1974.
Yaoz-Kest, Itamar. *Ha'mehager ha'baita—siporet 1970–2005*. Tel Aviv: Eked, 2005.
Yizhar, S. "Der gefangener." *Di goldene keyt* 2 (1949): 154–171.

Secondary Sources

Abrahamson, Mark. *Urban Enclaves: Identity and Place in America*. New York: St. Martin's, 1996.
Abramson, Glenda. "Theater Censorship in Israel." *Israel Studies* 2 (1)(1997): 111–135.
Abrevaya Stein, Sarah. *Making Jews Modern: The Yiddish and Ladino Press in the Russian and Ottoman Empires*. Bloomington: Indiana University Press, 2004.
Achimeir, Ora, and Haim Be'er. *Me'a shenot tarbut 1900–2000: Ha'yetzira ha'ivrit be'Eretz Israel*. Tel Aviv: Miskal, 2000.
A'had Ha'am. "Shelilat ha'galut." In *Al parashat derachim*. Berlin: Judische Verlag, 1921.
Almog, Oz. *The Sabra: The Creation of the New Jew*. Berkeley: University of California Press, 2000.
Almog, Shmuel. *Le'umyut, tzyonut, antishemyut: masot u'mehkarim*. Jerusalem: Ha'sifrya ha'tzyonit, 1992.
Appelferd, Aharon. *Masot be'guf rishon*. Jerusalem: Ha'sifriya ha'tzyonit, 1979.
Arbel, Michal. "Gavryut ve'nostalgya: keri'a be'*Hu halach ba'sadot* shel Moshe Shamir al reka benei doro." *Mada'ei ha'yahadut* 39 (1999): 53–66.
Arendt, Hanna. *Essays in Understanding 1930–1945: Formation, Exile, and Totalitarianism*. Edited by Jerome Kohn. New York: Harcourt Brace, 1994.
Arin, Asher. "Mas bulim ve'sha'ashuim." In *Hitpathut ha'misim be'Eretz Israel*, edited by Avraham Mandel. Jerusalem: Museum of Taxes, 1968.
———. "Misi ha'rashuyot ha'mekomiyot." In *Hitpathut ha'misim be'Eretz Israel*, edited by Avraham Mandel, 296–297. Jerusalem: Museum of Taxes, 1968.
Aslanian, Sebouh David. *From the Indian Ocean to the Mediterranean: The Global Trade Networks of Armenian Merchants from New Julfa*. Berkeley: University of California Press, 2011.
Azaryahu, Maoz. *Tel Aviv: Mythography of a City*. Syracuse, NY: Syracuse University Press, 2007.
Bachi, Roberto. *A Statistical Analysis of the Revival of Hebrew in Israel. Studies in Economic and Social Sciences*. Jerusalem: Magnes, 1956.
———. "Tehiyat ha'lashon ha'Ivrit be'aspaklarya statistit." Standalone booklet of *Leshoneinu* 21, no. 1 (1956).
Barak-Erez, Daphna. "Giyus bahurei yeshivot: mi'peshara le'mahloket." In *Tzematei hachra'ot u'parshyot mafteah be'Israel*, edited by Dvora Hacohen and Moshe Lissak

13–39. Sede-Boker: Ben-Gurion Research Institute for the Study of Israel and Zionism, 2010.

Bareli, Avi. "Politika miflagtit u'politika shel mimshal: hanhagat Mapai ba'ma'avar mi'yishuv li'medina." *Israel* 5 (2004): 31–60.

Bartal, Israel. "Yishuv and Diaspora in Changing Perspectives." In *Major Changes within the Jewish People*, edited by Israel Gutman, 387–397. Jerusalem: Yad Vashem, 1996.

Barzel, Hillel. "Ha'mesila." *Moznayim*, December 14, 1961, 61.

Bassok, Ido. "Tenu'ot ha'no'ar ha'yehudiyot be'Polin bein shetei milhamot ha'olam." In *Alilot ne'urim: otobiografyot shel benei no'ar yehudim mi'Polin bein shetei milhamot olam*, edited by Ido Bassok and Avraham Novershtern, 769–792. Tel Aviv: Tel Aviv University Press, 2011.

Berkowitz, Joel, and Barbara Henry. "Introduction." In *Inventing the Modern Yiddish Stage: Essays in Drama, Performance and Show Business*, edited by Joel Berkowitz and Barbara Henry, 1–24. Detroit: Wayne State University Press, 2012.

Berman-Assouline Dalit. *Shimur u'temura ba'Yidish ha'haredit be'Israel*. PhD diss., The Hebrew University of Jerusalem, 2007.

Bernstein, Moshe. *Balada al ha'ayara*. Ramat Gan: Unknown publisher, 1966.

Bialin, A. H. *Moris Shvarts un der idisher kunst teater*. New York: farlag Biderman, 1934.

Blau, Judith R., Min Thomas, Beverly Newhouse, and Andrew Kavee. "Ethnic Buffer Institutions: The Immigrant Press; New York City, 1820–1984." *Historical Social Research* 23, no. 3 (1998): 20–37.

Borovaya, Olga. *Modern Ladino Culture: Press, Belles Lettres and Theater in the Late Ottoman Empire*. Bloomington: Indiana University Press, 2012.

Bourdieu, Pierre. *Distinction: A Social Critique of the Judgement of Taste*. Translated by Richard Nice. Cambridge: Cambridge University Press, 1984.

———. *Sociology in Question*. Translated by Richard Nice. London: Sage, 1993.

Boym, Svetlana. *The Future of Nostalgia*. New York: Basic, 2001.

Bunim, Shmuel. *Kan Bunim*. Tel Aviv: Dvir, 1994.

Burstein, Pesach, *Geshpilt a lebn*. Tel Aviv: no publisher, 1980.

———. *What a Life! The Autobiography of Pesachke Burstein*. Syracuse, NY: Syracuse University Press, 2003.

Cammy, Justin. "Abraham Sutzkever." In *Writers in Yiddish*, edited by Joseph Sherman, 303–313. Detroit: Thomson Gale, 2007.

———. "Tsevorfene bleter: The Emergence of Yung Vilne." *Polin* 14 (2001): 170–191.

———. "Vision and Redemption: Abraham Sutzkever's Poems of Zion(ism)." In *Yiddish after the Holocaust*, edited by Joseph Sherman, 240–265. Oxford: Boulevard, 2004.

Caplan, Debra. "Attention Must Be Paid—Death of a Salesman's Counter Adapted Yiddish Homecoming." *Modern Drama* 58, no. 2 (Summer 2015): 194–217.

Caspi, Dan, and Yehiel Limor. *Ha'metavchim: emtze'ei ha'tikshoret be'Israel 1948–1990*. Tel Aviv: Sifryat Eshkolot, Am Oved, and The Hebrew Univeristy of Jerusalem, 1992.

Cassedy, Steven. *Building the Future: Jewish Immigrant Intellectuals and the Making of the Tsukunft*. New York: Holmes and Meier, 1999.

Chaikin, Joseph. *Yidishe bleter in Amerike*. New York: self-published, 1946.

Chaver, Yael. *What Must Be Forgotten: The Survival of Yiddish in Zionist Palestine*. Syracuse, NY: Syracuse University Press, 2004.

Chetrit, Sami Shalom. *Ha'ma'avak ha'mizrahi be'Israel, bein dikui le'shihrur, bein hizdahut le'alternativa 1948–2003*. Tel Aviv: Am Oved, 2006.

Cohen, Berl. *Leksikon fun Yidish shraybers*. New York: Raya Ilman Cohen, 1986.
Cohen, Nathan. "Itonut yomit yehudit be'polin." In *Kiyum va'shever: yehudei Polin le'doroteihem*, edited by Israel Bartal and Israel Gutman, 301–323. Jerusalem: Merkaz Zalman Shazar, 2001.
———. *Sefer, sofer ve'iton: merkaz ha'tarbut ha'yehudit be'Varsha, 1918–1942*. Jerusalem: Magnes, 2003.
———. "Sifrut ve'itonut 'shund'." In *Zeman yehudi hadash*, edited by Yirmiyahu Yovel, 1:314–315. Jerusalem: Keter, 2007.
Cohen, Uri. *Ha'har ve'hagiva: ha'universita ha'ivrit bi'tekufat terom ha'atzma'ut ve'reishit ha'medina*. Tel Aviv: Am Oved, 2006.
Conforti, Yitzhak. *Zeman avar, ha'historyografya ha'tzyonit ve'itzuv ha'zikaron ha'le'umi*. Jerusalem: Yad Yitzhak Ben Zvi, 2006.
Coren, Yitzhak. *Dos gerangl far Yidish in Yisroel*. Tel Aviv: Veltrat far Yidish un yidish kultur, 1982.
Dankner, Amnon. *Dan Ben Amotz: biografya*. Jerusalem: Keter, 1992.
Della Pergola, Sergio. "Merkaz u'periferya ba'olam ha'yehudi: hamishim shana be'perspektiva sotzyo-demografit." *Yahadut zemaneinu* 8 (1993): 269–299.
Deleuze, Gilles, and Felix Guattari. *Kafka—Toward a Minor Literature*. Translated by Dana Polan. Minneapolis: University of Minnesota Press, 1986.
Dinnerstein, Leonard, and David Reimers. *Ethnic Americans: A History of Immigration*. New York: Columbia University Press, 2009.
Dror, Yuval. "Reishit ha'technion ha'ivri be'Haifa, 1902–1950, me'ha'tochnit le'beit sefer gavoha yehudi ve'ad tom tekufat nihulo shel Shlomo Kaplanski." *Iyunim bi'tekumat Israel* 6 (1996): 333–334.
Drori-Pereman, Nitza. "Ne'ila." In *Kinus dumiyot, mivhar shirei Abraham Sutzkever*, edited by Nitza Drori-Pereman, 372–374. Translated into the Hebrew by Benjamin Harshav. Tel Aviv: Am Oved, 2005.
Drucker Bar-Am, Gali. *'Ikh bin dayn shtoyb'?, yitzug ha'havaya ha'israelit be'siporet Yidish be'Israel 1948–1968*. PhD diss., The Hebrew University of Jerusalem, 2013.
Dubnow, Simon. *Michtavim al ha'yahadut ha'yeshana ve'ha'hadasha*. Translated into the Hebrew by Abraham Levinson. Tel Aviv: Ha'hoker, 1936.
Dzigan, Shimen, *Der koyekh fun Yidishn humor*. Tel Aviv: no publisher, 1974.
Eisenman, Yehudit. "Moshe lo yelech bi'shevil ha'yedidut." In *Asufa le'zichro shel Moshe Yungman*, edited by Nava Gonen, 71–80. Tiv'on: self-published, 1985.
Eisenman, Zvi. "Ahi Moshe." In *Asufa le'zichro shel Moshe Yungman*, edited by Nava Gonen, 41–49. Tiv'on: self-published, 1985.
Eliav, Mordechai. "Meir Dvorjetski z"l, ha'ish, ha'hoker ve'hamore." In *Iyunim bi'tekufat ha'sho'a*, 11–18. Ramat Gan: Bar-Ilan University, 1979.
Enoch, Yael. *Aliya u'kelita: nituah sotzyologi. Israel ba'asor ha'rishon*. Tel Aviv: Open University, 2001.
Erel, Nitza. *"Beli mora beli maso panim: Uri Avnery ve'HaOlam Haze*. Jerusalem: Magnes, 2006.
Estraikh, Gennady. "Sovyetish heymland." *YIVO Encyclopedia of the Jews in Eastern Europe*, http://www.yivoencyclopedia.org/article.aspx/Sovetish_Heymland.
Ettinger, Shmuel. *Bein Polin le'Rusya*. Jerusalem: Zalman Shazar Center and Bialik Institute, 1994.

Even-Zohar, Itamar. "The Emergence of a Native Hebrew Culture in Palestine, 1882–1948." In *Essential Papers on Zionism*, edited by Jehuda Reinharz and Anita Shapira, 727–744. New York: New York University Press, 1996.

———. "Polysystem Theory." Edited by Itamar Even-Zohar, special issue, *Poetics Today* 11, no. 1 (1990): 9–26.

———. "Tahalichei maga ve'hitarvut be'hivatzrut ha'tarbut ha'ivrit ha'hadasha" In *Nekudat tatzpit: Tarbut ve'hevra be'Eretz Israel*, edited by Nurit Gertz, Dan Miron, and Shalom Reichman, 129–140. Tel Aviv: Open University, 1988.

Feingold, Ben-Ami. "Shenot ha'shishim ba'te'atron ha'isra'eli." In *He'asor ha'sheni*, edited by Zvi Zameret and Hanna Yablonka, 241–260. Jerusalem: Yad Ben-Zvi, 2000.

Fishman, David E. *The Book Smugglers: Partisans, Poets and the Race to Save Jewish Treasures from the Nazis*. Lebanon, NH: ForeEdge 2017.

———. "The Politics of Yiddish in Tsarist Russia." *From Ancient Israel to Modern Judaism* 4 (1989): 155–171.

———. *The Rise of Modern Yiddish Culture*. Pittsburg: University of Pittsburg Press, 2005.

Fishman, Joshua A. "Attracting a Following to High-Culture Functions for a Language of Everyday Life: The Role of the Tshernovits Language Conference in the 'Rise of Yiddish.'" *International Journal of the Sociology of Language* 24 (1980): 43–73.

Fishman, Joshua A., and David E. Fishman. "Yiddish in Israel: The Press, Radio, Theater and Book Publishing." *Yiddish* 1–2 (1973): 4–23.

Frakes, Jerold C. *Early Yiddish Texts 1100–1750*. Oxford: Oxford University Press, 2004.

———. Introduction to *Eyn shoyn mayse bukh*, excerpt in original older Yiddish in Jerold C. Frakes, *Early Yiddish Texts 1100–1750*, 296–322. Oxford: Oxford University Press, 2004.

Frankel, Jonathan. *Prophecy and Politics, Socialism, Nationalism and the Russian Jews, 1862–1917*. Cambridge, MA: Cambridge University Press, 1981.

Gabbai, Yehuda, ed. *Te'atron "Ohel"—sipur ha'ma'ase*. Tel Aviv: Mifalei tarbut ve'hinuch, 1983.

Gal-Ed, Efrat. *Niemandssprache—Itzik Manger—ein europaischer Dichter*. Berlin: Judischer Verlag im Surhrkamp Verlag, 2016.

Galnoor, Yitzhak. *Reishita shel ha'demokratya be'Israel*. Tel Aviv: Am Oved, 1985.

Gelber, Yoav, *Moledet hadasha: aliyat yehudei merkaz Eiropa u'kelitatam 1933–1948*. Jerusalem: Yad Yitzhak Ben Zvi, 1990.

Gertz, Nurit. *Makhela aheret: nitzolei sho'a, zarim ve'aherim ba'kolno'a u'va'sifrut ha'isre'aliyim*. Tel Aviv: Am Oved, 2004.

Giladi, Dan. *Ha'yishuv bi'tekufat ha'aliya ha'revi'it (1924–1929): behina kalkalit u'politit*. Tel Aviv: Am Oved, 1973.

Gingold, Pinhas. "Di role fun Yidish natsyonaler arbeter farband in dem yidishn kultur lebn in Amerike." In *Yidish-natsyonaler arbeter farband*, 339–385. New York: Jewish National Workers Alliance, 1946.

Glatstein, Jacob, Shmuel Niger, and Hillel Rogoff, eds. *Finf un zibetsik yor yidishe prese in Amerike 1870–1945*. New York: Y. L. Peretz farayn, 1945.

Glazer, Nathan. *American Judaism*. Chicago: University of Chicago Press, 1957.

Glinert, Lewis, and Yosseph Shilhav. "Holy Land, Holy Language: A Study of an Ultraorthodox Jewish Ideology." *Language in Society* 20, no. 1 (March 1991): 59–86.

Gonen, Naava, ed. *Asufa le'zichro shel Moshe Yungman*. Tiv'on: self-published, 1985.

Gorny, Yosef, Avi Bareli, and Yitzhak Greenberg. *Me'hevrat avoda le'irgun ovedim*, edited by Yosef Gorny, Avi Bareli, and Itzhak Greenberg. 1–4 Sede-Boker: Ben-Gurion University of the Negev Press, 2000.

Gramsci, Antonio. *A Selection from the Prison Notebooks*. Edited and translated by Quintin Hoare and Geoffry Nowell Smith. New York: International Publishers, 1971, 2014 reprint.

Greenberg, Lev. "Ovdim hazakim, ovdim halashim, zeramim ba'kalkala ha'politit ha'isra'elit, 1967–1994." *Teorya u'bikoret* 9 (Winter 1996): 61–81.

Gross, Nahum. "Kalkalat Israel." *Ha'asor ha'sheni, 1958–1968*. Edited by Zvi Zameret and Hanna Yablonka, 30–46. Jerusalem: Yad Ben Zvi, 2000.

Gross, Nathan. "Dzigan and Shumacher." *YIVO Encyclopedia of the Jews in Eastern Europe*, http://www.yivoencyclopedia.org/article.aspx/Dzigan_and_Shumacher.

Gutman, Israel. "She'erit ha'pleita: be'ayot ve'havharot." In *She'erit ha'pleita 1944–1948, ha'shikum ve'ha'ma'avak ha'politi*, edited by Israel Gutman and Adina Drechsler, 461–479. Jerusalem: Yad Vashem, 1990.

Habas, Bracha, and Eliezer Shohat. *Sefer ha'aliya ha'shenya*. Tel Aviv: Am Oved, 1957.

Hacohen, Dvora. *Immigrants in Turmoil: Mass Immigration to Israel and Its Repercussions in the 1950s and After*. Syracuse, NY: Syracuse University Press, 2003.

———. *Olim bi'se'ara: ha'aliya ha'gedola u'kelitata be'Israel 1948–1953*. Jerusalem: Yad Ben Zvi, 1994.

Halamish, Mordechai. "Mendl Mann." In *Mikan u'mikarov: antologya shel sipurei Yidish be'Eretz Israel mi'reishit ha'me'a ve'ad yameinu*, edited by Mordechai Halamish, 403. Tel Aviv: Sifriat Poalim, 1966.

Halperin, Liora R. *Babel in Zion: Jews Nationalism and Language Diversity in Palestine, 1920–1948*. New Haven, CT: Yale University Press, 2015.

Ha'negbi, Moshe. *Hofesh ha'itonai ve'hofesh ha'itonut be'Israel, dinei tikshoret ve'etika itona'it*. Ra'anana: Open University, 2011.

Harpazi, Michael. "Hofesh ha'itonut le'or hukei Israel." In *Sefer ha'shana shel ha'itona'im*, 22–30. Tel Aviv: The Association of Journalists in Tel Aviv, 1957.

Harshav, Benjamin. "Abraham Sutzkever, shira ve'hayim." In *Kinus dumiyot, mivhar shirei Abraham Sutzkever*, edited by Nitza Drori-Pereman, 11–30. Translated into the Hebrew by Benjamin Harshav. Tel Aviv: Am Oved, 2005.

———. *The Meaning of Yiddish*. Berkeley: University of California Press, 1990.

———. "Sutzkever: Life and Poetry." In *A. Sutzkever: Selected Poetry and Prose*, translated from the Yiddish by Barbara Harshav and Benjamin Harshav, 3–23. Berkeley: University of California Press, 1991.

Har-Tzion, Nachumi. "Mi'binyanei ha'uma ad holot Nu'eba: ha'zemer ha'ivri be'asor ha'shelishi." In *Ha'asor ha'shelishi, 1958–1968*, edited by Zvi Zameret and Hanna Yablonka, 217–230. Jerusalem: Yad Ben Zvi, 2008.

———. "Nitzanei ha'rok ha'isra'eli." In *Ha'asor ha'sheni, 1948–1958*, edited by Zvi Zameret and Hanna Yablonka, 299–314. Jerusalem: Yad Ben-Zvi, 2000.

Hever, Hannan. "Aharayut u'merhav be'*Ha'shavui* me'et S. Yizhar." *Mehkarei Yerushalayim be'sifrut ivrit* 23 (2009): 273–278.

Hobsbawm, Eric. "Introduction: Invention of Tradition." In *The Invention of Tradition*, edited by Eric Hobsbawm and Terence Ranger, 1–13. Cambridge: Cambridge University Press, 1983.

Holtzman, Avner. "Ha'sipurim shel dor ba'aretz." In *Ha'asor ha'rishon 1948–49*, edited by Zvi Zameret and Hanna Yablonka, 263–280. Jerusalem: Yad Ben Zvi, 1995.

———. *Mafteah ha'lev, omanut ha'sipur shel Hanoch Bartov*. Jerusalem: Mosad Bialik, 2015.

———. "They Are Different People: Holocaust Survivors as Reflected in the Literature of the Generation of 1948." *Yad Vashem Studies* 30 (2002): 337–368.
Howe, Irvin. *The World of Our Fathers*. New York: New York University Press, 2005.
Ilan, Rafi. "Nes Ha'megila, 1965: hatzagat mofet be'Yidish be'te'atron ha'Hamam be'Yafo." *Davka* 4 (2008): 44–47.
Inbari, Assaf. "Sipurei ha'kibbutz shel Yossel Birstein." *Keshet ha'hadasha* 21 (2007): 138–149.
Janowitz, Morris. *The Community Press in an Urban Setting: The Social Elements of Urbanism*. Chicago: University of Chicago Press, 1967.
Kaplan, Kimi. "Mosdot hinuch ba'hevra ha'haredit be'mahatzit ha'shenya shel tekufat ha'mandat ha'briti u'mekomam be'shikuma le'ahar ha'sho'a." *Israel* 21 (Spring 2013): 196–200.
Kazshdan, Haim. *Der kinstler un dertseyler Mendl Mann*. Paris: Undzer kiem, 1965.
Kimmerling, Baruch. *Mehagrim, mityashvim, yelidim: ha'medina ve'ha'hevra be'Israel bein ribui tarbuyot le'milhemet tarbut*. Tel Aviv: Am Oved, 2004.
Kitron, Naomi. *Bein shalosh yabashot: hayei Moshe Kitron*. Jerusalem: Carmel, 2005.
Kobrin, Rebecca. *Jewish Bialystok and Its Diaspora*. Bloomington: Indiana University Press, 2010.
Kohansky, Mendel. *Ha'te'atron ha'ivri*. Jerusalem: Weidenfeld and Nicolson, 1974.
———. *The Hebrew Theater: Its First Fifty Years*. New York: Ktav, 1969.
Kolat, Israel. "Ha'im ha'yishuv haya hagshamat ha'le'umyut ha'yehudit?" In *Leumyut u'politika yehudit: Perspektivot hadashot*, edited by Yehuda Reinharz, Joseph Salmon, and Gideon Shimoni, 225–252. Jerusalem: Merkaz Shazar, 1996.
Kritz, Reuven. *Erev rav: Al sefarim, sofrim ve'sugyot sifrut*. Tel Aviv: Pura, 1990.
Kronfeld, Chana. *On the Margins of Modernism*. Berkeley: University of California Press, 1966.
Krutikov, Mikhail. "Yiddish Literature: Yiddish Literature after 1880." *YIVO Encyclopedia of the Jews in Eastern Europe*, http://www.yivoencyclopedia.org/article.aspx/Yiddish_literature_after_1800.
Lahav, Pnina. "Governmental Regulation of the Press: A Study of Israel's Press Ordinance." *Israel Law Review* 13 (1978): 230–250, 489–524.
———. "Ha'oz ve'ha'misra: Beit ha'mishpat ha'elyon ba'asor ha'rishon le'kiyumo." *Iyunei mishpat* 14, no. 3 (August 1989): 492–500.
Laor, Dan. *Alterman, biyografya*. Tel Aviv: Am Oved, 2013.
———. "Bein metzi'ut le'hazon, al hishtakfuta shel ha'aliya ha'hamonit ba'roman ha'isr'aeli." In *Olim u'ma'abarot 1948–1952*, edited by Mordechai Naor, 205–220. Jerusalem: Yad Ben-Zvi, 1987.
———. *Ha'ma'avak al ha'zikaron, masot al sifrut, hevra ve'tarbut*. Tel Aviv: Am Oved, 2008.
Levin, Amos. *Le'darka shel havurat "Likrat."* Tel Aviv: Hakibbutz Hameuchad, 1984.
Levy, Emanuel. *Ha'te'atron ha'le'umi Habima, korot ha'te'atron ba'shanim 1919–1979*. Tel Aviv: Eked, 1981.
Liebman, Charlse S. "Diaspora Influence on Israel: The Ben-Gurion Blaustin 'Exchange' and Its Aftermath." *Jewish Social Studies* 36 (July–October 1974): 274–275.
Liss, Abraham. "Mordechai Tsanin—shtraykhn tsu zayn shafn." *Yerusholaymer almanakh* 25 (1995): 280–287.
Lissak, Moshe. "The Demographic Social Revolution in Israel in the 1950s: The Absorption of the Great Aliya." *Journal of Israeli History* 22 (Autumn 2003): 1–31.
———. *Iyunim be'historya hevratit shel Israel*. Jerusalem: Mosad Bialik, 2009.
Lomsky-Feder, Edna, and Tamar Rapport. *Yisra'elim be'darkam: sipurei hagira shel tze'irim mi'Brit Ha'mo'atzot le'she'avar*. Jerusalem: Magnes, 2013.

Luz, Ehud. *Makbilim nifgashim: dat u'le'umyut ba'tenu'a ha'tzyonit be'mizrah Eiropa be'reishita 1882–1904*. Tel Aviv: Am Oved, 1986.
Man, Rafi. "Ha'hashuv im ha'me'anyen, hesped le'David Giladi." *Ha'ayin ha'shevi'it*, http://www.the7eye.org.il/25210.
Mankowitz, Zeev W. *Life between Memory and Hope: The Survivors of the Holocaust in Occupied Germany*. Cambridge: Cambridge University Press, 2002.
Margalit, Mattityahu. "Ha'yetzira be'Ladino." *Moznayim* 87, no. 6 (2014): 28–30.
Megged, Aharon. *Shulhan ha'ketiva: kovetz ma'amarim be'inyenei sifrut*. Tel Aviv: Am Oved, 1989.
Mintz, Matityahu, "Tzyonim ve'Poalei-Zion ba'hprakh konferentz be'Tshernovitz, 1908." *Shvut* 15 (1992): 135–147.
Miron, Dan. *Arba panim ba'sifrut ha'ivrit bat yameinu* Iyunim bi'yetzirot Alterman, Ratosh, Yizhar, Shamir Jerusalem: Schocken, 1962.
———. *Ha'tzad ha'afel bi'tzehoko shel Sholem Aleichem, masot al hashivuta shel retzinut ba'yahas le'Yidish ve'sifruta*. Tel Aviv: Am Oved, 2004.
———. "The Literary Image of the Shtetl." In *The Image of the Shtetl and Other Studies of Modern Jewish Literary Imagination*, 1–48. Syracuse, NY: Syracuse University Press, 2000.
———. *Sheleg al kenaf ha'yona: Pegishot im Avraham Sutzkever*. Tel Aviv: Eked Le'shira, 1999.
———. *A Traveller in Disguise: The Rise of Modern Yiddish Fiction in the Nineteenth Century*. Syracuse, NY: Syracuse University Press, 1996.
Moss, Kenneth B. *Jewish Renaissance in the Russian Revolution*. Cambridge, MA: Harvard University Press, 2008.
Myers, David N. "History and Ideology: The Case of Ben Zion Dinur, Zionist Historian Par Exellence." *Modern Judaism* 8, no. 2 (1988): 167–193.
———. *Re-inventing the Jewish Past*. New York: Oxford University Press, 1995.
Naor, Mordechai. "Oman ha'milim." *Ha'ayin ha'shevi'it*, May 17, 2012, https://www.the7eye.org.il/6596.
Near, Henry. *The Kibbutz Movement: A History*. Oxford: Published for the Littman Library by Oxford University Press, 1997.
Niger, Shmuel, and Jacob Shatzky et al., eds. *Leksikon fun der nayer yidisher literatur*. Vols. 1–8. New York: Alveltlekher yidisher kultur kongres, 1956–1981.
Nora, Pierre. *Realms of Memory: The Construction of the French Past*. Translated by Arthur Goldhammer. New York: Columbia University Press, 1996.
Novershtern, Avraham. *Avrom Sutzkever, tsu zayn vern a ben shivim*. Catalogue of an exhibition at the Jewish National Library. Jerusalem: no publisher, 1983.
———. "Between Town and Gown: The Institutionalization of Yiddish in Israeli Universities." In *Yiddish in the Contemporary World: Papers of the First Mendel Friedman International Conference on Yiddish*, edited by Gennady Estraikh and Mikhail Krutikov, 2–20. Oxford: Legenda, 1999.
———. *Hasifrut ve'ha'hayim, tzemihat sifrut Yidish ha'hadasha*. Tel Aviv: Open University, 2000
———. *Kesem ha'dimdumim. Apokalipsa u'meshihyut be'sifrut Yidish*. Jerusalem: Magnes, 2003.
———. Modernizm yidi be'mizrah Eiropa." *In Zeman yehudi hadash* edited by Yirmiyahu Yovel. Vol. 3. 166–169. Jerusalem: Keter, 2007.

---. "The Multi-Colored Patchwork on the Coat of a Prince." *Modern Hebrew Literature* 8-9 (1992): 56-59.

---. "Sifrut ve'politika bi'yetzirata shel kevutzat 'Yung Vilna.'" In *Bein shetei milhamot olam*, edited by Chone Shmeruk and Shmuel Verses, 169-181. Jerusalem: Magnes, 1996.

---. "Outcasts: Representations of the Underworld in Modern Yiddish Literature." In *Margins and Centers in Yiddish Culture and Literature*, edited by Shlomo Berger, 33-64. Amsterdam: Menasse Ben Israel Institute, 2014.

---. "Walk through Words as through Minefields: Abraham Sutzkever z"l." *Yad Vashem Studies* 38, no. 1 (2010): 47-59.

Ofrat, Gideon. *Ha'shiva el ha'shtetl, ha'yahadut ke'dimui ba'omanut be'Israel*. Jerusalem: Mosad Bialik, 2011.

Olzak, Susan, and Elizabeth West. "Ethnic Conflicts and the Rise and Fall of Ethnic Newspapers." *American Sociological Review* 56, no. 4 (August 1991): 458-474.

Park, Robert Ezra. *The Immigrant Press and Its Control*. New York: Harper and Brothers, 1922.

Perry, Menachem. "Kavim yehefim u'tzelil." In Yossel Birstein, *Sipurim me'ezor ha'shalva*, 323-346. Tel Aviv: Hakibbutz Hameuchad, 2004.

Pikar, Avi. *Olim bi'mesura, medinyut Israel kelapei aliyatam shel yehudei tzefon-Afrika 1951-1956*. Sede-Boker: Ben-Gurion Institute, 2013.

Pilowsky, Arye L. "Itonut Yidish be'Eretz Israel mi'tehilata ve'ad hofa'at *Nayvelt* 1934." *Katedra* 10 (1979): 72-101.

---. "Lashon tarbut u'le'umyut ba'yishuv ha'hadash—ha'diyun ha'tziburi ba'tochnit le'hakim katedra le'Yidish be'Yerushalayim be'shilhei 1927." *Katedra* 21 (1981): 103-134.

---. *Tsvishn yo un neyn: Yidish un yidish-literatur in Erets-Yisroel 1907-1948*. Tel Aviv: Veltrat far yidishe kultur, 1986.

Pinsker, Shachar. "Ata marvad me'ofef, eincha yoter me'hazaya shel am te'atrali." *Ha'aretz*, December 11, 2009.

---. "Choosing Yiddish in Israel: Yung Yisroel between Home and Exile, the Center and the Margins." In *Choosing Yiddish: New Frontiers of Language and Cultures*, edited by Lara Rabinovitch, Shiri Goren, and Hanna S. Pressman, 277-294. Detroit: Wayne State University Press, 2013.

Poll, Solomon. "The Sacred-Secular Conflict in the Use of Yiddish among the Ultra-Orthodox Jews of Jerusalem." *International Journal of the Sociology of Language* 24 (1980): 109-125.

Ravitch, Melech. "A vort fun an eltern khaver." In *Di ban: dertseylungen fun Poyln, Rusland, Yisroel*, edited by Zvi Eisenman, 8-9. Yagur: Yung Yisroel series, 1956.

Ravitzky, Aviezer, ed. *Shas: hebetim tarbutiyim ve'rayoniyim*. Tel Aviv: Am Oved and Merkaz Yitzhak Rabin, 2006.

Raz Krakotzkin, Amnon. "Galut be'toch ribonut, le'bikoret shelilat ha'galut ba'tarbut ha'isra'elit." *Teorya u'bikoret* 4 (1993): 23-55; 5 (1994): 113-132.

Regev, Motti, and Edwin Saroussi. *Popular Music and National Culture in Israel*. Berkeley: University Press of California, 2004.

Riggins, Stephan Harold. "The Media Imperative: Ethnic Minority Survival in the Age of Mass Communication." In *Ethnic Minority Media: An International Perspective*, edited by Stephan Harold Riggins, 1-20. New York: Sage, 1992.

Rintzler, Abraham. "Randn." *Yung Yisroel, zamlung far literatur un kritik* (1956): 58-59.

Rojanski, Rachel. "Bein ideologya li'metzi'ut politit—yahasam shel Poalei-Zion be'Amerika le'Yidish 1905–1933." *Yahadut zemaneinu* 11–12 (1998): 51–71.

———. "Ben-Gurion and Yiddish after the Holocaust." In *The Politics of Yiddish*, edited by Shlomo Berger, 25–40. Amsterdam: Menasse Ben-Israel, 2010.

———. "The Final Chapter in the Struggle for Cultural Autonomy: Palestine, Israel, and Yiddish Writers in the Diaspora, 1946–1951." *Journal of Modern Jewish Studies* 6, no. 2 (2007): 185–204.

———. "'Ha'omnam safa zara ve'tzoremet?' li'she'elat yahaso shel Ben-Gurion le'Yidish aharei ha'sho'a." *Iyunim bi'tekumat Israel* 15 (2005): 463–482.

———. "Magbit ha'igudim ha'miktzo'iyim le'ma'an ha'histadrut u'Poalei-Zion be'Amerika." In *Me'hevrat avoda le'irgun ovdim*, edited by Yosef Gorny, Avi Bareli, Yitzhak Greenberg, 529–555. Sede-Boker: Ben-Gurion University of the Negev Press, 2000.

———. "Tsanin." In *Leksikon heksherim le'sofrim isra'elim*, edited by Zissi Stavi and Yigal Schwartz, 752–753. Or Yehuda: Kineret Zemora, Bitan-Dvir, 2014.

———. "Yiddish Journals for Women in Israel: Immigrant Press and Gender Construction (1948–1952)." In *Yiddish Studies Today (Leket)*, edited by Marion Aptroot, Efrat Gal-Ed, Roland Gruschka, and Simon Neuberg, 585–602. Dusseldorf: Dusseldorf University Press, 2012.

———. "A Yiddish Shtetl in Tel Aviv." In *Yiddish Cities: Montreal, Melbourne, Tel Aviv*, edited by Shlomo Berger, 65–81. Amsterdam: Menasse Ben Israel Institute, 2013.

———. *Zehuyot nifgashot: Poalei-Zion bi'tzefon Amerika, 1905–1931*. Sede-Boker: Ben-Gurion University of the Negev Press, 2004.

Rollansky, Shmuel. "Medines Yisroel in der yidisher literatur." In *Yidishe literatur-Yidish lebn: Shraybers, bashraybers un vizyonern in unzer literatur-geshikhte*, 614–622. Buenos Aires: A grupe fraynd fun der literatur-gezelshaft baym YIVO, 1973.

Roskies, David G. *Against the Apocalypse: Responses to Modern Jewish Culture*. Cambridge, MA: Harvard University Press, 1984.

———. "Di shrayber grupe Yung Yisroel." *Yugntruf* 27–28 (1973): 7–12; 33 (1975): 7–8; 34 (1976): 4–7.

———. *The Jewish Search for a Usable Past*. Bloomington: Indiana University Press, 1999.

Rosnboym, Mikhele. *Ondenk bukh fun Yisroel Khadash*. Tel Aviv: Naye Lebn, 1973.

Rotman, Diego. *Performans ke'bikoret tarbut: Mifal ha'te'atron shel Dzigan ve'Shumacher 1927–1980*. PhD diss., The Hebrew University of Jerusalem, 2012.

Rozin, Orit. *The Rise of the Individual in 1950s Israel: A Challenge to Collectivism*. Waltham, MA: Brandeis University Press, 2011.

Rubinstein, Amnon. *The Zionist Dream Revisited: From Herzl to Gush Emunim and Back*. New York: Schocken, 1984

Rubinstein, Joshua. *Tangled Loyalties: The Life and Times of Ilya Ehrenburg*. London: I. B. Tauris, 1996.

Rimon, Zeev, ed. *Sefer Yagur*. Tel Aviv: Kibbutz Yagur and Hakibbutz Hameuchad, 1965.

Sadan, Dov. "Grus fun nonte kroyvim." *Di goldene keyt* 69–70 (1970): 12–14.

Sandrow, Nahma. *Vagabond Stars: A World History of Yiddish Theater*. Syracuse, NY: Syracuse University Press, 1996.

Saposnik, Arieh. *Becoming Hebrew: The Creation of a Jewish National Culture in Ottoman Palestine*. Oxford: Oxford University Press, 2008.

Sarna, Jonathan. *American Judaism*. New Haven, CT: Yale University Press, 2004.

Schwartz, Yigal. *Ha'yadata et ha'aretz sham ha'limon poreah, handasat adam u'mahshevet merhav ba'sifrut ha'ivrit ha'hadasha*. Or Yehuda: Kineret and Dvir, 2007.
Segal, Louis. "Der yidish-natsyonaler arbeter farband fun 1924 biz 1945." *Yidish-natsyonaler arbeter farband 1910–1945—zamelbukh*. New York: Jewish National Workers Alliance, 1946.
Segev, Tom. *The Seventh Million: The Israelis and the Holocaust*. New York: Henry Holt, 1991.
Sephard, David. "Mordechai Tsanin." *Yidishe kultur* 46, no. 5 (September–October 1980): 33–37.
Shaham, Chaya. *Hedim shel nigun, shirat dor ha'Palmach ve'havurat Likrat be'zika le'shirat Alterman*. Tel Aviv: Hakibbutz Hameuchad, 1997.
Shaked, Gershon. *Ha'siporet ha'ivrit 1880–1980*. Vol. 4, *Be'havlei ha'zeman—ha're'alism ha'isra'eli 1880–1980*. Tel Aviv: Hakibbutz Hameuchad and Keter, 1993.
———. *Ha'moderna bein shetei milhamot, mavo le'dorot ba'aretz*. Jerusalem: Keter and Hakibbutz Hameuchad, 1988.
Shamir, Shlomo. *Be'chol mehir—li'Yerushalyim*. Tel Aviv: Ma'akharot, 1994.
Shandler, Jeffrey. *Adventures in Yiddishland: Postvernacular Language and Culture*. Berkeley: University of California Press, 2006.
Shapira, Anita. "Ben-Gurion and the Bible: The Forging of an Historical Narrative?" *Middle Eastern Studies* 33, no. 4 (October 1997): 645–674.
———. "Dor ba'aretz." *Alpayim* 2 (1989): 173–203.
———. "The Holocaust: Private Memories, Public Memory," *Jewish Social Studies* 4, no. 2 (1998): 40–58.
———. *Israel: A History*. Waltham, MA: Brandeis University Press, 2012.
———. "Whatever Became of 'Negating Exile'?" In *Israeli Identity in Transition*, edited by Anita Shapira, 69–108. Westport, CT: Praeger, 2004.
———. *Yehudim hadashim yehudim yeshanim*. Tel Aviv: Am Oved, 1997.
Shavit, Zohar. "Ha'shelabim be'hitpathuto shel ha'merkaz be'Eretz Israel ve'hafichato le'hegemoni." In *Toldot ha'yishuv be'Eretz Israel me'az ha'aliya ha'rishona—beniyata shel tarbut ivrit be'Eretz Israel*, edited by Zohar Shavit, 87–92. Jerusalem: Israel Academy for Science and Humanities and Bialik Institute, 1998.
———. *Toldot ha'yishuv ha'yehudi be'Eretz Israel me'az ha'aliya ha'rishona*. Jerusalem: Israel Academy for Science and Humanities and Bialik Institute, 1998.
Shenhav, Yehouda. *The Arab Jews: A Postcolonial Reading of Nationalism, Religion, and Ethnicity*. Stanford, CA: Stanford University Press, 2006.
Shimoni, Batya. *Al saf ha'ge'ula: sipur ha'ma'abara dor rishon ve'sheni*. Or Yehuda: Kineret, Zemora-Bitan, Dvir, 2008.
Shmeruk, Chone. *Ha'keri'a la'navi: mehkarei historya ve'sifrut*. Jerusalem: Merkaz Shazar, 1999.
———. "Le'toldot sifrut ha'"shund' be'Yidish." *Tarbitz* 52 (1983): 325–350.
Shtarkman, Moshe. "Vikhtikste momentn in der geshikhte fun der yidishe prese in Amerike." In *Finf un zibetsik yor yidishe prese in Amerike, 1870–1945*, edited by Jacob Glatstein, Shmuel Niger, and Hillel Rogoff, 5–54. New York: Y. L Peretz farayn, 1945.
Shur, Shimon. *Gedud meginei ha'safa be'Eretz Israel, 1923–1936*. Haifa: University of Haifa, Mosad Herzl, 2000.
Sikron, Moshe. *Ha'aliya ha'hamonit, me'afyeneiha ve'hashpa'oteiha al uchlusyat Israel*. Jerusalem: Merkaz ha'hasbara, 1989.

———. *Ha'aliya le'Israel 1848–1953*. Jerusalem: Falk Center for Statistical and Economic Research, 1957.

Spiegel, Charlotte. *Diyokano shel sofer: Yeshayahu Spiegel: mivhar bikorot al yetzirato*. Tel Aviv: self-published, 1985.

Spiegelblatt, Alexander. "*Di goldene keyt* un ir melukhisher maymed." *Yidishe kultur* 52, no. 1 (1990): 38–42.

———. *Durkh farreykherte shayblekh*. Tel Aviv: Leivick farlag, 2007.

Sprinzak, Yosef. *In vort un in shrift*. Buenos Aires: Kiem, 1954.

———. *Unzer zorg farn goles: Unzer flikht far der tsyonishtesher organizatsye*. Tel Aviv: Ihud Olami Poalei-Zion—Hitahdut, 1939.

Steinlauf, C. Michael. "Jewish Theater in Poland." *Polin* 16 (2003): 71–92

———. "The Kaminski Family." *YIVO Encyclopedia of Jews in Eastern Europe*, http://www.yivoencyclopedia.org/article.aspx/Kaminski_Family.

Sternhell, Zeev. *Binyan uma o tikun hevra, le'umyut ve'sotzyalism bi'tenu'at ha'avoda ha'isre'alit 1904–1940*. Tel Aviv: Am Oved, 1995.

Sutzkever, Abraham. *Baym leyenen penemer, dertseylungen, dermonungen, eseyen*. Jerusalem: The Hebrew University of Jerusalem, 1993.

Szeintuch, Yechiel. "Ve'idat Tshernovitz ve'tarbut Yidish." *Khulyot* 6 (2000): 255–285.

Tec, Nechama. *Defiance: The Bielski Partisans*. New York: Oxford University Press, 1993.

Tsanin, M. (Mordechai). *Iber shteyn un shtok: a rayze iber hundert khorev gevorene kehiles in Poyln*. Tel Aviv: Letste nayes, 1952.

———. *Oyf zumpike erd*. Warsaw: Shprayzn, 1935.

———. *Shabesdike shmuesn*. Tel Aviv: Letste nayes, 1957.

———. *Vivat lebn: novelen*. Warsaw: Shprayzn, 1933.

———. *Vuhin geyt Yapan: reportazhn fun vaytn mizrekh*. Tel Aviv: Eeygns, 1942.

———. *Zumershney*. Tel Aviv: H. Leivick farlag, 1992.

Turkow-Grodberg, Yitzhak. *Zygmunt Turkow*. Tel Aviv: Orly, 1970.

Turniansky, Chava. *Sefer masa u'meriva le'R(eb) Aleksander be'R(eb) Yitskhok Papen Hofen (1627)*. Jerusalem: Magnes, 1985.

Ulitzky, Yosef. "Ha'laaz be'rosh hutzot." In *Sefer ha'shana shel ha'itonaim*, 39–50. Tel Aviv: The Association of Journalists in Tel Aviv, 1954.

———. "Ishey ha'am al hanhalat ha'lashon." In *Sefer ha'shana shel ha'itonaim*, 53–55. Tel Aviv: The Association of Journalists in Tel Aviv, 1954.

Urian, Dan. *Yahaduto shel ha'te'atron ha'isra'eli: pirkei mehkar*. Tel Aviv: Hakibbutz Hameuchad, 1998.

Warhaftig, Zerah. *Huka le'Israel: dat u'medina*. Jerusalem: Mesilot, 1988.

Weinreich, Max. *History of the Yiddish Language*. Chicago: Chicago University Press, 1980.

Weiss, Yfaat. "Golem and Its Creator: How the Jewish Nation State Became Multiethnic." In *Challenging Ethnic Citizenship: German and Israeli Perspectives on Immigration*, edited by Daniel Levy and Yfaat Weiss, 82–106. New York and Oxford: Berghahn, 2002.

Weitz, Yechiam. "Bein mashak kanfei ha'historya le'vein yemei hulin: Harkavat ha'memshala ha'rishona u'mashma'uta." In *Politika be'milhama, kovetz mehkarim al ha'hevra ha'ezrahit be'milhemet ha'atzma'ut*, edited by Mordechai Bar-On and Meir Chazan, 127–154. Jerusalem: Yad Ben Zvi and Chaim Weizmann Institute for Zionist Studies, 2014.

———. *Ha'behirot la'knesset u'mashberim memshaltiyim. Israel ba'asor ha'rishon*, Vol. 9. Tel Aviv: Open University, 2001.

Wisse, Ruth R. "Avrom Sutzkever." *YIVO Encyclopedia of the Jews in Eastern Europe*, http://www.yivoencyclopedia.org/article.aspx/Sutzkever_Avrom.
———. "Yitzhok Leybush Peretz." *YIVO Encyclopedia of the Jews in Eastern Europe*, http://www.yivoencyclopedia.org/article.aspx/peretz_yitskhok_leybush.
———. *I. L. Peretz and the Making of Modern Jewish Culture*. London: University of Washington Press, 1991.
———. "Introduction: The Ghetto Poems of Abraham Sutzkever." In *Burnt Pearls: Ghetto Poems of Abraham Sutzkever*, edited by Ruth Wisse, 1–18. Translated by Seymour Mayne. Oakville, ON: Mosaic, 1981.
———. *The Modern Jewish Canon—A Journey through Language and Culture*. New York: Free Press, 2000.
———, ed. *A Shtetl and Other Yiddish Novellas*. Detroit: Wayne State University Press, 1973.
Wittke, Carl. *The German Language Press in America*. Lexington: University of Kentucky Press, 1957.
Wolitz, Seth. "Shulamis and Bar Kokhba: Renewed Jewish Role Models in Goldfaden and Halkin." In *Yiddish Theater: New Approaches*, edited by Joel Berkowitz, 87–104. Oxford: Littman Library of Jewish Civilization, 2003.
Yaar, Ephraim, and Zeev Shavit, eds. *Megamot ba'hevra ha'isra'elit*. Vol. 1. Raanana: Open University, 2001.
Yablokoff, Herman. *Arum der velt mit yidish teater*. New York: Herman Yablokoff, 1969.
Yablonka, Hanna. *Ahim zarim: nitzolei ha'sho'a bi'medinat Israel 1948–1952*. Jerusalem: Yad Ben Zvi, 1994.
———. "Kelitat nitzolei ha'sho'a bi'medinat Israel—hebetim hadashim." *Iyunim bi'tekumat Israel* 7 (1997): 285–298.
———. *Medinat Israel neged Adolf Eichmann*. Tel Aviv: Miskal, 2001.
———. *Survivors of the Holocaust: Israel after the War*. London: MacMillan, 1999.
Yeger, Moshe. *Toldot ha'mahlaka ha'medinit shel ha'sochnut*. Jerusalem: Mosad Bialik, 2010.
Yidish literatur in medines Yisroel. Tel Aviv: H. Leivick farlag, 1991.
Yungman, Moyshe. "Draysik yor Yung Yisroel." *Di goldene keyt* 108 (1982): 59–66.
———. "Shtrikhn." In *Yung Yisroel, literatur, kunst, kritik* (1954): 35–36.
Zach, Natan. *Mi'shana le'shana ze, pirkei biyografya sifrutit u'muva'ot*. Tel Aviv: Hakibbutz Hameuchad, 2009.
Zameret, Zvi. *Alei gesher tzar me'od: Ha'hinuch be'Israel bi'shenot ha'medina ha'rishonot*. Sede-Boker: Ben-Gurion University of the Negev Press, 1997.
———. "Ben Zion Dinur: Intelektual bone medina." *Ha'tzyonut* 21 (1998): 321–332.
Zer-Zion, Shelly. "Ha'vilner trupe'—prolog la'historya shel Habima." *Bikoret u'parshanut* 41 (2009): 65–92.
Zinger, Mendl. *Be'reishit ha'tzyonut ha'sotzyalistit*. Haifa: Yalkut, 1956.
Zipperstein, Steven J. *Imagining Russian Jewry: Memory, History, Identity*. Seattle: University of Washington Press, 1999.

INDEX

Page numbers in *italics* indicate figures.

Agranat, Shimon, 61, 112
Ahad Ha'am, 28
Aharonowitz-Aran, Zalman, 80, 251, 252
Al HaMishmar, 78, 122, 154; and Abraham Sutzkever, 159–60, 162
Almagor, Dan, 237, 238, 239, 254
Alterman, Nathan, 165, 230, 245n29–30
Am Oved, 191–92, 204, 205, 207, 285–86
Anderson, Benedict, 50
Appelfeld, Aharon, 191
Arab-Israeli War of 1973, 253, 254
Arbeter Ring (Brit-Avoda), 85–86. *See also* Bund in Israel
Arendt, Hannah, 51
Argentina: and Yiddish, 82, 119, 120, 189, 256
Asch, Sholem, 115, 118, 165, 172, 267
Ashkenazi: and Israel, 9, 19, 229, 270; and Mizrahi, 193, 262; and Yiddish, 3, 27, 125
Assaf, Simha, 61, 112
Association of Hebrew Journalists, 41, 72, 91n45
Association of Yiddish Writers and Journalists, 73, 136, 256, 259, 289
Atzmon-Wircer, Shmuel, 263–65, 266, 267–68, 269–70, 278n95, 287
Auerbach, Rachel, 69, 191–92
austerity regime, 59, 67, 91n48
Avnery, Uri, 66, 75–76, 86, 90n26
Aykhenboym, Yisokhor (Artusky), 251, 252

Bachi, Roberto, 9, 89n16
Ballas, Shimon, 193
Barash, Asher, 35
Bartov, Hanoch, 213–14
Bay zikh, 256, 257, 258, 261
Basman, Rivka, 188, 194, 199, 223n116
Becker, Israel: and Yiddish Theater, 264, 265
Begin, Menachem, 262
Beit Leivick (Tel Aviv), 251, 252, 288, 289

Beit Sholem Aleichem (Tel Aviv), 243, 251, 288–89, 292n9
Ben-Amotz, Dan, 227–28, 245n13
Ben-Gurion, David, 8, 29, 68, 81, 85; attitude toward Yiddish, 26–27, 30–31, 43n6, 112, 174, 176, 281, 282; and development of Hebrew culture, 32–35, 38, 179; and the Diaspora, 155, 177, 240; and *Di goldene keyt*, 166; and the historical leap, 29–30, 34, 38; and orthodox religious culture, 178–79, 187n120–121
Ben Zevi, Yitzhak, 29, 230
Benyomin, H., 194, 198. *See also* Harshav, Benjamin
Bergner, Yossel, 172, 228
Berkowitz, Y. D., 166, 236–37, 251, 286
Berdyczewski, Micha Yosef, 28, 29, 239
Bergmann, Samuel (Shmuel) Hugo, 34, 36
Besser, Yaakov, 272
Bialik Prize, 33
Bimot Theater, 238
Binetzky, Peysakh, 194, *196*
Biran, Ya'ad, 291
Birstein, Yossel, 1–2, 194, 195, *196*, 197, *199*, 221n91; stories of, 207–210, 285–86
Blumenfeld, Diana, 119, 147n121
Book Publishers Association of Israel, 62
Boreysho, Menakhem, 165
Bourdieu, Pierre, 234, 246n56
Boym, Svetlana, 14, 240, 241, 249n111
Boymvol, Rokhl, 256, 258
Brat, Yitzhak, 85
Broderzon, Moyshe, 132–33
Buber, Martin, 34, 239
Buloff, Joseph, 102, 122–23, 125, 130, 137; in Israel, 127–29, 258
Bund in Israel, 4, 5, 75; Brit-Avoda, 75, 86; Bund-Brit Avoda House, 288, 292n8
Bunim, Shmuel, 229, 232, 234, 235, 258

Burstein family, 119–20; and *Di megile*, 225, 232
Burstein, Motele (Mike Burstyn), 119; and *Di megile*, 225, 232, 235
Burstein, Pesach, 119; and *Di megile*, 225, 234, 242
Bustan sepharadi, 270–71

Cahan, Abraham, 55
Cameri Theater of Tel Aviv, 237
Carlebach, Ezriel, 59, 72, 88, 135–36
Chagall, Marc, 172, 231
Committee for the Foreign-Language Press of Mapai, 82, 83
Committee for Jewish Culture in Israel, 255–57, 258, 259, 260–61, 274n28
Communist Party, 26, 43n1, 76
Council for the Control of Films and Plays, 19, 104, 107, 108, 109–113, 135, 282
Council for Cultural Matters, 35
Council for Humanities and Culture, 35

Davar, 27, 62, 76, 80, 121, 126, 127, 131, 152n231, 176, 230–31, 237–38, 239, 251; and *Di goldene keyt*, 156–57, 168; and *Di megile*, 232
Der moment (Warsaw), 5
Der tog (New York), 8, 174
Der yidisher kemfer (New York), 115
Devar Ha'shavu'a, 54
Di goldene keyt: background of, 154–56, 162–64, 177, 184n83; content of, 69, 165–67, 171, 185n89; and poetry, 188; and post-Holocaust Yiddish culture, 169–73, 176, 179, 195, 199, 201, 205, 206, 207, 250, 256, 283; reception of, 168–69; and Yung Yisroel, 210–11
Di megile (play), 225, 226, 229, 232–34, 258, 266, 267; and post-Holocaust Jewish culture, 238–40, 241–44, 249n126, 250, 270–71
Di tsayt (Tel Aviv), 77, 78
Di tsukunft (New York), 169
Di tsvey Kuni Lemel, 109–10, 111–12
Di vokh (Tel Aviv), 78, 83, 84
Diaspora: and Ben-Gurion, 68, 155, 177–79; and Mizrahi Jews, 37; and Yiddish, 2–7, 15–16, 17, 50, 67, 74, 175, 269–70; and Yiddish literature, 168, 174, 191–92, 200–203, 205, 208, 214–216; and Yiddish theater, 109–110, 111–12, 121, 126–27, 129, 131, 138
Dinur (Dinaburg), Ben-Zion, 34–37, 44n37, 63; and promotion of Hebrew, 38–39, 40–41, 42, 60, 71; and Yiddish chair at the Hebrew University, 176
Dos Vort (Tel Aviv), 76–77, 78, 80–81, 85
Dunkelblum, Menachem, 112
Dvorjetski, Meir, 81, 98n197, 174
Dzigan, Shimon, 17, 53, 132, 138, 264
Dzigan and Shumacher, 17, 102, 108; in Israel, 134–39, 151n221, 152n231, 287; origins, 132–33

Editors Committee of the Hebrew Press, 88
Ehrenburg, Ilya, 159–60
Eichmann trial, 14, 69, 129, 226, 236, 285; and eastern European Jewry, 239, 240, 241
Einstein, Arik, 253
Eisenman, Zvi, 188, 193, 194, 195–96, 199, 204, 212, 218n35, 220n56; stories of, 200–3
Eretz Israel, 163, 253–54; Eretz Israeli Zionism, 6, 29, 174–75; Yiddish in, 17, 165–66. *See also* Mandatory Palestine; Yishuv
Eshkol, Levi, 235, 252
Even-Zohar, Itamar, 29

Fiddler on the Roof, 14; in Israel, 235, 236, 238, 247n80
Fishman, Joshua, 17, 255
Fishman, Rokhl, 194, 197, 199
Folk, velt un medine (*Folk un medine*) (Tel Aviv), 255, 261
Folkist Party, 5
Forverts (Jewish Daily Forward) (New York), 6, 53, 55, 256
Frank, Shlomo, 61
Fray Yisroel (Tel Aviv), 76

Galay, Daniel, 289
Galina, Gita, 118–19, 120
General Zionist Party, 61, 66, 73, 78; *Unzer fraynt*, 78, 85; *Unzer haynt*, 61, 78, 85
Gesharim-Brikn (Tel Aviv), 261

Giladi, David, 71
Givat Aliya, 109, 114–15, 139
Glantz-Leyeles, Aaron, 165
Glatstein, Jacob, 50, 211, 223n110
Gold, Zishe, 225
Goldenberg, Eliyahu, 264, 287
Goldfaden, Abraham, 102, 109, 110, 237, 267
Goldfaden Theater, 31, 105, 108, 109–113, 116, 118, 120, 121, 135, 139, 144n75; end of, 114, 117
Gordin, Jacob, 110, 113, 130, 267
Gouri, Haim, 33
Grade, Chaim, 192
Gramsci, Antonio, 12, 38
Greenberg, Chaim, 176
Gris, Noah, 166, 183n55, 183n62
Gross, Nathan, 133
Grossman, David, 216
Grossman, Moshe, 115
Gurin, Moyshe, 194, *196*, *199*

Ha'aretz, 59, 62, 115, 234, 237, 242
Ha'dor, 66, 80
Ha'molad, 80
Ha'po'el Ha'tza'ir, 80
Ha'shomer Ha'tza'ir movement, 78
Habima Theater, 110, 130, 213, 231, 237, 238, 264, 270
Hacohen, Dvora, 32, 46n66, 254
Hadash, Israel, 56; break with Tsanin, 64–65, 66–67
Haifa Municipal Theater, 238
Hakibbutz Hameuchad (press), 191–92, 202–3, 207, 259
Halamish, Mordechai, 138, 152n231, 255, 261
Halperin, Dina, 119
Hamam Theater, 225, 226–27, 245n18; and *Di megile*, 232, 234, 235, 241, 242
HaOlam Haze (Israel), 54, 66, 76, 86, 90n26
HaPoel HaMizrachi, 36, 74
Harshav, Benjamin, 157, 190, *196*, 289–90. See also Benyomin, H.
Hart, David, 108–9, 110, 111–12, 120, 128
Hasidism, 37–38
Haskalah movement, 3, 4, 37
Haynt (Warsaw), 5, 67, 126, 168

Hayntike nayes (Israel), 67, 70
Hebrew: inculcation of, 32–42, 70–74, 79, 81–82, 139, 168; in prestate Israel, 6–7, 17, 29, 45n58; and theater, 88, 106, 109, 110, 118, 122, 125–26; and Yiddish, 3–5, 11, 49, 69, 86, 126, 130, 165, 191–92, 198, 213, 232–33, 255, 290–91. See also hegemony
Hebrew Matate Theater, 118
Hebrew University, 8, 17, 33, 34, 36, 155, 228, 251, 257, 260; and *Di goldene keyt*, 172; and Yiddish chair, 173–75, 179
Hefer, Haim, 227–28, 234
Heftman, Joseph, 136
hegemony, 12–14, 18–19, 28, 32, 38–42, 44n25, 45n58; and Yiddish press, 79–82, 86–87, 155, 164, 168, 169, 189–90, 200, 205–10, 213–14, 216, 219n55; and Yiddish theater, 102–6, 122–24, 262–63. See also Hebrew: inculcation of
Hermoni, Matan, 291
Hershele Ostropolyer, 101, 110–12
Herut (daily), 122, 128, 241–42
Herut movement, 61; political party, 65, 262
Herzl, Theodor, 28
Heshin, Zalman Shneur, 112
Hirschbein, Peretz, 107, 110, 113, 126
Histadrut, 8, 36, 52, 76, 80, 230, 265; in the Yishuv, 154–55; and *Di goldene keyt*, 156, 163, 164–65, 166, 167–68, 171
Hobsbawm, Eric, 34
Hofer, Yehiel, 192, 232
Holocaust: and Jewish culture, 2, 31, 37, 158–60, 190–91, 224n127, 284; and the press, 55, 64, 67, 68, 69–70, 75; and Yiddish, 9, 11, 73, 87, 172, 269–71; and Yiddish theater, 103, 109, 124, 130, 132–33, 137; and Yiddish literature, 154–55, 163, 166–67, 169–70, 189, 192, 195–202, 205–6, 209–11
Holzer, Rachel, 107, 122

Idish natsyonaler arbiter farband (Farband), 174–176
Ilustrirte velt vokh (*Tsanins yidishe ilustrirte velt*), 85, 99n234, 250
Ilustrirter vokhnblat, 27, 49, 54–56, 57, 58, 61, 65, 87

Institute for Microfilmed Hebrew Manuscripts, 177
Israel: immigrant press in, 54–58, 70–75, 86–89; immigration to, 9–11, 17, 18–19, 23n45, 32, 51–52, 59, 81, 87, 114–15, 137–38, 191, 254–58, 283–85; and kibbutz life, 208–10, 212, 222n97; promotion of Hebrew in, 13, 28–29, 32–33, 36–40, 49, 105, 163–64, 283–84; regulation of the press in, 58–64, 70–75, 86–87, 90n41, 92n62, 95n141; regulation of theater in, 104–13, 129, 135, 141n17, 141n21, 282; and war of independence, 154, 165, 166, 171, 175, 205–56, 208, 214–15, 221n85; and Yung Yisroel, 195–208
Israel Defense Forces (IDF), 53, 166, 259; and the Chizbatron, 227
Israeli Journalists Association, 88
Itzik Manger Prize, 252

Jabotinsky, Ze'ev, 5
Jaffa Professional Yiddish Theater, 107
Jewish Agency, 36, 52, 79, 97n175, 161, 258, 260–61, 265
Jewish nationalism: and Yiddish, 3, 4–5; and Zionism, 29, 34
journalists' association of Tel Aviv, 162

Kaminska, Ester-Rokhl, 103, 129
Kaminska, Ida, 102, 108, 117, 123, 137, 225; in Israel, 129–31, 258, 259
Karpinovitsh, Abraham, 120, 194, 196, 199, 220n70, 257; stories of, 203–6, 216
Kassit coffee house, 230, 245n31
Kerler, Yosef, 256, 258
Kibbutz Yagur, 188, 193–94, 198, 210; significance of, 211–12
Knesset, 26, 65–66, 81, 85, 262; regulation of the press; 20, 62, 69, 70–75, 79; and Yiddish, 130, 163, 268–73, 282, 285, 287
Kol Ha'am, 26, 43n1, 242
Kol mevaser (Odessa), 4
Korczack, Rozka, 8, 30
Kovner, Abba, 160
Kitron, Moshe, 82–83

Labor movement: and Yiddish, 7–8, 38, 163; and Zionism, 29, 115, 174–75, 176
Labor Party, 88, 176, 191, 262. *See also* Mapai
Ladino (Judeo-Spanish), 10, 74, 80, 81, 175; and Yiddish, 270–73
Lahat, Shlomo, 264–65, 267
Lavon, Pinhas, 74, 178
Lebns-fragn (Tel Aviv), 75, 84, 85, 123, 251, 252
Leivick, H., 30–31, 110, 119, 165, 167, 172, 212, 230
Letste nayes (Tel Aviv), 48, 65–67, 71, 75, 76, 78, 250; content of, 67–70, 87–88; origins of, 56–58, 63–64, 79; and Mapai, 80–85; articles in, 101, 115; and Yiddish theater, 116, 121; and Yung Yisroel, 203, 204
Levanon, Haim, 42, 78, 119
Levinson, Abraham, 154, 156, 164, 165, 172, 183n55
Leybl, Daniel, 211
Leyeles, Aaron, 211
Liberal party, 262
Lichtenberg, Joseph, 107, 119–20
Likrat, 189, 198
Likud party, 262
Liss, Abraham, 257
Liton, Eni, 120–21, 122–24, 259
Lubitz, Jenny, 107
Luden, Yithak, 251, 252, 281
Lux, Lillian, 119; and *Di megile*, 225, 234–35

ma'abarot, 65, 66
Maariv 59, 62, 72, 73, 104, 231, 251, 287; and Abraham Sutzkever, 163; and Yiddish theater, 117, 122, 123, 138, 232, 235, 237, 270–71
Mandatory Palestine: multilingual nature of, 7, 17, 45n58, 60–61; theater in, 104, 125; and Yiddish, 53. *See also* Eretz Israel; Yishuv
Manger, Itzik, 212, 230–31, 269, 287; and *Di megile* (play), 225, 226–27, 228–29, 232, 234–35, 242, 266, 267, 270
Mann, Mendl, 192, 194, 196, 216, 221n86; stories of, 207–208
Mapai: and Hebrew, 80; and *Letste* nayes, 83–86, 86, 88, 250; political party, 12–13, 20, 65–66, 176, 205, 255; and Yiddish press, 50, 74–75, 76–83, 205, 256, 282–83; and Yiddish theater, 127

Mapam (political party), 65, 73, 77, 78, 83
Mark, Yudel, 255
Markish, David, 256
Masa (literary periodical), 229, 231
Megged, Aharon, 216, 267, 285–86, 287
Meir, Golda, 53, 74, 131, 182n43, 251, 252, 257; and Abraham Sutzkever, 161, 260
memory: and *Letste nayes*, 68; and post-Holocaust Jewish culture, 12–15, 69–70, 126, 226, 240–44, 254, 263, 267–68, 285. *See also* nostalgia
Mendele Moykher Sforim, 4, 197
Menora (press), 250
Mer, Benny, 290
Michael, Sami, 193
Mikunis, Shmuel, 26
Miller, Arthur, 127, 128
Miron, Dan, 157, 241, 244, 278n93, 286
Misgav Theater, 120
Mittelpunkt, Y. D., 115
Mizrahi Jews: in Israel, 18–19, 36–37, 254; and Ashkenazi, 193, 262
Mizrachi Party, 36, 62
Morgn zhurnal (New York), 6
Movement for Greater Israel, 262
muzika mizrahit, 262–63

National Authority for Yiddish Culture, 263, 268, 269, 271–73, 285
Navon, Yitzhak, 270
Nayvelt (Tel Aviv), 7, 8, 48–49, 53, 56, 61, 80, 88n2, 211
Negation of the Diaspora, 2–3, 10, 27–31, 37–8, 43n14, 47n78, 55–56, 176, 197, 225, 238–40, 272–73, 281–82
Neiman, Y. M., 126, 152n231, 168
Niger, Shmuel, 50, 165, 172, 211; and Sutzkever, 167
Nora, Pierre, 14, 126, 241
nostalgia, 12, 14–15, 238, 240–44, 249n111, 253–54, 267, 270, 285; and Yiddish press, 87, 212; and Yiddish theater, 128–29, 226, 236, 239, 250. *See also* memory
Nuremberg trials, 160, 162

Ohad, Michael, 234–35, 242–43
Ohel Theater, 110, 113, 126, 130, 134, 230, 234, 237, 264
Olshan, Yitzhak, 61
Opatoshu, Yosef, 165, 172
Organization of Democratic Women in Israel, 79
Osherovitsh, Hirsh, 256, 257
Oyf der vakh, 78–79, 85

Pale of Settlement, 4, 5
Palmach, 33, 166, 214, 227–28, 230, 231
Paner, Yitzhak, *196*
Papyernikov, Yosef, 27, 107, 165, 257
Peretz, Y. L., 5, 103, 107, 113, 122, 138; and *Di goldene keyt*, 170, 171; and Yung Yisroel, 197
Perlman, Max, 118–19, 120
Perlov, Yitzhak, 78, 107, 113, 145n85
Pines, Eliezer, 164
Pinkus, Yirmi, 291
Pinsker, Leon, 28
Pinsky, David, 116, 194
Pirsumim Publications Company, 81, 83, 84
Poalei-Zion, 5, 56, 82; and Ahdut Ha'avoda, 227–28; in Eretz Israel, 4, 6–8, 49; in Israel, 61; in America, 6, 174–75
Pollack, Israel, 264
Popular Yiddish Theater, 117
Preger, Jacob, 130
Press Committee for Imparting Hebrew, 72
Pyekatsh, Pesach, 81, 83

Ranger, Terrance, 34
Rapoport, Tamar, 10
Ravitch, Melech, 166, 200
Rintzler, Abraham, 194, 195, *196*, 198–99
Rochman, Leyb, 192, 257
Rodensky, Shmuel, 264, 287
Rogoff, Hillel, 50
Rokach, Israel, 73–75
Rollansky, Shmuel, 189, 200, 217
Rosenblum, Herzl, 42, 59
Rosenfarb, Chava, 238
Rosenfeld, Shalom, 252
Rotlevi, David, 264–65

Rubinstein, Amnon, 238, 272–73
Russian Empire, 5, 102

sabra: image of, 138, 227–28, 229, 231, 239–40
Sadan, Dov, 36, 175–76, 251, 255, 256, 257
Schwartz, Maurice, 102, 103, 123, 129, 130, 137; in Israel, 125–27, 148n157
Segal, Israel, 108–9, 111–12, 113, 114
Segal, Kalman, 256
Segal, Shmuel, 264, 287
Seltzer, Dubi, 227, 232, 235
Shaked, Gershon, 191, 192
Shamir, Moshe, 213–15, 216, 265
Shapira, Moshe, 110, 136
Sharett, Moshe, 74, 112–13
Shas (political party), 262
Shazar, Zalman, 36, 173, 235, 243, 251, 255
she'erit ha'pleita, 9, 23n38
Shechtman, Eli, 256, 257, 259
Shilanksy, Dov, 269–70
Shlonsky, Avraham, 231
Sholem Aleichem: and *Fiddler on the Roof*, 14, 236–38; and Yiddish literature, 138, 166, 243–44, 251, 286, 287–88, 290; and Yiddish theater, 107, 110, 113, 115, 118, 122, 130, 237–38, 259, 260, 264, 265, 266
Shprakh konferents (Czernowitz conference), 5
Shumacher, Israel, 17, 132, 135, 138
Shurer, Haim, 66, 131, 230, 231
Sifriat Poalim, 203, 259
Sinai Campaign (1956), 68, 119
Singer, Isaac Bashevis, 192, 257, 290
Singer, I. J., 125
Six-Day War (1967), 14, 238, 239, 253, 285
Smolyer, Hersh, 256
Sobol, Joshua, 267
Soviet Union: and Jewish Diaspora, 159, 160, 252, 254, 256, 257–58, 264, 268; Yiddish theater in, 129, 133, 137, 138
Spiegel Yeshayahu, 166, 191–92, 217n12, 257
Sprinzak, Yosef, 156, 163, 164, 171, 172
Stein, M., 60–61
Steinman, Eliezer, 34, 107, 239
Supreme Council for Cultural Affairs, 35, 38–39, 40–41; and the foreign language press, 59–60, 71; and Yiddish theater, 106

Sutzkever, Abraham: background of 157–62; and *Di goldene keyt*, 154–56, 163–65, 256, 283; and post-Holocaust Jewish culture, 17, 167, 169–73, 255, 257, 265, 269, 289–90; and Yung Yisroel, 188, 193–95, *196*, 199, 206–7, 223n116

Tami (political party), 262
Teatron Komedia, 118, 120
Telesin, Ziyama, 256
There Was a Pious Man (play), 238–39
Toplpunkt, 272
transnationality, 24n56; and Yiddish, 2, 15–16, 169, 171–72, 210, 213; and Yiddish theater, 103, 131–32
Tsanin, Dora, 67
Tsanin, Mordechai, 48–49, 77, 86, 90n36, 232, 251, 255; background of, 52–54; and *Di goldene* keyt, 164; Ilustrirter *vokhnblat*, 27, 49, 54–56, 57, 58, 61, 65, 87; and *Letste nayes*, 56–58, 63–68, 70, 79, 85, 87–88; and Mapai, 82–83, 84
Tsanins yidishe ilustrirte velt, 81, 84, 85
Turkow, Jonas, 119, 147n121
Turkow, Zygmunt, 108, 117–18, 120, 129, 147n121

ultraorthodox: and Yiddish, 16; military exemptions for, 178–79, 187n120
United States: and the immigrant press, 50–51; and Labor Zionist movement, 6, 115, 174–75; and post-Holocaust Jewish culture, 18, 124, 174, 240–41; and Yiddish, 3, 5–6, 7, 9, 15, 74, 115, 158, 165, 181n37–38, 190, 207, 211, 223n120, 236, 255; Yiddish theater in, 102–103, 118, 119, 125, 127, 129, 135

Veltshpigl (Tel Aviv), 75–76, 86
Vilna ghetto, 109, 81, 174; and Abraham Sutzkever, 156, 160, 194; and Rozka Korczack, 8, 30
Vilna Troupe, 117, 127
Vorzoger, Shlomo, 194, *196*, 211

Warsaw Yiddish Art Theater, 129
Weber, Shimon, 257
Weinreich, Max, 175, 186n107
Weisgal, Meyer, 252

Weislitz, Jacob, 107
Weiss, Shevah, 269
Witler, Ben-Zion, 119
World Congress for Yiddish, 257, 259–60, 277n65
World Council for Yiddish and Jewish Culture, 260–61, 267
World Zionist Organization, 52
Wulfowitz, Nathan, 101, 108, 110, 111–12, 113

Y. L. Peretz (publishing house), 203, 250, 257, 258
Yablokoff, Herman, 119–20
Yakir, Yankl, 256, 257, 258
Yanasovitsh, Yitzhak, 256, 258, 267
Yannai, Meir, 118
Yavnieli, Shmuel, 35, 39, 46n65, 60
Yerusholaymer Almanakh (Jerusalem), 256–57, 258
Yiddish: decline of, 250, 252–61, 280n124, 284–85; and the Diaspora, 2–7, 15–16, 17, 47n78, 50, 67, 74, 131–33, 174–75, 207, 215, 238, 254–58, 269–70, 281; and high court of justice; 60, 105, 111, 112, 116; and high culture, 15–16, 155, 156–57, 169, 171, 226, 235, 252, 283, 287; as a funny language, 285–88, 291; and Israeli political parties, 76–85; and Ladino, 270–73; and literature, 165–66, 169–72, 195–210, 218n16, 245n14; new developments in, 288–92, 292n10; perceived as threat, 33–34, 59; and poetry, 188–91, 212; in prestate Palestine, 6–8, 17; sources of, 19–21; transregional nature of, 6, 12, 58, 270
Yiddish Art Theater: in New York, 103, 125–26, 127; in Poland, 117, 129
Yiddish newspapers: and Hebrew, 41–42, 47n78, 71, 79–80; regulation of, 58–64, 70–75, 86–87, 90n41, 92n62, 95n141, 96n154, 232–33, 282–83. *See also individual titles*; Yiddish press
Yiddish press: 6, 41, 48–61, 69–75, 85–86, 232–35, 282. *See also individual publications*; Yiddish newspapers
Yiddish speakers (second generation), 9, 14–15, 31, 210, 248n110, 251, 261, 263, 267–68, 285, 287–88

Yiddish theater: attitudes toward, 121–25, 128–29, 226, 228, 236–44, 263, 286–87; background of, 102–3; companies of, 113–20, 264–68; and *Di megile*, 232–42; and the Diaspora, 111–12, 126–35, 137–38, 238–39, 257–59; regulation of, 104–13, 129, 135, 141n17, 141n21, 141n282
Yiddishpiel Theater, 263–69, 285, 288, 289
Yidishe prese (Tel Aviv), 64, 67
Yidish velt (Tel Aviv), 261
Yidishe bilder (Tel Aviv and Jerusalem), 61, 75
Yidishes tageblat (New York), 6
Yidishe tsaytung (Tel Aviv), 63–67, 70, 78
Yishuv: and Hebrew, 9, 29–30; and Histadrut, 155; Labor Party in, 262; newspapers in, 58; transition from, 155, 240; Yiddish in, 6–8, 17, 23n49, 48–49, 161–62, 174, 225. *See also* Eretz Israel; Mandatory Palestine
Yisroel-bleter fun ikhud olami (Tel Aviv), 76
Yisroel Bukh (Press), 250
Yisroel shtime, 79, 85, 97n188
Yisroel tog ayn tog oys, 77–78, 81, 83
Yizhar, S., 166, 206, 216, 221n84
Yoseftal, Giora, 81
Yung Yisroel, 17, 172, 188, 191, 219n47, 219n50, 257; background of, 189, 193–98; and Israeli culture, 210–11, 215–17; journal of, 198–99, 202, 210; and post-Holocaust literature, 195–210, 212; and Zionism, 199–200, 213
Yungman, Moyshe, 188, 193, 194, 195, 196–97, 198, *199*, 211–12, 219n40, 257

Zarai, Yohanan, 238, 239
Zavit (theater company), 264
Zeitlin, Aaron, 107, 165, 255
Zeitouni, Matzliah, 56–57, 66, 67
Zerubavel, Yaakov, 165, 231
Zilberg, Moshe, 112
Zionism: master narrative of, 12–13, 18–19, 104, 189–92, 200, 202, 205–6, 213–14, 283; and Yiddish, 2–11, 19, 27–28, 131, 168, 174, 190–91; and the Yung Yisroel, 189–90, 195–96, 200–10. *See also* hegemony; Negation of the Diaspora
Zusman, Yoel, 112
Zuta Theater, 118

RACHEL ROJANSKI is Associate Professor of Judaic Studies at Brown University. She is the author of *Conflicting Identities: Labor Zionism in North America 1905–1931* (Hebrew; Ben-Gurion University Press, 2004), as well as many articles on political and cultural history of east European Jewish immigrants in the United States and Israel.

www.ingramcontent.com/pod-product-compliance
Lightning Source LLC
Chambersburg PA
CBHW021343300426
44114CB00012B/1054